The Form of Greek Romance

———————————— ✳ ————————————

The Form of
Greek Romance

---- ✳ ----

B. P. REARDON

---- ✳ ----

PRINCETON UNIVERSITY PRESS

PRINCETON, NEW JERSEY

Copyright © 1991 by Princeton University Press
Published by Princeton University Press, 41 William Street,
Princeton, New Jersey 08540
In the United Kingdom: Princeton University Press, Oxford
All Rights Reserved

Library of Congress Cataloging-in-Publication Data
Reardon, Bryan P.
The form of Greek romance / B. P. Reardon.
p. cm.
Includes bibliographical references and index.
ISBN 0-691-06838-0 (alk. paper)
1. Romances. Greek—History and criticism. 2. Literary form.
I. Title.
PA3267.R4 1991   90-43220   CIP
883'.0109—dc20

This book has been composed in Palatino Typeface

Princeton University Press books are
printed on acid-free paper, and meet the guidelines
for permanence and durability of the Committee
on Production Guidelines for Book Longevity
of the Council on Library Resources

Printed in the United States of America by
Princeton University Press, Princeton, New Jersey

1   3   5   7   9   10   8   6   4   2

FOR JANETTE

✳

"Tenez, je vous rapporte votre Balzac, je n'ai pas pu le finir. . . . C'est trop triste, il n'a que des choses désagréables à vous dire, ce monsieur-là!"
Et elle lui demanda des histoires où il y eût beaucoup d'amour, avec des aventures et des voyages dans des pays étrangers.

—Zola, *Pot-Bouille*, chapter 11

* Contents *

* Preface *

THIS STUDY aims to provide a framework for the understanding of the surviving examples of the genre of the Greek romance, or novel. Its method is to analyze the genre in terms of ancient critical categories; although there is virtually no ancient discussion of the form, it is possible to reconstruct critical attitudes relevant to it, and to do so will, I believe, provide an illuminating perspective on these texts. The core of the book is thus Chapters 3, 4, and 5, which discuss the literary-theoretical background of romance and the problems arising in the creation of a new and revolutionary form of literature. The emphasis is on the general pattern of the genre rather than on discussion of individual texts; by way of illustration of that pattern I have taken one text, Chariton's *Chaereas and Callirhoe*, as my principal specimen.

I have tried to set the romance in its context in Greek culture; and also, in a limited degree, to offer general interpretation of the form and, in a final chapter, set it in the context of romance as a perennial form of literature. To that end I have made some use of the general theory of romance propounded by Northrop Frye. Apart from this excursion into archetypal theory, however, I have not attempted analysis in terms of modern theory. There is certainly scope for such examination—for instance in formalist terms—but that would be a different book.

Further discussion of the scope and method of the book will be found in Chapter 1.

Until recently English translations of some of the works discussed were hard to come by, but in 1989 a volume of new translations, *Collected Ancient Greek Novels*, including all the major texts discussed here, was published by the University of California Press under my editorship. These translations are used here, for the most part, the translators being: for Achilles Tatius, John J. Winkler; for Chariton, myself; for Heliodorus, J. R. Morgan; for Longus, Christopher Gill; for Xenophon Ephesius, Graham Anderson. Other translations are acknowledged as they occur, or else are my own.

I wish to thank a number of people who have helped me in the writing of the book. Tom Rosenmeyer suggested the topic and commented extensively on earlier drafts of the text; August Frugé, Christopher Gill, and Tomas Hägg all read the book at various stages and gave me valuable advice; anonymous referees made many helpful suggestions. I am grateful to all of them for their help; they should not, of course, be supposed to approve of everything in the book. Lastly, some of the writing was done in 1987–88 at the Institute for Advanced Study, Princeton, where I held a Visiting Professorship awarded by the Andrew W. Mellon Foundation; I wish to record my gratitude to both bodies.

✳ *Bibliographical References and Abbreviations* ✳

FULL BIBLIOGRAPHICAL information about books and articles is given in the notes on their first appearance, and also in the Bibliography.

The following works of reference are abbreviated, in the notes and Bibliography, as shown below:

CHCL *Cambridge History of Classical Literature*, vol. 1 (Greek). Edited by P. E. Easterling and B.M.W. Knox. Cambridge, 1985.

LSJ Liddell, H. G., and Scott, R., *A Greek-English Lexicon*, 9th ed. Revised by H. S. Jones. Oxford, 1940.

RE *Paulys Realencyclopädie der classischen Altertumswissenschaft*. Stuttgart, 1893–1970; Munich, 1973–1978 ("Pauly-Wissowa").

The Form of Greek Romance

———————— ✽ ————————

The Genre Romance in Antiquity

ROMANCE is difficult to define, but may be described generally as narrative fiction. It is usually idealizing and sentimental, and the specimens we shall be concerned with are in prose; but none of these attributes is essential to the genre, since the quality of romance is so ubiquitous that it readily dispenses with specific formal characteristics. Perhaps even realistic fiction, which we generally call "novel," tends towards romance—"all fiction has a way of looking like romance and in a sense this is just, since all fiction frees us into an imaginative world."[1] And that is really at the heart of the matter: romance inhabits an imagined world.

Let us situate the sort of work we shall be considering. In creating its imagined world, romance will not necessarily follow a recipe; rather, it will exhibit typical features: "a cluster of properties," in Beer's formulation—"the themes of love and adventure, a certain withdrawal from their own societies on the part of both reader and romance hero, profuse sensuous detail, simplified characters (often with a suggestion of allegorical significance), a serene intermingling of the unexpected and the everyday, a complex and prolonged succession of incidents usually without a single climax, a happy ending, amplitude of proportions, a strongly enforced code of conduct to which all the characters must comply."[2] Again, this should not be thought of as a checklist: any given element in this conglomeration may be absent in a particular work, but the overall flavor will remain distinctive. In practice we recognize romance readily enough.

Nor need we be unduly concerned about terminology. Although initially we may be disposed to consider "romance" trivial and re-

---

[1] Gillian Beer, *The Romance* (London, 1971), 5. This perceptive and stimulating monograph, in Methuen's *The Critical Idiom* series, is as helpful a brief treatment as any.

[2] Beer, *Romance*, 10. Later in the argument it will prove convenient to attempt a definition along the lines of Aristotle's definition of tragedy, and it may be of interest to anticipate it here: "Romance is extensive narrative fiction in prose, destined for reading and not for performance, describing the vicissitudes and psychological torments of private individuals, culminating in their ultimate felicity, and achieving through the presentation of their fears and aspirations the satisfaction of similar emotions in the reader."

serve our more serious attention for the "novel," it quickly becomes apparent that the forms cannot be neatly distinguished from each other, and if this study were being written in French or German the appellation *roman* or *Roman* would obviate the need to do so. Northrop Frye remarks that "the prose romance . . . is an independent form of fiction to be distinguished from the novel and extracted from the miscellaneous heap of prose works now covered by that term," but at once agrees that " 'pure' examples of either form are never found; there is hardly any modern romance that could not be made out to be a novel, and vice versa. The forms of prose fiction are mixed, like racial strains in human beings, not separable like the sexes. In fact the popular demand in fiction is always for a mixed form."[3] The ancient texts to be studied certainly do contain elements of both forms. In this book I shall for the most part use the term "romance," as being broader than "novel," but for present purposes I do not set great store by the distinction.

"Romance" itself has of course additional senses: besides signifying the specific genre of narrative prose fiction it may characterize a complex of genres (*e.g.*, epic, drama, lyric) that exhibit a romantic tone, or the quality of being romantic, whatever that may involve. The first of these senses will be the most common one here, but with the distinction once made there should not be any difficulty in recognizing the others where appropriate.

At this point we may set out the material to be discussed. Several kinds of narrative prose fiction existed in antiquity. The central texts, in their probable chronological order—none of the dates is very firm—are a group of love-romances: Chariton, *Chaereas and Callirhoe* (1st century A.D.); Xenophon of Ephesus, *Ephesiaca* or *Anthia and Habrocomes* (2nd century A.D.); Achilles Tatius, *Leucippe and Clitophon* (latter 2nd century A.D.); the familiar story of Longus, *Daphnis and Chloe* or *Pastoral Story* (end of 2nd century A.D.); and Heliodorus, *Ethiopica* or *Theagenes and Charicleia* (either 3rd century or late 4th century A.D.).[4] These texts have survived complete (it has been held that

---

[3] Northrop Frye, *Anatomy of Criticism* (Princeton, 1957), 305.

[4] The titles are given first in their most common form, then in alternative forms where these exist. The form *Jack and Jill*, which sufficiently indicates the content of the stories, is sometimes, in some cases, reduced to its female element: thus, Heliodorus's story is known in the Byzantine period as *Charicleia*, and Chariton's own title for his story may well have been *Callirhoe*. The geographical form of the name (e.g., *Ephesiaca*, or *Ephesian Story*) is of a type common enough throughout Greek literature. None of the dates is known with certainty, but it is unlikely that any is more than, say, half a

Xenophon's story is abridged). There are also fairly substantial fragmentary remains of several other stories of about the same period, of generally similar pattern, and less of yet others, including some mere titles. The outline of these stories is usually as follows: a handsome youth and a beautiful girl meet by chance and fall in love, but unexpected obstacles obstruct their union; they are separated, and each is launched on a series of journeys and dangerous adventures; through all their tribulations, however, they remain faithful to each other and to the benevolent deities who at critical junctures guide their steps; and eventually they are reunited and live happily ever after.

These are the texts that form the main subject of this study. There exist, however, some other kinds of work that cannot always be separated very clearly from the above group. First, there is a tradition of fanciful historiography going back to the classical period, ultimately to Herodotus. In similar vein there is a strain of romantic biography, stretching back to Xenophon's account of the boyhood of Cyrus the Great (*Cyropaedia*), and including notably the various forms of the Alexander-Romance. In the imperial period it is represented by Philostratus's life of the wonder-worker Apollonius of Tyana. In such texts travels and adventures naturally figure prominently, as they did also in some Hellenistic utopian travel stories (Iambulus, Euhemerus). An even clearer ideological content, and sometimes a love theme, are also to be seen in a group of Christian and para-Christian romance texts, such as some apocryphal *Acts*, recounting missionary travels and activities.

There is also a picaresque comic tradition. The well-known *Metamorphoses*, or *Golden Ass*, by Apuleius, belongs firmly to the second century A.D.; itself written in Latin, it is a descendant of a Greek original of which an abbreviated comic version is extant (*Asinus*, or *The Ass*), sometimes attributed to Lucian. Apuleius's book, however, de-

---

century out. The date of Heliodorus is a special case, and the subject of extensive argument, but he is almost certainly the latest of the group (possibly by a very wide margin). Some of these dates are discussed more fully in the notes to the next chapter. It will perhaps be useful to recall here what is indicated in the Preface: that a comprehensive collection of English translations of the texts discussed in this study is now available, namely B. P. Reardon, ed., *Collected Ancient Greek Novels* (Berkeley and Los Angeles, 1989). All of the translations are new and were made for the collection (with the exception of my translation of Lucian, *A True Story*, which was first published in 1965). This is the first such collection ever to appear in English. Collections exist in other languages, and English translations exist of individual works (several being out of print); see the Bibliography for details.

fies straightforward classification; it unquestionably has a serious side to it. More obviously comic is the celebrated *Satyricon* of Petronius. Both works must be mentioned here because they have connections with romance proper; but the nature of those connections is complex, and the works will be marginal to the present study. It will be noticed that the two principal ancient comic stories are also the only two unquestionably Latin novels.[5] That there was a comic strand in Greek prose fiction seems, however, established by the recent publication of a distinctly scurrilous fragment, *Iolaus*; as by the existence of Lucian's *True Story*, a second-century Baron Munchausen tale parodying incredible accounts of travel in strange lands, such as Homer and Herodotus offer.

Finally, romantic matter figures markedly in several other genres. The *Odyssey* itself is the fountainhead of Greek romance, and there is similar narrative in the romantic love story of Jason and Medea as told in the Hellenistic miniature epic of Apollonius of Rhodes, the *Argonautica*. There is romantic tragedy (some of the plays of Euripides), comedy (Menander) and lyric (Sappho). We shall have occasion to return to these works.

It would scarcely be possible to construct an analysis that would comprehend all of these forms.[6] For analytical purposes the Greek

[5] There is another story extant in Latin, the *Story of Apollonius King of Tyre*, known to us in a sixth-century text, but it is often thought to be a Latin version of a Greek original of the second or third century A.D.; see G.A.A. Kortekaas, *Historia Apollonii Regis Tyri* (Groningen, 1984) 107 ff., 118 ff., 125 ff. Its content places it in the same category as the Greek love-romances.

[6] I shall not attempt to draw in detail the literary-historical map of the texts to be discussed; it is certainly a complex one. The best extensive guide to the topic is Tomas Hägg, *The Novel in Antiquity* (Oxford, Berkeley and Los Angeles, 1983). Among histories of literature, see especially the *Cambridge History of Classical Literature*, vol. 1 (Greek), edited by P. E. Easterling and B.M.W. Knox (Cambridge, 1985) (referred to in the present study as *CHCL*). The chapter on "The Greek Novel," by E. L. Bowie, 683–99, gives an excellent account; in particular, it brings out well in short compass the range of prose fiction in Greek antiquity: some twenty "novels" are now known of, either fully extant or in fragmentary form (*CHCL*, 684)—this figure does not include the "fringe" texts such as romanticized biography and Christian or para-Christian proselytizing romance. A. Lesky, *A History of Greek Literature*, trans. J. Willis and C. de Heer (London, 1966; Berne [German orig.], 1957/1958), 857–70, remains very useful. Older standard histories of Greek literature, such as that of Schmid-Stählin, are now out of date on this topic. General accounts will also be found in N. Holzberg, *Der antike Roman* (Munich and Zurich, 1986), a well organized and coherent account that very largely replaces R. Helm's never very satisfactory handbook of the same title (Göttingen, 1948), and is fully up to date (though the format of the series precludes documentation) on recent scholarship and on the numerous fragments published in recent de-

love–romance, which probably began to appear in the late Hellenistic period and lasted until at least the third century A.D., has advantages over other forms of romance, for several reasons. A clearly defined corpus exists; the form has a recognizable and fairly standard plot, whereas other forms develop in several different directions; and it engages the imagination and emotions of the reader in a consistent, readily identifiable, familiar way. It is the form to which narrative prose fiction seems to gravitate; in antiquity as in other periods "the central element of romance is a love story."[7] Consequently this variety of romance will constitute the principal subject of the present discussion, although other forms will enter the picture to frame it.

The study of ancient romance poses special problems, however. The literary history of the form is difficult to establish, because of the insufficiency of our evidence, and there is virtually no explicit ancient theory on the matter such as exists for tragedy or, say, historiography. Aristotle does not say anything about the genre of romance, nor does anyone else. Prose fiction arrived late on the scene, centuries after the other genres, and when it did arrive it was at first apparently not thought to merit the serious attention of the cultivated. In consequence it did not exist officially, and was never discussed until late antiquity (and very little even then); no such critical category existed. It did not even have an agreed name. Several terms are indeed employed, such as *plasma* (fictitious creation), *diēgēma* (narrative), *historia* (account of what one has discovered), and *drama* (story of action); all relate to one or another aspect of prose fiction; but no one word in antiquity comprehends prose fiction adequately—or even inadequately, as do "romance" and "novel." So no theorist of literature would have been troubled by the question "what is romance?"

There was no lack of theorists, of a sort, at the very period of florescence of prose fiction. But the qualification "of a sort" is important; for better or for worse, they were not of our sort. In fact, remarkably little theory that we could wholeheartedly endorse ever did exist in antiquity: one ideologue, of massive imaginative power and

cades (it should be noted, however, that Helm's book includes useful summaries of the fringe and Christian texts); B. P. Reardon, *Courants littéraires grecs des IIe et IIIe siècles après J.-C.* (Paris, 1971), 309–403 (on the novel in its literary context); and O. Weinreich, *Der griechische Liebesroman* (Zurich, 1962), originally published as a postscript to a German translation of Heliodorus's *Ethiopica* by R. Reymer (Zurich, 1959).

[7] Northrop Frye, *The Secular Scripture: A Study of the Structure of Romance* (Cambridge, Mass., 1976), 24.

massive influence; one analytical genius; a handful of perceptive spirits (Gorgias, "Longinus"); apart from these, and especially at the period relevant here, a plethora of technicians of rhetoric, whittling away for centuries at a limited enough theory of expression. One can hardly suppose that an early outburst of genius stifled subsequent criticism. Plato's thought was wholeheartedly modified, throughout its range, and we cannot be sure whether Horace (of all people) even knew Aristotle's work. Strange, when so much writing, so many *genera*, came to us from antiquity. But it would be inappropriate to pursue this topic here. For the moment it will be enough simply to observe that, in some respects at least, the ancient world was not very good at literary criticism.[8] This creates a serious difficulty when we consider ancient prose fiction: we hardly have a handle by which to take hold of romance.

Other, related questions arise as well. First, the very notion of fiction is not one that fits readily with the literature of the classical world. It is, of course, central in our literary scheme of things. "Fiction" is, for instance, a principal classification in our libraries. Librarians are in no doubt that it is a thing, and put it on specific shelves. Ancient librarians had no such category, and we cannot say where Chariton's story would have been shelved; very few copies of it were ultimately shelved anywhere, other than in Egyptian garbage dumps.[9] Why is there no such category? How does it come about that the civilization we loosely think of as the source of modern literature is so distant from us in this respect? Is it in fact so distant? Another question concerns the medium, the vehicle. With us, the major form of fiction is the novel; that is, *prose* fiction. Now, not only is the ancient notion of fiction somewhat at odds with ours, but the idea of using prose for purposes of fiction is foreign to antiquity, in its classical periods. Fiction itself does exist in reality: in the *Iliad* and *Odys-*

[8] A similar judgment is reached, for different but converging reasons, by D. A. Russell in his *Criticism in Antiquity* (London, Berkeley and Los Angeles, 1981). See *e.g.*, page 6: ". . . this ancient rhetorical 'criticism', though undoubtedly useful in suggesting principles of judgment and helping to elucidate authors' intentions, is fundamentally not equal to the task of appraising classical literature."

[9] *Chaereas and Callirhoe* has survived complete in only one manuscript, Conventi Soppressi 627 (known usually as "F"), now in the Laurentian library in Florence; it dates from the late 13th century, and is not of good quality. Several papyrus fragments of Chariton have been found, from 1899 on, in relatively remote Greek settlements in Egypt (Oxyrhynchus, Fayûm); they have been of crucial importance in the dating of the work.

sey, to start with—no doubt they were thought of as historical legend, but obviously they are substantially fiction. Later, it exists just as clearly in drama; dramatists were anything but reluctant to invent. But it does not exist in prose. Almost all of what we should call "creative literature" in antiquity is in verse, until relatively late.[10] Why? These questions will need answers, to our minds; we have no such conventions. We have given full rein to fiction, we have released the tremendous vehicle of prose for creative purpose—and produced *Persuasion, War and Peace, The Heart of the Matter.* Perhaps we can properly feel superior to antiquity; but we should ask ourselves why.

The late appearance of prose fiction and the academic conventions surrounding its elements led to its being generally disregarded by the academic world in antiquity. This disregard is responsible for the loss of much of the literary history attached to the genre, and hence for the modern world's ignorance of it—which in turn explains, in part, the disdain that long attached to the ancient romance in the modern world. The monumental standard work on the form, Rohde's *Der griechische Roman,*[11] is the principal expression in modern times of that disdain. It was never likely that Rohde would think well of romance. Immensely erudite, young (the book was completed by the time he was thirty) and impatient of mediocrity, he was living in the tradition of Winckelmann and Goethe, and writing in the wake of ground breaking German work on early and classical Greek literature. Romance, a late form whose content he thought sentimental and trivial, was far from the center of his sympathies.[12] This attitude to such forms, in any culture, is common enough now, particularly in the academic world. The romance form is generously receptive; it will accept much that is repugnant to the cultivated reader, who is

[10] This topic is discussed at length by B. E. Perry in *The Ancient Romances* (Berkeley and Los Angeles, 1967), an important modern study of romance to which general reference may be made here; see his chapter 2, "The Form Romance in Historical Perspective." See chapter 3 of the present study for further discussion of the point at issue.

[11] E. Rohde, *Der griechische Roman und seine Vorläufer* (Leipzig, 1876) now commonly referred to in its 3rd edition, ed. W. Schmid (Leipzig, 1914), which is reprinted with the original pagination printed in the margin, and a foreword by Karl Kerényi, in the 4th edition (Hildesheim, 1960) and 5th (1974); referred to here as *Gr. Rom.*.

[12] For Rohde's attitude to the topic see particularly Hubert Cancik, "Erwin Rohde, ein Philologe der Bismarckzeit," in *Semper Apertus: Sechshundert Jahre Ruprecht-Karls-Universität Heidelberg 1386-1986,* ed. W. Doerr (Berlin and Heidelberg, 1986), 436–505, esp. 451–56.

9

not always as ready as a Northrop Frye to discern the nature and value of a massive design, a scriptural quality, behind it.

Perhaps more importantly, though, Rohde had his chronology wrong, seriously wrong, although not really through his own fault; and that had a major effect on his assessment of the genre. The dates of the extant texts were not known in his day—as we have seen, they are known only approximately now—and there was little to help him in establishing them. His general attitude perhaps made it difficult for him to approach the problem in a detached way. That could be done: Schmid did it for Chariton, simply by observing the nature, in particular the simplicity, of his language, and concluding that the text was therefore early.[13] Rohde did see the simplicity, but he took it for decadence, and concluded that the work was therefore late. Before his book was twenty years old, one revolutionary papyrological discovery was made that was destined to make the first breach in his chronological edifice, and consequently in his whole interpretation of the form.[14] A few years later other discoveries, almost as sensational, brought Chariton to a date at least three hundred years earlier than Rohde's date for him, to the beginning instead of the end of the series. Such discoveries have continued to the present day, and they have resulted in the total disruption of Rohde's scheme; hence, in a total reinterpretation of the whole form. Not, be it noted, in a fully adequate understanding of it. The old problems have been replaced by new ones, and if the picture is rather fuller, it is also more complicated. But that picture has unquestionably changed considerably in our century. Above all, it is now beyond question that romance constituted, in antiquity, a veritable genre. The texts are no longer isolated, discontinuous, odd; no longer inexplicable, as Longus and

[13] W. Schmid, "Chariton" *RE* 3 (1899), 2168–71. It is true that by 1899, after the publication of the *Ninus* fragment (see next note), Schmid's suggestion was less revolutionary than it would have been a few years earlier, since it was by then possible to contemplate an earlier date for the first romance texts than had so far been the case; but that does not detract from Schmid's achievement in redating Chariton in the face of prevailing opinion, on the internal evidence of the text itself.

[14] See U. Wilcken, "Ein neuer griechischer Roman," *Hermes* 28 (1893), 161–93; the text is discussed at length in Perry, *Ancient Romances*, 149–66. The fragments are part of a romance about the historical figures Ninus, King of Assyria in the 9th century B.C., and his wife Semiramis. On papyrological grounds the papyrus must have been written before A.D. 100, and the romance itself probably goes back at least to the 1st century B.C. A translation can be found in my *Collected Ancient Greek Novels* (see n. 4 above).

Petronius, for instance, once seemed to be. And they are no longer matter for simple contempt, as they were to Rohde.

Rohde's explanation of the appearance of romance had been, to use Perry's expression, a "biological" explanation characteristic of the nineteenth century:[15] two literary forms, love-elegy and travel story, were "crossed" and produced the love-and-travel story. The operation of social forces does not figure in his account. For us, this may seem to lead to miscomprehension of the very nature of the form. Romance is surely, above all else, the expression of a stage of society. In that perspective it will be a picture of a society—romance is "usually acutely fashionable, cast in the exact mould of an age's sensibility";[16] in the event, it was an open society. Unfamiliar as the texts and literary history may be still, to classicists as well as others, we shall hardly be likely to look for other kinds of explanation, unless indeed we adopt the entirely non-historical approach of some recent theories.[17]

Another, rather different perspective may also be of value in assessing this form-for-the-age: a spiritual perspective. The twentieth century is more prepared than was the nineteenth to look behind the impressive political structure of the Roman Empire; prepared to be disenchanted about empire in general, and correspondingly ready to see Greece and its culture as by no means played out in the early Christian era. But we are not yet—unless we are very cynical, or nihilistic—disenchanted about man-in-society. That does interest us, attract us, to the point of creating myths about him. Romance, in Frye's overall scheme of literature, slips into novel, into irony; and irony slips into myth; into Kafka. Man-in-society is a theme in ancient romance; we shall be considering it. We may think also, or alternatively, that ancient romance writers offer us man-in-divine-context. That too is myth. Myth and romance are close neighbors.

Whatever the circumstances of its genesis, whatever the nature of its reception in antiquity and in modern times, the ancient romance did arise. Creative artists are not dependent on academic approval. A priori it seems unlikely that antiquity would not have made its way sooner or later to "the structural core of all fiction."[18] In a sense, ro-

---

[15] Perry's comments on Rohde form an important part of his first chapter, "Greek Romance: Forms and Origins."

[16] Beer, *Romance*, 12.

[17] See, however, Chapter 7, n. 12, for a swing of the pendulum.

[18] Frye, *Secular Scripture*, 15.

mance material exists from preliterate times, in the form of myth and legend; it found expression, as we have seen, in various forms—oral tale, ballad and epic, drama. Eventually it acquired the written form now familiar to us. When social conditions and historical circumstances were propitious, some writers spread their wings in the new air and began to use the form, to use it to talk about the new society. They did not reach the regions explored by Stendhal or Dostoyevsky, but if we can disencumber ourselves of such expectations, we shall find in the ancient romance a form of what modern theory usually thinks of as having been born in eighteenth-century Europe.[19] The "novel" is undoubtedly a major literary genre. The broader term "romance" may well signify something bigger and more important than a mere literary genre. It may constitute a whole mode of thought, a frame of reference, an authority for our behavior: Frye's term "secular scripture" is a singularly felicitous formula.

Considered in these terms, ancient prose fiction deserves more than the obscure corner in literary history it has often had in our own day. These romances are not merely a literary-historical phenomenon; they have a claim to attention in themselves. Their main attraction is quite simply that they are good stories, in a strong and popular form. They offer adventure not the less interesting for being often improbable, and a romantic vision of life whose attraction lies precisely in that quality of romance. In sum, they offer a coherent imagined world. From the very beginning of the form, authors are clearly aware that interesting things can be done with it, and we can see them using their material inventively. Furthermore, although the art of romance writing no doubt had its primitive stage like all arts, what is striking in this case is rather the sophistication of even the earliest

[19] E.g. Ian Watt, *The Rise of the Novel* (London, 1957); see now Michael McKeon, *The Origins of the English Novel* (Baltimore and London, 1987). Occasional protests are heard, e. g., Paul Turner, "Novels, Ancient and Modern," in *Novel* 2 (1968–69), 15–24, questioning "the current belief in the parthenogenesis of the eighteenth-century novel": "If, as I have shown, the best of the ancient Greek novels [Longus] realistically describes the psychological development of two individual adolescents through a story constructed on principles of causation and set in a context of particularized time and place; if even the worst of them were based on plot-formulae which are still being used by novelists today—can anyone but a Tertullian remain convinced that the origin of this species was a special *fiat* 'round about 1700'?" (referring to a phrase of Walter Allen's). See also Arthur Heiserman, *The Novel before the Novel* (Chicago, 1977), on this topic and (3 ff.) the related topic of terminology (novel/romance, see above). McKeon finds modern scholars of ancient narrative "disarmingly relaxed in their use of generic terminology," a somewhat simplistic view of the matter.

surviving texts; the sophistication of attitude, of observation, of technique within a convention; the stance that authors adopt towards their own creations. Nor is it only the writer's own imaginary, self-contained world that claims our attention; these writers also reveal an external, objective world, the society of their own time. They do so not directly, by writing about it, reporting it, consciously representing it; but indirectly, by writing *in* it and unconsciously reflecting it, its assumptions, its aspirations: by simply appearing and working in that given time and place. In short, the ancient romance is interesting both as an artistic and as a social phenomenon.

Romance is in the air. From Tolkien to Hollywood to drugstore paperback, it is all around us. Perhaps we are in a romance cycle. Certainly we are familiar with more kinds of romance than ever existed in antiquity. With that in mind, I shall close this study by considering some general interpretations of Greek romance that may serve to set it in a broader conceptual framework. I have already referred to what is perhaps the most substantial single modern literary-theoretical construction on the topic of romance, Northrop Frye's expansion, in *The Secular Scripture*, of one of the elements in his celebrated "anatomy" of criticism; it will be useful to return to it, in some detail, at that final stage.[20] It constitutes, of course, nothing less than a rehabilitation of the whole concept of romance, as a serious major category of narrative expression. The term "romance" embraces a whole area of imaginative creation; "novel," correspondingly, denotes a category of romance, "ironically displaced" romance. An approach of this kind will help us in navigating the ancient romance between— Scylla and Charybdis, a classicist is bound to say: the Scylla of disdain, the Charybdis of not being "novel." The basic pattern of romance, critical authority will tell us, is that of "quest narrative." We shall do well to keep this pattern in mind, in our assessment of Chariton, Longus and their contemporaries. What is the relation of ancient romance to this perennial shape?

I shall try, then, to describe and analyse the generic features of Greek romance, and the theoretical considerations relevant to it in antiquity; and to situate it in its context and place in ancient literature. My aim is not to write a handbook but to set out some main lines of the form, and to keep a whole picture in view. In such a critical analysis we shall to some extent be thrown back upon extrap-

[20] An outline of the principal elements of Frye's analysis will be found in Chapter 7.

olation, or educated guesswork. We must try to see through what readers and critics saw and what writers did; to ask of antiquity questions that antiquity had no thought of asking. But with luck we may be able to make out the outline of our sort of question in some minds in antiquity.

The Practice of Greek Romance

IT WOULD be lèse-majesté to begin an analysis of romance in antiquity anywhere other than with its *fons et origo*, the *Odyssey*. The *Odyssey* appears to have all the elements of romance, to set out the coordinates of the genre; it subtends, as it were, all the travel-and-adventure stories in subsequent Greek literature, if not in the whole Western tradition. I shall begin, therefore, by setting out the pattern of romance as it appears in this prototype and exemplar of the form.

For our purposes here, the *Odyssey* may be seen as an imaginative narrative describing the vicissitudes and ultimate success of a resilient, glamorous hero whose adventures, in a varied and sometimes exotic setting, could be thought to constitute a national experience, even to symbolize human experience. Teasing out these basic features, we can see here several characteristics of romance. The *Odyssey*'s nature as essentially imaginative, and narrative in mode, forms the basis of its romance form. Whatever the claims to truthfulness of romance, whether as history, legend or myth, it is not *qua* true account that it attracts, but *qua* interesting account; and it is the author who is responsible for making it interesting. Accordingly he will simply invent, where necessary. And perhaps above all, it is the *story* that attracts, the imagined sequence of events: "tell us a story" is the oldest request in the world, and that is where the real strength of romance lies.

The principal features of the fictitious story thus narrated are as follows. First, it is a story of exciting and perilous adventure, and also of love. In one perspective a picaresque story, it is nonetheless held together by a plot which is also a love story: though the love involved is not the erotic passsion we meet in Euripides, Odysseus, in achieving his return, is after all reunited with a beloved partner. Second, the *Odyssey* offers us a central character on to whom we can project our own dream-image: a resourceful hero, *polymētis Odysseus*, an embattled, enduring, successful Superman, *polytlas dios Odysseus*. Next, the central concrete feature of romance—perhaps the one element that is indispensable to its success—is plot. In the *Odyssey* we are

15

offered a plot involving, essentially, a task to be carried out: the *nos-tos* or return of the hero to his home. This is the element of quest that Frye and others identify as the motor of romance. The quest involves much travel, and requires the hero to overcome various dangerous obstacles, such as shipwreck and the threats posed by enemies (and sometimes friends); it separates the hero and heroine, until near the end; and it enlists divinities in its cause, some helping, some oppos-ing the hero. The quest-story is extensive, of epic proportions, and it is architecturally conceived: the numerous episodes, individually at-tractive, form not simply a linear series but a mounting climax—and they also people the story with a wealth of secondary characters against whom the figure of the hero can be measured. The setting of this narrative is varied, and above all imaginative, even fantastical in places, with the fantasy ranging from nightmare to utopia. Finally, and crucially, the story ends with our wish fulfilled. This issues, as in most romances, in the restoration of the hero's identity, and in a happy ending, such as to fit the anterior story and thus be psycho-logically satisfying.[1]

This reads like a veritable ideal catalogue of the ingredients of ro-mance as they will be found in the prose love-stories. And that is why it has been worthwhile to set them out at this point: the list can stand as a table of contents, a bill of fare, for this chapter, and as the articulated skeleton for the whole book. Only the proportions of these contents will vary as we look at later texts. The shadow of the *Odyssey* will be ubiquitous.

This much said, we shall pass immediately to prose romance of the imperial period. That is a long haul. It should not be supposed, how-ever, that the *quality* of romance disappeared for eight or nine cen-turies. Far from it: it never did, in any civilization. It simply took other forms: in archaic lyric, in tragedy and post-classical drama, in Alexandrian poetry, in prose writings of various kinds. All these manifestations of romance can throw light on the mature form, and in due course we shall be turning to them for just that purpose. But for the present, with the vision of the *Odyssey* before us, it will be better to emulate the *Odyssey* itself and plunge into the heart of the matter. This can be done best by looking in detail at one specimen text to illustrate clearly the salient features of the genre. It will then

---

[1] Tragic romance of course also exists—*Tristan and Iseult* springs to mind, or, come to that, the *Iliad* itself. But often, as with the *Iliad*, in such a work the sense of tragedy overpowers even the narrative element, its aspect as story.

be possible to note what is similar and what is different in other examples, and thus to establish a pattern for the form.[2]

Chariton's romance *Chaereas and Callirhoe* has already been mentioned several times, notably as being in all probability the earliest fully extant romance text.[3] As such, its literary-historical importance is considerable, and the text has in this century been the subject of important literary-historical and also critical work.[4] It also happens, however, that *Chaereas and Callirhoe* is not only an early but also a particularly "ripe" specimen of the form, and it is for that reason that we shall use it here as our principal example of ancient romance. Curiously, it is the one text totally disregarded by Northrop Frye;[5] its

[2] It would be disproportionate to give more than very selective bibliographical information in the course of this chapter. Extensive work has been done on the form in recent decades. Some authors and topics will receive a certain amount of commentary for particular purposes relevant to the immediate discussion; for the rest, the reader is referred to the general bibliography and to the information to be found in the works listed in n. 6 to Chapter 1.

[3] Dates nowadays proposed range from mid-1st century B.C. (A. Papanikolaou, *Chariton-Studien* [Göttingen, 1973], 162–63, on linguistic grounds; rejected as too early by *e.g.* G. Giangrande, *Journal of Hellenic Studies* 94 [1974], 197–98 and B. P. Reardon, *Classical Review* 26 [1976], 21–23) to late 2nd century A.D. (R. Petri, *Ueber den Roman des Chariton* [Meisenheim am Glan, 1963], 47–58, as imitating Achilles Tatius and Xenophon Ephesius; shown to be too late by Papanikolaou, *Chariton-Studien*, 153–59). A date in the 1st century A.D. has been suggested on various grounds by a number of scholars, and seems likely. A useful summary of current suggestions can be found in C. Ruiz Montero, "Una observación para la cronologia de Caritón de Afrodisias," *Estudios Clásicos* 24 (1980), 63–69; she herself suggests ca. A.D. 100, on the basis of a possible identification and dating of the rhetor Athenagoras to whom Chariton was secretary. The extreme possible limits are early 1st century B.C., on historical grounds (Papanikolaou, 162) and ca. A.D. 200 (on papyrological grounds; see Petri, 47–51). My own guess is mid-1st century A.D., on stylistic grounds—before the full onset of the literary and stylistic "renaissance" dated by Philostratus (*Lives of the Sophists* 511) in the later 1st century A.D.

[4] Here, besides recalling Perry's *Ancient Romances*, whose second chapter is entitled "Chariton and the Nature of Greek Romance," and his article "Chariton and his Romance from a Literary-Historical Point of View," *American Journal of Philology* 51 (1930), 93–134, 129, I will mention only the standard modern edition of W. E. Blake (Oxford, 1938), with his translation (Ann Arbor and London, 1939), and a recent Budé edition by G. Molinié (Paris, 1979); the last of these is not impeccable (see T. Hägg, *Gnomon* 53 [1981], 698–700 and B. P. Reardon, *Revue des Etudes Grecques* 95 [1982], 157–73), but for those not greatly concerned with the quality of the text it does make available, in the original and in translation, a work which had become often difficult of access (Blake's work being long out of print).

[5] Frye not infrequently talks of ancient romances, but invariably omits Chariton from any list (*e.g.*, *Secular Scripture*, 3, 71–72, 114) and never discusses him. This may be a consequence of the relative inaccessibility of *Chaereas and Callirhoe* compared to other

use here may in some measure serve to repair this neglect. It will be worthwhile to set out more than the skeleton of the story, since the exposition will serve to illustrate the nature of Greek romance as well as its basic structure. It runs as follows.

The beautiful Callirhoe is the daughter of the famous Syracusan general Hermocrates. He is a historical figure, and the story is thus purportedly a historical romance, set rather vaguely in the late fifth and fourth centuries B.C. Callirhoe has as suitors princes and tyrants from all Sicily and beyond. Eros, however, has his own plans for her, and arranges that the girl, on her way to worship Aphrodite, should suddenly come face to face with the handsome Chaereas, son of Hermocrates's bitter political rival Ariston. The encounter is only fleeting, but the two fall passionately in love at once. Soon they are wasting away; Callirhoe is ashamed to tell her parents of her love, and Chaereas, when he reveals his plight to his parents, meets with strong opposition—he must not woo the daughter of a rival family. Soon Chaereas is at death's door, and the whole citizen body of Syracuse, in public assembly, implores Hermocrates to save him by consenting to the marriage. Hermocrates yields to this pressure, and a spectacular wedding takes place. But Callirhoe's other suitors, furious at being thus set aside for a mere private individual, mount an intrigue to break up the marriage. Chaereas is deceived into thinking that his wife is unfaithful to him, and in his anger kicks her violently in the stomach; Callirhoe falls apparently dead. The truth about the intrigue, however, soon comes out. Chaereas, in bitter regret, tries desperately to do away with himself, but is restrained from doing so; and Callirhoe is entombed, after a magnificent funeral, in a large funeral vault, together with untold wealth.

The second movement of the story now begins. The funeral display attracts thieves, who that night enter the vault to rob it of its treasures. To their astonishment the first thing they see is Callirhoe—alive! She had, we learn, merely been in a deep coma from which she has just awakened as the robbers enter. Chariton takes full advantage of the pathos, drama, and even humor of this situation:

---

ancient romance texts (see previous note). But it is the more curious in that he does refer to Perry's book in his very first note, and, as we have just seen, Chariton is central to Perry's thesis; a long summary of the plot is given in his third chapter, 124–37.

When they began to use crowbars and hammer heavily to open the vault, Callirhoe was gripped by a variety of emotions—fear, joy, grief, surprise, hope, disbelief. "Where is this noise coming from? Is some divinity coming for me—poor creature!—as always happens when people are dying? Or is it not a noise but a voice—the voice of the gods below calling me to them? It is more likely that it is tomb-robbers; there, there is an additional misfortune; wealth is of no use to a corpse." While these thoughts were still passing through her mind, a robber put his head through and came a little way into the vault. Callirhoe, intending to implore his help, threw herself at his knees; he was terrified and jumped back. Shaking with fear, he cried to his fellows: "Let's get out of here! There's some sort of spirit in there who won't let us come in!" Theron [the leader of the pirates,] laughed scornfully at him and called him a coward and deader than the dead girl. Then he told another man to go in; and when nobody had the courage to do so, he went in himself, holding his sword ready before him. At the gleam of the metal Callirhoe was afraid she was going to be murdered; she shrank back into the corner of the vault and from there begged him in a small voice: "Have pity on me, whoever you are—I have had no pity from husband or parents. Do not kill me now you have saved me." (1.9.3–5)

Theron at once realizes what has happened. Eventually he decides to carry off Callirhoe along with the plunder and sell her as a slave. The scene rapidly moves to Miletus, in Asia Minor, represented as at that period part of the Persian Empire. There Callirhoe is adroitly palmed off, with a plausible story about her provenance, on Leonas, the agent of the Greek seigneur of the region, Dionysius; and Theron and his crew remove themselves speedily from the scene. Here Callirhoe's fortunes take a yet more pathetic turn. Dionysius has recently been left a widower, and apparently inconsolable. When he sees Callirhoe, however, he takes her at first sight for Aphrodite, so beautiful is she, and soon is deeply in love with her. An honorable man, he will not take advantage of her misfortune, and he induces her to tell him her real story. Callirhoe does tell him much of it—the incident of the coma, and how she has come into his possession—but she remains silent about her marriage to Chaereas. Dionysius resolves to treat her with all the respect due to her; but he cannot bring himself to return her to Sicily, and hopes to win her as his wife—

against hope, because Callirhoe, despite her maltreatment by her jealous husband, still loves him passionately and is for her part desolate at the prospect of being separated forever from him. Here Fortune—almost a doublet or agent, in the story, of Eros and Aphrodite—brings about another dramatic turn of events: Callirhoe now discovers that she is two months pregnant by Chaereas. She thus faces a crisis. The solutions open to her appear to be either to let her child be born into the condition of slavery or to procure an abortion.

But Dionysius has allotted to her as servant one of his own slaves, a young woman called Plangon, who astutely manages the situation so as to earn her own freedom. She convinces Callirhoe that Dionysius will never allow her to rear her child, and persuades her to marry her noble-minded, unsuspecting new master and pass the child off as his. Callirhoe, after passionate heart-searching, and with the help of a vision of her husband, at last and with heavy heart resigns herself to this course:

> Callirhoe went up to her room and shut the door. She held Chaereas's picture to her womb: "Here are the three of us," she said, "husband, wife, and child; let us decide what is best for us all. I shall give my view first: I want to die Chaereas's wife and his alone. To know no other husband—that is dearer to me than parents or country or child. And you, my child—what is your choice for yourself? To die by poison before seeing the light of day? To be cast out with your mother, and perhaps not even thought worth of burial? Or to live, and have two fathers—one the first man in Sicily, the other in Ionia? When you grow up you will easily be recognized by your family—I am sure I shall bring you into the world in the likeness of your father; and you will sail home in triumph, in a Milesian warship, and Hermocrates will welcome a grandson already fit for command. Your vote is cast against mine, child; you will not sanction your death. Let us ask your father too. No, he has spoken; he came to me in person in my dreams, and said 'I entrust our son to you.' I call you to witness, Chaereas—it is you who are giving me to Dionysius as his bride." (2.11.1–3)

Meanwhile, the people of Syracuse have not been inactive. When the tomb-robbery is discovered, search parties are sent in all directions. Chaereas himself, forlorn, suicidal and passive as he is, participates in the search. By good luck he happens upon Theron's ship, tempest-tossed by an avenging Providence in the robbers' escape and drifting helplessly with all but Theron dead. The robber is seized, taken to Syracuse, and crucified, but not before revealing that Callirhoe is in Miletus—he does not say exactly where. A ship is sent to recover her, with Chaereas of course aboard, accompanied by his faithful friend Polycharmus. It reaches land in Dionysius's domains. There, Dionysius's steward Phocas—the husband of Plangon—discovers its mission and incites a Persian military unit to destroy it as a hostile vessel. Chaereas is as a result himself enslaved to Mithridates, the Persian satrap of Caria (a region near Miletus). Dionysius, meanwhile, hearing Callirhoe cry out the name of Chaereas in her sleep, learns that she has been married to him; but he remains quite without suspicion, even when Callirhoe's child is born after seven months of marriage.

Shortly after this, Callirhoe has reason to wonder whether Chaereas is in the vicinity. This leads to inquiries. Callirhoe hears of the destruction of the Syracusan ship and concludes that Chaereas is dead, of course to her intense distress. Dionysius, only too glad to be rid of this ghost, mounts a magnificent cenotaph funeral for Chaereas, in an attempt to console his wife. And here further complications ensue. The funeral is attended by all the great men of the area, among them Mithridates—now Chaereas's master—who inevitably falls passionately in love with Callirhoe. There follows a complex intrigue, in the course of which, when Chaereas is about to be crucified, his identity becomes known to Mithridates, who encourages him to try to win back his wife—though in fact Mithridates is hoping to win her ultimately for himself. A letter from Chaereas to Callirhoe is intercepted and taken to Dionysius; this leads to a quarrel between Dionysius and Mithridates. The quarrel reaches the ears of the Persian King in Babylon, and he summons both Dionysius and Mithridates before him to stand trial. They bring Callirhoe and Chaereas, respectively, but the separated couple do not yet meet, for more tribulations are in store.

The trial and debate which follow are handled dramatically and with great skill. Dionysius and Mithridates each accuse the other of stealing another man's wife; the tension mounts, as Mithridates holds his fire; and finally, when Dionysius challenges his rival to exonerate himself by producing Chaereas, Mithridates, to spectacular effect, does precisely that. Hero and heroine stand before each other for the first time since Callirhoe fell seemingly dead:

21

. While he was still speaking—that is how they had arranged things—Chaereas himself stepped forward. When she saw him, Callirhoe cried out, "Chaereas! Are you alive?" and made to run to him. But Dionysius held her back, blocked the way, and would not let them embrace. Who could fitly describe that scene in court? What dramatist ever staged such an astonishing story? It was like being at a play packed with passionate scenes, with emotions tumbling over each other—weeping and rejoicing, astonishment and pity, disbelief and prayers. How happy all were for Chaereas! How glad for Mithridates! For Dionysius, how sorrowful! As for Callirhoe, they did not know what to think. She was in total confusion and stood there unable to utter a word—she could only gaze wide-eyed at Chaereas. I think the King himself, at that moment, would have liked to be Chaereas. When men are rivals for a woman's love, they are always easily provoked to violence. In this case, the sight of the prize made them even readier to fight; but for the King's presence they would have come to blows. But they limited themselves to words. "I am her first husband," said Chaereas. "And I am a more reliable one," replied Dionysius. "Did I put away my wife?" "No, you buried her." "Show me the divorce papers!" "You can see her tomb." "Her father married her to me." "She married me herself." "You aren't fit for Hermocrates' daughter!" "You're even less fit—Mithridates had you in chains!" "I demand Callirhoe back!" "And I am keeping her!" "You're laying hands on another man's wife!" "And you killed your own!" "Adulterer!" "Murderer!" Such was their argument—and the audience enjoyed it. (5.8.1–4)

But they are not yet back in each other's arms. The contest now becomes a struggle between the rival claims of Chaereas and Dionysius, each armed with a strong case. Mithridates bows out honorably. But by now the King of Persia himself has fallen helplessly in love with Callirhoe—for him, a singularly delicate position (drawn with delicacy by Chariton). He postpones the trial, unable to solve his problem. But it is solved for him by Fortune, when Egypt suddenly rebels against the Persian rule. The King marches to war, taking Callirhoe in his train; Dionysius goes with him, subsequently to distinguish himself in battle. Chaereas, who has already been dissuaded from suicide a number of times by Polycharmus, now in desperation joins the rebel side, determined to achieve at least a glorious death. In the vicissitudes of war that follow, Chaereas proves a brilliant commander and, although the rebel army is defeated, defeats the Persian fleet. Among Chaereas's prisoners is not only the Persian Queen, but his own Callirhoe—although it is only in the nick of time that he learns of her presence. And this, at last, is the so-long-postponed reunion. Chaereas enters the room.

> When he saw her stretched out on the ground with her head covered, he felt his heart stirred at once by the way she breathed and the look of her, and felt a thrill of excitement; he would certainly have recognized her had he not been thoroughly convinced that Dionysius had taken Callirhoe for himself. He went up to her quietly. "Don't be frightened, lady," he said, "whoever you are. We are not going to use force on you. You shall have the husband you want." Before he had finished speaking, Callirhoe recognized his voice and threw the covering from her face. They both cried out at the same time: "Chaereas!" "Callirhoe!" They fell into each other's arms, swooned, and fell to the ground. At first Polycharmus too could only stand there, struck speechless by this miracle. But after a time he said, "Get up! You have recovered each other; the gods have granted your wishes, both of you; but remember that you are not in your own country, you are in enemy territory, and the first thing to do is to deal with that situation, so that no one separates you again." He had to shout; they were like people plunged deep in a well who could scarcely hear a voice calling from above. Slowly they came to themselves; then, when they saw each other and embraced, they were overcome again; and this happened a second time and a third time. All they could say was, "You are in my arms—if you really are Callirhoe!"—"if you really are Chaereas!" (8.1.8)

After the raptures of the hour, Callirhoe settles her own affairs— with Dionysius, with the King and Queen—tactfully; curiously, she leaves her child with Dionysius. There follows a triumphal return of hero and heroine to Syracuse. Callirhoe offers her thanks to Aphrodite for reuniting her with her husband—and, still tactful, lays her misfortunes at the door of destiny. Thereafter, Chariton hints, the couple will live happily ever after. "And that," says Chariton, "is my story about Callirhoe."

Whatever romance is, this is clearly romance. Several questions present themselves. We may ask: where did such a text "come from," and where does it "fit" in antiquity? In due course we shall do so; but the answers, in this study, will subserve other questions. How does this *kind* of text behave? What are its distinguishing characteristics? And how far is this story typical of romance in antiquity? We shall begin by looking first at what it is "like," trying to put our finger on its important features.

One could begin by a characterization. This text is a naive romantic fantasy, by turns sentimental and sensational in tone; historical in setting and dramatic in method, it is conventional in its attitudes, its content and its composition. This is not to say it follows a traditional literary pattern—as written literature it is in fact positively revolutionary; it is to say that it proceeds by formula, psychological and narrative formula. The clichés leap from the page, even in summary, clichés of action and situation as well as language. Love at first sight repeatedly sends this story on the next stage of its journey, like a booster rocket: a series of *coups de foudre* strikes Chaereas, Dionysius, Mithridates, the King in turn, incinerating them with love's heat. Dramatic turns of event, thrown into the story by Tyche, the goddess Chance, land hero or heroine in one pathetic plight after another; Callirhoe and Chaereas rise infallibly to every emotional situation, like trout to flies. The language is charged with pathos and drama: lament and entreaty jostle with paradox and antithesis, emotional debate with passionate soul-searching. The story regularly runs the gamut of the emotions; even in the brief extracts quoted we have twice seen Chariton set up a checklist—"fear, joy, grief, surprise, hope, disbelief." Action is rapid: "before he had finished speaking" the next step is taken, the emotional climax is that much nearer, our heartstrings are tugged once more. The author's strategy is to maneuver his heroes into situations, such as reunion scenes, that favor all the standard features of his narrative: rhetoric, pathos, drama. Chariton manages his plot adroitly to that end: Callirhoe is presented to us as the very embodiment, the very symbol, of emotion.

It would not be to the purpose to examine in any more detail the specific characteristics of this particular story. We are more concerned with what is generic. And though details of style and rhetoric naturally vary from one author to another, the features we have just been observing nonetheless constitute the standard language of Greek romance. We should now move more clearly from the particular to the general. To serve the purpose of assessment of the genre, let us dissect this story for its generic features: of action, character, situation, attitudes, writing.

24

For the action, it will here be pertinent to put some flesh on the skeleton already offered of the standard romance plot, in order to set out more fully the ancient form of that plot. The elements in Chariton's story that are typical of the Greek love-romance are the following. A beautiful young heroine and handsome hero meet by chance on the occasion of a religious festival. Love comes at first sight, and with it comes, to start with, pining and wasting and despair; of such stuff are these lovers made. In Chariton's story this situation is briefly resolved by marriage, before the real action begins; in others, the marriage may be postponed to constitute the climax. Whether married or not, the couple are separated by circumstance: Tyche, Chance, is a prime mover in romance plots. The separation involves travel anywhere in the Eastern Mediterranean and its hinterland— from Sicily to Babylon here, from Greece to Egypt, even Ethiopia, in other stories. Travel almost inevitably involves disaster—shipwreck, or capture by pirates or brigands—and hence, slavery for one partner or both. Inevitably, danger to chastity, or to virginity itself, ensues— invariably for the woman, often for the man as well. Typically, although as we have seen not quite invariably, these dangers are avoided or averted by a hair's breadth. Adventures dangerous to life and limb proliferate; war is involved, misfortunes multiply for both partners, coincidences abound. At some point, the heroine appears to suffer death in some form, but of course it is illusory, merely apparent death. Rivals, jealousies, intrigues complicate events in themselves hair-raising enough: the girl resists, the man dares, and at all points each remains inviolably faithful to the other, and invincibly hopeful of reunion somewhere, someday. In this optimism the heroes are sustained by mysterious promptings from one divinity or many: Aphrodite, Isis commonly, Apollo, Dionysus, others; yet the divinities seem often rather to be working against them than for them, and it is impossible to tell where the divinity Chance, as active as any, fits in this theology. The coincidences eventually coincide for the heroes' salvation—which may be overtly attributed to divine benevolence. In a last crisis of events, hero and heroine are brought finally to meet, and, somehow or other, to recognize each other. *Peripeteia* and *anagnōrisis* issue in ecstatic reunion; Frye's state of "identity" is achieved, "in which there is nothing to write about";[6] and after all this excitement, everybody lives happily ever after.

[6] *Secular Scripture*, 54. CF. p. 173 below.

For the characters, Chariton's gallery offers a good selection of romance types. Beautiful and hapless heroine, handsome and often rather passive hero, are the idealized protagonists of the action, the very doubles of those lovers around whom revolve the comedies of Menander, Plautus, Terence. The other characters are in general more realistic, if often melodramatic in type. Rascally brigand, noble seigneur, resourceful slave, unscrupulous rival, faithful friend, anxious parents form the basic cast; to them we may add for other stories the developed forms of noble brigand and *femme fatale*. Chariton's story is something of an exception in having no *femme fatale*—for the only "other woman" in the story, the Persian Queen, is far from representing a danger to the heroine. On occasion some of the characters may belong to a distinctive social group—rustics in *Daphnis and Chloe*, priests in the *Ethiopica*—but this does not substantially affect their basic function in the story, whose main lines follow those of *Chaereas and Callirhoe*.

Next, the situations created by the action and the ethical attitudes embodied in the story; they can be taken together, since they are two sides of the same coin. The general intellectual content of Chariton's story is that of a bourgeois idyll, with a distinct air of social snobbery about it. Beauty and love are the beacons in this landscape; beauty will be an appurtenance of social quality, and indissolubly linked with love—it issues unerringly in love, and feeds on love. Physical beauty is in unswerving alliance with virtue, which in its turn is identified as chastity, fidelity, and a sound respect for the gods. Given this respect, happiness will follow as a due condition; for the gods are finally beneficent, and the world is finally a blessed place for those born to suitable station, for people of quality. But there is nonetheless a fly in the ointment. It cannot be taken for granted that happiness will come to those who deserve it with no effort whatever on their part and at no cost to them. Though the gods are beneficent ultimately, in the short term they are inscrutable; Chance, who (one suspects) is their agent, has some poisoned arrows in his quiver, and is only too ready to fire them. Eros is rather fond of drama, paradox, spectacular reversals of fortune. At any moment he may plunge the happiest into misery; let him find the slightest chink in a man's armor—understandable jealousy, pride, even vulnerable innocence—and he certainly will do so. And in that case the world picture can be grim indeed. Misfortunes and tribulations are not the half of it; the worst is the awful loneliness, the isolation, the separation from one's beloved and one's own world. It is enough to drive a man—less often, perhaps, a woman, and that is worth remarking—beyond despair to suicide. But faith will win. Faith is the ultimate essential quality; and in the end it will win. Only survive despair; and happiness—tempered, now, by experience—will come.

As for the writing, that of course is more markedly a function of the individual author than are the structural and conceptual conventions of the genre. Chariton is particularly dramatic in his presentation of the situation of his heroes—especially Callirhoe, who comes across in the text as a veritable *grande dame* of drama, in the tradition of Phaedra, Hecuba, Andromache; time after time her very words recall theirs—"I am far away even from your grave, Chaereas!" she laments on being carried off to Babylon. "Who will pour libations over you, dear heart?" (5.1.7). He makes full use, that is to say, of the specifically *dramatic* opportunities the structure of his story offers him to bring the distraught Callirhoe vividly before us at the trial in Babylon; and he narrates relatively little and rapidly. Other authors have their own manner: Xenophon is breathless, Longus reflective. But the individual manner, important though it is, is not our first concern here. The structure and nature of such stories mean that for all the differences of approach, much of the machinery of narration and the devices of exposition and narrative movement is found regularly from one story to another. Oracles, dreams, apparitions occur in profusion; letters, debates, soliloquies, agonized apostrophes keep our emotions at high pitch; cliff-hanging is the very substance of the story; every author revels in the purple passage, the ecphrasis or set description of a heroine's beauty, a natural wonder, a shipwreck. Vocabulary is emotive and stylized. Antithesis and paradox color every page: "Treacherous beauty!" cries Callirhoe, besieged by the Persian King's attentions, "the cause of all my woes! . . . How often have you given me over to brigands, to the sea, to burial, slavery, trial! The worst of all my burdens is—the King loves me!" (6.6.4). Apophthegm and epigram, proverb and quotation, commonly enhance the text; every situation is milked. Structurally, too, fundamental problems recur from story to story: how to keep hero and heroine both alive at once but separately, in the reader's mind; how to keep track of an accumulating burden of incidents; how to initiate each new movement. Each author, of course, has to solve his own problems for himself. Some are more successful—Chariton is one of them; some, like

Xenophon, less. It remains true that these are the problems of romance writers and romance writing.

So much for dissection of this particular example of romance.[7] But we are not primarily concerned here to assess or demonstrate the ability of individual writers. It is the *kind* of story that most concerns us, and perhaps the kind is adequately suggested by this example of it.[8]

Such a story is not simply a fantasy of the individual author. It has a basis in social reality, in the world as Chariton saw it. That world is the late Hellenistic and imperial Greek world of the Eastern Mediterranean. Greek society had by now existed for centuries within the political framework of one large empire or another, Alexander's or his successors', or Rome's. While local life was assuredly busy, in the wider context of the cosmopolitan Greek world this was no longer the compact culture of Old Comedy, in which a man could aspire to having an effective voice in controlling his own social existence in his own autonomous community; now there was a large-scale, open society, in which the individual cut a much smaller figure, was swallowed up and lost in the mass—as we may feel lost in today's large-scale open society. Chariton's story was written for those who lived in that world, and it reflects that world and its inhabitants, their situation, their anxieties, their aspirations.

In short, this is fable, *mythos*; myth, even. This narrative expresses a social and personal myth, of the private individual isolated and in-

[7] See T. Hägg, *Narrative Technique in Ancient Greek Romances* (Stockholm, 1971) for analysis of Chariton's manner of telling his story, *e.g.*, 294: "The narration of concrete events takes up a comparatively small part of the text; they are generally related in 'summary.' The emphasis is instead on the reactions which they call forth in the minds of the participating characters. . . . Nearly half the text . . . is taken up by direct speech, monologues and dialogues . . . 'scene' is the predominant narrative type in the romance" ('scene' takes up nearly 90% of the story, in fact). Other writers, *e.g.*, Xenophon, *relate* more of the story. On Chariton's handling of his story in general see, besides the works of Perry and Hägg already mentioned, B. P. Reardon, "Theme, Structure and Narrative in Chariton," *Yale Classical Studies* 27 (1982), 1–27. Critical discussion, sometimes speculative, may also be found in Heiserman, chapter 6 (= "Aphrodisian Chastity," *Critical Inquiry* 2 [1975], 281–96); G. Molinié, introduction to Budé edition; and G. L. Schmeling, *Chariton* (New York, 1974) (Twayne's World Authors Series). The particular topic of Chariton's character-drawing, already treated in Perry, "Chariton and his Romance," 115–23, is developed at length in J. Helms, *Character Portrayal in the Romance of Chariton* (The Hague and Paris, 1966).

[8] Perry ("Chariton and his Romance," 129), calls *Chaereas and Callirhoe* "Greek romance as it should be written," and one sees what he means.

secure in a world too big for him, and finding his security, his very identity, in love. Chaereas, well-born and wealthy as he is, is nonetheless a nobody, on the world stage. He is not one of those who make the world move, a King of Persia, a Dionysius, a Mithridates. True, when pushed to the very limit of despair he can produce a flash of brilliance, though we have to wait long enough for it. But that over, he returns at once to his private occupation and preoccupation, namely Callirhoe. He is essentially a private individual, who does not impose himself on his world but takes his color from it. As for Callirhoe, she indeed moves the world, or at least moves the world's movers, one after another: Dionysius, Mithridates, the King himself. But this is her doom, not her glory, not her ambition: "treacherous beauty, the source of all my woes!" Her sole desire is to love and be loved, and nothing would suit her better than to *leave* the corridors of power. It is a private world that is the center of this story; the troubles of the big world are first and foremost a threat to private happiness. The world of great affairs is a bad dream, to the heroes of the story. When at last they come through it, they know not how, it is to disappear into love: love unperturbed, uneventful, conventional, respectable. Chariton takes aim quite explicitly at his readers as he begins his last book: "I think that the end of the story is going to be very agreeable to my readers," he says; "it will clear away all the grim events that precede it. No more pirates or slavery or trials or battles, no more suicides, or wars or taking of prisoners; no, now it is sanctioned love, and legal marriage"(8.1.4).[9] Private love and happy endings are clearly what his audience want at this stage of such stories. It is a pipe-dream, in short; wish-fulfillment is its essence. The vicissitudes of life are reduced, by vicarious exorcism, to acceptable proportions. It is as if the reader should say to himself, "I am nothing in the great world. Happiness is not after all to be found in the great world, as I may sometimes imagine in my distress; let me see creatures of nothing finding their own happiness."

Of course, it is anything but heroic. "Latter-day epic for Everyman" is Perry's trenchant categorization of Greek romance, and it is

[9] The vocabulary is interesting: *skythrōpos*, "grim," is one of the author's favorite words for the desperate situations of his heroes; *katharsion esti*, "it is purifying," "will clear away," recalls very clearly Aristotle's doctrine of *catharsis* in the operation of tragedy. It seems unlikely, however, that Chariton is consciously quoting Aristotle, or that he has any very profound or sophisticated concept of the psychological operation of his story. See Reardon, "Theme, Structure, and Narrative," 21ff.

easy enough to think up derogatory terms for it.[10] We may, if we wish, feel superior about such stories; but it is incumbent on us to interpret their terms. We shall consider in the last chapter how all of this corresponds to other concepts of salvation—of escapism, it may be. Given the date of *Chaereas and Callirhoe*, it is worth noting Frye's remark that "there are close connections between the imaginative universe of romance and of Christianity."[11] For the present, let us note that such an interpretation of Greek romance can be extended to all the examples of it that we shall be considering. Although of course the terms of the interpretation can be expected to differ substantially, all are in one way or another versions of what I have here called this myth. But the details are not a major issue here; for present purposes enough has been said to suggest general lines of interpretation.[12]

To give Chariton's story a context, and to suggest the dimensions of this literary genre, we may turn to other specimens of it: first, to a much less simple one, Longus's *Daphnis and Chloe*, of perhaps some century-and-a-half later than Chariton's day. Any summary of this story must be either very brief or very long. In one sense little happens, but in another sense a great deal happens, and every detail has its carefully calculated place. The present account will be fairly brief; it is intended mainly to emphasize the important difference between Longus's more familiar text and Chariton's.

The differences are considerable. Hero and heroine, to begin with, are only newborn babies as the story begins. They are found by shepherds in springtime, separately and at two years' interval, abandoned in the countryside and being suckled by animals; beside them are found various items of jewellery. They are adopted by the shepherds, and when they reach adolescence they are set to herd animals together. This proximity, and the incidents of a country life, produce in them strange feelings for each other. They neglect their flocks, lie awake at night, grow pale—and do not know what is happening to

---

[10] *Ancient Romances*, 48; elsewhere (47) such literature is "impoverished" (echoing Rohde's description, *Gr. Rom.*, 522/490, of the action of *Chaereas and Callirhoe* as *armselig*).

[11] *Secular Scripture*, 92; cf. Chapter 7 below for concepts of salvation.

[12] For a fuller exposition of this view see B. P. Reardon, "The Greek Novel," *Phoenix* 23 (1969), 291–309, and *Courants littéraires*. For a different view, see Bowie, *CHCL*, 683–88, "The Genre"; he prefers a "purely literary" explanation (as did Rohde), and minimizes the element of isolation in hero and heroine which seems to me central in the shape of such stories. See Chapter 7 and n. 12.

them. An old countryman, Philetas, instructs them in this knowledge, the theory of love (or as Longus puts it, "the name of Love"). He represents Eros as the greatest god in creation:

> Love is a god, my children: he is young, beautiful, and winged; and so he enjoys youth, pursues beauty, and makes souls take wing. Zeus has not so much power as he has; he rules the elements; he rules the stars; he rules his fellow gods—more completely than you rule your goats and sheep. All the flowers are the work of Love; all the plants are his creation; thanks to him, the rivers flow, the winds blow. . . . There is no medicine for Love, no potion, no drug, no spell to mutter, except a kiss and an embrace and lying down together with naked bodies. (2.7)

Longus, then, gives Love a psychological and theological dimension barely hinted at by Chariton.

The seasons progress, and pastoral occupations form the backdrop of the whole story: the tending of sheep and goats, poetic displays, pastoral sports and pastimes. Summer comes, and the youngsters' love progresses—less rapidly, though, than the explicitness of Philetas's instruction might suggest, for instinct makes them hesitate to plunge directly into the next degree of knowledge, the deeds of Love; though, Longus tells us, they come close to it. Rural incidents sharpen their feelings; and among them are some which in this pastoral and stable setting perform the function of the exciting and exotic adventures of the standard romance form. A rustic rival makes a pass at Chloe, but gets short shrift. A pirate boat makes a brief descent on the coast, and Daphnis is carried captive a few hundred yards out to sea—it is the farthest he ever gets from home, until the very end of the story. A quarrel breaks out between country and city, and in the ensuing brief conflict, Chloe is carried off; but no sooner have her captors covered a mile or so than Pan intervenes miraculously to bring her back, and the couple return to their pastoral and innocent joys. The worst that happens, in this idyllic world, is that the rigors of the winter keep the lovers apart—this is the nearest Longus comes to "apparent death"; but not for long, for Daphnis finds excuse to visit Chloe's home. When spring returns, the lovers' passions are unleashed again. They experiment, and come nearer and nearer to the deeds of love, but still without success. By now, one might well think (and many critics, including Rohde, have said) that Longus is being more than titillating. At this point, further instruction comes from outside: a neighbor's wife, smitten with Daphnis and guessing at his problems, decides to kill two birds with one stone, or as Longus puts it, "saw a two-fold opportunity—for rescuing them and satisfying her desire" (3.15). So Daphnis learns from her the deeds of love. Chastity, it seems, is less indispensable in the man than in the woman. Chloe will remain virgin until the very end of the story—for Lycaenion, Daphnis's instructor, has taught him gentleness as well.

But the year goes inexorably round; the season of mellow fruitfulness will soon be on the heroes. Chloe is very marriageable, and suitors multiply. Her foster-father is sorely tempted by their offers; Daphnis is in agony, for he cannot match them materially. Here the nymphs save him—as Chloe had been saved—and put him in the way of discovering enough money, at least, to present himself as suitor. In the final book, harvesttime has come. The master of Daphnis's estate, Dionysophanes, arrives from town; an intrigue develops, worthy of New Comedy; Daphnis finds himself the object of a parasite's homosexual attentions. This precipitates the dénouement. Daphnis's identity is finally discovered, by means of the tokens exposed with him when he was a baby: he is none other than the son of Dionysophanes. A similar discovery makes Chloe socially fit to be his bride. A brief visit to the city is enough to convince the couple that the country is where they want to live, and they are duly married there. At last

> Daphnis and Chloe lay down naked together, embraced and kissed, and had even less sleep that night than the owls. Daphnis did some of the things Lycaenion taught him; and then, for the first time, Chloe found out that what they had done in the woods had been nothing but shepherds' games. (4.40)

This too is romance, fantasy, quite as plainly as Chariton's story. But it is at the other end of the range. This is a consummately elegant work, polished in every detail, stylistically as well as structurally, fearing comparison with no such work ever written, infinitely self-conscious and fine. The theme of back-to-nature has of course caught the imagination of every age, the more insistently as society has multiplied its own complications. *Daphnis and Chloe* is by a long way the most often translated of the Greek romances (it is interesting that versions come thick and fast when the world is at war).[13] Deluxe edi-

---

[13] As an indication of its popularity in one modern society I give some figures culled from the catalogue of the Bibliothèque Nationale in Paris: from 1714 to 1959 well over

tions are a familiar sight; translation by a famous writer (unless it is a version of Amyot's as revised by Paul-Louis Courier; or the version of Geo. Thornley, Gent., 1657, "A most sweet and pleasant pastoral Romance for Young Ladies"); illustrations by an equally famous artist; hand-laid paper, elegant typeface, luxurious binding. And the idyll breaks out, of course, in other arts: in Watteau, Ravel.[14]

Yet this is not totally different from Chariton's melodrama. The elements are all there; the difference is in the presentation, not in the content. The disguise is not very difficult to penetrate. The most striking improvement, perhaps, is in the structure itself, in the very mechanics of the plot. No journey here, to need motivating: the journey is a journey in time, eighteen months of adolescence, and thus an inevitable one. Divinities intervene in the action, but they also *constitute* the action: Eros in effect *is* Dionysus, the great god of life, the irresistible life-force who carries all with him, natural element and human being alike. For they are integral parts of the same world; this Dionysus is less terrifying than that of Euripides, more benevolent, but still of massive power.[15] The revolution of the seasons *is* life itself:

---

100 French translations are listed; from 1870 the average for some periods is almost one per year; in the troubled decades of our century, especially the forties, there are sometimes two, three, and even four in a single year. These figures are far higher than the figures for all the other ancient romances put together, and assuredly cannot be fully explained by the alleged element of sexual titillation referred to; presumably they are due in large part to the compensatory virtues of the novel's idyllic pastoral setting. The notes (by Giles Barber) to a British Library exhibition ("*Daphnis and Chloe*: the markets and metamorphoses of an unknown bestseller") held from October 1988 to January 1989 tell us that "In all some five hundred editions of the work have appeared, for all sorts of markets and in all sorts of countries, since the first printed reference to the work in 1489—that is, on average, one a year for five centuries. Since the majority of these editions belong to the twentieth century, it would appear that *Daphnis and Chloe* is 'still going strong'!" See now Giles Barber, *Daphnis and Chloe: the markets and metamorphoses of an unknown bestseller* [The Panizzi Lectures 1988] (London: The British Museum, 1989).

[14] The fortunes of Longus in pictorial art are illustrated in Hägg, *Novel in Antiquity*, "Pictorial Supplement: Daphnis and Chloe in the Mirror of Art," 214–27 (fourteen black-and-white reproductions ranging from the 17th to the 20th centuries), and more fully in the Swedish original of the book, *Den Antika Romanen* (Uppsala, 1980), 276–319 (thirty-six black-and-white reproductions, with art-historical essay by Sten Karling). A volume of the Flemish journal *Kleio*, 13.4 (December 1983) contains a further art-historical article, by B. van de Wijer, "Enkele picturale voorstellingen van Daphnis en Chloé," 212–20, and a musicological article by I. Bossuyt on "Maurice Ravel en het ballet 'Daphnis et Chloé,'" 199–211.

[15] For Dionysus-worship in the Roman Empire see M. P. Nilsson, *The Dionysiac Mysteries of the Hellenistic and Roman Age* (Lund, 1957; New York, 1975); and now R. Merkelbach, *Die Hirten des Dionysos: Die Dionysos-Mysterien der römischen Kaiserzeit und der*

his heroes cannot avoid growing, with the natural world. Whether it is a more real or more acceptable, believable world than Chariton's—that may be another matter. This is, after all, a very special case of love. It is a carefully controlled clinical experiment, in large degree preserved from the pollution of normal society—which of course is what constitutes its attraction.

Again, as with Chariton, we are not principally concerned to assess the quality of the story, but rather to characterize it. Longus is as sophisticated as a writer may well be—the word is exactly right, for the composition of *Daphnis and Chloe* shows just those qualities of style and conception which mark the Second Sophistic, the literary movement of the second century A.D. in which many exotic plants flourished.[16] He is as self-consciously writing "artistic" prose as any writer who ever lived. There is a distinctly pre-Raphaelite flavor to *Daphnis and Chloe*; some have even thought the work decadent. So much, here, to situate the romance of Longus, very different from Chariton's. It will be enough to suggest the nature of this work, and thus to span the range of the extant Greek romances.[17]

The pattern of Greek love-romance, then, is as simple as it could be. Loving couple, their travels and trials; the vicissitudes of Fortune, which may take on a providential aspect; the happy ending. A perennial pattern. Its shaping may result in any kind of story, from merely exciting to symbolic, allegorical. Allegory, we have suggested, is in the pattern itself, which is easily seen as a figure of man's journey in life. It will be worthwhile at this point to spend a little time on the principal remaining romance texts, to fill in our picture of the *kind* of romance that was written; for there are not many extant, but each of them has its distinctive character, and the total range is quite remarkably wide. It will not be necessary in all cases to sketch plots, but only to indicate their nature in relation to the plots we have seen;

---

bukolische Roman des Longus (Stuttgart, 1988). The latter should be used with caution, since the author assumes that *Daphnis and Chloe* is a *Mysterientext*—that is, that it is built upon the rituals of the mysteries—and that therefore those rituals can be reconstructed from the action of the romance to some extent.

[16] See below, Chapter 6.

[17] There is a good deal of work on Longus. Here may be mentioned three general studies: H.H.O. Chalk, "Eros and the Lesbian Pastorals of Longus," *Journal of Hellenic Studies* 80 (1960), 32–51; R. L. Hunter, *A Study of* Daphnis and Chloe (Cambridge, 1983); and W. E. McCulloh, *Longus* (New York, 1970) (Twayne's World Authors Series). The standard text is that of M. D. Reeve, 2nd ed. (Leipzig, 1986) (Teubner). Dalmeyda's 1934 Budé edition has now been replaced by that of J.-R. Vieillefond, Paris, 1987. There is a Loeb edition by J. M. Edmonds (London and Cambridge, Mass., 1916).

and to suggest what kind of use is being made, in each case, of the basic pattern.

Perhaps nearest to Chariton's story is that of "Xenophon"—the name is certainly a pseudonym, indicating the current admiration for an earlier Xenophon, who in the age of Plato demonstrated a similar interest in people and their characters, a similar tendency to romanticize, and a similar simplicity of style; we shall have occasion to return to him. "Xenophon" may or may not have been from Ephesus.[18] His story is set there, and indeed several of these stories are based in Asia Minor—more flourishing, now, than mainland Greece, and closer to the Orient which figures so much in the romance; Chariton was from Aphrodisias in Asis Minor, the secretary of a lawyer there. Xenophon—we will drop the quotation marks—has clearly read Chariton, who wrote perhaps a hundred years before him and had become a minor popular classic.[19] This story, the *Ephesiaca*, is sufficiently similar to Chariton's to suggest direct imitation.[20] But it is maladroit, in the event. For Xenophon is clearly of a more religious cast of mind than his predecessor, and seems to want to make of his story a patently religious document. The gods appear at the very beginning of a story structured initially rather like *Chaereas and Callirhoe*, and they appear—there are several of them, Eros, Apollo, Artemis, Isis, Helius—at many of its principal junctures as well. Sometimes they smooth its passage, but more often they put it out of joint with their unpredictable intervention—as when, at the beginning, the love-sickness of Habrocomes and Anthia is diagnosed by an oracle, which then proceeds first to hamstring the action and then to rob it of its surprises, by predicting the fortunes of the voyagers. The he-

[18] B. Lavagnini, *Studi sul romanzo greco* (Messina and Florence, 1950), chapter 3, "La patria di Senofonte Efesio." As for the name "Xenophon," other romance writers took that pseudonym: "Xenophon of Antioch," who wrote a *Babyloniaca*, and "Xenophon of Cyprus," who wrote a *Cypriaca*, both of which are said by the *Souda* to be "erotic" (love stories, that is). All three writers are called "historians" (*historikoi*); Xenophon of Athens was also a *historikos*. See Perry, *Ancient Romances*, 166ff.

[19] That is a reasonable inference from the distribution of the papyri and from the hostility shown to him (apparently) by the literary "establishment figure" Philostratus some generations after Chariton's own time (see the beginning of the next chapter).

[20] Papanikolaou, *Chariton-Studien*, 153–59, demonstrates that it is Xenophon who is the imitator. Xenophon's date was probably after A.D. 117, since at 2.13 and 3.9 he mentions an official title ("Eirenarch") not so far attested before that date; J. H. Oliver, "Xenophon of Ephesus and the Antithesis Historia-Philosophia," in G. W. Bowersock et al. eds., *Arktouros: Hellenic Studies Presented to B. M. W. Knox* (Berlin, 1979), 401–406, offers some grounds for placing Xenophon in the reign of Hadrian (117–38), but his argument is not very cogent.

roes are soon separated, but nothing like the human interest vested in Callirhoe informs their fortunes. She is at least faced with an agonizing choice, melodramatic as the mounting of it may be, between love for her lost husband and love for her unborn child. Anthia, and Habrocomes too, face (repeatedly) nothing more moving than death—or a fate worse than death. Miracles accumulate, each more lurid than its predecessor; Xenophon can think of no very effective means of conducting the parallel actions, and ends up moving his characters more and more wildly around the Mediterranean, like demented chessmen.[21] It all ends happily, of course—if only from sheer exhaustion, for there seems little reason in the action itself why it should ever end at all. In this respect too Xenophon cannot match Chariton, who carefully builds his action to a crisis that must be resolved, be it only by chance and war.

This, then, is a clumsy, extremely melodramatic, and utterly solemn version of romance.[22] The *Ephesiaca* is of course full of interest from other points of view, notably in respect of religious history and its literary elaboration,[23] and the action itself has a certain hectic appeal to it; but it is not a notably successful literary construct. Romance accepts anything. It is not critical, intellectual, as the novel is; there is no guarantee that it will show good taste.[24]

But taste is in any case a changing thing; in a number of ways, second-century taste is not ours. This is evident in the romance of Achilles Tatius, *Leucippe and Clitophon*, a work as far removed from Chariton's as is *Daphnis and Chloe*, and in its way as sophisticated. The story is told in ego-narrative by the hero, Clitophon of Tyre. As

[21] Examples in Chapter 5.

[22] Most ancient romances contain at least some elements of humor, and some (*e.g.*, Achilles Tatius) contain a lot. It is only quite recently that this has been generally recognized. See now Graham Anderson, *Eros Sophistes* (Chico, Calif.: American Philological Association, American Classical Studies 9, 1982), which however perhaps somewhat overstates the case.

[23] See notably R. E. Witt, "Xenophon's Isiac Romance," in *Isis in the Graeco-Roman World* (London, 1971), 243–54. The religious question raised by the controversial book of R. Merkelbach, *Roman und Mysterium in der Antike* (Munich, 1962) (91–113 for Xenophon), will call for some discussion in Chapter 7; it may be said here that the thesis set out in these two books—that the *Ephesiaca* is a religious *roman à clef*—seems exaggerated. For the Isis myth, see Chapter 7.

[24] G. L. Schmeling, *Xenophon of Ephesus* (Boston, 1980), offers a more sympathetic, if not always convincing, analysis of the story. The best general study of the problems associated with the *Ephesiaca* is H. Gärtner's article "Xenophon von Ephesos," in *RE* 9A 2 (1967), 2055–89. The standard text is that of A. D. Papanikolaou (Leipzig, 1973) (Teubner); there is a Budé edition by G. Dalmeyda (Paris, 1926).

in Chariton, an adroitly handled initial movement gets the story off to a positive start, and hero and heroine find themselves escaping to Egypt (a country that figures quite often in these stories). Adventures follow, and the couple are separated. But in this text the adventures occupy only a relatively small place in the action, much of which is concerned with amatory intrigue of various kinds distributed among not one couple but two. Clitophon, who for a long stretch of the story believes himself deprived by death of his Leucippe, engages half-heartedly in a liaison with the beautiful Melite, who likewise thinks that she has lost her husband Thersander. Thersander, however, appears out of the blue, only to pursue the similarly resuscitated Leucippe. A complex four-part intrigue ensues, involving among other things an elaborate legal process, as a result of which hero and heroine are finally united in marriage. The basic construction, it will be seen, follows the standard pattern: travel, separate adventures, the buffetings of Fortune. What is different about this story is the writer's attitude to his material.

First, love is neither the simple and naive concept we saw in Chariton and Xenophon, nor the cosmic force which Longus represents it as being. It is above all a social movement. It is difficult in *Leucippe and Clitophon* to distinguish, or even separate, the romantic convention of love from the social act, from seduction, intrigue, and amatory complication. It is as if romance had been invaded by the spirit of Congreve and Wycherley. Long passages, at the beginning and the end of the story, are devoted to testing in various ways the chastity of the heroine—which very nearly fails to pass the test. As for the hero, *his* virginity is the subject of veritably philosophical scepticism: "is there such a thing as virginity in a man?"[25] Clitophon does in the event preserve his virginity, but only, as in his protestations he is careful to add, "[a]s far as Leucippe is concerned" (and at that, one must observe, it is not for want of trying). Throughout the work there are passages which it is difficult to interpret as anything other than lubricious. Longus, perhaps, leaves it up to the reader; but Achilles Tatius hardly does. He is almost guying the convention, in fact; making sport of the simple sentiments that inform a naive romance, setting them in a society long past that stage. And it is not only the convention of romantic love that he takes as his target, but the convention of romantic adventure too. The misfortunes that be-

[25] 5.20.5, repeated 8.5.7.

fall the heroine are more lurid than anything even a Xenophon can think up. She suffers apparent death not once but three times, and violent death it is too: on one occasion disembowelled, on another decapitated, before the horrified eyes of her lover; to end, finally, in a situation worthy of the most distressed damsel who ever graced Victorian melodrama, on every page about to be wronged by the villainous squire. It is in its way an extremely elaborate construction. An earlier generation of scholars was troubled by this romance: it really does seem a bit extreme, they muttered to themselves; presumably this is the Gothic horror to end all horrors? It seems easier now to see it as verging on parody, though perhaps not unmitigated parody—there is much in the work that would not after all be too out of place in another romance. But in all the key places the cup seems to spill over; and we are left with a curious taste in the mouth.[26]

Are we, then—if parody comes on to the horizon—moving from romance to novel, to the "realistic displacement" of Frye's scheme?[27] The idea has been suggested before now: "Achilles Tatius," said Rattenbury, "seems to have been to Greek Romance what Euripides was to Greek Tragedy. He broke down the conventions."[28] Clearly the possibility of disrupting the romantic scheme was there from the beginning; we have seen Longus, of whom Achilles Tatius was probably an earlier contemporary, at least look askance at it. Disruption, or perversion?

One further major text remains, the most massive of all: the *Ethiopica* of Heliodorus—to be dated, let us recall, at any rate substantially later than all the other extant works.[29] This is the romance to end all

---

[26] The idea that parody is involved has occasionally been adumbrated—sometimes by rejection—and is worked out by D. B. Durham, "Parody in Achilles Tatius," *Classical Philology* 33 (1938), 1–19; the suggestion is not altogether invalidated by the subsequent discovery that Achilles Tatius precedes Heliodorus, whom Durham supposed to be the principal target. But scholars generally prefer less categorical formulae; *e.g.*, Hägg, *Novel in Antiquity*, 53–54, who speaks of the author's "ironic tone . . . he sets out to 'humanize' the novel, with the result that some of its conventions tend to appear slightly ridiculous." This seems to me not to take sufficient account of the grotesqueness of some of the incidents. There is no full-scale study of Achilles Tatius; see Hägg and Bowie, *CHCL*, for the main issues and bibliography. There is a Loeb edition by S. Gaselee (Cambridge, Mass. and London, 1917; 2nd ed., 1961); the standard edition is that of E. Vilborg, 2 vols., (Stockholm, 1955/1962).

[27] *Secular Scripture*, 38.

[28] R. M. Rattenbury, "Traces of Lost Greek Novels," in J. U. Powell, ed., *New Chapters in the History of Greek Literature* III (Oxford, 1933), 256–57; Perry, *Ancient Romances*, 113ff.

[29] One date often proposed is sometime in the third century, because of the frequent

romances. Anything you can do, the author seems to be saying to his predecessors, I can do better, and at twice the length. It is spectacular as no earlier romance is spectacular: as dramatic as Chariton at his best, as tortuous as Achilles Tatius's lengthiest episodes, as learned as a library catalogue, as elaborate in its structure as Longus in the writing of his most careful poetic prose. And throughout, megalomaniac: Cecil B. de Mille let loose in the Bodleian—and with a cast of thousands. It is surprising that it has not caught the attention of Hollywood's moguls; perhaps it has, at that. Certainly it fired the imagination of writers and artists from the Renaissance onwards; witness the enormous canvases at Fontainebleau, in some of which, as in film

mention in the story of the Sun cult; two periods, ca. 220 and ca. 270, would fit this. J. R. Morgan (D.Phil. diss., Oxford University, 1978, "A Commentary on the Ninth and Tenth Books of the Aithiopica of Heliodoros," Introduction, xli ff.), has contested this argument and date, maintaining that the alleged prominence of the cult dissolves on inspection. The other date often favored is the latter part of the fourth century, this date being based on a clear resemblance between an episode in Book IX (the siege of Syene) and a siege described in two letters by the emperor Julian. The latter seems to be a historical siege of Nisibis that took place in 350. If it is, it would seem that Heliodorus is borrowing historical facts from Julian to decorate his narrative; in that case, he is obviously later than Julian's letters, which can be dated to 356 and 359. But it has been argued that it is rather Julian who is borrowing from Heliodorus, to enhance his account of historical facts; in that case the early dating becomes a possibility again. This stage of the debate is set out in more detail in Reardon, *Courants littéraires*, 334, n 57. More recently, it has been claimed that Julian's account is not historically accurate as a description of the siege of Nisibis; see T. Szepessy, "Le siège de Nisibe et la chronologie d'Héliodore," *Acta Antiqua Academiae Scientiarum Hungaricae* 24 (1976), 247–76. To my mind this article is not totally convincing. Yet more recently, see an article by another Hungarian scholar, M. Maróth, in the same journal (27 [1979], 239–43), "Le siège de Nisibe en 350 ap. J.-Ch. d'après des sources syriennes." J. Pouilloux, "Delphes dans les *Éthiopiques* d'Héliodore: la réalité dans la fiction," *Journal des Savants* (1983), 259–86, argues that Heliodorus's picture of Delphi fits the late 2nd or early 3rd century so well that Heliodorus could not have lived at a later period. C. S. Lightfoot, "Facts and Fiction: The Third Siege of Nisibis (A.D. 350)," *Historia* 37 (1988), 105–25, also prefers a pre-Julian date. There is a possibility also that Heliodorus is the sophist of that name mentioned by Philostratus in his *Lives of the Sophists*: this would fit the 3rd century date. But the matter is to my mind not as firmly settled as suggested by e.g., *CHCL*, 883–84. For present purposes the question is not crucial, but it will illustrate how little we know of the chronology of the genre. The extant romances may have been spread over four hundred years or more, or they may have been written within little more than a century, or a century and a half; that fact could have a great deal of significance—see Chapter 7, n. 12. The 4th century date still seems possible to me; in that case Heliodorus—the author of the "ultimate romance"—would be a throwback, like Julian himself. The standard text of the *Ethiopica* is the Budé edition of R. M. Rattenbury and T. W. Lumb, 3 vols., (Paris, 1935/1938/1943). On Heliodorus in general see Gerald N. Sandy, *Heliodorus* (New York, 1982) (Twayne's World Authors Series).

versions of books, it is hard to see immediately just what in the original has prompted the incident depicted.[30]

Summary of the plot is out of the question here; it is extremely involved, and the story is extremely long. The thread of the action is a journey from Delphi to Ethiopia undertaken—together in this case, at least for the most part—by the heroes, Theagenes and Charicleia, and studded with set pieces: games at Delphi, shipwreck at the mouth of the Nile, an elaborate siege, a religious ceremony in the heart of Africa. The structure of the book, however, introduces a device new to prose romance, the flashback. Heliodorus has clearly borrowed the idea from the *Odyssey* (as he borrows much from earlier literature), and contrives by this means to plunge directly into the center of the action. This creates forward movement and tension in the plot, which, with the weight of the anterior story subsequently added to it, builds up to an impressively staged climax. Of the principal characters, Theagenes can only be called muscle-bound; and Charicleia is a thoroughly determined, masterful and not very lovable young woman—one has the impression that had she been in Callirhoe's place in Babylon, she would have taken the trial firmly into her own hands and disposed of the various pretendants as effectively as in the *Ethiopica* she disposes of her father, foster-father, and fiancé.

The journey is at once a quest in search of Charicleia's real father, who is the King of Ethiopia, and a religious pilgrimage, from Apollo's shrine to that Eldorado of elevated religion which had fascinated the Greek world since Herodotus's time. The usual perils are in wait: pirates, bandits, shipwreck, wars, scheming and powerful rivals for the love of each of the couple—it is in this story, beloved of Racine, that is found the model for his *femmes fatales*, Arsace, the wife of the Persian satrap Oroondates.[31] Into the structure of the narrative is built a succession of priests, which adds to the impression of religious solemnity. This solemnity has usually seemed to scholars sincere enough, even if the religio-philosophical doctrine it entombs

---

[30] See Sandy, *Heliodorus*, 120ff., on these and other paintings, and 124 for echoes of the *Ethiopica* in *Aida*.

[31] The story is told of Racine that when he was a student at Port-Royal he twice had a copy of the *Ethiopica* confiscated by the authorities and burned as unsuitable reading. He procured a third copy, learned it by heart, and then voluntarily surrendered it for destruction. Presumably what he learned by heart was the story, or possibly Amyot's translation; hardly the 350 pages of Greek text. . . . See Hägg, *Novel in Antiquity*, 205–206, for this story, and Sandy, *Heliodorus*, 95–124, for the rich *Nachleben* of the romance, especially in France.

(the practice of human sacrifice in Ethiopia, for instance, is in the final scene forsworn) appears at times rather vague; the "message" seems both lofty and woolly. But Heliodorus has, with all his other qualities, a sardonic cast of mind, and recently the suggestion has been made that, after all, the religious paraphernalia are not more than "mental furniture," and the romance has no very serious theological content.[32]

Again, it is not to the purpose to elaborate further on any interpretation of this story. But we can usefully notice that several of these texts have been or are a critic's battleground, which may suggest that there is matter enough in them, and more than one approach to that matter. More than one general interpretation, indeed, has been proposed for all of these texts as a group; that is, for the Greek romance genre. I have suggested in this chapter that the romance is a popular form, in the sense that it is addressed originally to a fairly wide and probably not unduly cultivated audience, and reflects the kind of world outlook that might be thought to characterize such an audience in late Hellenistic and imperial times. On the other hand, one could say that to talk of a "world outlook" of any kind is to see too much in the form; that as well as being popular it is simply escapist, and nothing more than amusement was ever intended or achieved by these authors. One might think of romance as the relaxation of the literate.[33] Even escapism and entertainment, however, are not really simple ideas, since in themselves they imply a cultural context: one must ask what people are escaping from, what constitutes escape, why entertainment takes that form. There may be, for instance, an element of instruction involved.[34]

But, even if it is granted that ancient romance as we have it was

[32] J. R. Morgan, *Commentary*, Introd., xlviii ff., rejects the religious interpretation, arguing that "the many references to the supernatural do not shew a consistent view of divine intervention in human affairs and derive from a purely literary desire for unity and forward movement." Although this sceptical attitude seems rather modern for Heliodorus, the idea deserves consideration; cf. G. Anderson, *Eros Sophistes*, who attributes Heliodorus's "religiosity" to his "mischievous technique and personality" (33 n. 1).

[33] Cf. B. P. Reardon, "Aspects of the Greek Novel," *Greece and Rome* 33 (1976), 130, with other ideas discussed there. The question of the readership of these romances has attracted increasing attention recently—the "poor-in-spirit" (Perry, *Ancient Romances*, Preface vii and 90), women, the young, have been suggested. See now K. Treu, "Der antike Roman und seine Publikum," in H. Kuch, ed., *Der antike Roman: Untersuchungen zur literarischen Kommunikation und Gattungsgeschichte* (Berlin, DDR, 1989), 178–97.

[34] Beer, *Romance*, puts the point neatly: "Because romance shows us the ideal it is implicitly instructive as well as escapist." (9).

41

nothing more than popular amusement, it must be an open question whether it was bound to stay on that level. The form appears to have won, or to have been on the point of winning, its spurs (say, by the late second or early third century), when suddenly it dried up—as far as we know, and the qualification is important. The supply apparently failed; perhaps writers no longer wanted to write romances. Furthermore, it may well be the case that sophistication came much earlier than the second century. For as has been mentioned earlier, there is also a comic tradition in prose narrative—not very generously documented, it is true, in the remains we possess of it, and reflected indirectly in the Latin works of Petronius and Apuleius rather than exemplified in the Greek texts. These are very broad questions of cultural history, which cannot be elucidated as satisfactorily as we could wish for sheer lack of information. We simply have very little evidence to tell us who read ancient prose fiction; and in any event it is unlikely that the question could be answered simply, any more than it can for modern fiction. The best approach is probably to examine the cultural context of romance, the world in which it was read. We shall do that, briefly, in a later chapter.

But the mention of comic romance will serve conveniently to move us beyond the ideal narratives. Just as we began this chapter by characterizing the *Odyssey*, so it will be useful here, in order to put the love-romances in perspective, to look briefly at this different species of the genus romance. Petronius and Apuleius, whose works more clearly call for the label "novel," are roughly contemporary with Chariton and Achilles Tatius, respectively. We do not know how much comic tradition there was behind them, although recent discoveries of papyrus fragments suggest that there may well have been something in Greek.[35] Each of their works, it is true, seems to be *sui generis*. But comic writing often is *sui generis*, since it lends itself less readily than ideal narrative to formulaic treatment, and is more

[35] P. J. Parsons, "Narrative about Iolaus," *Oxyrhynchus Papyri*, eds. B. P. Grenfell, A. S. Hunt, *et. al.* (London, 1898–) (Egypt Exploration Society), vol. 42 (1974), 34–41 (= *POxy* 3010); the central figure (Iolaus) is apparently taking instruction in the mysteries of Cybele in order to impersonate a eunuch priest, for reprehensible purposes. Also M. W. Haslam, "Narrative about Tinouphis in Prosimetrum," *Papyri Greek and Egyptian . . . in Honour of E. G. Turner (P. Turner)* (London, 1981) (Egypt Exploration Society), 35–45; apparently a prophet is saved from execution by "a single brick" (?). A striking feature of each text is a recherché metrical structure, which recalls Alexandrian experiments; some elements of the contents seem to reinforce this impression.

clearly a product of the wit, taste and imagination of an individual writer.[36] It will nonetheless be useful to glance at them.

Of Petronius' *Satyricon* only fragments remain. One of them is very long, a lively description of a dinner-party given by a vulgar, nouveau riche freedman, Trimalchio. This is an episode in the adventures of the central characters, a pair of sophisticated homosexual rogues and a boy, who wander from town to town, mostly around Naples and in Southern Italy, in the pursuit of various disreputable occasions. The *Satyricon* was evidently a long work: the travel serves as a frame for inserted episodes and tales, and there are some passages in verse, in the manner of Menippean satire (*prosimetrum*). The purpose of the work is clearly satirical observation of society, and this makes it a very different thing from Chariton's kind of ideal romance based on an edifying conception of love; furthermore, the world it is set in is Italian, not Greek. In form, however, it looks as much as anything like parody of the ideal romance, and that is the reason for mentioning it in this chapter:[37] love is replaced by sexual perversion, idealizing morality by realism and even cynicism. Several other familiar romance motifs occur in a distorted form: the standard shipwreck, the machinations of Tyche, the intervention of a deity—in this case the phallic deity Priapus. The problem is the date (the age of Nero, in the sixties of the first century A.D.), which seems early for such parody. But if, as seems possible, Chariton's story predates Pe-

[36] Perry builds a good deal on this point, in the second part of *Ancient Romances*: "Comic romances," he maintains, "unlike the serious or ideal species, to which they are traditionally unrelated, are not produced in quantity in response to the steady demand of a naive reading public, but are put forth on isolated occasions by highly sophisticated authors addressing themselves ostensibly to the learned world of fashion for purposes of their own" (Preface vi; cf. 88ff., and his Introduction to Part II, 183–85). But he exaggerates. In our own day there is by now practically a tradition of comic "university novels"—Kingsley Amis' *Lucky Jim*, Malcolm Bradbury's *The History Man*, David Lodge's *Changing Places* and *Small World*—which, while not mass-produced, do have standard targets for their fun (British academic types, the American university system), and evolve in patterns recalling New Comedy (which certainly *was* produced in quantity in response to a steady demand). Furthermore, they are clearly related to the "serious" form of the species (J.I.M. Stewarts's Oxford quintet, *A Staircase in Surrey*) as Menander to Euripides. And there is also the academic detective story—a third branch of the family. But Perry is simply carrying too far an idea that is sound in itself, as he often does: comedy is harder to achieve than other modes.

[37] It seems increasingly likely, in fact, as the picture of ancient prose fiction begins to fill out, that the very title of the work was not *Satyricon* but *Satirica* (or *Satyrica*), "A Story from the Land of Satyrs" (the comic figures of ancient satyr-play, which parodies Greek tragedy)—just as *Ethiopica* is "A Story from Ethiopia." The form *Satiricon* or *Satyricon* would be a Greek genitive plural: *Liber Satiricon*, "A Book of Stories from. . . ."

tronius, and is itself already based on a tradition of no doubt more primitive sentimental romance, there may be no need to indulge in critical acrobatics in order to fit it into some other tradition (if it is necessary at all to equip such a work with familiar antecedents).

Apuleius's *Metamorphoses* is of a different kind, but also elusive. The story, set in Greece, is based on the widespread folktale of the ass-man and developed from an earlier Greek version. It described the adventures of an inquisitive young man who seduces the (very cooperative) servant of a witch and himself dabbles in the witch's magic, only to be transformed, by mistake, into an ass. In that shape he has various adventures, through which we are shown a tableau of provincial life in the Roman Empire at its apogee. Finally he succeeds in regaining human shape through the good graces of Isis, to whose service he thereafter dedicates himself.

This is unique among the narrative fiction texts in being a "wonder-tale," but it has strong similarities with both comic and ideal branches. As with the *Satyricon*, its picaresque structure gives opportunity for a series of varied episodes and for realistic observation of human follies (and virtues). In this story too, the hero is by no means ideal—in whatever shape, he is all too human; similarly, love is again reduced to sex, though this time some of it, at least, is vigorously, even athletically, normal. But this is not a parody of ideal romance (although we may recall here that this story is certainly descended from a Greek original); it is another narrative strain, on a similar base but without the lovers. One can readily see major features that the *Metamorphoses* shares with sentimental romance, namely its serious ending and its moralizing theme, which consists of a sermon against excessive human ambition and excessive sensuality, and an invitation to submit, like the hero, to divine will. It is mirrored in the most extensive inserted tale, the famous story of Cupid and Psyche. This is Apuleius's own creation, and itself *is* entirely serious (although not entirely solemn), being in fact patterned on the ideal romances.[38]

The principal problem raised by the *Metamorphoses* is the author's own ambivalent attitude to the story. Most readers, however, find it only superficially comic, though the comedy is certainly extensive. It *is* a moralizing story, even an allegory, of human vice become bestiality, of salvation attainable only through divine grace. But the allegory is not heavy-footed; rather, we have to do here with a form of

[38] See, *e.g.* Hägg, *Novel in Antiquity*, 182–86.

serio-comic writing not so very far removed, perhaps, from the purpose of Petronius, if that aesthete had a purpose. It has been held that the Isis-episode of the last book is nothing more than a cover for a story which for most of its length tends to raciness and even bawdy. But that seems unlikely; the religious sentiment in question is sophisticated, certainly, but seems genuine enough.

It would be inappropriate to discuss these Latin texts at any greater length, so different are they from the Greek ideal romance.[39] The point here is that in antiquity, as nowadays, the travel-adventure-love formula could be used for quite un-ideal purposes. The sentimental tradition is only one strand of what was probably a quite complex literary cloth; for all we know, texts of quite different kinds may have existed. Several papyrus fragments do appear to make the literary history more complex than it was once thought to be. We are justified in looking searchingly at apparently simple texts, and speculation should not be too readily discouraged. But this is not the place to embark on it, or on further information of a generally bibliographical kind. Certainly, other literary products have more or less marked affinities with romance; some of them will figure in later discussion. Here, I have tried to suggest the *kind* of thing romance was in antiquity, to situate the topic of the form of Greek romance. We may turn now to other, analytical considerations: first, to whatever theory we can find that may throw light on the nature and behavior of the romance.

[39] On the Latin novels see in general P. G. Walsh, *The Roman Novel* (Cambridge, 1970).

The Content of Romance: The Idea

of Fiction

O NE WAY to analyse a literary genre is to follow the example of
Aristotle and consider systematically its object, manner and
means. Literature, for Aristotle, represents people doing things,
mimeitai prattontas. Tragedy, for instance, represents people doing
notionally historical things, in a dramatic manner or mode, and by
the means or in the medium of verse. Romance represents people
doing things invented by the writer, fictitious things; it does so by
telling a story, that is in narrative mode; and it does so in prose.
Romance, that is, is narrative prose fiction. In this chapter and the
next I shall discuss each of these three elements, fiction, narrative
and prose, although it will scarcely be possible to keep them entirely
apart.

First, the most important of the three: fiction, the object or content
of romance; the imagined world is the heart of romance. Although
the genre we have been considering looks substantial enough, there
is little if any explicit theory of fiction in Greece, not surprisingly
since the thing hardly existed until late. But precisely for that reason
it is important to look hard for such theory as may be relevant to
romance; so strong and ubiquitous a thing as romance assuredly left
some traces in people's thoughts about literature. This chapter, accordingly, tries to collect some thoughts that in antiquity were directed to other ends. It will be convenient, before entering on this
analysis, to consider some general attitudes to romance that help il-
luminate this absence of theory.

The first explicit reference to romance is not even certainly a reference to romance at all, though it very probably is. There is attributed
to Philostratus, a writer of the early third century, a group of imaginary letters to various people, some of them long dead. Letter 66 is
to one Chariton. "You think Greece will remember your stories when
you are dead. But if a man is a nobody when he is alive, what on
earth can he be when he is dead?" A nobody—"nothing," strictly
(*mēden*). It is interesting that he chooses Chariton—not the much

more literary Achilles Tatius, for instance. We cannot be sure that the addressee is our Chariton—the name is not unique. If it is not, we do not know who the addressee is, though that in itself proves nothing. It seems probable, however: we know of no other Chariton who wrote "stories" (*logoi*), and Philostratus was a Bloomsbury figure, the biographer of the Second Sophistic—it is entirely likely that he was a literary snob, and would have a low opinion of tales like *Chaereas and Callirhoe*.

If it is our Chariton, the text tells us several interesting things about him. First, his memory was alive enough, perhaps as much as two hundred years later, for Philostratus to think him worth a snide remark. Second, Chariton apparently had pretensions, or at any rate Philostratus thought he had. The careful structure of his story, along with his pride in his handling of it (as at the beginning of his last book, quoted earlier), does not belie that at all; he was justified in having pretensions. Thirdly, it is possible that the Greek plural form *logoi*, here translated as "stories," is a real plural, not a conventional plural-for-singular. In that case, Chariton made something of a habit of writing romances; it has in fact been suggested that he is the author of extant fragments of two other stories.[1] All of this tends to enhance the literary-historical importance of Chariton and his book. But of course the main thing the letter tells us is what the literary Philostratus thought of Chariton—that is, not much; this, it may be added, coming from a man who wrote a *Life of Apollonius of Tyana* which may reasonably be suspected of containing not very much more real history than *Chaereas and Callirhoe*, and of romanticizing its hero as much as Chariton romanticized his.[2] Even if the attribution to the biographer Philostratus is incorrect,[3] the text is there: somebody wrote it, somebody thought little of Chariton.

The second reference is later. It comes from the middle of the

---

[1] *Chione*, see M. Gronewald, "Ein neues Fragment zu einem Roman," *Zeitschrift für Papyrologie und Epigraphik* 35 (1979), 15–20; and *Metiochus and Parthenope*, see A. Dihle, "Zur Datierung des Metiochos-Romans," *Würzburger Jahrbücher für die Altertumswissenschaft* NF 4 (1978), 47–55; see also T. Hägg, "The Parthenope Romance Decapitated?" *Symbolae Osloenses* 59 (1984) 61–92, 79. Chariton's own word is usually *logos* (the singular) (5.1.2, 8.1.1). See now Holzberg, *Antike Roman*, 60.

[2] See Chapter 6.

[3] There is an apparently insoluble problem concerning the relationship and literary production of three (or even four) Philostrati, but it is of limited relevance for the present point. On Philostratus see G. W. Bowersock, *CHCL*, 655–58, and Graham Anderson, *Philostratus* (London, 1986).

fourth century, and again is in a letter—a real one, this time. The apostate emperor Julian, attempting to reform or reconstruct pagan religion in an effort to counter the spread of Christianity, gives advice to budding pagan priests on what to read. "We should read history," he says, and at once qualifies his remark: "—accounts of real events, that is; as for historical romances, such as people used to write—love stories, that kind of thing—those are to be avoided."[4] This text too tells us several things: historical romances are familiar to Julian (*Chaereas and Callirhoe*, the *Ethiopica*, and others are historical romances); they seem, by Julian's time, to be things of the past; and Julian thinks no more highly of them than Philostratus does, though that judgment is in his case incidental to his main point.

This is virtually all the direct evidence we have of the reactions of the literary world to romantic prose fiction. It could hardly be more meager. Further evidence might be seen in the paucity of surviving material—but even for tragedy only a tiny fraction remains of what was written. Better evidence of that kind lies in the fact that only the three "sophistic" romance texts survived antiquity in anything like a decent tradition. Chariton and Xenophon survived the late middle ages as marginally as can be imagined, in one late thirteenth century manuscript, and not a good one at that. Presumably the ancient and early Byzantine tradition of their texts was thin. Yet the papyrus tradition of Chariton was at one time relatively extensive, and our evidence for it continues into the sixth or seventh century.

It might also be thought that evidence of writers' implicit attitudes to their work is to be found in one feature of contemporary literary practice. As was pointed out earlier, creative literature was traditionally offered in the form of verse, not prose. Some sophisticated writers of prose in the second century appear to keep their distance from fiction, to offer a justification for writing it. Thus, the romances of Longus and Achilles Tatius are theoretically both commentaries on pictures: the stories open with a narrator contemplating a picture and then constructing an exegesis of it, which *is* the love story. Lucian does something similar. He lived at the very time when romance was most popular, the second century A.D., and wrote in various forms

---

[4] 89B Bidez-Cumont. This remark has some significance for the date of Heliodorus, incidentally (see Chapter 2, n. 29): it seems unlikely that Julian would refer so slightingly to a genre he regarded as distant and defunct if he himself borrowed from Heliodorus; whereas the *Ethiopica* could perfectly well *postdate* this remark if, as has been suggested, it is a throwback.

(one being the "Menippean dialogue" which he invented[5]). Among them is prose fiction, although not romantic prose fiction. The *True Story* is one such work; as we have seen, it is a parody on travellers' tall tales, which takes us to the moon, Hades, the belly of a whale, and other such places. Elsewhere, in the *Philopseudes* (*Lover of Lies*), he offers a group of short stories (*The Sorcerer's Apprentice* is one of them) which pillory human credulity. This fiction too has another aspect: it is satire. Is Lucian's satire, is Longus's painting, really a gesture, on the part of an educated writer, to justify him in writing prose fiction—a bow to academic convention? Perry maintained that it was—it is one of his main themes in *The Ancient Romances*. He is perhaps too categorical about the matter; more probably these writers are not so much covering themselves in academic eyes as simply employing an artistic device for entering into their stories. But it is interesting that it should be these devices that they use; there *is* some distance between prose and fiction; the point is worth making.

To move on, it is not that the age of romance had no literary figures who might have commented on the form—far from it. In the Augustan period, the scholar and critic Dionysius of Halicarnassus is ready to assess the qualities of other kinds of prose—that of Demosthenes, of Thucydides. But not a word about romance, which must have been at least beginning to show its face; it is altogether likely that *Ninus*, and no doubt other romances like it, existed in his day. At the end of the first century A.D. and early in the second, the contemporaries Plutarch and Dio of Prusa, Dio Chrysostom "the golden-mouthed," both philosophers of a kind and both literary figures, are willing to talk in detail about several kinds of writing, from Homer through Herodotus and tragedy to Aristophanes and New Comedy;[6] Dio even writes a romantic novella himself, a picture of idyllic rural existence rather similar in tone to *Daphnis and Chloe*.[7] But neither of

---

[5] A protest should be uttered here in passing about the nomenclature adopted by Northrop Frye for another of his literary categories, "Menippean satire." We know virtually nothing about the original Menippean satire; certainly not enough to justify the use of the name as a catch-all title for whatever will not fit into any other category. The borrowing is very inappropriate; given Frye's authority, however, it is inevitable that it should be put to use.

[6] Plutarch *On the Malice of Herodotus* and *Comparison between Aristophanes and Menander* (see n. 10 below); Dio Chrysostom *Trojan Discourse* (Oration 11), *The Bow of Philoctetes* (Oration 52).

[7] Sometimes called *The Hunters of Euboea*; it is the first part of Dio's "Euboean" Oration, Oration 7.

them, prolific as they both are, says a word about romance: this is particularly striking in the case of Plutarch, who had read everything and was incurably garrulous about everything under the sun. The great critic known as Longinus may have been their contemporary;[8] he can write a treatise *On Great Writing* without saying a word about romance (so far as we know—the text is incomplete). Finally (that is, to close this selection, for it is only a selection), in the second century Hermogenes wrote quite exhaustively on style, in the form of pedagogic manuals which were in vogue a thousand years after his time— yet not a word about romance.

We shall return to "Longinus" and Hermogenes, for it will be seen that some of what they did say does have some bearing, albeit indirect, on the matter. But if they are witnesses to the standing of romance, it is, as with Dionysius and Plutarch and Dio, by their silence. The reception that romance received was clearly anything but enthusiastic. It looks as if it was not born in any context of theory or critical interest, but in spite of theory and critics' interests. Indeed, some of what may seem indirectly relevant theory probably hindered as much as it helped. This will be the burden of this chapter. But before we turn to it, let us make a preliminary observation of a general kind.

What, in the genre of romance, invited disregard? We have seen that among its principal characteristics are the importance it accords to the private individual, its sentimental tone, its fictitious content, and its prose form. What, among these, is calculated to set traditional teeth on edge? As we consider the question, we soon realize that some of these features are to be found in Greek literature, "creative" literature, well before the day of romance. What is more, they are found together, without evoking distaste—far from it. New Comedy shows us, just as romance does, private individuals going through various tribulations and achieving a happy ending. The tone is sentimental and romantic, and the content is entirely fictitious.[9] It is a singularly instructive example, for New Comedy is for all the world like a tamer predecessor of romance—minus the travel, violence, and divine intervention. Yet New Comedy was anything but unpopular.

[8] The two dates suggested are late 1st century A.D. and early 3rd century A.D.— either would suit the present point; see n. 48 below for this and other matters concerning Longinus.

[9] As for Old Comedy, its plots are highly fictitious; but its characters are in some sense contemporary Athenians, so that in a way Aristophanes' plays are historical documents.

On the contrary, Menander, at least, was highly popular in the second century. That very Plutarch who knows (or at least says) nothing about romance writes a whole treatise comparing him with Aristophanes, and coming down unequivocally in favor of Menander: "What good reason has an educated man for going to the theater, except to see Menander?"[10] Furthermore, there is specific warrant in the *Poetics* for fictitious content, when at 9.1451b[11] Aristotle observes that in Agathon's *Antheus* both the names and the events are invented, "and it gives just as much pleasure"; it would indeed be absurd, he adds, to stick at any cost to the traditional stories, since one cannot by any means assume that the audience will all be familiar with them. Another element of romance, the happy ending, is actually positively commended at 14.1454a: "the best use of traditional material is for example the case in [Euripides'] *Cresphontes*, where Merope means to kill her son and does not, but recognizes him instead." It is true that this is in flat contradiction to Aristotle's categorical statement at 13.1453a that the line of development should go "from good fortune to bad and not the other way round"—a matter to which we shall have to return. The point here is that there was interest in the matter, even if only in the mind of Aristotle himself. And Aristotle and Menander are both authoritative names from the critical period—the seminal period, as we shall see—of literary theory. What was good enough for them ought, one would have thought, to be good enough for Plutarch.

What then is it that was objectionable about romance? In a word,

[10] Trans. D. A. Russell, in D. A. Russell and M. Winterbottom eds., *Ancient Literary Criticism: The Principal Texts in New Translations* (Oxford, 1972), 532; from Plutarch, *Comparison between Aristophanes and Menander, Moralia* 854B (vol. 10 in the Loeb edition). This extremely useful volume will be referred to as Russell-Winterbottom.

[11] References to the *Poetics* will be given in the form used here: 9.1451b means Chapter 9, p. 1451b. This is for ease of location, since translations sometimes omit one or the other reference. A similar system will be used for Aristotle's *Rhetoric*. Plato's *Republic* will be quoted in the form (Book) 10.595 (from the numeration of the Stephanus edition of 1578). Simple text references will be given in the body of the text to avoid a proliferation of minor footnotes. With the exception of the short passages quoted in the present sentence, translations from these three works will be taken where possible from Russell-Winterbottom (see previous note). This collection is to be recommended very strongly as a comprehensive collection of ancient literary-critical texts; in particular, the translation of the *Poetics* by M. E. Hubbard is distinctly superior to others available, not least in that by virtue of its division of the subject matter, with analytical headings, together with its copious footnotes, it constitutes in practice a very helpful running commentary on Aristotle's conduct of his argument. Additional texts in ancient literary criticism are to be found as an appendix to Russell's *Criticism in Antiquity*.

it is a matter of taste. To start with, the very nature of the content of romance was evidently objectionable: the action, the incident, the tone. For though romance is similar in general "post-classical" outline to New Comedy, in that both are concerned with private individuals and happy endings, there are important differences. The urbane intrigue of comedy becomes, in romance, melodramatic incident; obstacles to happiness become danger to life; hairbreadth escape replaces social maneuvering. A mildly romantic tone becomes downright sentimentality; a domestic setting is replaced by exotic foreign lands, familiar friends by inscrutable deities. If the base remains New Comedy, romance is altogether more violent, lurid, sensational. Romance increases the stakes, heightens the drama, the tension, the emotional content—to the point where it provokes critical resistance. It is judged not worth the exercise of critical intellect. Nor should we exaggerate the acceptability of New Comedy itself. It was clearly popular; it was watched in countless examples by generations of people, like television comedies; but it was not thought worth preserving—only papyrus texts and fragments remain of even the most popular author, Menander. Romance was even less memorable.

Secondly, a Chariton is in some degree open to the charge of pretentiousness. Here we return to another aspect of a point already made. By its form as prose, Chariton's story encroached on the territory of historiography, philosophy and oratory, for until his day that is the kind of thing prose had been used for: essentially for information or analysis or persuasion—that is to say, for intellectual purposes. But romance is not aimed at the intellectual faculty; it is entertainment. Romance thus intrudes on an intellectual world, and the intrusion is resented. But perhaps more important than this is the question of the quality of the writing. It is common experience today that the cultivated reader will persist with an Agatha Christie where he will not with a penny dreadful on a similar subject. In early or unsophisticated romance, the writing was not in general pitched at a highly cultivated level, although it was to improve considerably with the more ambitious authors (who, significantly, are the ones who have survived best).

In short, many, perhaps all, of the constituent elements of romance—subject, action, tone, prose form—were in themselves acceptable enough to theory and to general taste. What is objectionable seems to be the combination of them, and the manner of their miseen-scène; in particular, the combination in some romances of cheap effect with cheap style.

Let us turn now to the matter of what elements of theory were available to the writer and to the reader of romance.

In the early period of Greek literature there is little in the way of explicit literary theory of any kind, certainly nothing that can be in any direct way linked to romance in any form. It is true that there is enough preserved, in fragmentary fashion, to suggest that (as one would expect) writers were thinking about their craft and critics assessing their performance and the nature of literature in general. When Xenophanes observed, for instance, that "Homer and Hesiod attributed to the gods all the things that call forth criticism and blame when men do them—theft, adultery, deceit," he was making a critical point that was to be developed by Plato into a whole ideology of literature.[12] But it is a very general point. Similarly, Simonides called painting "poetry without words" and poetry "painting with words." The point is interesting, and even more general.[13] Rather, however, than catalogue such *obiter dicta*, we shall attempt to gather together what can usefully be said. The process will not be systematic and complete; the purpose of this study is not to give an account of Greek critical theory, but to extract from it, in as clear a way as possible, what is relevant to the genre of romance.

Narrative, story-telling, is as old as time, in Greek as in any other civilization. The principal form surviving in literary shape from the preliterate period is epic, and we have already had occasion to think of romance as itself an epic form. We must remember, though, that for all the argument since Milman Parry, we cannot say that we know just how "literate" the extant *Iliad* and *Odyssey* are. We almost certainly do see an originally oral form, even if it was only ballad, assuming written shape, whether with or after "Homer," if he existed. And there are other literary genres of which it can plausibly be argued that oral precursors existed. In the case of drama there appear to be several lines of affiliation. First, in general terms, the legends and myths which form the standard subjects of tragedy certainly were originally cast in oral narrative form. Some kinds of dramatic material have been analyzed closely by Sophie Trenkner with a view

---

[12] Fragment B 11 Diels-Kranz (Russell-Winterbottom 4).

[13] Reported in Plutarch, *On the Fame of the Athenians* 3, *Moralia* 346F = Loeb vol. 4 (Russell-Winterbottom 5; see 1–6 for a collection of such apophthegmata).

to discerning such narrative models.[14] Euripidean tragedy, she concludes, goes farther afield than the legends employed in earlier tragedy, and uses romantic themes of adventure, intrigue and love—some of them similar to romance motifs, which appear to imply the existence of oral *novelle*.[15] Later, New Comedy extended this borrowing, using folktale and adapting for the stage themes which originally required narrative exposition (travel-stories, for instance, which could not be set out dramatically). Trenkner also analyzes some other genres, in particular historiography. Oral tales become catalyzed in literature notably in the *contes* of Herodotus, as well as in romantic historiographers such as Ctesias; Herodotus is particularly fond of using such oral *logoi* to create *novelle* in which characters suffer the same kind of fate as tragic heroes (the story of Croesus, for example, in Book I, whose wealth could not save him from suffering). Oral narration, that is, lies behind all narrative literature—sometimes not very far behind it—and other forms as well.[16] But we cannot say that any explicit thoughts remain extant either on the construction of oral tales or on the manner of their catalysis in written texts.

We shall be returning to the matter of the narrative characteristics of epic. In the fifth century there is clearly considerable thinking going on about how to produce the most effective literature in one field, the field of tragedy. One question, certainly, was how to tell a story on the stage. It is virtually impossible to separate the narrative from the psychological or affective aspect of tragedy, because tragedy is concentrated in its action and exclusively dramatic in its means of presenting a story. No doubt the telling of a story was not its primary function. Nonetheless, a story is told—and we should not forget that the theater must have been where many people actually learned traditional stories, and that according to Aristotle most people did not in fact know the traditional stories.[17] We cannot hope to chart the course of theoretical speculation where we have only fragmentary evidence of practice to cull it from, but we can be sure the interest was intense. There would be, for instance, unending ways to tell the story of Agamemnon and Clytemnestra—the actual ending of Aes-

---

[14] S. Trenkner, *The Greek Novella in the Classical Period* (Cambridge, 1958).

[15] Trenkner, *Greek Novella*, 77–78.

[16] Trenkner also examines realistic anecdote in the fabulists, notably Aesop; folklore themes in Old Comedy; and rhetorical narrative and character-sketch.

[17] "What is well known is known only to a few"—although he may be referring to the details of stories rather than their main lines (9.1451b [Russell-Winterbottom 103]).

chylus's version of it, let alone all the incidental detail, is invented. And even at the end of the fifth century, if not later, poets could try to get too much story into a play, instead of selecting dramatically manageable elements; Agathon was booed for doing so (*Poetics* 18.1456a). Beyond that we can hardly hope to go, here.[18] But experiment in narrative, and hence tacit theory of narrative, there certainly was. "One cannot interfere with the traditional stories—by saying, for instance, that Clytemnestra was not killed by Orestes"—but Aristotle adds in the same breath that "one should invent for oneself and use the traditional material well" (14.1453b).

Theory, however, is not very long in appearing. By the time tragedy has tried many ways of telling a tale, and by the time that oral *conte* is beginning to assume literary form—that is, by the time society had extensive experience of literature of several kinds: epic, lyric, drama, history—a veritable maelstrom of ideas about the nature and function of literature seems to be forming. For the nature of communication, the nature of truth, the power of persuasion are central ideas in the intoxicating intellectual adventure of the sophistic movement, in the second half of the fifth century. General ideas about literature are at issue first, rather than precise thoughts about this or that form of it. Of the little specific evidence we have, the most significant is no doubt the fragmentarily preserved remarks of Gorgias on *logos*—speech, words—and on tragedy; they are not numerous, but among them they will take us straight to some major topics of fourth-century literary theory, which in turn lead us directly to the remaining elements of romance, namely prose and fiction.

The first of Gorgias's perceptive utterances develops the point that "speech" (*logos*) "is a great prince." His point is worth reporting at greater length for our purposes:

He can make fear cease, take away pain, instil joy, increase pity . . . Those who hear poetry feel the shudders of fear, the tears of pity, the longings of grief. Through the words, the soul experiences its own reaction to successes and misfortunes in the affairs and persons of others. . . . Speech the persuader forces the persuaded mind to agree with what is said and approve what is done . . . The alliance of speech and persuasion shapes the mind as it wishes . . . by the skill of its writing, not the sincerity of its utterance . . . The effect of

[18] See Rosemary Harriott, *Poetry and Criticism before Plato* (London, 1969).

speech bears the same relation to the constitution of the mind as the prescribing of drugs does to the nature of the body.[19]

Clearly Aristotle and Plato were not the first to think such thoughts. And these thoughtful remarks should be taken together with others, on tragedy. Tragedy, says Gorgias, produces *apatē*, deception, but a deception wherein

> the deceiver is more just than the non-deceiver, and the deceived is wiser than the undeceived . . . because it takes a measure of sensibility to be accessible to the pleasures of literature.[20]

Among them, the ideas expressed here raise several fundamental issues. First, the issue of persuasion, of persuading an audience that what is not true is true, clearly leads in the direction of fiction, of saying what is not true; and also raises the question of the social function of literature. Both matters were to be taken up by Plato, who made the social function of literature the whole basis of his ideological literary theory—which in its turn was to provoke the critical ideas of Aristotle. Second, the means of achieving effective *logos*, already in the later fifth century a serious study (witness the *logoi* of Euripides' plays and those of Thucydides' history, the elaborate debates on both sides of a question), was to become in the next century *the* predominant issue: theories of "rhetoric," in principle referring to prose, arose which before long produced both a whole doctrine of style— effective *logos*—and a whole educational system, destined to last for several centuries and dominate both Greek and Roman literary practice at the very period when romances were produced. The whole process of affecting the consumer, of "getting through" to him, is not any less applicable to romance than to tragedy. Plato was to use the expression "psychagogy" for it,[21] and it is a term which will recur. The theory of it, as we shall see, was not developed; but it is there, in embryo, even in that one word.

Finally, in yet another respect Gorgias was a pioneer, in using prose for a purpose other than strictly functional. The very speech in

[19] Gorgias, *Helen* 8–14. His point is that Helen of Troy should be excused for her misbehavior, as she was persuaded by *logos*; see Russell-Winterbottom 6ff. (from which the translation is taken).

[20] Plutarch, *On the Fame of the Athenians* 348c; translation from Russell-Winterbottom 6. The reason given ("because it takes . . .") is usually attributed to Plutarch himself.

[21] *Psychagōgia*, *Phaedr.* 261a 7–8, 271c10; Gorgias, in the *Helen*, uses *goēteia*, "witchcraft" (10).

which he utters his pregnant remarks is itself one of the earliest examples of "epideictic" *logos*, that is, writing for display (and not for information). It is a category which grew out of all proportion to its origins. By the time romances were being written, the practice of prose writing had far outstripped the theoretical framework available to accommodate it, and everything in prose which had no immediate purpose of persuasion, in lawcourt or civic assembly, was bundled willy-nilly into "epideictic"—because it presumably had to go somewhere, and there was nowhere else for it to go. Thus not only history and biography, but romance itself, is in theoretical principle "display rhetoric." The point is worth retaining; if I have here rather anticipated its discussion later in this chapter, it is in order to establish a "program," as it were, a basis for that subsequent discussion. But we should turn now to the heart of the matter: to the fourth century, to Plato, Aristotle, and their contemporaries; to the ideas of "prose" and "fiction"—and we shall see that it is not possible to separate completely those two ideas.

The idea of fiction is a sophisticated one. Fiction lies somewhere between the ideas of true and false, between fact and non-fact. A work of fiction tells a story which is factually not true, but may in a sense be emotionally true: true to life, for instance, so that it offers us a picture of something that inevitably interests us; or true to our desires, our imagination, so that even if what it offers is fantasy, it can hold our attention by corresponding to our own fantasies, or by stimulating them. The sophistication, however, does not lie in the nature of fiction; it lies in *recognizing* the nature of fiction. A child makes up stories. They are neither true nor, except in a superficial sense, false. They are not historical accounts of things that happened, nor will our child offer his stories as veridical—or as *not* veridical. The idea has never entered his head that they are either true or not. At first, "true" and "not true" are simply not categories in his mind; the question does not arise. At some point, however, he will become aware that fiction, though it may not be reprehensible, is not fact. That is the point at which sophistication sets in.

Perhaps in the earliest stage of Greek story-telling, similarly, no awareness was shown of the distinction between "true" and "not true"—or, more accurately, no awareness that the distinction matters. No doubt this is a normal process with primitive civilizations. If this is so, the condition clearly goes back, in Greece, to prehistory, for Homer is not as simple as a child. He obviously knows very well that the stories he is telling are not historically true, because he is obviously shaping them himself with certain purposes in mind: to portray Achilles as heroic, Odysseus as resourceful. There would certainly be different levels of awareness of fiction at different levels of society or of intelligence, as awareness differs among children of the same age. These levels would differ also according to the purpose the fiction is serving, its social function. Tragedy embodied traditional stories—that Agamemnon was killed by Clytemnestra and Clytemnestra by Orestes, for instance—and they were evidently thought of as substantially true (perhaps some of them were true, at that). Comedy, on the other hand, was obviously known to be not true—even if it did represent larger-than-life, genuine contemporary events (the Peloponnesian War) or figures (Socrates, Euripides). As for myth— let us say, for example, the story of Io, told in the *Promethus Bound*— it is impossible to guess what degree of truthfulness was attributed to it. But it is clear at any rate that untrue stories known as untrue circulated from the earliest days of Greek literature. It is also clear that the distinction between true and untrue was recognized. Hesiod's Muses

> "Know how to tell many lies that resemble the truth,
> But we know also how to tell the truth when we wish."[22]

Personal lyric seems to have done the same thing. We have, of course, no way of measuring how far Archilochus or Sappho told the truth about their own lives. But to ask that question is to ask whether Wordsworth actually knew a girl called Lucy, who, alas!, died. Occasionally, in modern times, it is possible to find an answer. At that point we realize, or should, that that is not the question we should be asking; it is only an anterior question, which may or may not be relevant in considering the real one.

We cannot say when or how the practice of conscious fiction appeared in Greek literature, any more than we can for any other literature. But we can say that early writers did not articulate the mental processes that lay behind their practice. The Muses did not tell Hesiod why they might *want* to tell lies that resemble the truth. Would they have expected their audience to believe their lies? We have no way of knowing whether their listener would believe that what they

---

[22] *Theogony* 27–28, Russell-Winterbottom 3.

said was true, or whether he would know that it was not true, but take pleasure in resemblance to truth. But here, surely, lies the crucial question. At what point did willing suspension of disbelief begin to operate? And as its corollary, for the immediate purposes of the present study, at what point did both writers and readers become aware of, and begin consciously to operate on the basis of, that principle?

Theory always appears after practice, in literature at least. Perhaps we can see the beginnings of the theory of fiction, in Greece, in the later fifth century B.C. What we have seen of Gorgias's thoughts on *logos* and the power of persuasion, and on poetic deception, looks like the real psychological origin of overt fiction. When writers come to realize that they can "mislead," a major step has been taken in the direction of fiction; they are then subject to the temptation to do so, consciously and (so to speak) with malice aforethought. The possibilities of the writer's craft expand. The remaining step comes when the audience falls into conscious complicity, becomes accessory before the fact. At each stage the question will arise: what is to be gained by misleading—or by being misled? There is a range of answers, and most of them are "positive": there is something to be gained. Fiction is fully present when what the writer offers is not offered as veridical, when it is known by the audience not to be veridical, and when something is seen to be gained in the process of offering it: when it *matters*.

The consciousness of the distinction between true and (in whatever sense) not true, and of its importance, is visibly heightened by the time of the Sophistic movement. Herodotus was ready to include in his history matter of questionable factuality.[23] Stringency came with Gorgias's contemporary Thucydides, who at the beginning of his much more austere work implicitly criticizes earlier historiography for its inadequate critical standards and cavalier attitude to historical truth.[24] And with fact comes fiction. Fiction cannot be recognized as fiction until fact is recognized as fact. But once fact is so recognized, once its importance as fact is understood, fiction is born,

[23] Here I pass over the vexed question of how far Herodotus was consciously manipulating facts; see, *e.g.*, the 1987 issue (vol 20) of *Arethusa*, which is devoted to "Herodotus and the Invention of History," esp. J. Marincola's summary of work on "The Sources of Herodotus," 26–40.

[24] "I made it my business to base my history of the war not on casual inquiry nor on my own general impressions, but on personal observation and on reports from others which I checked in detail as carefully as I could" (1.22).

as a corollary and in the same movement. In a sense, the theory of romance appeared, by inversion, when Thucydides published his "manifesto" laying down the nature of true historiography. Furthermore, since fiction is a function of fact, this is the point at which, and the reason for which, fiction enters the aesthetic arena in prose form; since history was in prose, fiction—the complement of fact—was first recognized in prose dress. And it was in the generation following Thucydides that the first steps were taken in the direction of conscious prose fiction. They were taken almost simultaneously by Thucydides' historiographical continuator, Xenophon of Athens, and by Plato, the disciple of Gorgias's adversary Socrates. The confluence of historiographical theory and philosophy (in the form of what we call social theory) was ultimately, for good or ill, to determine in large part the form of ancient romance and the intellectual atmosphere in which it came into existence.

Since what we are concerned with in this chapter is the literary theory relevant to romance, for the present little will be said of the actual practice of historiography and its associated discipline, biography; we shall have occasion later to consider the similarities between romance and other forms of literature. The most significant name is indeed that of Xenophon, though other fourth-century writers of his kind also come into the picture. Xenophon is particularly significant. In the *Hellenica*, his continuation of Thucydides' work, as in large degree also in the *Anabasis*, he occupied himself with straightforward history, the history of political and military events, in the mold of (although not nearly as well as) his predecessor; but he also wrote a number of biographical works—on Socrates, Agesilaus the fourth-century king of Sparta, and notably on Cyrus the Great of Persia, the *Cyropaedia* or *Education of Cyrus*. It is this last work, dated about the second or third decade of the fourth century B.C., which was to prove of particular importance in the history of romance.

Xenophon gave his name to, or rather had his name taken by, several writers of the imperial age; among them was a real historian, Arrian, who thought of himself as "a second Xenophon"; and among them also, as we had occasion to note in an earlier chapter, were several romance-writers: "Xenophon of Ephesus," like "Xenophon of Antioch" and "Xenophon of Cyprus," was not taking his name in vain. They are labelled as "historians" in later antiquity;[25] and in us-

[25] See Chapter 2, n. 18.

ing Xenophon's name they were labelling themselves as historians. Early romance, that is, was, in theory, history. But that is because in Xenophon of Athens and some contemporaries, history, in at least some of its forms, was in practice romance. "We shall not understand what biography was in the fourth century," says Momigliano, "if we do not recognize that it came to occupy an ambiguous position between fact and imagination . . . biography was preceded or at least inspiringly accompanied by fiction."[26] For the *Cyropaedia* is a romantic biography, certainly not a historically reliable account of the life of its subject. While it presents a version of his life, it is dominated by the desire to show Cyrus as a cultivated and moral man, and is in large part constructed of anecdotes designed to illustrate his personal qualities. There is even embedded within this account a moving love story. It does not directly concern Cyrus himself, and its marginal place in the book is emphasized by the discontinuity of its narration; but the romantic nature of the *Cyropaedia* is not dependent on the presence in it of the episode concerning Abradatas and his faithful wife Panthea.[27]

The work is not an isolated example of its kind, and we need spend no more time here on its historiographical and biographical context. It has been introduced to suggest that behind the fourth century historiographical prose tradition there is a theoretical analysis in process, concerning how one should write history, what constitutes the proper field of this branch of information conducted in the developing medium of prose. Information about character is thought as important as a catalogue of events—Xenophon himself virtually says as much in another of his biographies, the life of Agesilaus.[28] "Truth" has different values, as the sophists had said. A writer may wish to purvey things other than facts; he may wish to influence his audience in what he considers a suitable direction, to "lead their souls," "psychagogize" them—for whatever purpose. *Logos*, properly used, will help him do so. "Socratic philosophy and Isocratean rhetoric joined hands in encouraging the introduction of fiction into biography."[29]

[26] A. Momigliano, *The Development of Greek Biography* (Cambridge, Mass., 1971), 46 and 56; I am here much indebted to the whole chapter (43–64) on 4th century biography.

[27] On the fictional aspect of the *Cyropaedia* see esp. James Tatum, *Xenophon's Imperial Fiction: On* The Education of Cyrus (Princeton, 1989).

[28] Momigliano, *Greek Biography*, 50–51; the life is divided into separate accounts of (a) events, and (b) Agesilaus's character.

[29] Momigliano, *Greek Biography*, 57.

Isocrates and the Socratics represent the stage beyond sophistic, beyond Gorgias.

It does not seem likely that Xenophon expected readers of his *Cyropaedia* to take every word of it, or perhaps even much of it, as literally true. We can be fairly certain, however, that he wanted them to take his version of Cyrus' life as "morally true," and worth reading for that reason. With his contemporary Plato we are in no doubt at all; he tells us explicitly his views on fiction.

Plato's views on fiction—the first, and virtually the only, conscious theorizing about fiction in antiquity—are inextricably linked with his whole literary theory, based as it is on his crucial concept of *mimēsis* and his ontology, his theory of Forms. These, in turn, are predicates of his views on the organization of society, that society which was in turmoil throughout the fifth century, and in particularly at the end of it, when sophists like Gorgias—not to say Socrates—and writers like Euripides and Thucydides pierced the surface of the words that inspire and describe action.[30] We are now no distance at all from Gorgias's pregnant thoughts on *logos*. No distance—but the surrounding area has filled up considerably.

Acquaintance with the main lines of the social philosophy set out in the *Republic* must here be assumed. There are two stages in Plato's account of fiction, corresponding to the two levels of writers' understanding of reality, which he treats first in Books 2-3 and later in Book 10.[31] In the initial discussion, which comes before Socrates has set out his theory of transcendental reality (the theory of Forms), writers are conceived as being capable of representing the truth in their works, and as being obliged to do so. Among the truths their fables (myths) should reflect are doctrines about God: God is good, and cannot be responsible for crimes. It follows that Homer should be censured, in fact censored, for representing gods acting immorally, fighting one another and so on; even were such stories true, they should not be told to those not fitted to hear them (such as children), for literature should impose patterns of virtue, should for instance maintain that citizens do not fight among themselves. In the same way, gods may

---

[30] See Thucydides 3.82: words change their value in times of stress: mindless aggression becomes courageous loyalty to one's cause; circumspection becomes a specious name for cowardice; etc.

[31] *Rep.* 2.377–3.392 and 10.595–607. For the following discussion I am particularly indebted to Christopher Gill, "Plato's Atlantis Story and the Birth of Fiction," *Philosophy and Literature* 3 (1979), 64–78.

not be represented as appearing in other shapes, nor as uttering falsehoods. It is equally unacceptable to show good men under the sway of emotions, such as grief and laughter: these are not patterns of virtue. All of this, of course, effectively wipes out virtually all literature as we know it (and as Plato knew it); familiar stories may seem pleasant to the reader, but that is not their proper purpose. Only the truth about reality may be represented; needless to say, the truth about reality is what Plato thinks it is. Fiction, in short, should be state-controlled; its purpose is didactic; it should be, quite simply, propaganda. The thesis needs no further exposition. It is only too sadly familiar to the twentieth century—and we have seen it put into practice, as Plato did not. It hardly needs saying that this has nothing to do with the way Greek romance was in fact written.[32]

Understanding of reality, however, is of crucial importance. Now, the ideal community's rulers, the guardians, are philosophers who know the truth about reality; that is why they are the rulers. If they judge it necessary, they may employ falsehood for remedial purposes, like doctors: "rulers of the city may appropriately use falsehoods, because of enemies or fellow citizens, to help the city" (3.389b).[33] Only rulers have this privilege, and literature must be under their control. But the interesting thing, for our purposes, is that Plato here clearly does conceive of writers *inventing* stories and offering them for consumption, if they have government's approval, knowing them to be false; not just composing versions, accurate or inaccurate, of historical events, which is what Thucydides still thought Homer was doing.[34] One essential quality of fiction, thus, is now on stage, namely fictiveness—provided, of course, that the fiction is based on the approved "truth about reality."

And Plato himself on several occasions practices what he preaches by creating just such fictions, or "myths," to underline and impress moral truths, where he is afraid that mere logical demonstration will not be sufficient to bring about real conviction. Two such cases are the myth of Er, at the end of the *Republic,* and the account of the Last Judgment at the end of the *Gorgias.* Both are eschatological myths. In

[32] Although it does have something to do with the way some Greek romances were eventually interpreted: the *Ethiopica,* notably, was interpreted in the Byzantine period as ethical allegory; see Sandy, *Heliodorus,* 96.

[33] Cf. 3.382d: "Falsehood can surely be made useful in mythology . . . because we don't know the truth about antiquity; what we do is to make the falsehood as like the truth as possible." See Russell-Winterbottom, 60, 56–57.

[34] Thuc. 1.3, 10; Gill "Plato's Atlantis Story," 65.

the former, we are given a glimpse of the afterlife via a soldier, Er, who is killed but comes to life again on his funeral pyre, having seen what happens after death; he is sent back to earth expressly to tell human beings what he has seen. What we learn, after a cosmological account of the universe, is that the soul experiences transmigration after death, with each person being responsible for the choice of his next incarnation; thus when the soul of Odysseus has to choose, "the memory of his former sufferings had cured him of all ambition and he looked round for a long time to find the uneventful life of an ordinary man."[35] The lesson Socrates wishes to inculcate is that "we should believe the soul to be immortal . . . and always keep our feet on the upward way and pursue justice and wisdom."[36] Similarly, in the Gorgias we learn that after death our souls are judged impartially by Rhadamanthus, Aeacus and Minos, naked and stripped of all our earthly trappings. This almost invariably means that the powerful of this world, who have the best opportunity of sinning, are consigned to the punishments of Tartarus, while the soul of the unambitious lover of wisdom goes to the Islands of the Blest. "Personally," says Socrates, "I put faith in this story and make it my aim to present my soul to its judge in the soundest possible state."[37]

Thus, whereas for Thucydides historiography should remain firmly glued to fact, philosophy, at least in the person of Plato, has no a priori, impregnable objection to departing from historical truth. This being so, it might seem that creative writers would have found philosophical writing a more propitious terrain from which to launch fiction. In fact they sailed against the current, so to speak, and opted to present their work rather as a kind of historiography, though no doubt it was conceived—to mix metaphors—rather on the wrong side of the historiographical blanket. But the earliest romance writers were anything but philosophers.[38] Furthermore, philosophy, or at

---

[35] 10.620c; this passage and the following one are taken from H.D.P. Lee's Penguin translation (Harmondsworth, 1955).

[36] 10.621c.

[37] Gorgias 526d, trans. W. Hamilton (Harmondsworth, 1960) (Penguin).

[38] For an interesting example of "philosophical fiction," see Chion of Heraclea: A Novel in Letters, ed. I. Düring (Göteborg, 1951). This is a collection of 17 letters purporting to have been written by one Chion to a number of addressees, including Plato (no. 17); they recount the progress of a successful plot to kill a tyrant on ideological grounds. The main lines of the action are based on a real episode of 4th century history (the assassination of Clearchus of Heracles in 353/352 by Chion and others, who were themselves killed in the attack). The (unknown) author appears to have written the work in the period of Augustus or in the 1st century A.D. (that is, it is roughly contem-

least this philosophy, has ideological imperatives. Fiction demands freedom from ideology just as much as freedom from fact; and historiography was a less strict taskmaster than Plato.

To return to Plato's argument in the *Republic*, at this stage of it the reader is not a conspirator, who is in on the secret of fiction; he *believes* what he is told—there is no point in sanctioning official falsehoods if their audience is not going to believe them anyway. Plato supposes that the governed, in his ideal society, will believe the authorized fables, true or false, as Greeks believed Homer and myths. This makes these falsehoods less than fiction in the normal sense of the term, since the reader's complicity is not involved. In the second stage of his argument, Plato turns to this element of complicity, in the course of developing his case for the suppression of virtually all literature (10.595–607). By now he has set out his theory of the nature of reality: reality lies in the transcendent Forms, of which the manifestations on earth are only imitations. A material bed is already at one remove from the Form of "Bed"; it is in that degree not "real." It follows that a picture of a bed is at two removes from reality;[39] an artist therefore is only imitating an imitation, he is a *mimētēs* of a *phantasma* or appearance. The artist does not himself know what reality is, what the Form of Bed is—unless he happens to be a philosopher. The reader, therefore—to turn from painting to literature—is reading something unreal.[40] He takes pleasure in reading it, but it is not a pleasure derived from reason, only from emotion; he becomes involved in the emotions represented (e.g. grief), and this encourages

porary with Chariton's story); he evidently wants to illustrate the ennobling effect of Plato's philosophy ("a tyrant can inflict all kinds of evils on my body, but he can never subdue my soul," Düring 17). The story is rather dull. The model for the epistolary form is clearly Plato's own letters.

[39] It seems to be a habit of those who discuss Plato to say that a picture of a bed is at three removes from reality. That is good Greek—in Greek, Wednesday is the third day from Monday, since Monday, Tuesday and Wednesday are all counted, in Greek convention. But it is not good English: Wednesday is *two* days away from Monday in English—and a picture of a bed is at *two* removes from Plato's Ideal Bed.

[40] Well formulated by Gill, "Plato's Atlantis Story and the Birth of Fiction," *Philosophy and Literature* 3 (1979), 68: "The aesthetic experience, in fact, is a 'closed' experience that discloses nothing to us about the real world." Plato thus in a way anticipates modern constructs, such as that of Frye in *Anatomy of Criticism*: "Pure literature, like pure mathematics, contains its own meaning" (*Anatomy*, 351)—"literature as autonomous language"; see Chapter 7. Similarly, in the *Gorgias* Socrates maintains that "rhetoric" as taught by the sophists does not address itself to the reality of justice, as philosophy does; rhetoric is to philosophy as cooking (the art of pandering to the appetite) is to medicine (the art of inducing health).

like emotions in his own soul. But conduct should be governed by reason, not emotion; the writer, therefore—who is merely an imitator of what people do—"rouses and feeds this part of the mind [emotion] and by strengthening it destroys the rational part . . . The imitative poet . . . produces a bad government in the individual mind" (10.605). Plato puts his finger exactly on the operation of literature as "sympathy," a sharing of emotion: "the consequences of others' experience invade one's own, because it is difficult to restrain pity in one's own misfortunes when it has grown strong on others' " (10.606).

It would be hard to formulate more accurately than does Plato the romantic case *for* "creative literature": the writer represents what he sees, and in so doing engages our emotion on behalf of those involved in the action he represents. That Plato draws a non-romantic, in fact anti-romantic, conclusion—namely, that to engage the reader's emotions produces "bad government" in his mind—is neither here nor there; that is Plato's business, and we are not immediately concerned with it here. The point is that he sees exactly what writers of fiction try to do. Aristotle differs from Plato on just this point: such spectacles, far from debilitating the mind, "effect through pity and fear the *catharsis* of such emotions" (*Poetics* 6.1449b); whatever that may mean, it is a good thing, for Aristotle.

Here, however, we find ourselves in general literary theory, and should withdraw once more to our specific inquiry, concerning fiction. The application of the above argument to fiction is that Plato does not appear, at this second stage of his analysis, to think that a reader really believes the story he is reading: "when the best of us hear Homer or some other tragic poet imitating a hero in mourning . . . you know how we feel pleasure and give ourselves up to it, how we follow in sympathy and praise the excellence of the poet who does this to us most effectively" (10.605). Plato does not say explicitly that the listener doesn't really believe the story he is listening to, but no other conclusion could be drawn from what he does say. This can be nothing other than willing suspension of disbelief. And with this, the final requirement of fiction is fulfilled. The reader is accessory to the fact of fiction; Plato is aware of the process of complicity.

The foregoing pages do not demonstrate, and do not purport to demonstrate, that Plato ever arrived at our conception of fiction. His "fiction"—the "authorized fable" of his ideal state—is meant to be believed. What he sees as involving the reader's complicity, on the other hand, is not fictional in our sense. It is anterior (and perhaps contemporary) Greek literature, it is Homer and tragedy; and that is in principle veridical, though it is also "creative," arranged. But this is only to say that he evidently did not quite fit the pieces together as we do. The pieces are all there, however. "At a time when factual and fictional writing were not generally distinguished," Gill remarks, "Plato's account of the surface-level falsity of *muthoi*, and of the phantasm-world of the poet, went far to isolate the notion of fiction; and it did so in advance of the creation of any wholly fictional genre of literature."[41]

It may even be the case that in his own practice as a writer Plato came closer to the idea of fiction than we have so far allowed, for he more than once shows concern over this very question of whether the reader is or is not to believe the fiction he reads. Of the several major fictional stories with which he seeks to impress his philosophical points—we have just glanced at two of them—, most are offered as worthy of belief but not likely to attract it. Always there is an "underlying truth" which will be beneficial to the reader. It is clear, however, that belief is what Plato really hankers after, not simply acquiescence in the fiction and engagement of the emotions. Too much a realist to suppose that people will believe tales not (like Homer's) hallowed by antiquity and bearing resemblance to history, he is yet not prepared fully to trust mere acquiescence, not prepared to trust readers' emotions to operate in the right way unless they are underwritten by credence. But in the absence of real credence, perhaps a middle way is possible and may be advantageous: the way of willed credence, that willing suspension of disbelief that has just been evoked.

It is possible that towards the end of his life Plato was himself edging closer to what has become normal literary practice: the use of active literary artifice—as opposed to mere pious hope—to encourage such willed credence. The *Timaeus* and *Critias*, an umbilically linked duo, are usually taken to be late works, written in the period preceding the *Laws*; the *Laws*, a second attempt at describing an ideal state,

---

[41] "Plato's Atlantis Story," 69. Gill is, however, perhaps not quite right in speaking of the two descriptions of the writer as "distinct and not easily reconcilable with each other." They are distinct, certainly, but there is no occasion to try to reconcile them. The writer of *Rep.* 2–3 is a government servant in the ideal state; the writer of *Rep.* 10 is a "real" writer, to be ejected from the ideal state precisely because he does not do what the government (*i.e.*, Plato) wants him to do—or more accurately, because he does what Plato wants him not to do.

could in fact be regarded as a third member of this set, which would thus constitute a final trilogy. In the *Timaeus* and *Critias* he twice begins to tell a story he never finishes, the story of the lost city of Atlantis. Atlantis was, in his account, a powerful civilization which degenerated and attacked Athens in a mythical past in which Athens was itself an ideal society. In the *Critias* Plato does launch into a detailed account of Atlantis; and it is this account, this story, that concerns us at this point. For present purposes two things are interesting about it; neither, as it happens, is concerned directly with the description itself. First, in the *Timaeus*, Plato (or his character Critias) is oddly insistent that this is a true account, which is authenticated by its descent as a tradition, originating with the legendary Solon, within his own family; it thus has the authority of history. Secondly, in the *Critias*, its narrator, Critias himself, is nonetheless worried that he may not be able to present his story in a convincing way: "you should make allowances," he says, "if my narrative is not always entirely appropriate; for you must understand that it is far from easy to give satisfactory accounts of human affairs."[42]

It has been suggested that here, in what was to be the last of a series of literary experiments in such "myth-making," we see Plato himself aiming at that kind of result which in the *Republic* (10) he describes as achieved by great writers, such as Homer, who have the art of inducing their audience to suspend their disbelief and become accomplices in the act of fiction; to allow themselves, that is, to imbibe the values enshrined in the story.[43] Plato, in short, would use "rhetoric" to its true end; his story is an *approved* myth; so its values are true ones, whose absorption will benefit its audience. This is to say that Plato here accepts the idea of complicity in fiction, which is the ultimate sophistication of the idea of fiction. "He is not only writing fiction," suggests Gill, "but, consciously, playing the game of fiction, the game, that is, of presenting the false as true, the unreal as real. And in his preface, he is inviting his reader to take part in the same game, to pretend (to himself) to be deceived when he is not, to take as true what he knows is false . . . what Plato wants is a willed

---

[42] *Critias* 107e, trans. H.D.P. Lee (Harmondsworth, 1965) (Penguin).

[43] Gill, "Plato's Atlantis Story," 70–76: "In the presentation of Plato's myths, written around the time of the *Republic*, we can see an increasing awareness on Plato's part of the ambiguity of their truth-status" (70); the works in question are (in their probable order) *Gorgias, Phaedo, Republic, Phaedrus, Statesman, Timaeus/Critias* (see on the chronology also Gill, "Plato and Politics: the *Critias* and the *Politicus*," *Phronesis* 24 [1979], 148–67).

self-deception . . . . This new element of intended complicity in the fictional game makes his work the first piece of deliberately fictional narrative in Greek literature."[44]

Even if the basis for this judgment is tenuous and the idea itself speculative, we are looking in the right direction: both in theory and in his own practice, Plato had come to the very brink of a break-through in the analysis of the possibilities of literature. "The game of fiction was not a familiar one in Plato's day, as it is to us."[45] People surely played the game long before Plato's day, or Homer's. But it takes a genius to see the obvious.

It may then be that Plato had arrived at the heart of fiction, in the fourth century B.C. There is, at any rate, something very suggestive about the *Republic*'s two layers of theory about a kind of literature that is essentially fiction. Perhaps all literary theory, like all philosophy, is footnotes to Plato; in that respect at least, some recent literary-critical reflections are in an old tradition. It is true that literary theory is part of a total social ideology for Plato, and that literary practice in his ideal society is indissolubly linked with an authoritarian social structure, and thus is shaped by what modern authoritarians would call "correct thinking." Fiction, therefore, is not any more free than any other form of literature to "explore" the human mind or experience. No doubt most readers of these pages would indignantly reject such fiction. But the point is that Plato is at least close to seeing how fiction operates, and to writing fiction consciously on the basis of his theory. What Xenophon was doing by instinct, Plato was doing in the same generation as the culmination of an intellectual process. The fertile fourth century sowed the seeds of romance.

We may extend these thoughts, and stay directly on the subject of narrative fiction, by remaining with Plato and one of the major authors of footnotes to him, Aristotle, on the topic of imagination. The basis of Plato's theories was his view of the effect of literature on the imagination and emotions—and if fiction has a purpose, it is to affect the emotions in one way or another. An audience's emotions, for Plato, will be most directly affected, its sympathy most immediately engaged, when a representation is mimetic in mode, that is in dramatic form (*Republic* 392–98). Drama is the most dangerous form of

---

[44] Gill, "Plato's Atlantis Story," 76.
[45] Ibid.

literature because it is entirely mimetic; the spectator cannot, for practical purposes, detach himself from what is being enacted before his eyes by living actors, whereas it is much more feasible to detach oneself from what is merely being reported as having happened. Plato himself makes a distinction between this most vivid form of representation and narrative, the latter being at least less corrupting than drama because less directly affecting.

Aristotle's position is exactly the opposite, because his view of *mimēsis* is exactly opposed to Plato's: far from being psychologically harmful, it is actually "cathartic," that is, in some way therapeutic. Drama, in the form of tragedy, is a higher form than epic (26.1461b–1462b) because it is more unified and concentrated and because it is mimetic; Homer is superior to other epic poets in that he uses narrative relatively little and is "directly" mimetic (24.1460a).[46] We may note that Aristotle does not dispute Plato's analysis of the effect of literature; it is on the evaluation of that effect that he differs.

The point that is relevant here concerns the nature of narrative. Relatively (though only relatively) innocuous for Plato, narrative is apparently (and by the same token) less effective than drama for Aristotle, precisely because the reader is less personally engaged by it than the spectator is by drama. But Aristotle notices something else, which Plato does not notice (or does not discuss), about the narrative mode: the manner of the reader's engagement is different. In the case of epic, which for present purposes is equivalent to romance in being narrative and non-dramatic, "its size can be considerably further extended . . . one can tell of many things as at the moment of their accomplishment, and these if they are relevant make the poem more impressive. So it has this advantage in the direction of grandeur and variety for the hearer and in being constructed with dissimilar episodes. For it is similarity and the satiety it soon produces that make tragedies fail" (24.1459b). Furthermore, "epic is more tolerant of the prime source of surprise, the irrational, because one is not looking at the person doing the action. For the account of the pursuit of Hector would seem ludicrous on the stage, with the Greeks standing still and not pursuing him, and Achilles refusing their help; but in epic one does not notice it" (24.1460a).

Epic narrative is extensible, and it accepts the irrational. Put in

---

[46] It is true that Aristotle seems to be using "mimesis" in a more restricted sense here (to mean "dramatic") than he does elsewhere in the *Poetics*, where in general all poetry is "mimetic."

70

other words, Aristotle's point becomes: romance is infinitely comprehensive, and its appeal is purely to the imagination, not to the senses. Comprehensiveness and appeal to the imagination are precisely two of the major features that emerge in the romance even in antiquity, that are put to use instinctively by a Heliodorus, a Chariton. Though there is no theory constructed about these features of narrative, and their application to literature, we see that they did not go unnoticed. At a time when narrative fiction is in the air, Aristotle—laconically, as usual—sets out *en passant* the principal features of narrative fiction.

It would seem to follow that a writer can have the best of both worlds by employing dramatic narrative, by telling his story, in Aristotle's formulation earlier in the *Poetics*, "sometimes in narration and sometimes becoming someone else, as Homer does" (3.1448a); he can have both extensiveness and emotion. For Plato, of course, "imagined drama" would offer the *worst* of both worlds: it would make the imagination work overtime, and thus be particularly debilitating. We have seen that that is exactly what Chariton in particular does do. He plays on the emotional effect that directly presented drama can create, by moving rapidly from "scene" to "scene," by presenting his Callirhoe living before our eyes, in pathetic monologue and vivid, theatrically charged personal crisis. His whole aim is to tug at our heartstrings. Plato would have despised Chariton.

We may with some profit here pursue this point a little farther. If it is true that narrative gives more scope than drama to imagination, it is also true that imagination is a private thing, an individual and personal faculty. Narrative will more readily than drama spark individual and personal reactions, untrammelled by specific visual perceptions. In the unlimited world of narrative, characters can move and act entirely at the author's will; and the reader will move and act with them in the same unlimited way. Narrative appeals more readily to the individual, narrative fiction more readily yet; the reader can be bounded in a nutshell, yet count himself king of infinite space, and master of his fate.

Drama appeals to the eye, narrative to the mind. Drama is more suited to public performance and a collective audience, narrative to private reading, to the individual. We begin here to enter the country not of Aristotle, nor yet of Northrop Frye, but of Marshall McLuhan. If narrative fiction talks to the individual, it is likely that it will talk *of* the individual, for that is the message he is, in his capacity as individual, best conditioned to receive. And in fact, when narrative fiction does emerge, we find it talking not about kings and princes, whose doings are of concern to a public audience, but about less socially important people. Chaereas, Callirhoe, Daphnis, Chloe may be well-born, but they are important only to themselves and their families; and to the reader who in the mind's eye can more readily see himself or herself in them than in Oedipus or Clytemnestra. Such fiction treats of private matters, of the personal situation and fortunes of characters readily enough accessible to the reader's sympathies.[47]

These theoretical considerations, occasioned by early and classical Greek literature within the classical period itself, formed part of the philosophical tradition that helped inform the attitudes of writers and readers of romance. At this point we shall pass over several centuries directly to the age of romance; for somewhere in its intellectual penumbra is another theory of clear relevance to the present topic. It will here be presented in brief form; for it is not fully developed (or fully known, given the state of the text), its application to our topic is difficult to determine, and in short, it seems best to leave the reader to make of it what he thinks justifiable. But major it is; it is nothing less than a whole theory of "imagination," almost of "sensibility" in a Romantic, Coleridgean sense. In the fragments that remain to us of "Longinus" 's famous essay *On the Sublime* lies the skeleton of a whole new approach to literature as a creative process, an approach that might well be thought capable of constructing a theory of narrative fiction.[48]

[47] The terms "reader" and "spectator" no doubt oversimplify the complex question of the "consumption" of literature in antiquity, but they are not misleading. Chariton, for instance, hopes that the last book of his story will be agreeable *to his readers* (8.1; the verb is *anaginōskō*, the normal verb for "read"). We do know, however, that in the second century A.D. Homer could be "performed" (in *Leucippe and Clitophon* one important episode depends on a piece of equipment used by "one of those who declaim Homer in the theater" [3.20]); and it may be that there were public readings from romances. There may also have been readings to small groups, such as families; that would be consonant with the fact that numerous papyrus fragments of romance, including several of Chariton, have been found at country sites in colonial Egypt. In that case, readings could easily have taken serial form (which might account for Chariton's frequent recapitulations of his action). See Hägg, *Novel in Antiquity*, 90ff. On the general topic see B.M.W. Knox, *CHCL*, 1–41.

[48] See especially the edition by D. A. Russell, *'Longinus' On the Sublime* (Oxford, 1964), for analysis of the treatise and full discussion of the problems of date and authorship; here I shall call the author Longinus, without apology, and suppose that the date is late 1st century A.D. (rather than early 3rd century; cf. n. 8 above). Russell

The basis of the theory is set out in the eighth chapter, where the author tells us there are five main sources of greatness in writing (which is what "sublimity" means). They may here be reduced to two: "the power to conceive great thoughts" allied to "strong and inspired emotion," on the one hand; and, on the other, a group of stylistic concepts. It is the first of these sources that concerns us immediately. Thought and emotion represent a radical departure from all earlier criticism. We have been looking in this chapter at the factor of imagination in the literary theory of Aristotle and Plato, at its function and operation. It was the imagination of the reader or spectator that was at issue there. How, these theorists both ask, will such-and-such a kind of work affect its audience? What difference will there be between his reactions to drama and narrative, for example? How will he react to a fictitious story, or to a tragic story? That is to say that their theory is audience-oriented. It is the audience who are the important players in the game; they are the target of literature. This is understandable enough in a context where rhetoric, in the sense of the art of persuasion, is dominant: the speaker (or writer) is essentially concerned to affect his audience. Plato and Aristotle, that is, appear to be primarily concerned with the destination of a work of literature. Longinus, on the other hand, is concerned with its source. Now it is the writer who is at the center of the critic's thought: a work of literature is first of all an emanation of the human mind; the activity of literature is the expression of the writer's thoughts and emotions.[49]

This is by no means to say that the reader has disappeared from view; but it is to change the critical emphasis substantially. It is obvious that Sophocles and Pindar thought great thoughts, and may as well as any other writer have felt great emotion; in that sense there is nothing new about the process of literary creation, as seen by Lon-

---

returns to the topic of the shape of Longinus's argument in "Longinus Revisited," *Mnemosyne* 34 (1981), 72–86. Quotations will be taken from a translation by Russell, which (like Hubbard's translation of the *Poetics*) also functions as an analysis, in Russell-Winterbottom 460–503.

[49] For the distinction between audience-oriented and writer-oriented approaches in antiquity, see esp. D. A. Russell, "Rhetoric and Criticism," *Greece and Rome* 14 (1967), 130–44, 141ff. (this is the best brief account known to me, incidentally, of the relationship between rhetorical theory and literary criticism, and sets out clearly the activities of the teacher of rhetoric). For a modern point of contact, cf. Wayne Booth, *The Rhetoric of Fiction* (Chicago, 1961), 39: "Critical programs still divide . . . according to their emphasis on work, author or reader."

ginus, in itself. But this source of literature has not previously been analyzed, or even observed and identified explicitly, by earlier theorists; not by Plato, who had other fish to fry; nor by Aristotle, who was concerned with the philosophy and logic of the matter, and only secondarily with its aesthetics. And it may be observed that this development in critical orientation in a sense mirrors the development of literary creation. The literature of the earlier, classical period is in great part concerned with public issues, or with the public effect of private vicissitudes—the fate of an Oedipus affects a whole community. Romance, however, concerns primarily the individuals that it talks about: only Chaereas is really interested in Callirhoe. In the same way, in Longinus' view of literature, the critic is interested more in the individual writer than in his faceless audience.

The most direct application to romance of Longinus's revolutionary idea—that great literature springs from great thoughts—is simple to the point of being obvious: a writer will write about what he thinks about. The story of a Chariton will reflect the thoughts of a Chariton. In the fifth century dramatists employed the material of legend, it is true, but they fashioned it according to their view of their own age: ambitious for Aeschylus, individualist for Sophocles, often social for Euripides—the formulae will serve well enough for the present argument. Chariton and his fellows had similarly to reshape their material, which they found in New Comedy: the story of the more-or-less happy family. In reshaping it, they gave it the impress of the world they knew, wider and more unpredictable than the Athens or Ephesus of the early Hellenistic period. They uttered *their* thoughts.

Whether they were great thoughts may be another matter. Their audience, as we have seen, had its doubts. But great criticism is no more predictable in its occurrence than great literature. Longinus, like many of his time, is little enough concerned with contemporary literature. Homer, Sappho, and Demosthenes are all his study, or almost. That is in large measure true of the romance writers themselves; Chariton is always ready with a tag from Homer, or a reminiscence of Thucydides or Demosthenes.[50] Longus is soaked in

[50] He quotes Homer over two dozen times. C. W. Müller, "Chariton von Aphrodisias und die Theorie des Romans in der Antike," *Antike und Abendland* 22 (1976), 115–36, sees these quotations, and many more general reminiscences of Homer in Chariton, as evidence of a whole consciously epic "fabric" in *Chaereas and Callirhoe*—which is thus even more "epic" than it is "historiography." But this overstates the case. For Chariton's not inconsiderable knowledge of classical authors, see esp. A. D. Papanikolaou, *Chariton-Studien*, 13–24. As for Thucydides, Chariton's very first sentence is

pastoral, Heliodorus in tragedy. Nor is this literature altogether devoid of the quality that Longinus calls *hypsos*—"grandeur," "loftiness." The same Longus and Heliodorus possess qualities that he might well have admired. But the critical point remains valid whether a writer's thoughts are sublime or not: literature springs from the writer's thoughts. Emotion is there too, in the romance texts: the emotion of a society, caught by the writer and embodied in hero and heroine. If the heroes of romance are colorless, they are the more fitted thereby to carry anonymous aspirations.[51]

Longinus says nothing whatever about the structures of literature. He appears to have a fine disregard for the difference between one literary form and another, for all that Aristotle had demonstrated the structural basis of the major forms. But Longinus says what Aristotle does not say: that literary creations can be born only in the author's mind. In the age of romance people are thrown back upon their own thoughts. Romance reflects that fact, in various ways. The theorist of literature reflects it too.

Finding in Longinus's treatise this much about the importance of what goes on in the writer's mind, we should naturally expect to find more. There may very well have been more, but the text has not survived complete. Notably, it is not clear whether or not Longinus discussed emotion systematically.[52] For there is evidently a close connection between emotion and imagination, and we have just been considering, in effect, how in romance the writer appears to call on his imagination in projecting himself into the situation of his hero

---

visibly modelled on that of the historian: "I, Chariton of Aphrodisias, secretary to the rhetor Athenagoras, am going to tell you a love story that took place in Sicily"; cf. "Thucydides of Athens wrote an account of the war between the Peloponnesians and the Athenians"; see Papanikolaou, 16–17, 21. For Demosthenes, Chariton adapts a famous passage from the orator (quoted by Longinus 10.7, among others) describing the panic in Athens when news was brought of the capture of Elateia by Philip in 339, as an episode in the advance that was to rob Athens of her liberty: "It was evening when news was brought to the city officials that Elateia had fallen. Some of them at once got up, in the middle of dinner . . . the town was in uproar." In Chariton the alarming news is that Chaereas's father is ill: "It was evening when news was brought that Chaereas' father Ariston had fallen from a ladder on his farm and was very unlikely to live" (1.3.1); see Papanikolaou for other such references.

[51] As Beer expresses it (*Romance*, 9), romance "allows us to act out through stylized figures the radical impulses of human experience."

[52] He seems at the very end to have reserved it for a separate treatise—but it is not clear where (or whether) in the body of *On the Sublime* he has abandoned it as a topic in that book, because of a lacuna at 9.4 where the subject appears to have been "lost." See the two discussions by Russell referred to in n. 48.

and heroine. Aristotle had already observed that it is those who actually feel passion who will represent it the most convincingly (*Poetics* 17.1455a). But the closest Longinus comes in the extant text to discussing imagination specifically is to recommend what he calls *phantasia*, the power of visualizing particular scenes. "Enthusiasm and emotion," he tells us, "make the speaker *see* what he is saying and bring it *visually* before his audience" (15)—the very point Aristotle was making in the passage referred to; in fact, a clear echo of his actual words elsewhere in that passage. The point is of only limited relevance to the present discussion, and it would not be profitable to discuss it further. We cannot look to Longinus, therefore, any more than to any other theorist in antiquity, for a systematic discussion of that most romantic of topics, imagination.

It is not clear that there is any very distinct or immediate connection between Longinus's general thoughts on literature and the particular form of literature that is narrative prose fiction. It is rather a matter of what was in the air in the age of romance; of what was somewhere in the back of the romance writer's mind when *he* expressed *his* thoughts. We can at any rate see, at the very time when romance was being developed, the kind of critical sensibility that seems to recognize the romance writer's personal creative outlook.

Fiction, operating via the imagination on the emotions, is the primary constituent of romance. Prose form can be replaced by verse, and narrative manner can accommodate large elements of dramatic action; but imagination is indispensable. With these thoughts on fiction, imagination and emotion we will close here the first part of our analysis of the theory associated with romance, and turn to its more concrete constituent elements, its narrative manner and its prose medium.

THE MANNER AND MEDIUM OF ROMANCE: NARRATIVE PROSE

IT WILL be interesting to see whether other elements of Aristotle's *Poetics* are useful for the analysis of romance. First, its narrative manner. An obvious candidate is Aristotle's theory of plot, *mythos*. Can it throw any light on the plot of romance narrative?

Aristotle's theory identifies elements of story, which can be variously deployed in this or that character or legend or action, and can be variously used, disposed and combined to produce this or that effect—tragic or happy ending, moral outrage, human feelings, pity and fear; all of which is to say that Aristotle was a structuralist. But Aristotle was talking about tragedy. The purpose of romance is other than the purpose of tragedy, and this entails a different disposition of the elements of plot. We shall see, however, that the elements remain largely the same. It is their articulation that is different, and that entails a difference in their psychological effect. No doubt this did not help the writer write romance, but it does help us dissect it.

The elements of romantic narrative that can be found in Aristotle's account of *poiēsis*, literary creation in general, are as follows. First, in chapter 6, plot (*mythos*), character (*ēthos*, or the plural *ēthē*), "the expression of thought" (*dianoia*), and verbal expression (*lexis*);[1] chapter 11 adds, as sub-elements of plot, *peripeteia*, *anagnōrisis* and *pathos* ("an act involving destruction or pain"—that is to say, unpleasant things that happen to people in stories). In chapter 24 Aristotle says explicitly that these are all found in epic, that is in narrative as distinct from drama. Second, in two places Aristotle discusses happy endings, on both occasions specifically in contrast to tragic endings. He is thus equipped to analyze comedy as well as tragedy, *Odyssey* as well as *Iliad* (as he himself implies at the beginning of chapter 24). The actual constituents of an "action" (*praxis*), as represented in a successfully

---

[1] *Dianoia* is the way people's minds work, "intellectual capacity revealed in speech or action by the characters in drama" (*LSJ s.v.*, V). The remaining two elements in Aristotle's analysis, spectacle and music, can be disregarded here.

executed story, differ little from tragedy to comedy, or from drama to narrative; it is the use the writer makes of them that changes, and hence also the effect they will produce.

That effect depends on what the audience wants, what it is psychologically equipped to stand. Happy endings, says Aristotle the first time he raises the matter, exist "because of the weakness of the audiences; for the poets follow the lead of the spectators and make plays to their specifications. But this is not the pleasure proper to tragedy, but rather belongs to comedy" (13.1453a, end). He could hardly be more categorical or more clear, and we cannot be in doubt what he would think of the readers of romances. All the more surprising, then, that a mere page or two later he says exactly the opposite: the best plot will have the hero "through ignorance intend to do something irreparable, and then recognize the victim-to-be before doing it," and finally not do it (14.1453b). Nor is there anything fortuitous or incidental about this statement. It is the conclusion of an extensive and rigorous logical analysis of how stories *may* proceed, and is illustrated by three examples; among which Euripides' *Iphigeneia in Tauris*—the very model of an exciting escape-story, a cliffhanger if ever there was one, in which everything comes out right at the very last minute—is picked out as the best kind of play (14.1454a), the kind most apt to rouse fear and pity.

It is no part of my purpose here to elucidate this mystery; I am not convinced that it can be satisfactorily elucidated, or the problem argued away. The *Poetics* notoriously contains inconsistencies. Aristotle had as much right as anyone else to hold logically irreconcilable views; we call the chessboard white, we call it black; *de gustibus non est disputandum*, and anyone's taste may change. Two kinds of plot figure in the *Poetics*: one shows linear decline to destruction, the other a series of ups and downs and salvation in the nick of time; the latter is the more relevant here. Or perhaps more palatable is the suggestion that Aristotle changed his mind in later years, as Shakespeare moved from *Lear* to *The Tempest*. The point is that such an ultimate disposition of the events of a story was in Aristotle's mind, and he tells us in so many words that it was in other people's minds too— the happy ending is "the sort of arrangement that some people say is the best" (13.1453a, end). Clearly there was argument going on in the fourth century about literary theory, and not only on the part of the Platos and Aristotles. If further evidence were needed, it can be found in the tenacity with which the same Aristotle insists (in chapter 6) that plot and not character is the most important element in tragedy; evidently not everyone agreed with him. This perceptible background argument adds to the tally of those who were speculating in this period about the effects of literature and *logos*, and experimenting with them. Fiction is in the air, and narrative is in the air; romance is in the air too, it seems.

To return to the elements of narrative, the ending of a story is obviously of critical importance, since it is what finally constitutes the psychological effect. Nahum Tate could not stand Shakespeare's ending for *Lear*. In tragedy, or tragic narrative, the whole cathartic effect, one would suppose, is likely to be ruined by a happy ending. A good man, by a process of *metabolē* (change in fortune), comes to a bad end via some *hamartia*, and this is what produces the *catharsis*.[2] Can the story have the same effect if its hero does not come to a bad end? What conclusion might a Nahum Tate have concocted for *Oedipus Tyrannus*? Certainly it would seem that the effect of romance is to reassure the reader, not to drain him emotionally; to comfort him, not to let him end up with despair even in purified form. The basic structure of romance, at any rate of Greek romance, is isolation—tribulation—survival: pity and fear are, if anything, exorcized rather than refined, or purged, or "tuned"; they are countered rather than modified.

Can we measure more accurately the distance between the theory of narrative available in Aristotle—in which form, as much as in tragedy, we may reasonably suppose him to be prepared to consider the possibility of a happy ending—and the specific form of narrative fiction seen in the Greek romance of love and adventure? In the happy-ending narrative (or drama), as we have seen, the *metabolē* or change of fortune does not ultimately take place. This will involve other major structural consequences. First, there will not be the same need for any element of *hamartia*, and there may even be no need for it at all. *Hamartia* in Aristotle, it may be well to recall, is not "flaw in character" but "getting something wrong," even though no moral fault may

---

[2] I do not propose to enter the lists systematically on the subject of exactly what *catharsis* is: see *e.g.*, D. W. Lucas's commentary on the *Poetics* (Oxford, 1968), 273ff.; more recently R. Janko, *Aristotle on Comedy* (Berkeley, 1984), 136ff.; and S. Halliwell, *Aristotle's Poetics* (London, 1986), 168ff. My own view is that it is not purgation but some form of purification or refining, so as to produce some kind of mean between extremes; and my favourite metaphor for the process is that of tuning the emotions as one tunes a radio accurately on to a station. Chariton, we will recall, thinks that his story does have it (8:1.4; cf. Chapter 2 at n. 9).

lie with the character in question.[3] It is introduced into Aristotle's exegesis of the operation of tragedy, as Margaret Hubbard points out, to justify our reaction to the fall of a man who is not wicked but ends badly; without it, the spectacle of a good man ending badly would simply provoke moral outrage. *Hamartia* is in effect a buffer or cushion between our moral and aesthetic senses, necessitated—let us repeat—only by the hero's ultimate misfortune.

No such element exists in Greek romances. We do not need thus ominously to be prepared for the worst, since the worst is not going to happen—the hero is going to survive. All that may be thought useful is some initial but passing show of imperfection on the part of the hero: Chaereas's suspicions about Callirhoe's conduct, or in Xenophon's story the arrogance of the young hero Habrocomes in being contemptuous of Eros. Even in those two stories, however, this theme of imperfection is not really used after it has got the story off the ground: both heroes have repented amply by chapter two, and clearly will never do it again. And in the other extant texts it is difficult to find even so much motivation for the subsequent misfortunes. In Greek romance, "justification" for the slings and arrows of outrageous Tyche is neither necessary nor even possible. Falling in love is *hamartia* enough: love in itself will guarantee vicissitudes. Life just is like that. There is nothing anyone can do about it—except have faith. Understanding—such as Oedipus achieves, or Achilles—is not now within mortal grasp.

It is not surprising that the fourth century produced no theory to accommodate such a concatenation of events. It is not literary theory that is lacking; it is a whole view of life that is different. In Aristotle's day it was still possible for a community to determine events for itself—or so Aristotle's contemporary Demosthenes thought. In the time of Chariton or Xenophon (of Ephesus), the most it could do was

---

[3] It is of course perfectly possible for the person who makes the mistake also to have some "fault" of character—Oedipus *is* hot-tempered, Pentheus *is* puritanical—and this quality may indeed render him vulnerable to some retribution. But Oedipus's *hamartia* lies squarely in killing his father and marrying his mother, for neither of which can he really be held morally responsible; Pentheus's *hamartia* lies in underestimating the power of Dionysus, even though he had no reason simply to abdicate before the god's absolute demands. Here of course I simplify considerably this extensively debated question. The reader may be referred especially to T.C.W. Stinton, "Hamartia in Aristotle and Greek Tragedy," *Classical Quarterly* 25 (1975), 221–54; Stinton concludes that *hamartia* (in the *Poetics*) "does not mean only 'mistake of fact' or 'ignorance of fact.' It embraces a wide range of meanings. . . . What is common to all these is that the agent has some excuse for his act . . ." (254).

to send an embassy to do obeisance to Nero or Hadrian, and hope that he would graciously consent to build a new bridge.

The point seems fundamental; it has already been suggested that what is involved in romance is no less than a whole world-vision. Further and similar consequences follow. In tragedy, *peripeteia* and *anagnōrisis* are crucial in the operation·of the irony which constitutes the tragedy, they are its very means: the unforeseen reversals that take Oedipus and Achilles to their fate, the understanding that floods into Oedipus and Achilles when they recognize where they are in life as a result of them ("the best sort of recognition is that accompanied by *peripeteia*," (*Poetics*, 11.1452a). In romance, reversal is not irreversible; it is merely a vicissitude. Recognition involves no radical change of spiritual condition; it merely evokes from the hero another despairing cry of "What do I do *now*?" as the screw is turned yet tighter.

In this context, *pathos*—Aristotle's remaining element of plot, unpleasant things that happen to people—becomes less charged, less grim. Incidents, in romance, are exciting, hair-raising even—our hearts surely beat faster when the pirates appear on the horizon—but they are not fatal. And they are not in any very important degree connected to the hero's personality or his doings. The fate of a Chaereas, even a Daphnis, is a function of his situation merely as a human being: he is vulnerable by merely existing; Tyche will find him, will come at him out of the blue, whatever he does. Some philosophies might make the case that that was always so, is always so. But in tragedy of the classical period the hero *acts*. He may indeed not be master of his fate, but he is part of it; he is not merely its target.

That is to say that the elements of Aristotle's theory of plot remain substantially the same for romance as for tragedy, but they do not add up to the same effect. This in itself, however, sets the procedures of romance in relief, for the reader.

Let us turn to another of the major objects of literary *mimēsis*, character. *Mimēsis* of character plays only a limited part in the structure of romance. With few exceptions, things happen *to* heroes of Greek romance, not because of them. It is not because they are *as* they are that they suffer, but—as we have just seen—because they are *what* they are, namely, the principals in the story; one can hardly call them principal actors, because their most obvious characteristic is passivity. On this matter Aristotle has almost anticipated romance. "There could be a tragedy without *mimēsis* of character," we read during the discussion of plot, "and the tragedies of most of the moderns are in fact deficient in it" (6.1450a). If by "the moderns" Aristotle means his own contemporaries, as he probably does, we may observe that they lived only a generation or so before New Comedy, the most obvious precursor of romance. Aristotle's analysis of New Comedy might have filled much of the gap in theory we have been discussing.[4]

Passitivity is most marked in the male hero, the *jeune premier*. Minor characters are often altogether more alive. This is true for all the texts: the pirate Theron in Chariton's story, along with the "royal soul" Dionysius and a Persian king acutely embarrassed by his passion, will serve to make the point. And romance can produce a range of other figures: heroes' friends (few are as wooden as Polycharmus), older men, and in particular the women portrayed in the genre. This is true even of the female principals, some of whom at least have more to them than their male counterparts—perhaps because a woman is more at risk in a male world. Callirhoe is compelled to make a positive choice between lost husband and unborn son; Chariicleia, in the *Ethiopica*, has enterprise enough, and a distinctly malicious side to her; Leucippe has spirit, at least in the early part of her story.

But it is more markedly true of the gallery of *femmes fatales* to be found in the Greek romance: Arsace in Heliodorus, Lycaenion in Longus, Melite in Achilles Tatius, Cyno and Manto in Xenophon (Chariton's Chaereas, it will be observed, is not subjected to temptation from another woman). These are all sexually passionate creatures, who are in the story only in order to pursue the hero. In their case it is clearly *mimēsis* of character that constitutes their interest and their contribution to the plot: they represent love of a predatory kind. In the case of the female principals, however, love is not of a predatory kind at all, and is not altogether a manifestation of character. It is rather one of the fundamental ideas in romance: love makes the world go round. Love is part of the fiction, so to speak, one of the things the writer invents, an aspect of romance's *mimēsis* of human actions. There will be occasion to return to the topic in a later chapter.

The third element to consider is *dianoia*, the demonstration of the way people's minds work; we could think of it as an aspect of character. For the case of tragedy, *dianoia* is the expression of thought *in*

---

[4] R. Janko proposes a reconstruction of the lost second book of the *Poetics* in *Aristotle on Comedy*.

speech, "those parts in which they demonstrate something in speech" (*Poetics* 6.1450a), "their ability to say what the situation admits and requires" (6.1450b). As such, it is the province of rhetoric (*ibid.*) and is covered in Aristotle's *Rhetoric* (as he himself points out at *Poetics* 19.1456a). But that is because speech is the only medium of expression in drama. The essence of the matter is the thought expressed, not the medium. In the narrative medium it is mostly the author in his authorial voice who expresses "what the situation admits and requires" (though some texts, notably Chariton's, are in fact particularly dramatic in method). He demonstrates *his* ideas, the way *his* mind works. Those ideas are what create the action of romance, and as such they form the continuing subject of this whole book; they have been set out above in chapter 2. Beyond that, *dianoia* merges into the actual expression of ideas in words, *lexis*, the element of language and style that is the province of rhetoric. That takes us directly to our next major topic, namely the formal medium in which the texts are written: the medium of prose, the third and final element in the analyses of romance as narrative prose fiction.

The study of prose conditioned the composition of romance. If Xenophon of Ephesus affects a simple style, he has learned it at school; the same is true of the much more elaborate prose of Heliodorus. Not only the composition but also the reception of romance was affected, for reader as well as writer had been to school and read his classics. We should here consider in what ways writer and audience were conditioned.

The thoughts sketched earlier on the topic of truth and fiction relate essentially to prose expression. Historiography was a prose form, and rhetorical theory about persuasion springs from the social need to influence people in speeches, which are in prose. It is true that Plato's principal illustration of literary art, his principal target, is Homer, but that is because Homer was the most affecting existent writer; Plato by no means excludes prose, and his own fictitious creations are in prose. It appears that "false-writing," in whatever sense the term is conceived, is thought of in the fourth century essentially as creative prose rather than verse. Though drama continues to be a verse form, and to become with the development of comedy more and more frankly fictitious, this fictiveness of drama does not appear to arouse as much interest or disquiet as does prose rhetoric with its capacity for more specific, deliberate and covert deception of the consumer.

It was in this context that was built up such body of theory concerning prose as existed in antiquity. Prose was not originally a form used for literary, "creative" purposes. The effect of this upon the prose literature that did eventually develop is, not surprisingly, far-reaching. The form in which romance is cast affects its nature considerably: to summarize the matter rather simplistically, romance could be composed only as a form of rhetoric, of *persuasive* writing. And here we must return at greater length to a point sketched earlier in the discussion of Gorgias's thoughts on the power of words: the growth of the category of epideictic rhetoric. For it is under the aegis of rhetoric that the prose medium develops; when romance came into being, it was rhetoric that supplied the theory of its expression, and supplied it in highly developed form. That was not an altogether satisfactory theory, for the romance-writer's purpose; it was aimed essentially at persuading the audience to do this or that, or that such and such is the case; and that is not the same thing as telling a story. Writers of narrative had to carve out prose narrative expression for themselves from what rhetoric had to offer. We shall see that they did do that, with more success than might have been predicted from the nature of early theory of expression.

That is to say, literary prose—as opposed to oratorical prose—got in by the back door, a door held open by the art of rhetoric. The marks of rhetoric, in a somewhat pejorative sense, are there in all our texts, as they are in virtually all Latin creative literature, and as they are in the other major body of prose literature, historiography, both Latin and Greek. The original impression was to prove indelible. The crucial step was the expansion of rhetorical practice to accommodate the category of utterance known as "epideictic" oratory, or display oratory; this category came to embrace all prose which was not directly "persuasive" in function. Let us trace that expansion.

The cryptic comments of Gorgias on *logos* were accompanied, from the fifth century, by more practical utterance: handbooks of rhetoric, vade mecums of the public speaker.[5] The industry of rhetorical education expanded rapidly, for it was evidently a familiar feature of intellectual society by the time of Plato and Aristotle. Aristotle's own

---

[5] For this stage of rhetorical theory see George Kennedy, *The Art of Persuasion in Greece* (London, 1962), 52ff.

treatise on rhetoric was for practical purposes the summation of this first stage of the rhetorical tradition, and at the same time—as one might expect—it raised the level of the discussion and pointed the art of persuasion in the direction it was to take for centuries thereafter. The major constituents of the *Rhetoric* are its discussion of the disposition of the elements in argument (such as introduction and demonstration of a case); its analysis of what constitutes proof (what we should call logic); and its examination of the characteristics of prose style and the differences between, for instance, periodic and unstructured prose, or oral and written expression. It is the last of these that concerns us here, for it was to develop into the major topic of subsequent ancient critical theory: the art of effective composition, the production by stylistic means of conviction in the audience. This sense has been extended in modern critical theory, and applied to the whole technique of presentation of one's subject, as in Wayne Booth's *The Rhetoric of Fiction*; there, various non-stylistic authorial devices are treated as "rhetorical," such as manipulation by the writer of the "point of view" from which the reader is led to see the action of a story. This is a helpful metaphorical application of the term "rhetoric," but for present purposes it must be emphasized that metaphor is what it is. In ancient theory, the term "rhetoric" refers to the actual language used, not to an author's overall strategy.

Aristotle's *Rhetoric* was fundamental to the later history of rhetoric generally. The originators of "style" in language, says Aristotle, were the poets, and "since the poets, because what they said was naive, were held to have earned their repute by the way they said it, [prose] style was at first poetical, for instance that of Gorgias: and even today the majority of the uneducated think such speakers the best" (*Rhetoric* 3.1.1.1404a). The text is extremely interesting. It confirms the idea that the last decades of the fifth century saw the beginnings of deliberate analysis of the nature and functions of the new form of expression that prose was to constitute; for in the practice of his poetic prose, Gorgias was consciously experimenting with "Gorgiastic figures"—antithesis, equivalent-length phrases, rhyming phrase-ends,[6] and so on. But the educated, such as Aristotle, were by now discerning other virtues in prose: "let us define the excellence of prose style as being clear (for as speech indicates something, it will not do its job

---

[6] See E. Norden, *Die antike Kunstprosa* (Stuttgart 1898 [1958]), 15ff. Gorgias's prose is untranslatable; the nearest thing to the "bizarre verbal effects" (Russell-Winterbottom 6) of his epideictic speeches is what we call "euphuistic" style.

if it does not make that thing clear) and neither mean nor too elevated for its purpose, but appropriate; for a poetical style is perhaps not mean, but it is not appropriate to prose" (3.1.1–2.1404b). Clarity and appropriateness are thus the cardinal virtues. They are not in themselves restricted to prose, as the *Poetics* makes clear.[7] What is just as significant is Aristotle's recognition that "prose has much more restricted resources, as its theme is less grand" than that of poetry (3.1.2.1404b). Later writers spend a great deal of time analyzing those resources, working out what exactly the qualities and the "characters" ("types" or "impressions") of style are in Greek prose.[8]

We need not go into detail about these "types" of style.[9] *Mutatis mutandis*, they are the varieties of style one finds in prose expression in all languages. Greek commonly used, as basic categories, such terms as "high" or "grand," "middle," and "thin." The theory of the Hellenistic and imperial periods distinguishes an ever-increasing number of qualities associated with these principal types of style: variously "solemnity," "vehemence," "sweetness," "restraint," and the like. These terms correspond in large degree to the labels attached by critics to the prose of this or that modern writer, "limpid," "economical," "tortuous," and so on. This study formed one of the staple elements of the education received by writers of romance.

For all educated people went through much the same mill, certainly at the high school level. A great deal of the student's time was spent reading, commenting on, and analyzing the style of the "classics"; this educational program is the origin of the "canon" of "the ten best Attic orators" that survived right through and beyond antiquity.[10] We can see what kind of study was involved by glancing at almost any of the several surviving treatises on style. "Demetrius,"

---

[7] "Verbal expression is good if it is clear without being mean" 22.1458a.

[8] Here it should be mentioned that some notion of the wider "nature" of prose is to be found in other, contemporary writers. Notably, Isocrates offers some hints—they are hardly more—in *Evagoras* 9–11; see G.M.A. Grube, *The Greek and Roman Critics* (London, 1965) (Methuen University Paperback edition, 1968), 42–43. It is significant that one of the great educators of the age (see, *e.g.*, H.-I. Marrou, *A History of Education in Antiquity*, tr. G. Lamb [London, 1956 (original ed. Paris, 1948; 6th ed., 1965)], I.7) should perceive the possibilities of this mode of expression.

[9] See, *e.g.*, Kennedy, *Art of Persuasion*, Index, under "Characters of style."

[10] The lists varied slightly, but some names were permanently in anybody's Top Ten; the way to set a literary fashion, at the period of the romances, was to displace Demosthenes from the head of the list in favor of someone else such as Critias (as Herodes Atticus seems to have done: see Philostratus *Lives of the Sophists* 564).

for example, sounds like all the teachers of composition (or "rhetoric") the world has ever known in explaining patiently that

> A period is a combination of clauses and phrases which has brought
> the underlying thought to a conclusion with a neatly turned ending,
> as in this example: "It was especially because I thought it in the in-
> terest of the state for the law to be repealed and secondly because of
> Chabrias's son that I have agreed to be, to the best of my ability, my
> clients' advocate . . . For by saying 'period' we immediately imply
> that it has a beginning, will have an ending, and is hurrying to a
> definite goal. . . ."

He then points out that Demosthenes had a definite goal in view,
which would not be attained if the idea were expressed as

> I shall be my clients' advocate, Athenians; for the son of Chabrias is
> dear to me, and much dearer still is the state, whose interests it is
> right for me to defend.

As Demetrius points out, "the period is now lost."[11]

The relevance of rhetorical theory and education to romance does
not end there. Another essential component of standard rhetorical
education was the composition of endless passages, *progymnasmata*
or "preliminary exercises," according to predetermined patterns; the
undisciplined "free composition" of modern times would have been
alien to Greek habits of mind. A composite but typical list of these
exercises would be: fable, narrative account, moralizing anecdote,
philosophical maxim, proof and refutation of a position, "commonplace," speech of praise or blame, comparison of two items, character-sketch, description of a sight (town, river, etc.), general topic
("Ought one to marry?"), and statement in support of a legal proposal.[12] Any romance text contains very numerous examples of such
passages. When Callirhoe debates whether or not to procure an abortion for herself (2.11.1–4), she is "comparing two items" ("for" and
"against"), and discussing a "general topic." When Dorcon and
Daphnis indulge in competitive self-praise for Chloe's kiss (1.16),
they are uttering "encomia." Perhaps most familiar of all, the "description" or "ecphrasis" occurs times without number in romance.
And "narrative account" is the very basis of romance.

It was in such a manner that the theory of rhetoric became a major

---

[11] Demetrius *On Style* 11 (Russell-Winterbottom 175–76, trans. D.C. Innes).
[12] See Kennedy, *Art of Persuasion*, 270.

part of the cultural fabric of society, from the Hellenistic period to the end of antiquity. Much more than relatively esoteric philosophical or aesthetic treatises, this—the everyday application of rhetoric to form a common educational stratum—constitutes literary theory in practice. It has been emphasized, earlier in this study, that there was no theory of, or critical interest in, Greek romance. No; but its writers had—whether they wanted it or not—a thorough schooling in applied theory. If we leave aside the design of the romances, their expression in prose was the very embodiment of theory.

Theories of style proliferated. In the heyday of romance, the first three centuries of the Roman Empire, numerous treatises were produced on the theory and practice of prose expression. We may cite as examples the extensive and acute critical writings of Dionysius of Halicarnassus, who worked in the period of Augustus, on writers by then considered "classical," such as Demosthenes, Thucydides, and Plato;[13] also his theoretical treatise *On the Arrangement of Words*.[14] In the second century Hermogenes also wrote a great deal on stylistics, much of which was to constitute standard rhetorical theory right through the Renaissance.[15] His name will serve also to lead to the major point, already adumbrated, that must be made here, namely the fact that by the time romance was beginning to attract the notice of practicing writers like Lucian and Apuleius, the theory of rhetoric had patently burst its bounds and had come to be applied to *all* prose writing. That this was so in practice is indeed clear at a much earlier date, when (as we have just seen) a professor of rhetoric could dissect the work of not only the orator Demosthenes but also of the historian Thucydides and even the philosopher Plato—a singular peripety in literary history. But Hermogenes quite explicitly applies the theoretical classification of "panegyric" to the work of the historians Thucydides, Herodotus, and Xenophon among others.[16] Now "pan-

---

[13] See Grube, *Greek and Roman Critics*, chapter 13; Russell-Winterbottom 307–21.

[14] Russell-Winterbottom 321–43.

[15] See Russell-Winterbottom 561ff. for his *On Types*. There is now available a translation of the entire text: Cecil W. Wooten, trans., *Hermogenes' On Types of Style* (Chapel Hill and London, 1987).

[16] *On Types* 404–405, 408–11 (Russell-Winterbottom 575–78; 404): "The best panegyric must possess grandeur with charm, ornament and clarity, as well as realistic representation of character. . . . Not only poetry and prose in general (*logographia*) possess these qualities. History has them in abundance. Historians must therefore definitely be placed among the panegyrists." Of Thucydides we are told that "it might be doubted into which category he falls; he is as much forensic and deliberative as pane-

egyric" is nothing other than an alternative name for the third of the categories into which rhetorical utterance had been divided since the fourth century: forensic rhetoric, deliberative or "parliamentary" rhetoric, and "display rhetoric," or epideictic (*logos epideiktikos*), otherwise, as here, called "panegyric,"—rhetoric originally meant for use at "panegyries" or public assemblies of a ceremonial kind (such as games or festivals).

That is to say, "display rhetoric" is now taken to cover all non-oratorical prose. As we have seen, it is here that romance would fit in ancient literary theory if it could gain any footing in theory at all. To put the matter otherwise: epideictic rhetoric includes all non-technical prose—philosophy (such as Plato) and belles-lettres (such as Xenophon's minor works) as well as biography and history: it is "prose literature." Prose is now an acknowledged medium for literature. But it must be emphasized that it has got in under pretense of being something else. Consequently it is not fully accepted, and its possibilities are far from fully recognized. Still, in a sense it has arrived. The age of the romance is in fact the age of creative literature in prose; for the prose epideictic rhetoric of the Second Sophistic is nothing if not "creative."

Here a word should be said about the Second Sophistic, since it forms the context in which most of the novels were written. Briefly, in its purest form it was a literary movement whose central activity consisted of rhetorical declamation on unreal themes—unreal in the sense that they had no connection with contemporary life. "Sophists," in this sense of the word, were thus far removed from the philosophers and intellectuals of the late fifth century B.C.; in the second century A.D. they were orators who performed in concerts of oratory intended purely as a fine art—epideictic or display oratory. Their themes were usually drawn from Greek history of the classical period: thus, a speaker might assume the character of Demosthenes defending himself—five hundred years earlier!—against a charge of corruption (as in Philostratus's *Lives of the Sophists*, 538). In another type of sophistic performance, the subject might be a fictitious legal question—a defense of a wrongly disinherited son, for instance, as in Lucian's *Disinherited*. The topics, that is, were trivial in themselves, but they provided matter for virtuoso displays of rhetoric comparable

---

gyrical, in his thoughts and the elaboration with which he introduces every point" (409; translations by D. A. Russell). See following text for these classifications.

to, say, piano recitals.[17] The point was to show mastery of language, of style, of the technique of composition in prose. Skill in such an art—on the part of the audience as well as of the performer—implied a considerable literary education and taste. This taste, this skill, these attitudes overflow into much of the surrounding literature of the age, including the romance. Some novelists may even have been accredited sophists; in any event they use all the techniques of this highly specialized trade.

Other creative prose is more readily recognizable to us: the belletristic miscellany of Plutarch, the dialogues and essays of Lucian (who today might write for *Punch* or the *New Yorker*), and the more or less interesting work of many other writers of occasional pieces (Philostratus, who despised Chariton, is one of them); a later chapter will touch on some of them. Creative prose is not new; there is no sudden explosion of novelty in the early Empire. But the degree of it, the range and intensity of prose writing, *is* rather new. Prose is in the air.

In fact, there is some theory about the nature of prose. It is not very fully developed, but it is significant. One or two writers had given some thought to the nature of their medium. One, in particular, goes beyond the point of observing that prose is not verse and is governed by different formal requirements, and sees that prose has its own nature. He is Aelius Aristides, perhaps the brightest star in the Second Sophistic constellation, and altogether the prize pupil of the rhetorical tradition. In his prose *Hymn to Sarapis* he complains almost bitterly that poets have all the advantages a writer can have. They have apparently unlimited license to say what they will about any topic they choose, with no regard for order, consequence, or clarity:

> Sometimes they tell the beginning of something and leave out the rest, as though they have given it up; sometimes they rob it of the beginning, or take out the middle, and think all well; they have a despotic power over their thoughts.[18]

Perhaps he had been reading Pindar. The panegyrist-in-prose, he complains, has to fight for the right to use *his* tools for the honorable work of praising the gods:

[17] See D. A. Russell, *Greek Declamation* (Cambridge, 1983); also G. W. Bowersock, "Philostratus and the Second Sophistic," in *CHCL*, 655ff., and other articles in that chapter (XX) by Bowersock (Aelius Aristides) and E. L. Bowie (Dio of Prusa, Maximus of Tyre, Lucian).

[18] This passage and the others quoted in this section are taken from the translation by D. A. Russell of the *Hymn to Sarapis* 1–13 (Russell-Winterbottom 558–60).

For all other occasions we use prose speech (*logos*)—encomia of festivals and heroic deeds, narratives of wars, invention of fables, con-
tests in court. *Logos* is at hand for everything—but towards the gods
who gave it us we do not think it right to use it!

Prose is orderly and logical, claims Aristides, not arbitrary like verse;
it "makes us give everything its due"; it is more useful; it came first—
"it is not true that metre was invented first, and then speech and
conversation"—and is more natural, "just as it is more natural to
walk than to ride" (we may recall that the standard term for "prose"
in Greek is actually *logos pezos*: "words on foot," or "pedestrian" utterance). What poetry does is to add *psychagogia*—the term, Plato's
very word, hardly needs translating. Psychagogy, it seems, is not the
business of writers in prose. Their function is other: they are "like
soldiers keeping formation."[19]

Again, it all sounds as if argument were going on in the background. But one swallow does not make a summer. The argument
stays in the background. Rhetorical prose theory has come, long
since, to be theory of style; no-one steps forward to set out formally
and fully what a writer may do with the prose style he has acquired.
The practice of creative prose is established—but the revolution has
no theorist.

And yet there were some near misses. From the earliest days of conscious theory there are noises offstage, as it were, in the matter of the
use of prose, and also in the broader matter that we might describe
as general literary sensibility. This matter arose in an earlier chapter,
in relation to the topic of imagination, and there the name of Longinus was evoked, as a practitioner of "sensibility." We can here return to another aspect of Longinus's thoughts on what produces and
what constitutes great literature. One basis of great writing was for
him, as we saw, thought and emotion—the particular contribution of
the individual writer. The other ingredient in his recipe is style. Longinus does not suggest that the two ingredients are readily separable—he says in so many words that they are not: "Thought and expression are of course very much involved with each other . . .
beautiful words are the light that illuminates thought" (30.1–2). And

---

[19] For hymns in prose—the prose-poetry *par excellence* of the period, of which Aristides wrote several examples—a whole prescription existed; see Menander Rhetor *On
Epideictic Oratory*, ed. D. A. Russell and N. G. Wilson, with translation and commentary (Oxford, 1981); and Russell-Winterbottom 579–80. For Aristides, see Chapter 6
below.

he spends a great deal of time discussing, in a very detailed way, many of the topics in stylistic analysis and criticism that have occupied critics for centuries: figures of speech, similes, diction, composition, technical devices like hyperbole, the whole battery, in fact, of technical rhetorical matters. He offers, thus, a bridge between the strictly philosophical approach to literature and the technical, practical approach of the rhetorician.

Here we are seriously hindered in our assessment of his own critical practice by the fragmentary condition of the text. We may however guess, from for instance his treatment of Sappho's famous poem "To me he seems a peer of the gods," that emotion in literature is, ultimately a matter of the organization of significant matter, the selection and juxtaposition of its elements.[20] That is to say, it is a matter of choice of material and its expression in words. And at once we are back to style, to "rhetoric." "Even . . . permanent, universal responses embodied in the work," observes Wayne Booth, ". . . are unlikely to move us strongly . . . without the author's rhetoric. . . . The distinction between expressive and rhetorical theories of literature disappears. . . . The author cannot choose whether to use rhetorical heightening. His only choice is of the kind of rhetoric he will use."[21] Imagination flows into rhetoric; what we are faced with is "the text," in modern parlance, the speaking text. The fusion is perfectly illustrated in Longinus; and it issues in what we might call literary sensibility, the awareness of how thoughts are fashioned in words.

In passage after passage Longinus demonstrates—what generations of European critics have recognized in him—the sureness of taste that a fine mind could acquire by means of an education in rhet-

[20] "Every topic naturally includes certain elements which are inherent in its raw material. It follows that sublimity will be achieved if we consistently select the most important of these inherent features and learn to organize them as a unity by combining one with another. . . . Sappho's excellence, as I have said, lies in her adoption and combination of the most striking details" (10.1–3). The Sappho poem is the one adapted by Catullus as "Ille mi par esse deo videtur" (see Chapter 6 for a translation of it). "Do you not admire," asks Longinus, "the way in which she brings everything together—mind and body, hearing and tongue, eyes and skin? She seems to have lost them all . . ." (10.3). As Booth observes, "The meaningless accumulation of accurately observed detail cannot satisfy us for long; only if the details are made to *tell*, only if they are weighted with significance for the lives shown, will they be tolerable" (*Rhetoric of Fiction*, 114). Perhaps Longinus would have accepted the "sincerity" of emotion in literature.

[21] *Rhetoric of Fiction*, 113, 109, 116.

oric. He is a judge of expression, in the quite precise sense of the actual words in which great thoughts are clothed. In this he is totally a product of his rhetorical age, a contemporary (nearly enough) of Hermogenes and Aristides; and he must be seen in his rhetorical context. He was also a contemporary of other artists in words, like Longus. Longus has read what Longinus has read; he too can quote Sappho.[22] His sensibility to literature is similar to the critic's; for they were nurst upon the self-same hill. The track from Aristotle to Longinus is parallel to the track from tragedy to romance.

Finally, still in the field of rhetoric, we should consider the theory of history. For romance is in theory a form of history, and, as we have seen, history is comprehended in the category of epideictic rhetoric—because there is nowhere else to put it. Thucydides was just as much a model for "*mimēsis*" (in the other, more restricted sense, of imitation of *style*[23]) as Demosthenes; he had therefore to be fitted into the only theoretical framework that existed. Hermogenes was not concerned to distinguish between history and encomium, but his interest lay *only* in style. His contemporary Lucian is more critical: "the isthmus that divides history from encomium is no narrow strip. There is a great wall built between them," he tell us, in a treatise entitled, precisely, *How to Write History*.[24] And he proceeds to analyze the qualities of good historiography: respect for, and patient research after, fact; dispassionate critical judgment, based on understanding; and clarity of expression; the whole exercise being directed towards truth, and ultimately utility. It is very much what Thucydides had established in his own program (1.22).

Not all historians followed Thucydides' example, as we have seen. Very soon after Thucydides' own day, Ctesias allowed his fancy even more rein than Herodotus had, in his untrustworthy account of Persian history; and the same Lucian, in his *True Story*, names Ctesias, along with Herodotus and Homer, as one of the principal liars he is aiming his satire at. And what we know of Hellenistic historiography suggests that often enough it went the way of Xenophon's biography of Cyrus, along the romantic road, or at least was often less than diligent in establishing the truth.

---

[22] Of the one apple remaining on a tree: "The apple-picker must have been frightened to climb there and failed to take it down" (3.33); cf. Sappho 105A Lobel-Page (93 Bergk).

[23] For this secondary sense see Chapter 6.

[24] *How to Write History* 7, trans. D. A. Russell (Russell-Winterbottom 537).

The classic example is the third century A.D. historian Phylarchus, criticized by the much stricter Polybius for his emotive writing. It is worth while here quoting Polybius's strictures at some length, since they illustrate well the nature of such pathetic historiography and the use to which prose was being put in the Hellenistic period.

> In his eagerness to arouse the pity of his readers and enlist their sympathy through his story he introduces graphic scenes of women clinging to one another, tearing their hair and baring their breasts, and in addition he describes the tears and lamentations of men and women accompanied by their children and aged parents as they are led away into captivity. Phylarchus reproduces this kind of effect again and again in his history, striving on each occasion to recreate the horrors before our eyes.

It sounds just like Chaereas bewailing the death of Callirhoe. "It is not a historian's business," Polybius continues,

> to startle his readers with sensational descriptions, nor should he try, as the tragic poets do, to represent speeches which might have been delivered . . . ; it is his task first and foremost to record with fidelity what actually happened and was said, however common-place this may be . . . ; the historian's task is to instruct and persuade serious students by means of the truth of the words and actions he presents, and this effect must be permanent, not temporary. . . . Apart from these considerations, Phylarchus merely relates most of the catastrophes in his history, without suggesting why things are done or to what end, and in the absence of such an analysis it is impossible to feel either pity or an anger which matches the circumstances.[25]

All of this is so close to romance that a further thought suggests itself. We recall Momigliano's remark, quoted earlier, to the effect that biography "came to occupy an ambiguous position between fact and imagination." Polybius is here saying much the same about history "proper"—although that adjective is singularly inappropriate! One way of looking at this is to say that historiography was in practice anticipating what we formally call romance. People want exciting stories at all times; in the Hellenistic age it was the historian's job to supply them. It is perhaps not so much the "historian" who is rep-

[25] Polybius *Histories* 2.56, trans. I. Scott-Kilvert (Polybius, *The Rise of the Roman Empire* [Harmondsworth, 1979] [Penguin]), 168.

rehensible for writing such romantic stuff, as the literary historian, for calling the purveyor of such romantic stuff a historian.[26]

The picture had scarcely changed, however, by the second century A.D., when romance itself was in full spate; so it would seem from Lucian's treatise. Lucian himself was quite clear-headed about the matter—"creative writer" as he himself was. But just as evidently many of his contemporaries were romantic in the extreme, because extensive stretches of *How to Write History* are concerned precisely with how *not* to write history—that is, in the "encomiastic" manner of those currently exuding fulsome panegyric of the emperors then conducting war in the East.[27] There is prose and prose, in short, for those who bothered to see a difference. Not merely the expression but the thought could be manipulated. A couple of generations before Lucian's day, Plutarch had levelled the charge of deliberate misrepresentation against Herodotus—of all people, one might think, because what Thucydides complained of in him was closer to naiveté than to the "malice" of Plutarch's title.[28] And misrepresentation, observes Plutarch, can be pursued by subtler devices than plain lying; it is less conspicuous when it is attained by means of insinuation, unavowed *parti pris*, and sins of disingenuous omission, in the conduct of narrative.

The historiographer, that is, could teach the writer of romance to shape, even to skew, his *diēgēma*, his account of events. But some critics, at least, would notice the skewing. It may very well be Lucian himself who wrote a version of the man-in-animal-shape fable known as the *Onos* story. He skews the tale, in *Lucius or the Ass*, in the direction of racy humor, which becomes at times plain pornography; we have seen that Apuleius in the *Metamorphoses* turned the tale into something much more complex. And the same Plutarch can make his own distinctive use of historical material. Biography, in his

---

[26] See the thoughtful remarks on the relation between historiography and romance in J. R. Morgan, "History, Romance and Realism in the *Aithiopika* of Heliodoros," *Classical Antiquity* 1 (1982), 221–65, esp. 221–26, "History and Romance": "A certain popular corner of the literary market was apparently being satisfied by something with the outward form of historiography" (225). Aficionados of Max Beerbohm will recall that chapter 11 of his comic tragic romance *Zuleika Dobson* contains some perceptive observations to similar effect.

[27] Lucius Verus, the adoptive brother of Marcus Aurelius, and indirectly the emperor himself, whose Parthian campaigns took place, amid great publicity, in the 160s. The histories in question are fortunately lost.

[28] *On the Malice of Herodotus*; the malice consisted in not playing down the temporizing behavior of Plutarch's native Boeotia during the Persian Wars.

conception, is not merely the vehicle of historical truth. His *Lives* are moral lessons. They have an affective purpose: history can be used to inspire as well as to record. Representations in narrative prose of people acting thus and thus in life are not confined to the romances.

None of this is quite theory; it is theory in inchoate state, as it were lying around in the back of people's minds, and forming part of what was in the romance writer's consciousness when he put pen to paper. Historiography and biography were very present to the mind of some such writers, it seems, perhaps especially in the earliest stages of the form. The point will receive further illustration when we look at some contemporary literary practice in a later chapter. The purpose of the present remarks is to show the kind of contribution historiographical theory may have made to romance.

This effectively exhausts the list—an unexpectedly long one, as it has turned out—of the elements available in literary theory that might be thought relevant to romance. From here we must turn to extrapolation from the romances themselves.

Problems and Solutions

C HAPTERS 3 and 4 have discussed the theoretical background of narrative prose fiction, the attitudes, thinking and practice already existing in the literary tradition inherited by the first writers of romance. In the creation of a new genre, however, writers face new problems, new tasks. No doubt they do not always think in terms of theoretical problems that need solving, but for the student of the form following in their tracks it may be profitable to analyse their procedure in such terms. That is the purpose of this chapter. The following pages will thus be an extension of the preceding chapters, a reprise of their main topics—fiction, narrative, prose—seen in another perspective: not of what might or might not have been expected to happen, but of what did happen, as an aspect of the literary history of the form.

Literary theory, stimulated by social pressures and the literature they generated, had issued in a largely agreed body of rhetorical doctrine, which came to constitute the predominant educational practice of society. In so doing, it sanctified tradition. When in new social circumstances romance appeared, it ran counter to tradition; it was not likely to be welcomed by the cultural establishment. The cloudy beginnings of romance that we see in the fourth century B.C., in Plato, Xenophon and New Comedy, long remained cloudy. The changes in literary sensibility of the new age were not so far-reaching as to suggest major new literary structures. It was a long time before the literati would touch romance—which is regrettable when one considers what an Apuleius, or a Longus, eventually did manage to do with it.

Chariton and his successors managed without theory and tradition, even in the teeth of theory and tradition. They used what drama had to offer, and historiography, and rhetoric; but they made of them something other. In thinking about romance they found themselves facing major problems, technical problems of how to manage narrative. But before that there was *the* major problem: what was the story to be? What was its purpose, its nature? We should look at the other side of the coin, the gaps in theory; for those gaps were filled in practice.

Before launching on to that topic, however, it may be interesting to ask, *why* is there no theory of romance? To set out what theory there was, and demonstrate its grip, is merely to invert the philosophy of Pangloss and explain why all was for the worst in the worst of all possible worlds. What brought about this state of things? It is evident enough that even to a Hermogenes, an Aristides, a Philostratus, the intellectual structures available were not adequate—and how much more evident it must have been to those among the accredited "literary men" who, like Lucian, possessed an unmistakable taste and talent for narrative fiction? If social circumstances produced the literary theory of Plato, Aristotle and the rhetoricians, why did not social circumstances in a different world produce other theory to correspond to it? Why is romance not legitimized?

Ultimately, a sufficient theory would have entailed a new act of imagination, just as it was Plato's imagination that set on its way the theory of literature-as-a-social-act. And among academics, imagination is often enthralled by tradition—they live by tradition, after all. The post-classical society that was satisfied to have rhetoric settle like rigor mortis on its literature had, it would seem, little motive for striking out in new directions in its literature. It was content to live in the past; understandable enough, when the past covers several centuries, in which a Homer, a Sophocles, a Plato are merely the brightest stars in a galaxy. Its experiments lie in other fields: in philosophy, in sheer living. Such literature as the Alexandrian age has to offer is an end, and its writers knew it; not perhaps a dead end, but an esoteric firework display. Only comedy looks forward.

Hellenistic Greeks had no doubt little motive for reexamining the condition of their world; enough if they could come to terms with it. The society of the Greek world, as political institution, is not going consciously "forward" until centuries after Alexander; not at the level of the man-in-the-street, the descendant of those citizens who had attended tragic festivals as vital civic functions. There are exceptions among those who wrote history and those who made it. Polybius, in the second century B.C., is well aware of the reality of Roman power, as later, in the Roman Empire, are a growing band of his successors (Appian and Dio Cassius, for example); and from the last century of the Roman Republic, establishment figures in the Greek world are ready and eager to merge with the master-race—the sophists of the time of Hadrian and Marcus Aurelius are political as well as literary figures.[1] But in all this there is nothing to inspire a major literary form. Even in intellectual circles, the habit of living in the past is a way of life, an outlook on the world.[2] This is what lies behind the survival of the rhetorical tradition. It cannot even be maintained that this archaizing is unconscious; Philostratus, of all people, can attribute to one of his own characters—a non-Greek—the remark that "you Greeks have ruined yourselves talking about Troy."[3]

Once enshrined in an educational process, a world-outlook is all the harder to change. We have seen in our own day how powerfully conservative an educational establishment can be; how hard to move and change in any society, without a positive need to do so, such as has been provided in the twentieth century by demographic and social forces. In the early Hellenistic world, at least, there was no social pressure to construct a new educational theory. Theories of literature are not born in a vacuum. Whether in a city-state, an industrial revolution, or a centripetal or disintegrating twentieth-century society, they are born of social circumstance. None of the Hellenistic monarchies ever attained a position of sufficient dominance to constitute a durable political fact. Rome was only making her way in the third century and much of the second. Later, her leading figures were for long too busy winning the respect of the cultured to offer a Roman view of the world—too busy, also, learning and using what the established rhetorical tradition already had to offer them. It is only with the formal establishment of empire and principate that Roman mythographers (Livy, Virgil) can offer that Roman view; but, notoriously, it comprehends no indigenous cultural theory.

Meanwhile, a "view of life" is indeed forming, under the amorphous umbrella of religion, of Isis and her congeners. It will of course merge with the political fact of Rome, to produce a vision of the city of God. That construct is itself a cousin of the vision implied in the Greek romance, whose salient features are human love and human

---

[1] G. W. Bowersock, *Greek Sophists in the Roman Empire* (Oxford, 1969), maintains that the political importance of sophists was actually greater than their literary importance. This is contested by E. L. Bowie, "The Importance of Sophists," *Yale Classical Studies* 27 (1982), 29–59. But their political *activity* is not in question (see, *e.g.*, Philostratus's account of Polemo, *Lives of the Sophists* 1.25).

[2] See E. L. Bowie, "Greeks and their Past in the Second Sophistic," *Past and Present* 46 (1970), 3–41.

[3] *Life of Apollonius of Tyana* 3.19; cf. *Lives of the Sophists* 1.22: "To take refuge in your ancestors is to admit that you do not expect praise for your own achievements."

need of God. But this has come from underneath, where people do not construct or extract theories of literature, but live the life it represents. Such people read early popular romance; they did not theorize about it. And when religious outlook hardens into religious ideology, we need not expect to find literary theory. Creative literature itself is hardly more likely to survive, in a religious world, than literary theory. Creative literature and literary theory are hardly more necessary or desirable in the closed world of early Christianity than in early Communist Russia or China—and for the same reasons: there is nothing for writer or critic to discuss. There are no problems, by fiat; literature and literary theory are merely particular applications of ideology, of correct thinking. All the writer can do (as in Plato's world) is expound, and praise. It is perhaps not surprising that there never was any theory of romance.

There are, then, gaps in literary theory which the would-be romance writer has to fill. What are those gaps? Where does the writer have to exercise his inventiveness? To get some idea of the problem areas, it will be useful to ask ourselves what kind of theory we might imagine. We might start from Aristotle's definition of tragedy and, without attempting too close a correspondence, formulate a working definition of romance that will bring out the principal differences between the forms, and thus situate the questions we should ask—the questions to which the writer had to find answers. Romance might be "extensive narrative fiction in prose, destined for reading and not for public performance, describing the vicissitudes and psychological torments of private individuals, culminating in their ultimate felicity, and achieving through the presentation of their fears and aspirations the satisfaction of similar emotions in the reader."[4] The effect of such a working definition is to highlight three things proper to romance whose theory has already been considered: the vision and its embodiment (that is to say, the fictional aspect of the form); its destination,

---

[4] Compare Perry's definition: "An extended narrative published apart by itself which relates—primarily or wholly for the sake of entertainment or spiritual edification, and for its own sake as a story, rather than for the purpose of instruction in history, science or philosophical theory—the adventures or experiences of one or more individuals in their private capacities and from the viewpoint of their private interests and emotions" (*Ancient Romances*, 44–45). Aristotle's definition of tragedy is: "A tragedy is a *mimēsis* of a high, complete action ('complete' in the sense that implies amplitude), in speech pleasurably enhanced, the different kinds [of enhancement] occurring in separate sections, in dramatic, not narrative form, effecting through pity and fear the *catharsis* of such emotions" (*Poetics* 6.1449b; see Russell-Winterbottom 97).

and hence both content and expression (that is, its formal aspect, both as story and as prose); and the plot and its management (that is, its aspect as narrative).

Starting from such a definition, we may ask what is the nature of the form, and what are its procedures? The events in a romance did not happen: it is fictional, and that is its nature. That in itself does not differentiate romance from epic or drama. Even granting that a Trojan War took place, the essence of what the *Iliad* offers is not its historical kernel. History was never concerned with the states of mind of Achilles, at the various stages of the *Iliad*-episode, nor with the state of mind of the blinded or the exiled Oedipus. They are fiction, and no one ever objected to them as such; even for Plato the problem is not that they are fiction, but that they are fiction of a socially undesirable kind. No one ever objected to totally invented fiction in its place—in Aristophanes or Menander for instance—so long as it stayed within the tradition of what constituted literature. It is not free invention, but free invention in prose, that was unacceptable. Perry's point is central, and we should expect to find it facing us often in thinking about romance from different viewpoints.

But undoubtedly a writer's thoughts—his "great thoughts" and "great emotions"—will, if they are new thoughts as Chariton's were, new emotions, be more free to issue forth in a *form* that is not pre-empted by tradition. There is more room, simply, to think new thoughts. And there is more need to think afresh. Old forms do not inhibit new thoughts—Euripides poured the new wine of the *Bacchae* into an entirely conventional bottle. But new forms demand them. Not all composition is generically determined; it cannot be if there is no *genus* to determine it. Chariton, or the *Ninus*-author, was given a good start by historiography, certainly, by what did happen to people—what does happen to people is, after all, enough to set anyone's imagination working. But Chariton very soon left that behind and turned to what did not happen but might happen to them, to generalization. Like the generalization of *Oedipus Tyrannus*, it is cast in (immediately) very unlikely terms. Unlike the *Oedipus*, Chariton's generalization ends happily.

The first novelist, the inventor of the form if there really was one, must have felt that he was voyaging through strange seas of thought, alone. Chariton himself clearly did, to judge from his attitude to his own creation. But if the thought was rather less demanding than

Newton's, Chariton did—like Columbus, to modify the figure—make it to the new world. For all that we may stress the passivity of the characters, and the sentimentality of the story, what is more important is the newness of the subject—the Hellenistic and also non-parochial, infinitely extensive subject, which Chariton reflects vividly. He is not as embarrassed by his free invention as are the classicists, ancient and modern. It is they, not he, who have problems with romance. We, leaning on Coleridge and Wordsworth, may feel inclined to wonder how Chariton can have got through to the New World without their help. But he did. Hellenistic, Mediterranean life took him there. The problem is not the fiction; it is the prose form.

What is striking about the content of the fiction is what is new about it: its openness, its breadth, its sentiment. Romance is not just private individuals, love-and-adventure, and happy ending; that is there already in New Comedy, for Menander offers family, intrigue, marriage. Romance opens up these issues, broadens and deepens the themes: it discusses human beings in life and in love, a dangerous journey in life, a resolution that is physically and spiritually a homecoming. These are human mysteries; that is the scale of romance, the nature of the writer's vision. It is romantic, yes; it is what he wants to happen; it is not as stern as what does happen. For all that, it is a more disturbing *mimēsis* of human affairs than New Comedy. And more promising; a larger scheme. What the writer is representing is a wide world that he has recognized, a pattern in life that, for all the simplistic melodrama of the writing and the naiveté of the people whose actions are set out, offers a structure as valid as that of drama.

This vision, this fiction, does, however, need shaping. Here drama will not serve as a sufficient model, since the medium of its presentation is different. In an earlier chapter we touched on the elements of that structure, the specific qualities of narrative perceived by Aristotle: its extensiveness, and its appeal to the imagination rather than to the senses. No analysis like Aristotle's analysis of the procedure of drama—through reversal and recognition to a crucial change of condition—survives for romance. It is at this point that extrapolation from the texts becomes necessary. We turn now to the structural problems and spiritual content evidently perceived by the authors themselves in this vision of man-in-the-world.

In the familiar schema of boy-meets-girl/love-and-adventure/obstacles-and-reunion, the essential structural elements may be seen as: problem, conflict, development, solution. Now these elements, it

102

may be observed, exist in drama, although with a difference. There, they constitute the *praxis* or action whose *mythos*—plot, sequence of events—is analyzed by Aristotle, for the case of tragedy, as follows: (1) initial situation (= "problem");[5] (2) operation of some *hamartia* (= "conflict"); (3) events leading to a crucial *peripeteia* and *anagnōrisis*, and involving *pathē*, unpleasant things that happen to people (= "development"); (4) dénouement involving *metabolē*, a change of condition for the worse (= "solution"). But this is for the case of tragedy; and we are not concerned with tragedy, but with "drama," for which New Comedy, and some non-tragic plays of Euripides, offer a more relevant model. The elements will be functionally the same, but their nature is different, less grim. As we have seen at an earlier stage of the discussion, the *hamartia* is not needed since there is no final disaster to explain; there is no *metabolē* of any profundity, certainly no ultimate fall from happiness; and in consequence the *peripeteiai* and *anagnōriseis*, whose function in tragedy was to precipitate and reveal calamity, are reduced to being merely *pathē*, which may be unpleasant but are not fatal.

The romance author could find all of these elements already in Menander. What we are concerned with, then, is not where he found them but what he did with them, the difference in their treatment brought about specifically by the use of a narrative instead of a dramatic medium. It will be profitable at this point to examine the successive stages of the *praxis* thematically and systematically.

(a) *Problem*. An initial situation needs to be thought of, but Menander offers it: a young couple are in love. Normally in comedy we are simply told this fact; or rather, that the young man is in love with a young woman, whose own feelings may not enter very far into the reckoning. The fact of this love is usually not particularly justified in comedy; it is a convention. In romance, however, normally the author takes pains to explain it: the falling in love is a result of the beauty of the couple, a result presented as inevitable since it is going to be put to use more than once in the story. We shall see that Chariton in particular has good reason thus to elaborate his opening situation. For him the fact that beauty engenders love itself constitutes

---

[5] Not, it is true, specifically mentioned by Aristotle in the *locus classicus* (*Poetics* 13.1452b–14.1454a), but implied in the statement that "the best tragedies are about a few families only, for example, . . . Oedipus, Orestes . . . whose lot it was to suffer or commit fearful acts" (13)—that is, who were "accident-prone," and whose *metabolē* derives from a particular kind of initial situation.

the problem as well as the initial impulse. And we shall see that there is yet more to it.

(b) *Conflict*. This corresponds in some degree to the *agon* in tragedy, or in Old Comedy. In romance the conflict consists of the separation of the lovers; it is the fact against which they find themselves struggling, the situation which needs resolving for the *praxis* to come to a conclusion. This of course itself constitutes a "problem," but it should be emphasized that functionally, organically, it is not of the same order, for the writer, as the problem incorporated in the initial situation, to which it is subordinate. It is the characters' problem, not the author's, so to speak, and as such it is one of a series they face. The difficulties it creates for the writer will shortly require more examination. Once again, the kernel of this element is in Menander, who provides obstacles to the union of hero and heroine. But once again, it is elaborated substantially by the romance author. Where, for Menander, opposition to the marriage on the part of a miserly or old-fashioned father, or something of similar dimensions, is sufficient for the limited action of a play, in romance it is not. The obstacles are wider, deeper, more far-flung—the narrative is going to take the principals far beyond their domestic circle in Athens or Ephesus, into the wide Mediterranean world, and confront them with danger not just to love but to life itself. This is of course a function of the extensiveness of the narrative form, which thus begins to operate very early in the story.

(c) *Development*. Yet again, New Comedy affords a pattern, in the intrigue (conducted, for instance, by a scheming slave) and incident (Cnemon, in the *Dyscolus*, falling into the well) which lead from problem to solution. But again the sheer extensiveness of narrative is of first importance. Intrigues and incidents can be developed endlessly, they do not have to be rationed and tailored to size. And because they can be, they will be. It is the nature of the form to be generous of incident and description. To see the truth of this, we have only to write out in prose a plot from comedy. If the writing is done well, we may end with a short story—of Daudet, or Maupassant, or Herodotus himself (the story of Gyges, or Rhampsinitus[6]); and if it is not, we find ourselves with an operagoer's summary of the plot of *The Barber of Seville*. But the art of the short story is in its

---

[6] Herodotus 1.8–12 (Gyges), 2.121 (Rhampsinitus).

economy and point; the art of romance or novel is other. We expect something large-scale, with "grandeur"; the larger scale is what is specific to romance.

This scale brings its own problems. If point, economy and dexterity are not the characteristics of romance, romance must have other characteristics; the writer must have some other goal. Progression will involve cumulation; the snowball will gather weight and momentum; and that weight will have to be put to some positive use. What use the several writers do put it to, we shall see. Likewise, the incidents will differ from incidents in drama not only in number and extent, but in nature also; they can have "variety," can be imagined, and made more interesting thereby. Anything can happen in romance; not just a debate in Babylon, which might perhaps be staged, but a bullfight in Ethiopia, which only Hollywood could stage—or the human imagination. And again, they will *need* this added quality, to avoid tediousness. The writer *needs* "imagination" in that simple sense. Just what each writer does do in that respect, we shall also see; the immediate point is that he must do something. He has an ace in his hand, but he *has* to play it, he cannot discard.

In practice this will amount to the real test of what he is made of, what stuff he has in him, whether he does after all have "great thoughts." If he has, here as much as anywhere is where it will show. And if he has not, that will show too. Since the line of his plot does not offer him *metabolē* as a resounding dénouement, and its extent disbars a "witty," merely neat dénouement, he must conceive some other kind of dénouement that will make the whole enterprise seem worth while to the reader, who will expect due reward for his time and patience. What can the writer offer him? The challenge grows. The writer does not have to contrive ironic *peripeteia* and *anagnōrisis*, subsumed as they now are under the heading *pathē*. But if the *pathē* are not to lead to irony and tragedy, they must lead somewhere else; they carry much of the weight now. In the age of romantic imagination, if that really is what Longinus's treatise is witness to, imagination has to work overtime, for narrative prose fiction is a total enterprise.

(d) *Solution:* The preceding paragraphs have suggested the main point to be made here. Happy endings, in themselves, come from comedy, yet again. But a conjuring trick, by now, is not enough. Altogether too much water has now passed under this bridge. The

105

mountains have labored, and must produce something more interesting, more satisfying, than a mouse. The writer will discover now, if he has not discovered it before, that he has to have—to have had—something in mind: a purpose, a climax, of some kind. This cannot but reveal his "vision"; it will be all the better than he should have one. He cannot borrow that from Menander, or from legend, except perhaps indirectly. He has to think of it himself.

The features specific to narrative, then, turn out to be what Aristotle, almost casually, put his finger on: extensiveness and variety, scale and imaginative range; other features are functions of these two. In the actual elaboration of the plot of a romance, these issue in the following structural elements specific to the form: separation, journeys, parallel plots, and adventures (including escape from adventures). And the existence and nature of these elements give romance a dimension that the more confined form of drama cannot have; this also modifies the less specifically narrative elements of the *mythos*, notably in respect of its beginning and its ending. The initial situation—the problem—requires more justification than a bald statement that love exists. In romance, love is constantly justified by beauty. This constitutes a problem which will recur as often as it is needed, since hero and heroine are destined to move outside their family circle. And that in turn evokes a further characteristic of their love: it is durable, it comprehends fidelity—a central feature of their relationship, destined to be tested by their journeys and adventures. The dénouement, in turn, can and must now carry the weight of a more-than-ephemeral issue: it is to be the issue of trials, their climax; it must carry any aim or message the story may have.

That is to say that as a result of the extensive and imaginative treatment entailed by its narrative form, romance can carry a spiritual content similar in dimension to that of tragedy, and more impressive than is achieved normally by comedy. It can do so; it does not, however, necessarily always do so in fact. Romance can move, and we have seen that Greek romance does move, towards the condition of social comedy. It is getting close, in that case, to "novel." The way is wide open to the form that has dominated literature in recent centuries.

The non-limitation of narrative form makes possible a new kind of literary, aesthetic experience. The effect of this is that Chariton and his fellows have, whether they want to or not, to think of what they

106

want their stories to be about. They have to have an aim. It seems highly likely that the earliest romance writers had no conscious aim at all, in the sense of the "message" once dear to critics. Almost certainly all they aimed to do was tell a story. But the writer cannot get away with it as easily as that. He cannot write without writing *something*; the very narrative form ensures that. As in any other of the affairs of life, privilege involves responsibility; the privilege of wielding a new form entails the responsibility of doing something new with it. The writer needs a vision (however cautiously we employ that term). And this is what Chariton himself discovered. We see his mind at work in public at the beginning of his last book, where, as there has already been occasion to observe, he tells us as plainly as can be what he thinks his readers want: after all the pirates, slavery, battles and crescendo of misfortune, they want sanctioned love and stable marriage. His vision, or that of his readers, is of that kind.

All of that does after all take us into the realm of Northrop Frye as well as Marshall McLuhan. The practice of this form is assuredly, at first, something of a hand-to-mouth affair. Even with the relatively thoughtful Chariton we can see his general intentions breaking the surface of his plot in a hesitant, one suspects improvised, fashion. It is not at all clear, for instance, whether he does or does not want his story to include as a firmly conceived element some kind of theology, some conception of the world which will establish his human story as a manifestation of a divine economy in man's affairs. Aphrodite and Eros appear to be not very sure what they are doing in the story, though they poke their noses into it now and then, in rather fitful fashion.[7] The point, in the present study, is that practice involves theory, whether before or after the event. Handling a new form is *ipso facto* a theoretical problem: how it is to proceed is necessarily a function of what it is about. The writer of romance cannot evade thinking about what he is going to say in all those unlimited, unprescribed, formless pages; how he will navigate, and therefore where he will go, on this uncharted sea.

Let us consider in rather more detail just how this does work out, in the extant texts. What solutions are found by individual writers to

[7] The evolutions of Aphrodite and her underlings Eros and Tyche are discussed in Reardon, "Theme, Structure, and Narrative," 23–25. For instance, at the beginning of the last book Aphrodite has to overrule Tyche, who wants to keep hero and heroine separated still longer; but it is difficult to see anything systematic in her or their behavior. K.-H. Gerschmann, *Chariton-Interpretationen* (diss. Munster, 1974), argues for a more coherent divine intervention in the action.

the problems here raised? For assuredly, if one thing is true about the extant Greek romances, it is that they are emphatically *not* "all the same." Writers' minds are in fact busy, with these problems of structure and aim, in quite remarkable degree. Even within the corpus of the five extant complete texts that we possess of Greek romance, this is abundantly clear. Here we shall not go outside that group; but we should suppose that in the still largely submerged body represented by the known fragments, as well as by the scarce Latin texts, we should find quite as much variety if not more. The elements of structure we shall consider, again systematically, are: separation mechanism; motivation of journeys; management of parallel plots; nature and management of adventures; and pendant to these, the two other features we have brought forward, namely conclusion and "message" or "vision." We may hope, in thus looking at the machinery at close quarters, to see the various modifications in its design; to see the gaps in theory being filled. Though systematic, however, our analysis will not be a complete account of the practice of Chariton, Xenophon, Achilles Tatius, Longus and Heliodorus. What we shall look for is characteristic methods, which may reveal typical romance-writers' procedures; what is certainly visible is different depths of treatment, different levels of writer's craft, and of thought. The net result is five very different texts, literary creations.

It is evident immediately that chronology and sophistication do not go hand in hand, for in respect of the first problem specific to romance that we must consider, Chariton is palpably more adept than his imitator Xenophon. That problem is the separation of the couple. We have seen that in the new kind of myth that romance constitutes, separation is a major element, and one can reasonably posit, in the primitive narrative elaboration of the myth, a fundamental structure in which it happens quite simply by chance or through some violence; chance and violence are, after all, the leitmotifs that run through all adventures in romance. The adventure which issues in the separation of the lovers is, however, particularly important in the structure; it is emotionally more highly charged than other adventures, and will tend to be a unique event, at least in the putative primitive story. It will also tend to be initial, and to be closely connected with the Mediterranean journeyings of the heroes. An obvious resource for the writer faced with the need to arrange such an event is piracy or shipwreck; to try to guess the statistical incidence of such calamities, and hence to assess the story's degree of realism, would be to miss the point, which is simply that they occurred often enough to be familiar to the reader—a modern equivalent would be the hijacking or forced landing of a plane.[8] It is a crude enough device, and is seen at its crudest in Xenophon, who can think of no very plausible reason why Habrocomes and Anthia should ever set out on their journey in the first place, and when he has got them to sea, in the very teeth of his own plot, simply summons up a convenient storm so that things can begin to happen to his heroes.[9]

Xenophon, in short, evidently saw the problem, but just as evidently he was unable to solve it. This is in strong contrast with Chariton, who not only solves it neatly but manages actually to make capital, in an almost Shakespearian manner, out of what ought to be a disadvantage. For he too has a journey and, in his case, a pirate (Theron), but the two elements are so skilfully articulated and integrated into the basic love-plot—via the rivals' intrigue, Chaereas's jealousy, Callirhoe's coma and burial, and the tomb-robbery—that the author kills several birds with one well-aimed stone. Before we have even reached the end of Book I we have had proof of Callirhoe's shattering beauty, pathos fit for *La Dame aux Camélias*, and an exciting, tensely-written scene of melodrama in the capture of the resuscitated heroine; and not only that, but it is all so managed that Theron, and hence Callirhoe, and hence in due course Chaereas, have the very best of reasons for their journeying. These heroes have been sped on their way like an arrow from a bow, not (like Habrocomes and Anthia) with a ball and chain tied to their ankles. To boot, they have been well and truly separated, by nothing less than the Great Separator, Death itself; or so it seems. If we are prepared to accept the tone of Chariton's story, we can only applaud Chariton for

---

[8] I owe the point to E. L. Bowie, "The Novels and the Real World," in B. P. Reardon, ed., *Erotica Antiqua: Acta of the International Conference on the Ancient Novel 1976* (Bangor, Wales, 1977), 91–96: "The statistical rarity of hi-jacking today does not make its exploitation in a story unrealistic" (95).

[9] The oracle (1.6) predicts that Habrocomes and Anthia will suffer misfortunes abroad—so the parents send them abroad (1.10) in order to *paramythēsasthai* the oracle, whatever that means. It would normally mean "console," but has been translated as, *e.g.*, "conjure" (Dalmeyda, Budé ed.), *i.e.*, "disarm"—which explains nothing; or (by K. Nickau in a paper at the conference mentioned in the previous note, unfortunately not available for its *Acta*) as "temper, moderate the effect of" (on the basis of a scholium to *Iliad* 5.662), or "give a meaning other than the obvious one" (cf. Plutarch *On the Bravery of Women* 248B), *i.e.*, "reinterpret." Whatever the word means precisely (if it means anything precisely), the device is singularly limp.

his management of it. He has dealt royally with the initial problems of this kind of literary creation.

Perhaps alerted by the care he has evidently taken with the beginning of his story, his successors (apart from Xenophon) pay just as much attention to building the initial movement into the very body of their stories. Thus, Achilles Tatius follows the same pattern as Xenophon in that his heroes are not separated until their travelling has begun. But although he does have a shipwreck, like Xenophon, it is not itself the immediate cause of the separation of Clitophon and Leucippe. The shipwreck merely deposits them in a foreign land (Egypt), where they are captured by brigands, though still not separated. The separation itself arises through an accident of the fighting in which the brigands become engaged. The weight of the plot is thus not laid directly on the fortuitous shipwreck, but on a rather more readily acceptable circumstance. In fact the shipwreck itself is not in any way necessary to the plot, but is employed simply for the sake of the elaborate description, the rhetorical set piece that Achilles makes of it; such ecphrases are a conspicuous feature of *Leucippe and Clitophon*. There was no need of a shipwreck simply to get the heroes to some particular foreign land; they had in any case simply jumped on the first ship they could find when they left their home, without caring where it was going, and as far as the plot is concerned they could have arrived in Egypt, or anywhere else, safe and sound. The weight of the movement falls rather on the journey itself, and the reason for it; and that is motivated by the author with almost cynical skill.

The first two books are largely given over to an elaborate attempt by Clitophon at seducing Leucippe. He is on the point of succeeding when the girl's mother, alarmed by a dream, bursts into the room. Clitophon escapes unseen. Leucippe is accused by her mother of having given away her honor. She protests violently (2.25), with all the disingenuousness of one who six chapters earlier had agreed to do precisely that but had not quite reached the point of doing so. Her mother flatly refuses to believe her; whereupon Leucippe is mortified—but above all furious at being disbelieved when, as it happened, she was in fact telling the strict truth, if not the whole truth. Under the impulse of this emotion she demands urgently that Clitophon abduct her; and the story is on its way. As with Chariton's story, this initial movement has got the narrative off to a flying start, and has similarly set the tone of the whole romance. One is here

110

strongly tempted to use the term "novel," since psychological realism is clearly one of the author's achievements.

Evidently, then, it was possible, given thought, to avoid awkwardness in the initial movement demanded by this new kind of story: the trick would seem to be to conceive first the general direction and nature of the whole narrative; from that, to create the characteristics of its principal actors; and on this basis to construct a departure and separation that arise so to speak internally from the story, rather than being simply imposed on it by the "blueprint." Aristotle would have approved: "in the representation of character as well as in the chain of actions one ought always to look for the necessary or probable" (*Poetics* 15.1454a). This kind of drama, then, can be made to fit the prescription that has long applied to staged drama. The narrative form helps greatly to this end, for although it cannot be assumed that the reader will know what the initial situation is (as can be assumed for almost all plays), the writer has plenty of space, more than in a play, in which to maneuver. Achilles Tatius does use this space; Chariton's economy, in his Book I, is quite remarkable.

But it was also possible to modify substantially the very basis of the love-and-adventure romance, to make it much less dependent than it might at first sight appear to be on these very elements of separation and journey. By the time the two remaining authors, Longus and Heliodorus, have finished working out the theoretical problems of starting a romance on its way, it almost seems as if they had become quite disenchanted with conventional separations, and journeys, and lurid adventure-sequences generally. Achilles Tatius himself, as we have just seen, adopts at the very least an ambivalent, if not a positively satirical stance towards them. But Longus, in particular, disengages himself visibly from all the blood-and-thunder of the early romance, "defuses the romantic bomb," in the excellent phrase of McCulloh.[10] And Heliodorus, while he certainly does use the most patently romantic elements of the form, does so in an altogether less mechanical way than Chariton, Xenophon, and Achilles. The net effect is that journey, separation, and adventure itself are much less dominant in the structure of his story—although this becomes apparent only on fairly close inspection of his plot, for in this respect (as in many others) Heliodorus is a master of *trompe l'oeil*.

Longus' solution to the problem of the separation is essentially not

[10] *Longus* 68.

to have a separation; his solution to the problem of the journeying is essentially not to have a journey. Essentially—for there are in *Daphnis and Chloe* vestiges of both, in the short-lived capture first of Daphnis, by pirates, then of Chloe, by an invading army. But these episodes, hardly even ephemeral, are mere grimaces in the direction of conventional romance, just as Achilles makes grimaces of a different kind. Longus gives the broadest wink to indicate this when he brings Daphnis safe back to land between two cows, holding on to a horn of each as they swim—for cows can swim, we learn; oh yes, cows can swim very well!—not as well as fish, of course, but very well for all that, and without any risk of drowning unless their hooves become sodden and drop off. . . .[11] For, after all (we may imagine Longus thinking to himself), what is the point, for the writer of a story about lovers, in having a separation? The answer is, of course, that separation will naturally impede the progress of their love. But if that is the point, cannot the progress of love be impeded just as effectively, and far less bombastically, by more natural obstacles—ignorance, for example, and inexperience? Not everybody is really familiar in his own life with travel and adventures and consequent disruption in his affairs. Even in the wide Mediterranean world, the experience described by a Xenophon must have been entirely vicarious for nine people out of ten. Not that this is good reason for not inventing it—our thesis has been exactly the contrary. But another kind of adventure, in that general line, is after all imaginable: one in which the hero can get lost without ever stirring from home, can have all the emotions that adventures provoke without having anything more exotic happen to him than kissing a girl he has known all his life. Psychologically, that is very much closer than Chariton's story to what really does happen to people, to many more than one out of ten: my story will remind him who has loved what it was like to love, and if any there be by chance that has not loved, why then, him it will instruct; though truly, there never was nor shall be such as to escape love entirely, so long as men can breathe, or eyes can see; as Longus says, in so many words, in his preface.

[11] 1.30. Critics have suspected that the passage is interpolated, misplaced erudition of a kind common in the period (and found notably in Achilles Tatius and Heliodorus). That is possible, but it is fatally easy to be too solemn in reading Longus. The whole incident which lands Daphnis in the sea in the first place is Longus's comic version of the conventional shipwreck; and to my mind undue solemnity has been exercised here.

This is a considerable step in the theory of what romance is about: it is about people. Of course it is less immediately exciting than *Chaereas and Callirhoe*, less sensational. And by the same token it is the more likely to strike the educated as worthy of survival; that may well be why it survived rather more vigorously.[12] Longus has dug below the surface structure of the "conventional" form, to what that structure was used to represent, to relationships between people. It is a very special case, we have seen earlier, that he has invented, and the outlines of the conventional plot are visible, if only dimly. But perhaps this example of the now not-quite-new form comes closer to the "quest narrative" that critics have seen as underlying all romance than does the crude adventure story. Furthermore, Longus exploits the occasions readily offered by his story for detailed description of psychological processes. As Chalk showed, he builds these processes into an elaborate triptych structure, setting out the progress of the seasons, the events associated with each season as it comes round, and the emotional developments prompted thereby in hero and heroine. This is a particularly careful use of the possibilities offered by extensive narration.

Heliodorus, looking back by his time over a whole romance tradition, appears to have learned from Longus's fundamental reshuffling of the cards, but at the same time does go back in some degree to traditional features. Theagenes and Charicleia are separated, for a relatively short time; the most splendid adventures, however, happen to them when they are together, and are thus made the more impressive by being double-barrelled. There is little of love in the story, although there are many declarations of love and acts inspired by love—from the very beginning of the tale, where the heroine is discovered nursing her wounded hero back to life at the same time as she loudly proclaims her chastity, and her intention of protecting it against all aggressions (including, as it is to turn out, the occasional attempt by Theagenes himself, under provocation from the girl, who promptly slaps his wrist). Thus, not very much is lost by abandoning the theme of separation, for the story is less of a love story than are the earlier texts, and more of an extensive adventure of epic dimensions.

The journey itself is substantially changed in function of this

---

[12] Even so, the text depends on only two manuscripts; see the introduction to Reeve's Teubner edition.

changed overall purpose. One way of dealing with the problems of a journey, as we have just seen, is not to have a journey. Another, the one Heliodorus adopts, is to make it the whole point of the story, instead of being merely an endless thread on which to hang a series of episodes. In Chariton, Xenophon, Achilles, the journey is circular: though the heroes go to many places, they get nowhere in the end except back where they started (although it is of course true that their spiritual condition may have changed in the process). In Heliodorus, the journey (or at least, the part of it that we see) is from A to B, from Delphi to Ethiopia; it is a pilgrimage, it has a destination as well as an end, and thus itself constitutes the main beam of the edifice.

That the author did consciously contrive so to present matters is indicated by the care with which he envelops the anterior story in mist. For the truth of the matter is that in reality the journey is after all every bit as circular as in Chariton. The heroine Charicleia was born in Ethiopia, as it eventually transpires, but taken from there to Delphi when very young; so that in fact she is returning home just as did Callirhoe, Anthia and Leucippe. But here again, *trompe l'oeil* comes into play—this is the principal instance of such illusion. The *Ethiopica* begins not at the beginning, far from it, but *in mediis rebus*— just like the *Odyssey*. In fact, when the story opens, not only has the first leg of the heroine's journey (Ethiopia to Delphi) been completed many years earlier, she is actually halfway through the return journey, since the opening scene shows her stranded on the beach in Egypt; and in the meantime she has picked up the hero Theagenes en route, so to speak, at a festival in Delphi. When eventually we do learn how it has come about that Charicleia is where she is, we find the wool pulled very firmly over our eyes. It is at no point clear whether Charicleia's departure from Delphi is or is not fortuitous, for we are given two accounts of the matter which conflict directly with each other. According to one, her departure is motivated by an oracle; in the other, it was destined from the beginning of her history; and while it may be possible to reconcile the two reasons theologically, in terms of the detail of the structure of Heliodorus's story it is not. Heliodorus knew very well it was not; but he was intent on building both unity and dramatic effect into a story which by its nature cannot have both. So complex is his story that it takes a singularly tenacious literary detective to keep track of that particular thread when so many others are being simultaneously woven into a grandiose pattern; the reader is likely to be simply relieved when the whole design is at last completed, and little inclined to worry over-much about whether the story can be entirely straightened out or not.[13] The narrative technique of Heliodorus is extremely sophisticated. Patently he gave considerable thought to the whole structure; in particular, he realized fully what disadvantages and also what advantages are inherent in the mandatory journey. We are a long way from Xenophon of Ephesus.

It would seem, then, that the crucial elements of separation and journey were the subject of considerable practical experiment on the part of romance writers. If there is no explicit theory about these elements of romance (and Aristotle does not go into such detail in his brief remarks on narrative), there is much implicit thinking. And in every case, the sheer extensiveness and the infinite plasticity of the prose medium contribute substantially to the solutions found by one author after another. By the time of Longus and Heliodorus, the problems posed by these elements of a conventional and obvious structure are hardly problems at all. Like Jane Austen deploying "point of view," the most advanced of the Greek romance authors have turned such "problems" inside out, to make of them not an embarrassment but a pleasure. The art of prose narrative is visibly advancing.

Let us turn now to the remaining elements of structure specific to prose romance, namely parallel plots and adventures. We shall take them, this time, in sequence; they are less closely linked than are

[13] The detective who put his finger on the problem was V. Hefti, *Zur Erzählungstechnik in Heliodors Aethiopica* (diss. Basle, 1940, published Vienna, 1950), who sets this *grundsätzlicher Widerspruch* (6) at the center of his examination and discusses it fully in his Chapter 40, 73–78; the matter is summarized in Reardon, *Courants littéraires*, 390ff. and notes. At 4.13.1—nearly halfway through a very long text—Heliodorus does finally give the game away; but it takes a sharp eye to spot it, as the author does his best to confuse the issue and paper over the crack with a trick of language inevitably either over- or under-translated in modern versions (*men . . . de*). A quite different kind of explanation is advanced by J. J. Winkler, "The Mendacity of Kalasiris and the Narrative Strategy of Heliodoros' *Aithiopika*," *Yale Classical Studies* 27 (1982), 93–158: what Hefti sees as a fundamental fault in construction is attributed to the deviousness of Calasiris, the story's narrative "anchor man" for much of its length. While Calasiris does sometimes give the impression (like Odysseus) of never willingly telling the truth if a lie will do, this interpretation seems to me to outdo him in elaborateness. For the general complexity of the *Ethiopica*, see particularly the excellent study of S. L. Wolff, *The Greek Romances in Elizabethan Prose Fiction* (New York, 1912); his metaphors of "a nest of boxes," "a juggler keeping three oranges in the air at once" (193–94), put the matter well.

separation and journey. For parallel plot, once again Xenophon's romance can be taken as a base, in that it sets out a problem without providing an adequate solution. The problem consists in the difficulty of maintaining interest in what happens to each of two separated lovers, while at the same time maintaining sufficient organic unity in the plot for the reader's interest not to dissipate entirely. It is a perennial problem in a love story; the fact that it can be solved does not mean that there is no problem. What complicates it most in the primitive romance of love-and-adventure is the travel; physical separation is bound to create an effect of lack of contact. Basically, the writer has to report what happens to A and what happens to B. If he piles up all the adventures of A before turning to B, the perspective will be awry. If he adopts an alternation-technique, he may create a "ping-pong" effect that soon becomes wearisome. We can see the Greek romance writers at grips with the difficulty; it is caused, let us recall, by the extensive prose form of the genre, and does not arise in drama, where unity appears (it may be an illusion) to be imposed on the plot by the concentration of the audience's attention on a locally and temporally limited, and visible, arena of action.

Xenophon tries simply to give each of his heroes equal time, and darts from one to the other in largely unpredictable manner. At the most, we soon learn to expect that after two or three pages of Anthia, we shall have two or three pages of Habrocomes, for nothing in the nature of either partner's adventures raises any particular expectation in respect of what the other partner is likely to be doing; the two series have little logical connection. We may look more closely at this rudimentary structure, for later comparison with a more careful writer. For the first half of the *Ephesiaca*, Habrocomes and Anthia are either together or following each other's tracks coherently at least. But thereafter occurs a series of journeys which move them separately around the Mediterranean. In 3.8-10 they move from Cilicia to Egypt. In the case of Anthia, the journey is the sequel to the plunder by robbers of the tomb in which she is lying apparently dead (the epidose is lifted, that is, from Chariton, although it is handled less adroitly). She laments the situation passionately:

> Once again . . . pirates and sea! Once again I am a prisoner! But now it is worse because I am without Habrocomes. So what land will

116

have me? And who will I see there? . . . My only prayer is that I
may go where I shall at least see the tomb of Habrocomes.

And she is on her way; her role is to be pushed about. No less passionate is Habrocomes when, wildly casting about to find her, he
hears by pure chance what has become of her:

> I, poor wretch that I am, have been deprived of your body, my only
> consolation. So I am absolutely determined to die. But first I will go
> on until I find your body, embrace it and bury myself with you.

Eluding his companions he makes for the sea. There he

> found a ship weighing anchor for Alexandria. He went aboard and
> sailed off, hoping to catch in Egypt the pirates who had plundered
> everything.

And that is why, and how, hero mirrors heroine's movements, in
this piece of parallel plot: the correspondence is totally fortuitous and
meaningless. Similarly, Habrocomes next goes to Italy, "expecting to
find out there something about Anthia"; why Italy, rather than Ethiopia, Ultima Thule, or the Antipodes, we are not told.[14] At that, he
does not even get to Italy without an unplanned detour to Sicily ("the
wind carried his ship out of its route"), there to contemplate the edifying spectacle of a mummified woman kept in the bedroom by her
otherwise inconsolable husband ("now I truly realize that true love
knows no age limit!" . . .). *This* is what constitutes parallel action in
Xenophon, this spastic antiphony: Anthia and Habrocomes darting
quite unpredictably around the Mediterranean.[15]

To give Xenophon credit where credit is possible, he is clearly
aware of this inadequacy, and in an effort to counter it he creates a
third character, the "noble brigand" Hippothous, who moves a number of times from the Anthia-line to the Habrocomes-line. This clearly

[14] The "bareness" (*Knappheit*) of the narrative led Rohde to suspect that the extant
version of the *Ephesiaca* is abbreviated (the *Souda* mentions ten books; the extant story
has five); see Schmeling, *Xenophon*, 76–77. It seems more likely that this barren manner
is inherent in the work; but there are occasional indications of gaps, and conceivably
some of them have swallowed better motivation for the characters' travels. The argument against the "epitomization" theory is set out in T. Hägg, "Die Ephesiaka des
Xenophon Ephesios—Original oder Epitome?" *Classica et Mediaevalia* 37 (1966), 118–
61.

[15] It may be true, as was suggested by Garin (see Budé, 54 [note]) that here too
Xenophon is imitating Chariton, in making his heroes visit the same lands as Chaereas
and Callirhoe. But the correspondence is only partial; and, in any case, the point is
that Xenophon does not *motivate* their travels adequately.

introduces a degree of unity, a connection to which the reader can cling; and the device of a go-between of some kind was to become in the European novel a fairly standard means of focussing the story.[16] But at this unsophisticated level it causes as many problems as it solves. The very point and nature of the separation of Habrocomes and Anthia is that neither has the slightest idea where the other is, or whether the other is even still alive; the pathos of the story lies in this total isolation. Hippothous, inevitably, is apt to short-circuit such a plot. The reader may be aware that he is the common contact, but the heroes must not, if the story is to maintain its own kind of tension. Consequently Hippothous, who is aware of Habrocomes' side of the story, must be made to fail to recognize Anthia the second time he comes across her.[17] Xenophon finds himself thus, not only playing ping-pong, but jumping from the frying pan into the fire.

The foregoing remarks will illustrate sufficiently the nature of the problem; it would be unprofitable to examine this particular story in more detail. Reverting to Chariton, we can see this earlier but more thoughtful writer adopting, essentially, the other solution: recounting the adventures of one hero as a narrative block before turning to the other. He does not do so crudely. We are made well aware of what is happening to Chaereas while Callirhoe's story is building up to its climax, and Chaereas is adroitly built into that climax when Mithridates, at the trial in Babylon, is able to play him as the trump card at the very crisis, so dramatically staged by the writer. Nevertheless, up until the trial the story is really Callirhoe's. Its organic unity is kept firmly before us; it is presented *crescendo*; and it ends, effectively, when the impasse is reached. Thereafter Chaereas takes over. His story is in itself less emotionally powerful, and at several points we see Chariton straining to achieve a pathos which came naturally in Callirhoe's story. But all that is really needed is a sufficient flourish to bring about an acceptable solution to Callirhoe's problem. There can be no Callirhoe without Chaereas, but the romance is Callirhoe's story.[18]

[16] For example, Lady Catherine de Burgh, though she has a personality of her own, serves the function of intermediary between Elizabeth Bennett and Mr. Darcy in *Pride and Prejudice*. Of course such a character can be put to ancillary uses, such as directing sympathy to one of the pair. At a similarly early stage of the European novel the device of epistolary narrative may be seen as a primitive attempt to justify the relation of unconnected adventures. The difficulty is unavoidable.

[17] 4.3.6; at 5.9.5, however, he does recognize Anthia—but this time she does not recognize him!

[18] We may recall that *Callirhoe* may have been Chariton's own title for the book (see

In a sense, then, Chariton had already solved the problem that Xenophon later proved unable to handle; he did so by *choosing between* his two heroes, for the main direction of his story. That does, certainly, leave Chaereas as a rather mechanical hero. If he had shown, while in Mithridates' hands, the same ingenuity as he shows in the latter part of the romance (in capturing Tyre, for instance), we might be less inclined to wonder just what it is that Callirhoe sees in him. But that would have turned the whole narrative into another story. The initial ineptitude of his hero is the price Chariton has to pay to write the story he wants to write. Everything suggests that although he could not quite manage everything, Chariton—unlike Xenophon—knew very well what he was doing. It is interesting, finally, that in opting to make Callirhoe the center of his romance, Chariton was choosing the more fruitful subject. In romantic psychology, the female is a better focus for romance than the male.

Parallel plot, then, a basic element of primitive love-romance, is intrinsically difficult, though not impossible, to handle satisfactorily. The prose writer, even if as unskillful as Xenophon, finds himself unable to disregard its difficulty, and therefore is forced to think about the structure of his story. In doing so, he is likely to find himself faced with further problems—which will, however, offer correspondingly greater rewards in respect of complexity of narrative or the whole direction of the plot.[19] This tendency is seen in the so-called "sophistic" romance-writers as well; some of its effects have already been adumbrated in preceding pages, for it is scarcely possible to change one major element of narrative, such as separation or journey, without affecting substantially the relation of the adventures undergone by the separated pair or of the journeys they embark on.

In the case of Achilles Tatius, a major innovation lies in the ego-narrative structure he undertook. Ego-narrative is notoriously a difficult technique to handle. Authorial omniscience can be accepted without difficulty (for all the caveats prompted by recent critical discussion, it is after all the basis of any story, in the sense that the relator must be believed if the story is to be accepted at all). But to risk ego-narrative is to invite the question, "How do you know?"

Chapter 1, n. 4); cf. K. Plepelits's German translation, *Chariton von Aphrodisias: Kallirhoe* (Stuttgart, 1976), 28–29 (this book contains a very good introduction).

[19] The matter is well illustrated by the *Odyssey*; there the parallel-plot problem is solved by the flashback, which holds back one line of the plot, the Odysseus-line, until sufficient tension has been created to justify the change of subject.

How can the narrator, who is also character A, credibly claim to know what characters B and C and D think? How can he know what happened in places where he was not present? No doubt these problems can be solved, although Achilles does not always solve them;[20] but they are singularly intractable, and the fact that Achilles sustains the effort almost all the time, over a long text, argues considerable sophistication in him.

While it is of course impossible to know just what led him to this technique, it is worth while noting that to put the narration in the mouth of one of the main actors does in a way solve, or at least make it easier to solve, the problem of parallel plot. For one of the parallel tracks is that of the storyteller himself, a track which it is perfectly natural for the reader to follow from the beginning of the story, and which consequently does not appear to need any attention or explanation. As a matter of narrative illusion, then, only one line of adventures, not two, needs to be presented "authorially" (that is, as an objective reporting of what happened to someone other than the teller of the story). We are "inside" the story, and apart from other advantages this technique may offer, it will appear to simplify the complexity of a parallel-plot narrative. In fact Clitophon, in Achilles Tatius's story, is forced into rather elaborate explanations to the effect that he heard later (and is now telling the reader) all that happened to Leucippe. It is true that on occasion he uses Clitophon's temporary ignorance to dramatic effect (we are, for instance, kept waiting a long time before we discover how Leucippe could survive decapitation, which had appeared conclusive enough). But the device is as clumsy in one way as it can be effective in another. One problem has been exchanged for another, in fact. That, however, is the process of all creative endeavor. In the meantime, we note it simply as another approach to the problem of organizing plural narratives.

We have seen that for practical purposes neither Longus nor Heliodorus has to trouble himself substantially over the difficulty of parallel plots, since Daphnis and Chloe, in Longus, and Theagenes and Charicleia, in Heliodorus, are together most of the time; this is a function of what these authors decided to do about the basic element of journey in romance. But that does not altogether dispense the critic from analyzing their narrative procedures in this respect, since once again one problem is solved only at the cost of creating another,

[20] See Hägg, *Narrative Technique*, 303.

richer one. When two heroes go about their business not separately but in tandem, our attention is merely removed from the physical to the psychological aspect of their duality. Longus uses this duality to bring the narrative closer to the heart of the love-theme than was readily possible with separately wandering lovers. We see here what appears to be a fairly advanced stage of the process whereby the balance swings from history to romance in romantic-historical narrative, whereby the relatively superficial element of physical travel gives way to the profounder element of relations between human beings. But there remains, in a changed form, as much element of parallel plot as ever there was. For there are still two heroes involved, two people who both have to be presented; what has happened is that the plot, the adventure, becomes a story of emotional rather than physical adventure. And in this respect Longus is meticulously careful in setting out the parallel but different emotional development of a young boy and a young girl. For instance, in 1.14 Chloe sees Daphnis bathing, and is stung by love; in 1.18 Daphnis kisses Chloe, and is fired by love; their *love* is parallel. We may usefully set out these passages in full, to make the comparison with the structurally similar passages from Xenophon quoted above:

Now I feel ill [says Chloe] but don't know what my illness is; I feel pain, although I've not been injured; I feel sad, although I've lost none of my sheep; I feel hot, although I'm sitting in deep shade. How many times I've been scratched by brambles, and I've not wept! How many times I've been stung by bees, and I've not cried out! But the thing that's stinging my heart now is sharper than all those things. Daphnis is beautiful—but then so are the flowers. His pipes make a beautiful sound—but then so do the nightingales. And yet I care nothing for those things. I wish I were his pipes, so he could breathe into me. I wish I were his goat, so I could be led to graze by him. You wicked stream! You only made Daphnis beautiful; I bathed in you, and nothing happened. I'm dying, dear Nymphs; and even you are doing nothing to save the girl who has grown up at your side. Who will put garlands on you when I am gone? Who will bring up the poor lambs? Who will look after the chattering grasshopper I took such trouble to catch so that it could put me to sleep by singing in front of the cave? But now I cannot sleep because of Daphnis, and the chattering of the grasshopper does me no good.

121

And Daphnis in counterpoint:

> Whatever is Chloe's kiss doing to me? Her lips are softer than rose-petals, and her mouth is sweeter than honeycomb, but her kiss is sharper than the bee's sting. I've often kissed kids; I've often kissed new-born puppies and the calf that Dorcon gave her—but this is a new kind of kiss. My breath comes in gasps; my heart leaps out of my breast; my spirit dissolves—and yet I want to kiss her again. Oh, what a terrible victory! Oh, what a strange disease! I don't even know what to call it! Did Chloe take poison before she kissed me? But then why didn't she die? How the nightingales sing while my pipes are silent! How the kids jump around while I sit still! How the flowers bloom while I make no garlands! But while the violets and hyacinth flourish, Daphnis wastes away.

This, then, is how Longus does things. Earlier, Xenophon's "ping-pong" parallel action came under criticism. Is Longus's counterpoint better? Yes, because Longus is not darting unpredictably from hero to heroine merely to keep both in the picture. On the contrary, given his whole perspective, his whole manner of handling his story, what happens to A implies that something significantly similar will happen to B—and this is especially true of their psychological conditions, as we have just seen in the extracts quoted. This interplay is the very point of the whole story; these parallel and reciprocated feelings constitute the very growth of love. Our reaction is not, as with Xenophon, "what on earth do we get next?" but, "If this is what Daphnis experiences at this point, how does Chloe fare in the same situation?" The parallel action is in fact, with Longus, at the very center of our interest in the story; we ourselves are quite capable of navigating in this emotional world. Longus has no need of an intermediary Hippothous to solve his structural problem. He has not only taken hold of the difficulty of parallelism, he has actually turned it into a principal virtue in his story. This is ping-pong with a purpose.

As for Heliodorus, we have seen that he is not really interested enough in the love-theme to make it the center of his story. He prefers to present impressive people in dramatic situations, rather than to analyze the relationships among those people. Here, then, there is not much parallel plot at all, and not much parallel love; only adventures in tandem, lovers acting as a team. Heliodorus is clearly more at ease with the female of the couple, in which respect he resembles not Xenophon (to whom he is sometimes compared), but

Chariton. His Charicleia, though not in all respects a very desirable young woman, is at least more interesting than Theagenes; Theagenes is better at wrestling with bulls than with his future wife, and would no doubt get on well with Chaereas.

But there is no need to pursue the details of these developments. The point is that here again romance writers have found themselves forced to think about, and to modify substantially, a basic structural element in prose narrative form: the handling of two plots at once. In essence, what we see is the two plots tending, in the more advanced writers, to coalesce.

There is little need either, by this point, to treat extensively the fourth element specific to romance, namely the adventures. The general tone established by the structure of the several stories is naturally found in the detail of the episodes they incorporate, and it will be sufficient to recall what for the most part has been suggested in earlier pages. Chariton takes every opportunity to place his heroine in pathetic situations from which he can wring the last drop of melodramatic sentiment. Xenophon's adventures become more and more lurid as his book continues: Anthia is confined in a trench with two fierce and starving hounds (4.6); Habrocomes escapes from crucifixion, burning at the stake, and crocodiles (4.2). It would seem that Xenophon is conscious that he cannot rely on his plot to sustain interest, as Chariton can, and indulges more and more feverishly in sensational incident in order to give his reader something to look forward to. The grotesque nature of the episodes in Achilles Tatius has already been described; it may be added simply that they are of a piece with the ingenious construction of the story and with the regularly tortuous Greek of the passages of ecphrasis. In Longus, the simplest incident of idyllic country life can constitute an adventure: a grasshopper takes refuge in the bosom of Chloe's dress (1.26); Daphnis's father Lamon relates the myth of Syrinx (2.34). Equally, matters of real moment break into the idyll, as when the city woman Lycaenion makes a man of Daphnis (3.15-18). In Heliodorus, finally, the adventures are relatively few in number, but the most typical of them are elaborated into dramatic, colorful episodes: the games at Delphi where hero and heroine fall in love, the passionate intrigues of the Persian satrap's wife Arsace, the colossal siege of Syene.

In moving from narrative structure to episode we come to what is really the heart of romance: the element of fiction. For the adventures just touched on are what romance is about, what the authors wanted

123

to present. Technical problems of narrative are certainly important; we have just seen that central ideas cannot be handled effectively unless they are liberated, released, by skill in managing narrative—Longus has it, Xenophon has not. But that skill is the skill of a workman handling tools; what he creates with them is more important than the tools themselves. The extensive nature and loose prose form of such narrative is the frame; what fills the frame is imagination. Individual episodes and adventures are the constituent elements of the imagined world each writer is creating, and of course reflect that world.

This imagined world varies considerably from author to author. Sentimental romance based on psychological imagination; melodrama built of suspense and sensation; social comedy verging on parody of the romantic dream; the special world of controlled idyll; spectacular epic—even within the limited canon of extant *Liebesromane*, the range is wide. Each of these creations constitutes, one might say, an "object of literature" for its creator, what he is writing about; in each case it is an amalgam, though varying no doubt in its proportions, of the world he observes and earlier created worlds, from the *Odyssey* to Alexandrian elegy. Above all, it is an act of imagination embodying what the author sees as worth observing about life, about the world and people in the world; what he wants to say. This "writer's truth" holds, in romance, the place that philosopher's truth holds in Plato's idea of fiction: it is the purpose of the exercise. It is founded, however, upon what Plato did not accept: the engagement and stimulation of the emotions. We find ourselves with Aristotle again: such literature is the *mimēsis* of a *praxis*, and a generalized representation of human conduct. And such literature is not the worse, in Aristotle's view, for being mimetic. Nor is it less seriously conceived truth for being fictitious. Rather, it corresponds closely enough to Longinus's contemporary formula of "great thoughts and strong and inspired emotion" as the basis of great writing.

Longinus was looking behind the forms and procedures of literature to its source; which is as likely to be found in fictive creation as in stories whose outline was already determined by legend. If we may suppose that Aristotle's as well as Plato's critical thoughts on the function of literature were more or less in general circulation; and if, as seems reasonable, we may also suppose that other people besides Longinus, in the early Empire, were prepared to conceive the function of literature in romantic terms; then no doubt the kind of writer's truth that is embodied in Chariton and Longus would in practice mean something to contemporary readers—whether or not their academic spokesmen were prepared to give it formal approval. Chariton and Longus were presumably aware of that. The gap between practice and theory may not be unimaginably great after all. In the early days of film similar considerations obtained. Greek romance has often enough been compared to the silent cinema of the early decades of this century,[21] and the resemblances are striking. It seems probable that the similarity extends beyond the content and procedures of the films themselves, to the reception of the new form and the attitudes of its exponents: mild amusement and formal scorn, on the part of the audience; perseverance through initial discouragement, on the part of the creators of the new form. The chief obstacle to early fiction was in all probability contemporary conventional attitudes to a form born of a new society.

Literary-historical analysis has generally concentrated on the process involved in that birth, the problem of "origins," about which much has been said over the last century and more. The question would appear to be answered as well as need be, or as well as it can be answered in "bibliographical" terms, by observing the similarity of some early texts (*Ninus* and Chariton) as well as some others (notably Heliodorus) to romantic historiography. It may now be useful to ask, rather, where was romance going? The intention of the present chapter has been to show that the new form has its own independent direction and positive content. All of the writers under discussion offer a clear enough message. Each has his vision of the world, which, when all is said about the structural problems with which he wrestles and the devices he employs, informs his story from the very start and emerges from its conclusion. It may be a vision of love as domestic felicity, or as the motor of a social world, or as an orgasmic natural rhythm—it is not the purpose of the present study to examine in detail the different visions of particular authors.[22] Perhaps some of these authors could not have set out their thoughts very co-

---

[21] *E.g.*, by G. Dalmeyda (Budé edition of Xenophon, xxv); J. Ludvíkovský, *Řecký Román Dobrodružný* (*Le roman grec d'aventures*) (Prague, 1925) (French summary 147–58), 153–54—a now outdated but lively and still valuable study. It is interesting that even the titles of early films resemble the titles of romances: *The Perils of Pauline* and *Callirhoe* (heroine named); *The Mysteries of New York* and *Babyloniaca* (Iamblichus; cf. *Ethiopica*) (exotic theater of action).

[22] My analysis of these different visions, adumbrated in earlier passages of the present text, is set out systematically in the works cited in Chapter 2, n. 12 above.

herently in any more analytical, philosophical way. But how many writers can? And even if they can, why should they? Writers tell stories; that is their language. The story is told of Schubert that, asked to explain a composition of his own that he had just played, he sat down at the piano and played it again.

Creative artists are not likely to be seriously hampered for very long by tradition. It may be as Perry maintained, that the use of a historiographical form in early romance is in part a bid for the attention of the literary establishment. But in the perspective that has been adopted in this chapter, it seems likely that there was another, more positive motive at work. The *Ninus*-author used his historical figures because Ninus and Semiramis were interesting people, with whom one could do interesting things; also because their names would mean something to his readers—their stories were in a sense half-written already, and the writer takes advantage of that. Chariton sets his story in classical Greece because the antiquity of the setting adds a certain glamor to the actions of unexceptional people. What they are both interested in is what they can make of such people, not what the critics will think of them. Historiography had little to do with the crucial matter of fictiveness. Historiographical form, prose narrative form, was available, certainly, and surely suggested possibilities to the earliest romance writers. For fictiveness, however, they were more likely to look to comedy, and particularly to New Comedy—and the purposes of a Chariton are totally fictive, though elements of his material may not be. The revolution is in the use of prose for such purposes. Using prose meant dealing with the problems inherent in its extensiveness, formlessness, and narrative basis. From Chariton to Heliodorus we see these problems being faced.

Context and Contacts

So FAR romance has been considered in isolation; but it was not isolated, either in the overall history of Greek literature or in its own time. We should now look at its context, its surrounds and penumbra. In other periods there are works which could quite suitably be comprehended under the simple title "romance"; and there are works in the imperial period which we would not call "romance" but which share important features with romance. At the very beginning of this study it was pointed out that romance could be understood not only as a particular literary genre but as a complex of genres and, more broadly yet, as a quality. This is confirmed by the fact that some theory available about other forms (epic, drama) is relevant to romance; which suggests there can be something romantic about them.

In launching and developing the new form, romance writers were anything but aggressively non-traditional. Even at the beginning they were by no means uneducated men; it was natural that they should be sensitive to cultural trends. This is merely one aspect of an attitude normal in the period, summed up in the world *mimēsis* in its secondary, non-philosophical sense: the practice of deliberately recalling in one's writing the great works of the Greek tradition, as Milton actively recalls the language and content of the Authorized Version.[1] It is partly a result of the education described earlier: a writer soaked in Homer and Demosthenes may well reflect them in his own work. We have seen Chariton reflect those writers and others;[2] Xenophon himself, incompetent as he may be, consciously models his language in some respects on the classicizing, "atticizing" tradition, notably in his use of the optative, which has virtually disappeared from popular *koinē* (as found, for instance, in the Gospels). In the case of Achilles Tatius, Longus, and above all Heliodorus, their cultural level, their erudition even, leaps from the page, and is not disguised by even a disingenuously simple style. It is consequently nec-

---

[1] See esp. J. Bompaire, *Lucien écrivain: imitation et création* (Paris, 1958), Ière Partie, "La doctrine de la Mimésis"; for serious reservations see now, among others, C. P. Jones, *Culture and Society in Lucian* (Cambridge, Mass. and London, 1986), chapter 13.

[2] See Chapter 3, n. 50.

essary to consider the literary context in which romance was written; this question will be cousin to the familiar topic of "the origins of romance." The question of origins, it may be said in passing, is a lottery, a lucky dip—and everyone comes up with something in his hand; like the race in *Alice in Wonderland*, it is a contest in which everybody gets a prize, because it is hard to think of any earlier form of literature that did *not* affect romance, in one way or another. By its very nature, as we have seen, romance is receptive and elastic. But we are here concerned rather with other facets of the same question. What, in earlier literature, performed in some degree the function of romance, did what romance was to do in the imperial period? Next, what in its own day surrounded the form, constituted its literary and cultural context? Finally, what subsequently took the place of romance? For this question too may have value, in affording perspective: what sort of shadow did ancient romance cast?

In dealing with the first element of this multiple question we shall be in part rounding up ideas set out elsewhere. Epic, drama and historiography can all carry romance, and the writers themselves point to the paternity of their stories: Chariton when staging the trial in Babylon, Heliodorus in a score of places (including his very first chapter), fall naturally into theatrical metaphor.[3] Romance could be described as imagined dramatic action set out in the extensive manner of epic, in the guise of a consecutive historical account of events. Let us look more closely at these similarities and try to identify the most significant generic overlaps between romance and other forms.

As we saw earlier, the *Odyssey* recounts a quest, involving love, obstacles, travel and adventure, in an imagined world comprehending projected wishes and a happy ending. We can here see at a glance the power of Aristotle's analysis when he identifies the characteristics of epic as extensive form and freedom of imagination. Romance is above all not realistic—that is the imagined world; and it has room, simply, to recount an extended story, by narrative means and without having to select a limited number of critical points in the action in order to pinpoint conflicts and depict crucial choices, as drama

---

[3] Chariton: "What dramatist ever staged such a scene?" (5.8.2); Heliodorus: "Such a *theatron* (dramatic spectacle) did the gods set before the Egyptian brigands' eyes . . . they could not comprehend the scene" (1.1.6–7). For Heliodorus, see J.W.H. Walden, "Stage Terms in Heliodorus's Aethiopica," *Harvard Studies in Classical Philology* 5 (1894), 1–43, still a standard study.

does (that is really the central difference in function between drama and epic). Not all epics will fit the romance formula. Most archaic epic outside the *Iliad* and *Odyssey* appears to have been simply heroic,[4] and a major quality of Hellenistic and late epic was often erudition. The *Iliad* itself is at several points a different animal, notably in not depicting an imagined world (not in the same sense as the *Odyssey*, at least), or offering wish-fulfillment or a number of elements of plot, such as travel and adventure. But a certain connection with romantic epic at least is confirmed by a glance at a Hellenistic poem, the *Argonautica* of Apollonius of Rhodes, the story of Jason and Medea and the quest for the Golden Fleece, on which the shadow of the *Odyssey* lies especially long. It too is a story of love and adventure, on a similar theme; much of the narrative is an account of travels, as in the *Odyssey*, with several well told episodes. Often thought to lack structural point and coherence, in recent decades it has been extensively reassessed, along with other Alexandrian poetry. "Apollonius's epic poem," it has been said, "demonstrates . . . the inclination to shape narrative in the way novelists will eventually do it; it is a poem at the crossroads."[5] The point to be made here, however, concerns not the architecture of the poem, nor its general interpretation, nor indeed the basic story—that was given—but the way Apollonius, reflecting the changed sensibility of his own age, orients it. One of the most striking episodes is the portrait in Book 3 of Medea succumbing to love. She is represented as dominated by love, as her literary ancester Phaedra had been, and as her literary descendant Dido was to be. The issue of her emotional conflict, of the struggle in her heart between loyalty to family and all-powerful passion for her lover, clearly foreshadows the central impulse of the later romances.

The qualities of vision (or "imagination"), generous scale, and sustained description of character and action that are seen in romance found their outlet, then, in earlier periods, in epic. In romance these qualities are found most notably in Chariton and Heliodorus. The most striking difference is in level, in boldness of imagination. Chae-

[4] A *Telegony*—a sequel to the *Odyssey*, carrying the story to the death of Odysseus— would seem to have had a romantic plot.

[5] C. R. Beye, *Epic and Romance in the* Argonautica of Apollonius (Carbondale and Edwardsville, 1982), Preface, xiii; the Bibliographical Essay, 169–75, discusses developments in the study of Apollonius. See also Heiserman, *The Novel before the Novel*, chapter 2, "Resourceless Jason" (11–29).

129

reas is no Odysseus; the struggles of romance heroes, where they rise at all above passivity, are puny by comparison with those of the man who wrestled with Poseidon, Polyphemus, Circe; but this *is* a latter-day world, and latter-day epic—for Everyman. The structure of romance is that of epic; its action and emotional content are often dramatic. This is true of all the romance texts, in one way or another: Longus and Achilles Tatius take much of their intrigues and dénouements from New Comedy, while Chariton, Heliodorus and Xenophon recall Euripides and Sophocles with their melodramatic high points, crises and choices. Inverting this proposition, we may ask what features of drama are propitious to romance; in what ways can the quality of romance emerge in dramatic form? This amounts to considering in a different perspective some ideas that figured in the last chapter, where the features of romance were set against a structural grid of drama, and seen in their functions as problem, conflict, development and conclusion.

Drama operates by representing a progression of climaxes—a circumscribed number of climaxes—in which characters find themselves in conflict with one another, or caught in crucial situations; in either case forced to react, to choose this or that course of action before our eyes, and hence to make their way towards the outcome. The emotion of the action is concentrated by the playwright in these critical moments, not diluted as in epic by episodes or varied, discursive narration. Thus, by way of illustration, our interest in Antigone's situation is focused by Sophocles on the stages of her conflict with Creon, not allowed to dissipate itself on (for instance) her relationship with Haemon. The full story cannot be set out, as it can in narrative forms, but critical moments can; at these points choices, gestures can be made which can carry the quality of romance. The consequence is that where romance exists in a play, it will tend to gravitate towards these crucial conflicts, where the visual medium, the visible crisis itself, preempts the spectator's attention and constitutes the point of discharge for his imagination and emotions. In what ways does this show?

We saw in the previous chapter that two forms of drama, in antiquity, can readily accommodate romance: non-tragic "tragedy," as represented by some (mostly late) plays of Euripides, and New Comedy, especially as represented by the relatively serious Menander. What they have in common in that they occupy the middle ground between the grim events of the most brutal tragedy (*Oedipus Tyran-*

nus, Hippolytus) and rumbustious, hard-edged Old Comedy. We may characterize this middle ground as the province of melodrama, romantic melodrama—without leaning too heavily on the term.[6] Perhaps the best way to observe the typical operation of romance in drama will be to look in a fairly systematic way at appropriate examples of such drama. We shall consider the *Helen* of Euripides and Menander's *The Arbitration (Epitrepontes)*, enough of which survives for us to be able to see the relevant features of its action.[7] In the previous chapter the main stages of a drama were seen as problem, conflict, development, solution. Of these, the "conflict" seemed relevant mainly to full tragedy, where the fatal mistake (*hamartia*) is responsible for a fatal change of condition (*metabolē*). *Hamartia* and disaster are clearly not appropriate to romance, so we may discount the element of conflict in drama of the kind now in question. There remain problem, development, solution: that is, initial situation, stages of the action (incident, intrigue), and conclusion (invariably a happy ending). These will constitute the crises or climaxes in which emotion—and romance, where it exists—are concentrated.

In the *Helen*, the material is patently romantic before the play even gets under way. The glamorous Helen herself is the occasion of the action; she is presented here as not culpable, though still fatally attractive, since it was a phantom Helen who went to Troy, while the real one was taken to Egypt by the gods. In Egypt she can do nothing but wait to be rescued by her husband Menelaus, here shown as rather more of an enduring hero than in the *Iliad*; in fact, as a kind of pale doublet of the wandering Odysseus, separated like him from the wife he loves. All is thus set up for reunion. But clearly this is not going to come about without incident and adventure—that will be the very body of the action. The opening itself represents the dangerous crisis in events when Helen herself is in special danger from the King of Egypt, Theoclymenus, who seeks to make her his wife, just as Menelaus is about to find her again after many years.[8] Clearly,

---

[6] It has often been observed that Euripides' *Ion*, technically a tragedy, in fact has many of the characteristics of New Comedy: the seduction of a girl, the consequent exposure of the child born to her, an intrigue, and the subsequent recognition of the child by means of tokens.

[7] The only more or less fully extant Greek New Comedy, Menander's *Dyscolus*, is less suitable for present purposes; so too are Plautus's plays, in general, inasmuch as the element of slapstick is often emphasized in them.

[8] It is true that he thinks he has already found her—but it is the Trojan phantom Helen who so far has been travelling with him (she disappears at this point in the

here in this situation is the quintessence of romance, remarkably like the novelists' opening gambits. And the action follows readily predictable lines: intrigue, incident, adventure, as the reunited couple plot and effect their escape despite the obstacle offered by Theoclymenus. There is no need to set out the details of this action, except for one element, the intervention of the priestess Theonoe, who is the King's sister. Theonoe's assistance is crucial to the escape: at the critical juncture she chooses, romantically, to connive with Menelaus and Helen, and refrain from betraying them to her brother. For that she is threatened with death by him, when he is undeceived too late; but she is saved, and the reunited couple's escape confirmed, by the appearance of *dei ex machina* in the shape of Castor and Pollux, who impose their blessing on the reunion (thus, yet another romance feature, an intervening deity, appears in the action). The fortunes of Menelaus and Helen resemble strongly, in all essential respects, those of Theagenes and Charicleia; only, the romantic features are concentrated in initial situation and characters, two main items of intrigue (a mock funeral and Theonoe's intervention), and a dénouement assisted by the gods. The plot, which could serve as a major episode of a prose romance (in Xenophon, let us say), serves in the play as the whole action of this truncated romance. Even the atmosphere is romantic, in that hero and heroine find themselves in an exotic land. In *Iphigeneia in Tauris* a similar setting is used; in Plautus's *Rudens*, the emotionally milder climate of the North African shore fulfills the same function of casting a foreign glow over the action; in Menander's *Dyscolus*, the country atmosphere of Pan's shrine adds to the idyllic feel of the situation (which is not spoiled by the ill humor of the bad-tempered Cnemon himself).

In this drama, then, romance is ubiquitous. It manifests itself principally in the succession of high points in the action, from beginning through successive crises to end, by means either of the impulses of the heroes themselves, bent on escape, or of external assistants human and divine, appearing at turning-points to abet the suffering couple whose fate depends on their choice of action. It is these scenes—these choices, these turning-points, rather than the overall direction of the story—that constitute the excitement, the interest, of this piece of *mimēsis* of human behavior. It may be added that there

---

action). The purpose of this is simply to prolong the false situation right up to the point of the romantic recovery of the "truth."

is a characteristically pungent taste to this romance, a somewhat acid scepticism about divine participation in human affairs.[9] A similar acidity is even more evident in other plays by its author. In *Iphigenia in Tauris*, a very similar plot is set against an altogether grimmer background of human sacrifice. In *Ion*, the romantic naiveté of the protagonist is visibly dismantled as the play progresses and Apollo's duplicity becomes more and more evident. In *Alcestis* the central action is the decision of the herione Alcestis to offer herself as the victim of Death in place of her husband Admetus—a supremely romantic abnegation of self, but a gesture which is soured by a conspicuous lack of dignity on the part of the ignoble Admetus; the play is redeemed from an almost "sick" condition only by the near-comic contribution of Hercules, who averts disaster at the last moment by descending drunk to the underworld to bring Alcestis back to life. All these plays are romance à la Euripides—which is to say, not a sunny kind of romance.[10]

In Menander's *Epitrepontes* there is altogether more human warmth in the *mimēsis* of people. If there is also realism in the character portrayal, that is because the romantic outlook is bedded more deeply in a knowledge of the limitations of human nature, and less vulnerable to ideological commitment on the part of the author. Menander takes people as he finds them; he does not preach. The plot is a veritable pattern of this kind of human comedy. Once again, romantic possibilities are inherent in the elements of the initial situation: a seduced and wronged girl, an exposed child, a young and potentially happy match frustrated by circumstance. The girl's partner, Charisius, misled into thinking himself deceived by his young wife, takes up with a hetaera, and this leads at once to a classic romantic situation, the eternal triangle; the whole picture is thrown into relief by paternal anger. Again, quintessentially romantic material. The succeeding in-

[9] Much more could be said about the *Helen*, which is by no means a simple play; see, for instance, Ann Pippin Burnett, *Catastrophe Survived: Euripides' Plays of Mixed Reversal* (Oxford, 1971), 76–100, and Charles Segal, "The Two Worlds of Euripides' *Helen*," *Transactions of the American Philological Association* 102 (1971), 553–614, on the theme of "appearance and reality." The present comments are intended merely to point to the "romantic" material Euripides uses.

[10] *Alcestis*, it should be said, is exceptional in this group of Euripidean plays in being pro-satyric—that is, less serious in content than the group of three tragedies properly so-called which it accompanied; it is also considerably earlier than the other (438 B.C.—in fact, the earliest extant play of Euripides). For discussion of Euripides' "romances" in general see Burnett, *Catastrophic Survived*, including discussion of their relationship to the *Poetics* 1–21.

trigue revolves around the device of recognition; the exposed child is recognized by means of trinkets associated with it. This results in the other kind of happy ending: the rediscovery of happy union by the young couple, and the concomitant satisfaction of the supporting characters, slaves and parents. These are the mechanics of the plot; what sets them in motion, however, is again a crucial choice at a climactic moment. The hetaera Habrotonon reacts generously in a critical situation to intervene in the young couple's affairs, taking upon herself the burden of the situation by pretending to be the mother of the exposed child, and thus precipitating the events which lead to the dénouement; the interaction of Habrotonon with young wife, slave and angry father is played off against a set of misunderstandings to form a typical New Comedy intrigue. This whole movement reposes on a classic romantic figure, in one of her earliest incarnations: the prostitute with a heart of gold.

In essence, this play exhibits the same kind of movement as the adventure romance of Euripides: from an initial situation carefully loaded with enough matter to construct a whole action, through a sequence of climaxes dominated by a romantic gesture, to an emotionally satisfying ending—more satisfying than those of Euripides, in that it depends solely on human behavior. The atmosphere this time is anything but exotic; it is domestic, sentimental, a hymn to togetherness; its tone is the opposite of acid—it is humane, philanthropic.[11] Romance has many faces; this is its Menandrean aspect. Such romance appears in various shades; not only Menander, but other poets of Greek New Comedy assuredly, and Plautus and Terence to our knowledge, offered their own variants of the recipe, and they would range from sentimental to brittle. So do the prose romances; that of Achilles Tatius is the most brittle, and by that token the least romantic. Once again it can be instructive to set them against their like in another genre.

We may suitably pass at this point to the topic of lyric poetry, in the broad, English sense of the term: that is to say, poetry expressing

---

[11] If Menander had been Euripides he would have wallowed in indignation at the contemptible behavior of his *jeune premier* Charisius, who had himself when drunk been the violator of the girl (Pamphile), whom he later married without recognizing her. But being more concerned to observe and paint human behavior than to castigate it (or so it would seem from what we possess of the play), he simply uses the situation for dramatic purposes. The only criticism of Charisius's behavior (in what is extant) comes from Charisius himself (Act IV 878 ff., speeches of Onesimus and Charisius). This is to say that this play is more purely romance than the similar *Ion*.

personal sentiments (and thus embracing other ancient forms, notably elegiac). In a sense this will not take us very far from drama, because all such poetry is itself dramatic in offering a representation of the emotions of a "character," a persona. Here, as with drama, it would be inappropriate to do more than suggest the possibilities that exist in literary expression of this kind for presenting romantic sentiment; for such possibilities are numerous, given that lyric verse is the occasion of individual sentiments unhindered by the needs of a story. We shall, then, simply glance at the kind of matter and treatment that come to mind; the reader will readily fill out the picture.

There is of course one very important difference, for immediate purposes, between lyric and drama. Lyric is static, most commonly, whereas drama, like epic and prose romance, is essentially fluid. We have so far seen the romantic quality inhering in *action*; if we now look for it in lyric, it will necessarily be romance frozen in time. That is not to question the reality of such a manifestation of the romance quality, but its utility for the romance writer will be different from what he could extract from a play of Menander: romantic moments— a thought, an attitude, an expressed ideal—may serve him as navigational points in his progress through the events of a story. To turn to cases, lyric will of course be fertile of love-sentiment. For a concrete example we may look at what is no doubt the most famous poem of the most famous ancient lyric poet; we have already had occasion to allude to Longinus' discussion of it. The following version is deliberately prosaic, to restrict the poem to its thought-content and reduce the linguistic "interference." We should observe that the poem has not been preserved complete—not a single poem of Sappho does survive fully, in fact—, so we simply do not know what point Sappho was moving towards; but that is not the issue here.

> Equal to the gods that man seems to me
> who sits opposite you
> and from near to you hears you speaking sweetly,
> laughing your lovely laugh.
>
> It makes my heart tremble in my breast!
> As soon as I look at you,
> at once I can no longer utter a thing.
>
> No, my tongue is fixed in silence,
> liquid fire at once runs over my skin,

my eyes see nothing,
all I can hear is a blur of sound,

cold sweat runs down me,
my whole body is seized with trembling,
I am paler than grass,
I feel near to death.

But all must be endured, since . . .[12]

One lyric moment, two related thoughts: the divine happiness of the loved one's companion of the moment, and the startling physical effect on the lover. Clearly, such sentiments will be the very lodestar of the love story; and in fact we find comparable sentiments in the romances. Clitophon, in Achilles Tatius's story, when he first sees Leucippe, is seated near her at dinner (and is thus himself her divinely happy companion): "I swear by the gods," he tells his interlocutor, "that I have no idea what I ate—I was like a man eating in a dream"; he has already told us that at first sight of Leucippe, "I was thunderstruck by her beauty, my heart was quivering, I gazed at her at once shameless and embarrassed." And we have already in another context seen Longus taking up exactly this *topos* of the physiological effects of love upon the lover, when both Daphnis and Chloe are overwhelmed by their emotions (although they do not understand what is happening to them).[13] Likewise Chaereas and Callirhoe, and Habrocomes and Anthia, and all the romantic lovers in the world. Orlando is merely playing at love, is Rosalind's charge in an only slightly different context: "There is none of my uncle's marks upon you: he taught me how to know a man in love; in which cage of rushes I am sure you are not prisoner.—What were his marks?— A lean cheek, which you have not; a blue eye and sunken, which you have not; an unquestionable spirit, which you have not; a beard neglected, which you have not." Orlando is no such man; he is too much master of himself; rather point-device in his accoutrements, as loving himself, than seeming the lover of any other. The dramatist, and the novelist, can always use a lyric glimpse of romance.

There is one special case of overlap between prose romance and poetry which is not so much an overlap as an extensive borrowing, not just of isolated moments but of the very matter and themes of

---

[12] 31 Lobel-Page, 2 Bergk and other editions.
[13] See Hunter, *Daphnis and Chloe*, 73–76 for Longus's use of Sappho.

poetic predecessors. That is Longus's adaptation of Alexandrian pastoral. This is not the place to launch into an account of this process, which has been well studied recently.[14] But it should be recalled that the whole topic of love in a pastoral setting is one of the major themes of Theocritus's *Idylls*; a figure called Daphnis occurs in several of them, and seems to be an Alexandrian prototype of such lovers. How far the term "romantic" can properly be applied to pastoral poetry itself is a debatable question; that is allusive, learned verse, whose general atmosphere is that of Watteau rather than Wordsworth. But the theme of love is certainly there. Broadening the topic to Alexandrian erotic poetry in general, we find ourselves in the area of literature in which Rohde saw the roots of romance, which he considered the product of love-elegy and travel-narrative. We know very little directly, however, about this love poetry, although something can be speculatively reconstructed from Latin elegists of the first century B.C.; and we do possess the *Love Stories* of Parthenius, a collection of prose outlines of romantic plots (mostly mythological) intended for use by the Roman elegist Cornelius Gallus. Apart from general assertion on *a priori* grounds, we cannot say much about what Longus (or other romance writers) may have borrowed from such sources. One thing that does seem certain, however, is that Longus took the name of his character Philetas (the old countryman who gives Daphnis and Chloe their first, theoretical lesson in love) from the historical Philetas (or Philitas) of Cos, who lived in the third century B.C. and was one of Theocritus's models. Philetas was thought of in antiquity as the founder of Alexandrian poetry, and along with Callimachus one of its greatest names. This being so, it also seems likely that Longus drew more than a name from Philetas.[15]

The forms discussed so far in this chapter have all contained love-motifs. Love is naturally one of the major ingredients in romance narrative, whether as active sexual passion or as a cosy state of togetherness. In particular, a constant feature of the whole economy of the

[14] See Hunter on Theocritus and Philetas, 73–78; McCulloh's chapter in *Longus* on "Pastoral Infusions"; L. R. Cresci "Il romanzo di Longo Sofista e la tradizione bucolica," *Atene e Roma* 26 (1981), 1–25; B. Effe, "Longos: zur Funktionsgeschichte der Bukolik in der römischen Kaiserzeit," *Hermes* 110 (1982), 65–84.

[15] See Hunter, 76–83 for detailed examination of the question; and see now E. L. Bowie, "Theocritus' Seventh *Idyll*, Philetas and Longus," *Classical Quarterly* 35 (1985), 67–91. The fundamental study on the whole question of romance borrowing from Alexandrian love-poetry remains Rohde, *Gr. Rom.*, Part I.

form is a final happy-ever-after condition that is disturbed by no further adventures. Aristotle's theory of *mythos* conceives of the happy ending, but does not specify in what that happiness is to consist— except in the last-minute avoidance of disaster. Romance has its own formula for the happy ending: where epic and tragedy are built from early myth, in the late Greek world romance constitutes its own myth, in which private love is both problem and solution.

Though love as a motive force is far from new in literature, this form of it is; it is foreshadowed in New Comedy, but more is made of it in romance. In Chariton and Xenophon, however, it is a rather shallow motive, because no attempt is made to show how it operates, except that it is an effect of beauty. If a girl is beautiful, everyone will fall in love with her; it is as simple as that. Now, though the consequences of this *donnée* may be interesting, the *donnée* itself is anything but interesting. It simply leaves us helpless, and if anything a little exasperated, even resentful: where do we go from there? Are we to be allowed no hold on love all? Not all the romances are as simplistic as that, however, as we have seen in the cases of Longus and Achilles Tatius. Both of their interpretations of the nature of love—as natural force, as psychological movement—have precedent in classical Greece, in the sophistic movement and its surroundings and aftermath.

One of the earliest theories about the place of "love" in the universe is that offered by Empedocles, for whom "Love" and "Strife" are the two fundamental cosmic forces—the tendencies for things to come together or to fall apart. This is philosophical analysis of the material world rather than an observation about human beings; but the concept of Eros as an objective force in the operation of the cosmos attracts creators of literature right through to the period when, in their different ways, Longus, Chariton and Xenophon still see human beings as the "victims" of this external power. Somewhat later Gorgias, possibly a pupil of Empedocles, and himself living in the full flood of the Sophistic movement, may refer to this concept in attributing the misbehavior of Helen of Troy to the irresistible power of love.[16] But the two major sources for later antiquity were Euripides

---

[16] Gorgias, *Encomium on Helen*; at Chapter 3, n. 19 above the reference is to another possible cause of her desertion of her husband: Paris persuaded her, by the power of speech, *logos*. Gorgias offers two further reasons: the gods willed her to act thus, or she was forced to do so; the whole encomium is a sustained paradox on the theme "Helen was innocent."

and Plato. "Women in love" were notoriously a favorite theme of Euripides; he is chastised for it in *Frogs*,[17] particularly for his portrait of Phaedra in *Hippolytus*. Apart from the mimetic representation of Phaedra (and of Hippolytus) there is clearly also a theoretical position on the nature of *erōs* in Euripides's mind, and it is built into his play in the shape of Aphrodite in the prologue: erotic passion is an irresistible power in life, its demands are absolute. A highly promising position on which to build a narrative of love; it is built into minor figures in romance, as we have seen. But it is hardly surprising that it never forms the major theme since the whole point of it—as the basis of *mythos*—is that such love will meet resistance (as Phaedra initially resists it, and Hippolytus rejects it) and end in disaster. In the hands of a Heliodorus, however, a figure such as Arsace can suggest a whole new dimension for love-narrative, and realistic treatment will end up with the female figures of the nineteenth-century French novel. But realism is precisely what is not present in the psychology of romance heroines. Here, *erōs* is for practical purposes an external force: human beings can do nothing but submit (or not submit) to it; they can in no way control, or analyze, or sublimate such passion, and their attempts to do so are what produces the dramatic spectacle.

To turn to the other and more strictly theoretical (if fanciful) approach, the idea that love is an integral part of every human being's make-up, and that it looms large in the behavior of all of us, is delightfully symbolized in Aristophanes' speech in Plato's *Symposium*. The central thought in this fantasy is that the human soul, originally complete, has been split into two complementary halves, and spends its time seeking its own reintegration. Thus each of us is eternally in search of his or her "other half," and to be half of a couple is the fundamental situation of any individual. The point here is very close to what seems a fundamental position of romance, namely that each individual is separated, in the world, from what is needed for his completeness, his ideal condition; and the force which makes for reunion is love. Once more, love is an external force, abroad in the world at large. This time it is not a destructive force, but on the contrary a constructive, reconciling movement, present in each one of us inevitably, not merely at the will of those unseen powers who descend fortuitously on chosen victims. The idea is however based on a conception of the "ideal state of things" more coherent than can be

[17] 1040ff.

posited for any harmony dependent on the caprice of the *tychē* of romance, who unites partners at a street corner, or a religious festival—at a cocktail-party, as it might be in an Anthony Powell novel, across a crowded room. Of the extant romance texts, only *Daphnis & Chloe* suggests such coherent philosophical and imaginative power; Plato would recognize the Eros of Longus. Elsewhere in the *Symposium*, in Socrates' speech, there is recognition above all of the elevating, purifying power of love; but it is hardly the love of the romances.

Certainly little sense of elevation emerges from the romance texts. The romance ethos is thoroughly bourgeois; it is not in the least intellectual. As we have seen, it is probably this absence of intellectual ambition, more than anything else, that is responsible for the disregard of romance shown by contemporary critics. For all that, some substantial pieces of theory about the psychology of love are to be found in romance texts. Besides the passages cited from *Daphnis & Chloe*, the first part of *Leucippe and Clitophon* is studded with disquisitions on the nature of Eros, the psychology of love.[18] And in one of the fragments occurs an interesting analysis of what love is: in *Metiochus and Parthenope* it is described as "a movement of the mind caused by beauty and strengthened by familiarity." It is not clear from the context in what spirit this rationalistic remark is made. Possibly it is a disparaging remark, and Metiochus is rejecting the claims of love—as Xenophon's hero Habrocomes at first disdains Eros (he is soundly punished for his arrogance). Or possibly Metiochus is for some reason misrepresenting his true feeling of love for Parthenope, who is also present at the discussion; she apparently bridles at his remarks, and accepts a conventional view of Eros as a young boy with wings and a bow. Whatever the purpose of the remark, it does suggest that the author could rise to a theory of love; and it is not impossible that the author of this story is none other than Chariton.[19]

Undoubtedly, romance authors had read their Euripides and Plato, and at times it shows; but only in the margins. These texts are certainly not written to illustrate theories of love; they are written to

---

[18] 1.9–1.10 (how to seduce a girl), 17–18 (love in the animal, vegetable and mineral world), 2.4, 2.8, 2.35–38 (a whole syncrisis on the topic of "girls—or boys?," a question treated extensively in the probably contemporary ps.-Lucian *Amores*).

[19] See Chapter 3, n. 1. The story is historically-based, like Chariton's; it is set at the court of Polycrates, the tyrant of Samos in the 6th century B.C.; and the discussion is being led by the philosopher Anaximenes. The historical model in this case is Herodotus (in *Chaereas and Callirhoe* it is principally Thucydides). There are significant linguistic similarities between this text and Chariton's romance.

represent people acting or suffering as willed by Eros, in that form of Eros which finds sympathy with a sentimental audience.

Another Hellenistic form that clearly offers an analogy to prose romance is the kind of travel-romance that constituted the other pillar of Rohde's literary-historical construction.[20] In *Reisefabulistik* we may justifiably see another form that merits, as does the *Odyssey*, the unqualified appellation of romance. Romance, that is, without a love-motif; but it is salutary to recall that no single element, including love, is indispensable to the romance genre. Remains exist of two writers, Euhemerus and Iambulus, who both described island utopias in the Indian Ocean which no doubt reflected the travels of Alexander the Great, and possibly also the Atlantis conceived by Plato. They described the way of life of ideal communities, incorporating some of the social theory of the Hellenistic world (such as communistic features in society). Such works are plainly similar to some romances; they find a specific echo in Heliodorus, the action of whose story terminates in the legendary ideal community of Ethiopia. More generally, in a sense any fictitious story is a Utopia, in that it is a vision of society (even though all may not be well in that society). It has been argued in this study that projection of a vision is the most important single element in romance, the essence of the whole genre. That view does not of course contribute anything to the literary-historical question of why such visions should be extensively projected at one time more readily than at another. What is pertinent here is that such visions do exist throughout Greek literature, from Phaeacia through Cloudcuckooland and Plato's Republic to these Hellenistic never-never lands.

In moving to *Reisefabulistik* we have shifted to prose form, and shifted also to a form akin to historiography, or at least fanciful historiography. The similarities between Hellenistic historiography and biography and romance have already been discussed, and do not need repeating here. It is evident that not only do we see such similarities, early novelists saw them too, and used them to launch the genre; we have clearly now renewed contact with one of the main beams of the romance structure. And this will close the list of the major analogues of romance to be found in antecedent literature; we may move on to consider those forms that were contemporary with the new genre, in the early Empire.[21]

[20] *Gr. Rom.*, Part II.

[21] Several authors and topics treated in the following pages are discussed in my

The most natural thing is to continue with historiography, imperial historiography. If "degenerate" Hellenistic historiography—the term is Schwartz's[22]—was the seedbed for fictional narrative, what was the condition of historical writing at a slightly later period, in the early and middle Roman Empire? Briefly, there is not as much difference as there should have been between the historiographer and the less specifically committed "man of letters"—as we have already seen Lucian observe. Many of the extant historiographers display a tendency to treat their work as literary divertissement as much as inquiry into historical truth. One cannot, in fact, classify writers very precisely in this period, for the most part; a Plutarch or a Philostratus is apt to write on anything under the sun, and the age displays something like the tendency of some later periods of European literature to spawn all-rounders, or at least writers of rather extended range. The most noteworthy historians, for present purposes, are Arrian, whose principal but by no means only work is his *Anabasis* of Alexander the Great, and Dio Cassius and Herodian, who offer accounts of Roman history.

Two features bring this historiography into some proximity with romance: its biographical nature, and its penchant for sensationalism and rhetorical manner (a feature we have already seen in Hellenistic historiography). In this approach, world events are seen in their aspect as personal history; what seems important is what happens to this or that individual, and not for instance the grand historical design that Herodotus sees in the confrontation of East and West, or the social forces that Thucydides, in his account of the revolution at Corcyra or the Melian Dialogue, discerns in operation. That of course is substantially what romance is about: life is what happens to people. It may seem an attractive position; it is certainly a romantic one.

But it should not be supposed that there is no sober history. Arrian's account of Alexander and his adventure, written about the middle of the second century, is sober, and reliable for the most part;[23]

Courants littéraires grecs; general reference may be made here to that work, which will not be mentioned except for special points.

[22] E. Schwartz, *Fünf Vorträge über den griechischen Roman* (Berlin, 1896 [1943]): "Die den Roman erzeugende Zersetzung der historiographischen Kunstform" (156); this has been one of the seminal works, or rather one of the seminal ideas, in literary-historical scholarship on romance.

[23] For Arrian see Philip A. Stadter, *Arrian of Nicomedia* (Chapel Hill, N.C., 1980); and now the excellent study by P. Vidal-Naquet, "Flavius Arrien entre deux mondes," in

by far our best and most extensive source for Alexander. Its relevance to romance is rather different from that of Dio Cassius and Herodian. First, the adventure itself was in all conscience romantic enough, or could seem so to an age inclined in that direction; but the work is in fact a good example of historiography that had not degenerated, and is in that respect notably different from another account of its hero, the *Alexander Romance*, which thus forms a kind of companion-piece to Arrian's. The *Alexander Romance* attaches incredible adventures of all kinds to the life of the Macedonian conqueror. It was destined to have a very long history, which stretched into the Middle Ages, in various European and Oriental languages and widely varying versions. Alexander, like Arthur, was a figure to whom legend attached itself readily. The oldest extant version of this work dates from shortly after the period of the romances, although the putative original must have been produced just after Alexander's death; it exists in several forms, all highly fanciful. The *Alexander Romance* lies in the margin, or the hinterland, of romance in the sense adopted in the present book, although it too is distinctly the projection of a vision, of a different kind; it belongs with the *Cyropaedia* of Xenophon of Athens, the Greek translation of the Egyptian *Dream of Nectanebus*, and the *Ninus*-fragment, in the dim prehistory of narrative fiction. It offers, in contrast with Arrian's work, a paradigm of how far history could degenerate. The second interesting feature of Arrian's topic is that it is itself archaizing, and is thus typical of almost all of the literary production of the age. Greek writers of the romance age are much more interested in earlier Greece than in the contemporary world, or in Rome in general. It is in the light of this that the historicizing tendency of romance should be seen.

Much of the historiography of the period, then, tends to the condition of romance by virtue of its very approach.[24] This tendency is strongly reinforced, in Dio Cassius and Herodian in particular, by the way in which it is written. Dio's models are Thucydides and Demosthenes; he is far from practicing the critical austerity of the former, but only too ready to follow the latter in the deliberate creation of an emotional climate, even if he has to embellish or actually distort the

Arrien: Histoire d'Alexandre, trans. (of Arrian's *Anabasis*) Pierre Savinel (Paris, 1984), 309–94.

[24] That is not to say that there are no other serious historians; Appian is one who (like, for instance, Tacitus in Latin) has no point of contact with romance.

historical facts in order to do so.[25] He is ever ready to take advantage of a battle scene (Pharsalia, Cremona), a political crisis (Sulla's proscriptions), or some natural phenomenon, to deploy all the stock procedures of the rhetorician—speech, ecphrasis, dramatic narration, antithetical comparison, and the rest. This is sensational history, written for effect as much as for more intellectual purpose. His manner is for all the world that of a Chariton magnifying the pathos of Callirhoe's lot, or an Achilles Tatius piling detail on striking detail in describing the city of Alexandria, or in elaborating the drama of the wicked Thersander's assaults on Leucippe.

An example will make the point. The reader may like to guess which of the following two passages is history, which romance.

1. At about noon the sun was utterly extinguished; we saw one another as by moonlight. Lightning's fire danced through the air, thunder bellowed from the skies, the air was alive with the sounds of moaning, and the waves in civil war answered them from below. Somewhere between the sky and the sea the winds were having a cat fight, spitting and snarling; a resonance as of muted horns echoed in the air. The mast ropes flailed about, screaming through the air and whipping against the sail. As the ship's timbers cracked and shivered, we were afraid that the nails would tear loose one by one, and the hull would soon be wide open. Wicker shields had been set up on all sides of the ship, for the storm water was flooding over; we crawled under their shelter as if into a cave and waited there, abandoning ourselves to fortune and giving up all hope.

Three-decker waves rose up on all sides—from the bow, from the stern—and crashed into each other. The ship by turns was either elevated to the very apex of a swelling sea-dome or sliding down sudden chutes between the waves, which seemed at one moment like mountains, then like canyons. But the waves that struck us amidships from either side were even more frightening. The sea came onto the ship, washed through the wicker shields, and covered the whole deck. The billows rose high and seemed to touch the very clouds. At a distance from the ship they seemed the size of mountains, but watching them advance you were sure the ship would be swallowed up. Wind and waves were at war. We could

[25] See F. Millar, *A Study of Cassius Dio* (Oxford, 1964), 43. I here cite the historian's name in its less accurate but more familiar form.

not stay in any one place, so violently did the deck quake and heave beneath us.

It was a pandemonium of noise: roaring waves, blustering wind, the shrill shouts of women, the hoarser cries of men, the sharp commands of sailors, an utter welter of various wailings.

2. There had been many thunderstorms and portentous winds, but no one would ever have expected so many evils to result from them. First there came, on a sudden, a great bellowing roar, and this was followed by a tremendous quaking. The whole earth was upheaved, and buildings leaped into the air; some were carried aloft only to collapse and be broken in pieces, while others were tossed this way and that as if by the surge of the sea, and overturned, and the wreckage spread out over a great extent even of the open country. The crash of grinding and breaking timbers together with tiles and stones was most frightful; and an inconceivable amount of dust arose, so that it was impossible for one to see anything or to speak or hear a word. As for the people, many even who were outside the houses were hurt, being snatched up and tossed violently about and then dashed to the earth as if falling from a cliff; some were maimed and others were killed. Even trees in some cases leaped into the air, roots and all. The number of those who were trapped in the houses and perished was past finding out; for multitudes were killed by the very force of the falling débris, and great numbers were suffocated in the ruins. Those who lay with a part of their body buried under the stones or timbers suffered terribly, being able neither to live any longer nor to find an immediate death.

The first passage is from Achilles Tatius, the second from Dio Cassius.[26] Without some accidental features it would be difficult to tell, from translations at least.

Even closer to romance is biography. Two examples will serve, of major writers who illustrate well what was evidently a popular trend (the biographical activities of Arrian have already been mentioned). They are Plutarch and Philostratus, one active at the beginning, the other towards the end, of this literary period: the conception of biography held by both was particularly "romantic," though in different senses.[27] We have already had occasion to touch on Plutarch ear-

[26] Achilles Tatius 3.2.2; Dio Cassius 68.24, trans. E. Cary (Loeb).
[27] For Plutarch, see A. W. Gomme, *A Commentary on Thucydides*, vol. 1 (Oxford,

lier, when considering elements of theory available about the nature of prose narrative. With Plutarch it is a matter of practice more than of theory, but he does theorize explicitly about what interests him.

> I am writing biography, not history, and the truth is that the most brilliant exploits often tell us nothing of the virtues or vices of the men who performed them, while on the other hand a chance remark or a joke may reveal far more of a man's character than the mere feat of winning battles in which thousands fall, or of marshalling great armies, or laying siege to cities. When a portrait painter sets out to create a likeness, he relies above all upon the face and the expression of the eyes and pays less attention to the other parts of the body; in the same way it is my task to dwell upon those actions which illuminate the workings of the soul, and by this means to create a portrait of each man's life. I leave the story of his greatest struggles and achievements to be told by others.[28]

Hence the unwearying string of anecdotes so familiar to his readers: Caesar reflecting on the politics of an Alpine village ("I would rather be first man here than second man in Rome"), Alexander making the difference between himself and Parmenio ("I would stop here, sir, if I were you"—"And so would I, Parmenio, if I were you"). Of course his value to the historian is immense, because of his erudition, his sheer industry; and he can be singularly irritating for those who are forced to use him for historical purposes. But that is not to the point here. What is more relevant is his endless interest in human beings (as well as countless other topics), and particularly in those who moved the world; and with that, his incorrigible preference for virtue in human beings. His *Lives* are so presented as to offer models to imitate; while he does not indiscriminately whitewash, he is in his element when he can demonstrate that virtue can triumph. If this is characteristic of him, this persistent optimism is also characteristic of romance; it is one of the marks of a complex age.

There is another respect in which Plutarch is on occasion within sight of romance. Romantic novelettes are to be found among his *Moralia* (*Amatorius, On Socrates' Divine Sign*). There is also much dramatic narrative (or romanesque history) in the *Lives* themselves;

1945), 54–84; D. A. Russell, *Plutarch* (London, 1972); A. Wardman, *Plutarch's Lives* (London, 1974).

[28] *Life of Alexander* 1, trans. I. Scott-Kilvert in *Plutarch: The Age of Alexander* (Harmondsworth, 1973) (Penguin), 252.

Shakespeare recognized vivid drama when he saw it in the life of Caesar, and took over parts of Plutarch's account little altered. For all that, however, and omnivorous as he is, Plutarch—as we have seen—does not so much as mention romance. That, and the similar silence of people like him in the second century, must remind us that contacts we may think we discern between narrative fiction and other more "official" forms of literature remain for the most part distant and indirect, and matter for speculation. There is after all a major difference between his character-sketching (*ēthopoiia*) and the representations of human beings in romance: Plutarch draws from life. Even if he sometimes omits the warts, his figures are real people, and real things happened to them. Callirhoe, whose story he may very well have read, is a figment of wishful thinking.

Philostratus is a very different case; he is himself a writer of "romance," nominally biographical, but in practice, almost certainly, very largely fictitious.[29] His *Life of Apollonius of Tyana* figures among the "fringe" romance texts, and deserves at this point more extended comment than can be accorded to other non-romance texts of the period. For if any one literary work represents this age, it is this one; it is situated, so to speak, in the midst of romance, biography, and the wider rhetorical and literary currents of the time. Here we do see, clearly, the effect that romance-writing had on an author of a different kind—ironically, the very writer (probably) who is so contemptuous of Chariton. Apollonius was undoubtedly a real person, who lived in the first century A.D. Philostratus, in writing his life over a century after his death,[30] was doing so at the request of Julia Domna, the cultured wife of Septimius Severus; she wished to see this strange figure elevated to the level of pagan saint, and the mixture in him of neo-Pythagorean philosophy and sun-worshiper (this element is added in Philostratus as a compliment to Julia Domna, whose father was a priest of the cult) does seem to make of him a rival of Jesus Christ.[31] What sort of man Apollonius really was is not clear at all: no

[29] See E. L. Bowie, "Apollonius of Tyana: Tradition and Reality," in H. Temporini and W. Haase, eds., *Aufstieg und Niedergang der römischen Welt* II.16.2 (Berlin, 1978), 1652–99. There is a translation (with some abridgment) by C. P. Jones, *Philostratus: Life of Apollonius* (Harmondsworth, 1970) (Penguin), with a useful introduction by G. W. Bowersock. Most recently, Graham Anderson, *Philostratus*, chapters 7–12.

[30] Apollonius was born in the first years of the Christian era and lived to over ninety; the *Life* seems to have been written about 217 or 218.

[31] It has been thought that the resemblance is not fortuitous, but is a result of a

doubt a moralizing philosopher, like his near-contemporary Dio Chrysostom, but he is presented also as a magician, who can cure the sick, speak all languages, effect miraculous escapes from captivity, and predict the future. His life, according to this account of it, was devoted to wisdom and to good and holy works, not only in the Greek and Roman Mediterranean but farther afield, in India and Ethiopia; his wanderings thus recall those of Habrocomes or Theagenes, while his doings, albeit quite different in kind, bring to mind the picturesque adventures of Apuleius's Lucius—with this difference, however, that they include no erotic element of any sort.

This, then, is romantic, if not quite romance in the sense that most concerns this study. The form of fictitious narrative in prose has made much progress since Chariton, more than a hundred years earlier. That Apollonius lived is not in doubt, but almost everything else is: his travels to Ethiopia, for example (which is probably an exotic place for such a hero to visit rather than a place that this hero did visit) his good works, his encounters with Nero and Domitian, his death. The sources of the book are themselves uncertain; Philostratus tells us that he has used the biographical notes of a certain Damis, a disciple of Apollonius, but this has often been questioned. This work falls, rather, into the category of *Reisefabulistik*. The *Life of Apollonius* is clearly reflected in Heliodorus's *Ethiopica*, in which the holy man Calasiris, himself an Egyptian, recalls Philostratus's hero in many ways. Religiosity is one of the marks of the age, and there is nothing exceptional in finding such an atmosphere in both biography and romance. It is found even in the avowed historians, for Dio Cassius (to take only one case) believed in a "divine spirit," in a oracles, in dreams. In both Philostratus's *Life of Apollonius* and Heliodorus's romance such religiosity is a principal feature of the atmosphere of the whole text.[32]

We may turn now to other prose forms, no longer even ostensibly informative in nature: the considerable strictly rhetorical activities of the professed sophists of the period, such as Aelius Aristides, and

---

deliberate attempt so to present him; as in the early 4th century Hierocles, in his *True Gospel*, did so present Apollonius.

[32] Mention has been made (Chapter 2, at n. 32) of the suggestion that this religious atmosphere is in fact only "mental furniture," not real conviction on the part of Heliodorus himself. If this is so, it does not disprove the point made here, but reinforces it: if a novelist goes to the trouble of filling his text with such furniture, that suggests that it would be welcomed by his readers. But it is hardly necessary to demonstrate that this is a religious age (whatever Heliodorus's date).

the extension of these activities by Lucian and others. A good deal has been made earlier in this book of the rhetorical practice and theory whose domination, beginning in the fourth century B.C., continued and expanded, until by the second century A.D. it was a major feature of the cultural activity of the period. It has been suggested that educational programs fostered the practice and appreciation of literature, and we have seen some evidence at least of interest in prose as a medium for literature. It is time now to build on this basis by indicating what kind of literature such theory produced at the time when romance writes were themselves being conditioned by it.

For the formally rhetorical writing, again two specimens will be adduced; in both, distant connections with romance will be seen. They are Dio Chrysostom, the almost exact contemporary of Plutarch, and Aelius Aristides, born circa A.D. 117, about the time of Dio's death, and himself the almost exact contemporary of Lucian.[33] Much of Dio's extensive corpus consists of formal orations in traditional "symbouleutic" (that is, deliberative or legislative) form, relating to real situations in the provincial politics of his time, especially in his native Bithynia. Another large part of his work consists of philosophical discourses—on Fortune, Covetousness and the like. Some topics are drawn from his personal life (Dio was exiled for a time); others, drawn from literature and legend (such as Homer and the capture of Troy—or rather the idea that Troy was *not* captured), give a clear glimpse of the attention evidently given to literature and literary criticism.

Here, then, is a good example of what standard rhetorical training did typically produce. Time after time, the orator Dio presents his material in exactly the manner and kind of style we find in abundance in the romances. We have already seen some examples of this, and may now glance at some more. When Mithridates and Dionysius in Chariton, or Thersander and the priest of Artemis at the end of Achilles Tatius's story, launch into their formal speeches in court, in prosecution or defense, they are doing what a Dio had been trained to do in a formal *logos dikanikos* (forensic oration) and they follow closely the precepts of the genre. The *logos dikanikos* figures in Char-

---

[33] For Dio, see esp. C. P. Jones, *The Roman World of Dio Chrysostom* (Cambridge, Mass. and London, 1978); J. P. Moles, "The Career and Conversion of Dio Chrysostom," *Journal of Hellenic Studies* 98 (1978), 79–100; and the voluminous study of P. Desideri, *Dione di Prusa: un intellettuale greco nell' impero romano* (Messina and Florence, 1978).

iton in particularly pathetic fashion when Chaereas, invited to defend himself before the magistrates against the accusation that he has
murdered Callirhoe, actually accuses himself of that act (1.5.4–5):

> And something strange happened, that had never happened before
> in a trial: after the speech for the prosecution, the murderer, when
> his time was allotted him, instead of defending himself, launched
> into an even more bitter self-condemnation and took the lead in
> finding himself guilty. He used none of the arguments he could rea-
> sonably have used in his defense—that he was a victim of malicious
> slander, that he was moved by jealousy, that his action was invol-
> untary; instead, he begged them all: "Stone me to death in public; I
> have robbed our community of its crowning glory! It would be char-
> itable to hand me over to the executioner; that would have been my
> proper punishment if it had been merely Hermocrates' servant-girl I
> had killed; try to find some unspeakable way to punish me. I have
> done something worse than any temple-robber or parricide. Do not
> give me burial; do not pollute the earth—plunge my criminal body
> to the bottom of the sea!"

Earlier in the movement of the book, two men take up different positions in their advice to their fellows, rivals of Chaereas, on how to
separate the loving and now married couple (1.2.2–6). Their speeches
are *logoi symbouleutikoi, suasoriae*—brief, certainly, but in essence exactly what Dio offers in advising the citizens of Tarsus or Rhodes to
do this or that. Later in the same book the pirates debate what to do
with the resuscitated heroine (1.10)—again, deliberative speeches.

All of the romances contain such situations and such passages.
Even in the least obviously dramatic of them, *Daphnis and Chloe*,
Daphnis has to defend himself formally against a formal accusation
by the Methymnaeans, before the herdsman Philetas as judge, of
having negligently lost them their ship (2.15–16):

> The Methymneans put the case for the prosecution first, putting it
> in clear and concise terms, since they had a cowherd for a judge "We
> came to these fields wanting to go hunting. We left the boat tied to
> the shore with a green willow shoot while we used our dogs to look
> for game. Meanwhile, this man's goats came down to the sea, ate
> the shoots, and let the boat loose. You saw the boat carried away on
> the sea; but have you any idea how many valuables it contains?
> What good clothes we've lost, what fine equipment for the dogs,

how much silver! Anyone who had all that could buy up these fields. In return for our losses, we demand to take this man with us. He must be a terrible goatherd, since he puts his goats to graze on the sea like a sailor!" This was the Methymneans' case for the prosecution. Daphnis was in a bad way because of his beating. But when he saw Chloe there, he rose above everything and spoke in this way "I am a goatherd and a good one. Not one of the villagers has ever held me responsible because a goat of mine has been feeding on anyone's garden or has broken down a young vine. But these men are bad hunters and have dogs that are badly trained, which run all over the place, barking noisily. These dogs were like wolves chasing the goats down from the hills and plains to the sea. They say the goats ate up the willow shoot. Yes, they did; but in the sand they didn't have any grass, wild strawberry or thyme to eat. They say the boat's been lost because of the wind and the sea. Well, that's the work of the weather, not my goats. They say it contained clothing and silver. But what man with any sense will believe that a boat holding so much stuff had a willow shoot for its mooring cable?"

Thus, even before we turn to the much broader category of epideictic rhetoric, there is much in the romance texts that is taken directly from rhetorical exercises. When we turn to epideictic, which in effect is undefined in range, Dio offers one speech which comes so close to the atmosphere of romance that we should pick up here an earlier brief mention of it: the Seventh Oration, the "Euboean," which turns into the *novella* sometimes called *The Hunters of Euboea*. In it Dio has occasion to tell his audience how he once found himself cast on a desolate shore in Euboea. Found and cared for by the country people who managed to scrape a living from the land, he eventually returns to civilization, but not before he has learned a salutary lesson in how to live truly well: not, that is, by indulging all one's desires, but on the contrary by limiting them, in true Stoic fashion, to the barest necessities, which are available to even the humblest beings. Freed from desire for material wealth, the hunters of Euboea had in consequence no quarrels among themselves, no envy, no hostility to others; satisfied with what a parsimonious Nature provided, they were an example, which Dio now takes it upon himself to transmit, of human nature at its best. The spirit of *Daphnis and Chloe* is at once recognizable, of course: the eternal "rustic dream"—and there is even a sketch of a rustic love affair, which brings the piece closer yet to Longus. What is just as interesting, however, is the extensive treatment Dio sees fit to accord to these themes. There is no real plot, it should be said, so the text cannot properly be set alongside the romances. But Dio feels himself at liberty to develop incidents into a lengthy narrative episode which might well figure in a romance—just as Xenophon develops the picture of the fisherman who lives in contentment with the mummified body of his beloved wife.

With Aristides the case is quite different: it is not the form but the content of his work—of some of it, that is—that comes into proximity with romance. But the contact is altogether more substantial, and for once we are left with the feeling, even if it is only a guess, that a writer working in the accredited tradition might have had, by temperament, at least some degree of sympathy with the romance writers. Those familiar with Aristides' principal work may find this a rather surprising remark, for if anyone is the high priest and classic executant of formal rhetoric, it is Aristides. He is stricter than Dio Chrysostom in his adherence to the standard formulae for rhetorical composition, and much less ready to admit into his speeches miscellaneous matter from the life of the period. At first sight, therefore, he is at the other end of the literary scale from, say, his near-contemporary Achilles Tatius. That is true enough, for that part of his work which won him the considerable reputation that lived into the Byzantine age. But Aristides was a two-sided literary personality, and in some respects his formal art is the less interesting part of his *oeuvre*. We have already seen that he was capable of having ideas of his own, on the matter of the nature of prose; he also had a distinctive personality and interests. It is these that particularly merit attention at this point.

As with Dio, his more formal work may here be treated more cursorily.[34] His favorite medium was the epideictic speech in praise of a city (the *Panathenaic Oration*, the celebrated speech *To Rome*), or an individual (a funeral speech, for instance) or a god (*Sarapis*—the occasion of his remarks on the use and function of prose—or *Hercules*). These are in due economiastic form; to them may be added a group of orations that purport to offer political advice but in fact differ little from the first group. One group, the *Hymns* in praise of gods, pursue

[34] The major study on Aristides is still A. Boulanger, *Aelius Aristide et la sophistique dans la province d'Asie au IIe siècle de notre ère* (Paris, 1923). For a thorough detailed analysis of a *meletē* (a speech on a topic drawn from Greek history), see L. Pernot, *Les discours siciliens d'Aelius Aristide* (New York, 1981).

quite strictly a formal plan, such as is set out in the manual of Menander Rhetor,[35] and their expression not infrequently rises to a certain height of dignity; evidently Aristides took trouble over them.
What is interesting about them is their content, of which the main
element is the enumeration of the good deeds and the virtues of the
god in question—that is to say, an "aretalogy." It includes as a standard feature an account of the god's essential nature (*physis*), lineage
(*genos*) and power (*dynamis*), as illustrated by his achievements; this
last section will contain at least a reference to, and perhaps a development of, the myths concerning the deity, especially those that
demonstrate his *philanthrōpia* and *pronoia*, his loving forethought for
mankind—Zeus, for instance, established the rule of law on earth,
and sent Honor and Justice among men for their preservation. Other
elements may appear as well: praise of places associated with the
god, and accounts of dreams inspired by him.

There is already, even in these formal compositions, an evident
point of contact with romance, in which gods do regularly manifest
their goodwill to men and their prowess. In the earliest stage of the
systematic analysis of the religious content of the romances, Reitzenstein saw at their heart just such an "aretalogy" as appears in these
Hymns;[36] and his analysis, as we shall see in due course,[37] has been
pursued farther subsequently. In this view, the addition of human
personality to the hymns, the free invention of their adventures, and
the literary elaboration of the whole would constitute the romance
genre as we have it. But in fact there is no room for human activity
in these hymns, or in any of the rhetorical formulae for literary composition; they are merely recipes setting out how to influence people
or how to praise them. This is the major shortcoming of the whole
rhetorical tradition: it simply cannot accommodate the representation
of human activity—which happens to be Aristotle's definition of the
function of creative literature. Rhetoric is not creative literature; nor
is rhetorical theory an adequate basis for literary analysis.

But we have already seen rhetorical theory leaking on all sides. In
the case of the rhetorician Aristides we see it actually overflowing.
The remaining element of his writings, not so far mentioned, presents a veritable cascade of extremely bizarre personality, as exotic as

[35] See Chapter 4, n. 19.
[36] R. Reitzenstein, *Hellenistische Wundererzählungen* (Stuttgart, 1963 [Leipzig, 1906]),
94–99.
[37] See Chapter 7.

anything that ever came from the pen of Euripides, or Tennessee Williams for that matter. That element is the group of six *Sacred Tales*; the personality is that of Aristides himself. The *Sacred Tales*[38]—translated perhaps better, but more cumbrously, as "Account of Religious Experience"—are an intermittent diary kept by the author of a period of some sixteen years in his life, during which he was under the care of Asclepius himself, in a way very common in antiquity and familiar to those who have visited Epidaurus or Pergamum: by the method of incubation, the god appearing to the patient in dreams. It would take a lot of space to set out Aristides' illnesses in detail; let us simply say that he was evidently a consummate hypochondriac whose basic complaint appears to have been asthma, often categorized as a psychosomatic ailment.[39] What we read in the *Tales* is a description of the god's interventions in the author's life, not merely in his medical regimen but in his everyday activities as well. Very often the cure seems more likely than the illness to kill the patient: plunging in midwinter into water on which the ice had first to be broken, horse-riding when Aristides was hardly able to move—a frightening medical obstacle course whose very rigor seems only to fire his religious enthusiasm the more. Other dreams recount vicarious suffering on the author's behalf, to the point where on two occasions other people actually die in his place, without the slightest expression of regret from him. Elsewhere nature itself is in sympathy with Aristides, whose prayers bring to an end an earthquake in Smyrna. Yet again, and this is a recurrent theme, Asclepius has nothing better to occupy him, it would appear, than acting as tutor, literary agent, and even impresario for the author in his literary activities, telling him what to write and when to perform, and making sure that when he did perform he had a packed house while his rival ("a piddling little Egyptian"), deserted by the crowd, slunk away with his tail between his legs. These examples will be enough to demonstrate the nature of the "book," which is a record—written, it should be said, in extremely

---

[38] See esp. C. A. Behr, *Aelius Aristides and the Sacred Tales* (Amsterdam, 1968) (translation and study) and also *id.*, *P. Aelius Aristides, The Complete Works*, vol. II (Leiden, 1981), 318–52 and 435–46 (translation and notes). For discussions of the *Sacred Tales* and their place in the religious activities of the period, see A. J. Festugière, *Personal Religion among the Greeks* (Berkeley, 1954), 85–104 (his translation, with introduction and notes, appeared posthumously in *Aelius Aristide, Discours Sacrés: rêve, religion, médecine au IIe siècle après J.-C.* [Paris, 1986]); and E. R. Dodds, *Pagan and Christian in an Age of Anxiety* (Cambridge, 1965), 39–45.

[39] The dreams are analyzed in G. Michenaud and J. Dierkens, *Les rêves dans les "Discours Sacrés" d'Aelius Aristide: essai d'analyse psychologique* (Brussels, 1972).

lively manner—of a hair-raising egocentricity hardly matched by any merely fictitious invalid. Aristides, inexpressibly proud of Asclepius' attentions, says explicitly that his case beggars description: "it goes beyond miracles." If we are looking for personality in the sophistic literature of the period, there is more than enough of it in this extraordinary work.

Technically, the *Sacred Tales* are very different from the rest of Aristides' work; they are totally devoid of form, and are a long way from fitting into any formal rhetorical category. But there is a very real link between the *Tales* and Aristides' *Hymns*: the *Tales* are one long aretalogy, an extensive account of the benefactions of the god Asclepius towards the human race, or at least that part of the human race which interested Aelius Aristides. Here is a human myth, with one human being participating very fully in the doings of deities. Evidently Aristides himself lived in two worlds, as many people do. One was the world he had learned about at school., The other was the real world, or at least the world that was real to him. The *Sacred Tales* do have a connection with romance, in that they show us, in vivid colors, one of the leading figures of the age of romance constructing his own vision of the world.

To return briefly to the formal aspects of rhetoric, it is in such writers as Dio and Aristides that one finds in fullest bloom that sophistication in expression, carried even to excess, that is so marked a feature of the actual language of romance. In Aristides in particular, even where he has really very little to say—it is often the case—that little is exquisitely said; exquisitely done, one is inclined to think, as the work of a porcelain painter, or a craftsman in ivory, may be exquisitely done; as if words themselves, language itself, were a material, plastic matter from which works of art may be wrought. As indeed they are, in poetry: in Xanadu did Kubla Khan a stately pleasure–dome decree, where Alph, the sacred river, ran down to a sunless sea. Demonstration is impossible, in any other language; one can only evoke similar cases. Aristides' disposition of his elements of composition recalls some formal art, like Japanese flower-arrangement; and his language, at its best, is as delicate, as conventional as his matter, recalling the Plato and Demosthenes he so carefully imitates, and evoking admiration even from a Wilamowitz, who saw Aristides with clear enough eyes.[40] At this level, in this mode, the

---

[40] U. von Wilamowitz-Moellendorff, *Der Rhetor Aristeides, Sitzungsberichte der Preussischen Akademie der Wissenschaften,* 5 Nov. 1925, 333–53—a "thank-offering" for Boulanger's book.

reader of romance will at once think of the prose of Longus, similarly elaborate and delicate. This prose is the poetry of the age. One may of course ask whether prose *can* be so used, whether it can "communicate" without communicating something, as Longus does communicate something. Aristides' own claim for prose was that it is logical and disciplined, not arbitrary; if so, he himself is not the best advertisement for it.

We may leave this topic for another aspect of rhetorical language: its striving after dramatic expression. The constant raising of tension is its most wearisome feature, and contributes as much as anything to an impression of falsity, of insincerity, which is one of the reproaches commonly leveled at "rhetoric" in this sense. In our own day handbooks set out the battery of technical terms—*chiasmus, homoioteleuton, meiōsis, hypallagē, aposiōpēsis*; some of them, such as "hyperbole," have become everyday terms. Their source is of course Greek theory; they flourish riotously in the prose of this period, and are as visible and even obtrusive in romance as anywhere else.

One instance may stand for all: the device of antithesis, which is the basic rhetorical device; the setting of one thing against another, to make both stand out in the contrast. The most striking example in the sophistic prose of the period is a rather obscure pair of speeches—for and against, in the manner of the age—written by a certain Polemo, one of the flashiest of the stars of the Second Sophistic. Polemo purports to be setting out the rival claims to the title of premier hero at Marathon of Cynegirus and Callimachus, whose exploits are reported by Herodotus (6.114). Callimachus was a general, Cynegirus a private soldier. Callimachus is represented in these speeches as having been killed first, at the critical point of the battle, and Cynegirus later, in pursuing the defeated enemy (incidentally, Herodotus says they died at the same time). In one speech, Callimachus was therefore a hero and Cynegirus a fool; in the other, Callimachus was fighting only because in the crisis he could not avoid it, and Cynegirus was the hero in going far beyond the call of duty.

The two constitute a prolonged and ingenious tour de force; they have no content whatever other than antithesis in its purest state.[41]

---

[41] See H. Jüttner, *De Polemonis vita operibus arte* (Breslau, 1898 [Hildesheim, 1967]), 46–112, for these speeches. Pernot, *Discours Siciliens*, 86 and notes 37–38, rightly points out my error in describing these speeches as "disordered" (*Courants littéraires*, 108); in fact they are constructed on "canonical" lines, as Pernot shows. In Jüttner's terms (60), "eum rhetorum scholasticorum praecepta accurate observasse . . . vidimus."

And they are very much in the spirit of Callirhoe debating whether or not to kill her unborn child:

"Am I," she said to herself, "to bring Hermocrates' descendant into the world to serve a master? Am I to bear a child whose father no-one knows? Perhaps some envious person will say, 'Callirhoe became pregnant among the pirates!' It is enough for me alone to suffer misfortune. It is not in your interest to come into a life of misery, my child—a life you should escape from even if you are born. Depart in freedom, while no harm has befallen you, without hearing what they say about your mother!" And then again she changed her mind, and pity came over her for her unborn child. "Are you planning to kill your child? Was ever woman so wicked! Are you mad? Are you reasoning like Medea? Why, people will think you yet more savage than that Scythian woman! She did at any rate hate her husband—but you want to kill Chaereas's child and not even leave behind any memorial of that celebrated marriage! What if it is a son? What if he is like his father? What if he is luckier than me? He has escaped from the tomb, from pirates—shall his mother kill him? How many stories are there of sons of gods and kings born in slavery, then coming into their rightful ancestral rank—Zethus, Amphion, Cyrus? You too, my child—you will sail to Sicily, I am sure! You will go and find your father and your grandfather and tell them your mother's story! A fleet will sail from Sicily to rescue me! O my child, you will restore your parents to each other!" All night long she pursued these thoughts. (2.9.2–6)

Chariton probably predates Polemo, but this taste for antithesis above all things lives at full strength in his successors, who will turn any situation inside out to squeeze from it every last drop of drama and pathos. The device can be fruitful; it can be wearing.

This sketch will perhaps indicate sufficiently what the relationship was between the prose of sophistic theory and practice and the prose of romance. A similar relationship obtains with the linguistic practice of "Atticizing," or returning to the vocabulary and syntax of classical Greek in reaction against the "decadence" of *koinē*. No late writer fully achieves this ideal, and we may wonder whether any of them really intended to do so. Perhaps it would not have been possible for the syntax to be "purified" completely and remain comprehensible.[42]

---

[42] A case in point is the complex of conditional constructions which notoriously offers, in classical Greek, so wide a range of delicately differentiated expressions in re-

Vocabulary is easier to "purify," although it takes a very alert person to spot every neologism, and some are very hard to dislodge because they are useful ("hopefully" springs to mind—alas!—in modern English). There were such alert persons at the time, of course. Some of them were also pedants, like Phrynichus, who issued lists of unacceptable words together with their classical counterparts.[43] Others with common sense, like Lucian (whose views on precisely this matter are set out in his *Lexiphanes*), simply wrote a language rather closer to classical Greek than had been current for some time. The details are of course very complex—and important, for they are close to the heart of the matter of the relationship between romance and epideictic. But the topic is too extensive, and too closely bound up with the Greek language, to be dealt with here, even summarily. The present point is that all the romance writers atticize in some degree; Chariton does so much less than others (that is one major reason for dating him before the "revival"), and Achilles Tatius and Longus do so frequently but not by any means invariably. Writers find their own levels in the matter, and romance writers are as capable of doing so as anyone else.

Some writers of fiction are known themselves to have been accredited sophists: Apuleius is one, and there may be others lurking in Philostratus's *Lives of the Sophists*.[44] Narrative prose fiction begins to force itself on sophists and the literary establishment. Conversely, some romance writers take upon themselves another of the academic

---

spect of hypothetical circumstances. Demosthenes and Plato deploy them, of course, with accuracy and subtlety. Aelius Aristides knew his Demosthenes and Plato inside out; yet Aelius Aristides does not use conditionals as they do. He will use, for instance, *ei* with the optative followed by a future indicative, thus mixing remote hypothesis with "more vivid" future conditions; as who should say, "If I were to come tomorrow I shall give you the book." Here the decline in the use of the optative complicates matters. For a sketch of the matter see Reardon, *Courants littéraires*, 82–88. The term "purify" is taken from the Modern Greek *katharévousa*, "purifying (language)," meaning formal "establishment" Greek, as opposed to *demotiké*, popular Greek: roughly speaking, *katharévousa* corresponds to "Atticizing," *demotiké* to *koinē*.

[43] Phrynichus was prepared to reject even Attic usage if he found it linguistically unsuitable; ancient mistakes, he held, are no better than modern mistakes. For Phrynichus, even the language of Menander (end of the 4th century b.c.) is already decadent.

[44] Apuleius's sophistic works include an *Apology* (his defence against a charge of magic practices), a declamation *On Socrates' Divine Sign*, and a collection of *Florida* or "flowery pieces"; for these see James Tatum, *Apuleius and* The Golden Ass (Ithaca and London, 1979), chapters 4, 5. For Lollianus and Heliodorus (the sophists: Philostratus *Lives of the Sophists* 1.23 and 2.32), see CHCL, 879, 884.

functions of prose, the dispensing of miscellaneous information—as occasion arises in the plot, but often without contributing very much to it. It is interesting that Chariton and Longus do not do this to any extent; they are particularly careful about the movement of their stories, and economical of matter irrelevant to it.[45] Achilles Tatius and Heliodorus, on the other hand, are altogether more leisurely in their progress, and amidst so much complex intrigue readily find room to develop tempting incidental topics. In Achilles there are passages about (for instance) various exotic animals and assorted natural phenomena as well as disquisitions on psychology or love—this in addition to numerous ecphrases and myths.[46] Likewise, Heliodorus is ready to instruct us in the mysteries attaching to the river Nile, discuss the provenance of Homer, or describe the camelopard:[47]

> To convey their compliments on his recent successes they too brought various gifts, including a specimen of an unusual and bizarre kind of animal: in size it stood as tall as a camel, but its hide was marked with garish leopard-spots. Its hindquarters and rear parts were squat and leonine, but its withers, forelegs and chest were disproportionately taller than the rest of its anatomy. Notwithstanding the bulk of the rest of its body, its neck was as slender and elongated as the crop of a swan. In appearance its head was like a camel's, in size not quite twice that of a Libyan ostrich. Its eyes were rimmed with a black line like mascara and darted hither and thither with an expression of pompous disdain. Even its method of locomotion was unique, since it rolled from side to side like a ship at sea, in a manner quite unlike any other creature, terrestrial or aquatic: it did not advance each of its legs individually, in rotation, but its two right legs moved forward in unison, separately from the two left legs, which also functioned as a distinct pair, thus leaving each side of its body in turn without support. It was so halting in its gait and so docile in its temperament that its keeper could lead it on

---

[45] In Longus there is an ecphrasis of a garden (4.2–3) and the myths of Syrinx (2.34) and Echo (3.23) are recounted; but their attachment to the psychology is clear, as they are both about frustrated and violent love. Chariton offers hardly anything beyond a brief description of a hunt (6.4) and an equally brief comment on the Persian system of military mobilization (6.8.6–7).

[46] E.g.: animals: elephant (4.4), crocodile (4.19), phoenix (3.25); natural phenomena: purple dye (2.11), affection among plants and animals (1.17–18); psychology (2.29, 6.7, 7.4); love (1.9–10, 2.35–38); ecphrases: a garden (1.15), a picture (1.1, 3.6–8); myths: Syrinx (8.6), Styx (8.12).

[47] Nile: 2.28, 9.9, 9.22; Homer: 3.18; Camelopard: 10.27.

a slender cord wound around its neck, and it obeyed the directions of his will as if it were a chain that brooked no disobedience.

The arrival of this beast produced universal amazement. The people spontaneously invented a name for the creature derived from the most prominent features of its anatomy: *camelopard*.

It is interesting to observe that it is in later specimens of the form that this happens, ambitious and elaborate literary constructions by obviously educated and confident writers who clearly expect an appropriate readership. The taste for such information is evidently widespread in this period of potted knowledge, in which handbooks and florilegia abound. The information may be an expression of serious intellectual activity: sometimes as being genuinely useful (Pausanias's *Guide to Greece*); sometimes as reflecting a real commitment to the Greek intellectual tradition (Diogenes Laertius's *Lives and Opinions of the Famous Philosophers*); at other times as forming a sheer mass of undiscriminating erudition, like the mountain of quotations from classical literature embedded in Athenaeus's *Table Talk* (*Deipnosophistae*). Or it may be nothing better than paradoxography, like Aelian's *Miscellaneous Information* (*Varia Historia*), displaying just that taste for the unbelievable that Lucian satirizes in *The Lover of Lies*. On occasion it may be strung onto a theme, as when Philostratus discourses on gymnastics in Greek tradition. It will be observed that in its content such literature often reflects the great age of Greece rather than the contemporary world. But equally it can express the religiosity of its age—a topic we shall turn to in due course. In both respects it is in evident contact with romance.

It has been maintained that these digressions show that Achilles Tatius and Heliodorus were not wholly committed to their novels, but used them simply as a thread on which to string such rhetorical set pieces; in this view *Leucippe and Clitophon* and the *Ethiopica* are really closer to Aelian than to Chariton. A very different view has also been maintained: that the digressions are not digressions at all, but are integral in the text, and far from being extraneous to the development of the story actually offer an important key to its interpretation.[48] Both views are extreme. Heliodorus's principal concern *is* his

---

[48] For the first of these two views, see e.g. Perry, *Ancient Romances*, 119: these authors "do not tell the love story for its own sake . . . but rather use it as a framework within which to display their sophistical wares." For the second, see Shadi Bartsch, *Decoding the Ancient Novel: The Reader and the Role of Description in Heliodorus and Achilles Tatius* (Princeton, 1989).

plot; he spends so much care on it, in fact, that it is hard to see how any other view can be held. Being an erudite man, however, Heliodorus is readily tempted to decorate his story with matter drawn from learned pursuits: pieces of "genuine" enough zoology or assorted similar information, which he does try where he can to fold suitably into the action, but which he does not feel absolutely constrained to justify. The sophistic novel can absorb them without strain; but for all that they are subordinate, in the design of the novel, to the story.

Romance, then, is flexible, and receptive to the Greek cultural currents of the time. It is thoroughly Greek in spirit: imaginative, flexible, self-propelled. Not Roman: the only two Latin texts are special cases, and one of them originally Greek at that. All of this raises a question. In Augustan and early imperial Rome there were major forms in existence at about the time Greek romance was coming into shape. We have had brief glimpses in passing of elements of romance in some Latin genres—in Plautus sometimes, in love-elegy more frequently. And the quality appears perhaps above all in the *Aeneid*—in Dido, of course, but also in a series of doomed warriors, Pallas, Nisus and Euryalus in Book IX, and especially the proud Turnus whose death closes the poem on an unresolved note of pathos. If we transfer our gaze, is anything discernible in Greek romance of Latin epic, drama, lyric?

The short answer is no, and it needs little qualification. Here we verge on the difficult topic of the relations between Greece and Rome, or more particularly the influence of the two literatures on each other. What is difficult is to avoid being simplistic. By the time Rome had settled as mistress of the Greek world, certainly by the second century A.D., relations were defined not on simple national lines, but rather on lines of social levels; there was extensive contact, and a good deal of cultural mixing, between Greeks and Romans in the upper strata of society. Greeks could achieve political importance at Rome—Arrian was consul, although it was exceptional that he went on to hold the office again. On the other hand, philhellenic and Greek-speaking emperors were common enough. The most familiar case is Hadrian, but Nero had toured Greece as a privileged performer, and Marcus Aurelius wrote his *Meditations* in Greek, the language of philosophy. The influence of Greek scholars and teachers in Rome is well known, and it is hardly thinkable that they did not read any Latin literature. Lucian appears to know Latin, Plutarch is well versed in Roman history, to take only two examples.

For all that, there is very little trace of any influence of Latin on Greek literature. The Lucian who lets us know he understands Latin never, as far as we can tell, refers unmistakably to any Latin treatment of his themes; if in *Hired Companions* he sounds in places very like Juvenal, we shall remember that the subject of the vulgar rich and the Greek parasite are well worn by Juvenal's time, let alone Lucian's. Aristides, in *To Rome*, cannot find enough to say in admiration of the organization of the Empire, and the illness which dominated his life was contracted when he undertook that journey to Rome which was *de rigueur* for all provincials who would succeed; but he feels no need to express any homage to Latin literature. In the case of romance, there is at most perhaps an occasional echo in some detail. For the rest, where similarities occur, where at first sight we might be tempted to think there could be contact, it is more likely that we should have recourse to that familiar scholarly solution, the common source; and it will be a source found in Greek antiquity. Thus, as we have just seen, in the *Aeneid* there is one of the most romantic characters in all of classical literature, Dido. She has all the passion of Achilles' Melite of Heliodorus's Arsace, and more magnetism; and much more dignity than the predatory females who figure in episodes of Xenophon's story, Manto and Cyno. But attractive as it might be to think that Heliodorus had read Virgil, which is by no means impossible, it is a commonplace of literary history that Dido first saw the light in the guise of Medea, and there is no doubt whatever that both Virgil and Heliodorus had read Euripides and Apollonius of Rhodes. If there is no need to bring Virgil into the picture, there is less need to look to his successors in epic, even though one of them also wrote about the Argonauts. Similarly, scenes abound in the tragedies of Seneca that are as dramatic, as sensational as anything in Chariton, who perhaps might just have known about them. But Chariton, the secretary of a rhetor, and Seneca, the nephew of his uncle, were alike nourished on rhetorical exercises, with their melodramatic, improbable situations, and there is no call to ransack the tragedies of Seneca in search of models for romance— fortunately, for we should only find that in lurid qualities they upstage even Achilles Tatius, which is quite a feat.[49] Chariton certainly

[49] Achilles Tatius merely disembowels and decapitates his heroine in narrative; Sen-

knew his drama, as we have seen, but it is in Euripides' words, not Seneca's, that Callirhoe bewails her lot. Chariton very probably heard them, in a performance of a classic play, in that late Hellenistic theater in Aphrodisias which now appears on tourist postcards. That was his theatrical tradition; that, and the enormously popular contemporary entertainment of mime.[50] Centuries later, Heliodorus re-

---

eca would have had it happen on stage, and another character would have tried to glue the pieces together again: see *Oedipus, Thyestes*. I am of those who (unfashionably) cannot take Senecan drama seriously. As for his uncle, who composed (or retailed) fictitious court cases as rhetorical pabulum, my own favorite is the case of the Vestal Virgin who, having broken her vow of chastity, was thrown from the Tarpeian Rock as the law prescribed. But the lady proved tougher than expected: she survived the incident, and the matter at issue is, what should now be done with her? Should the State call it quits, as is alleged to happen when a condemned man survives the electric chair? One suggestion is that a special rock should be constructed for the lady; another, that she should be taken back up the rock and invited to jump down as often as is necessary to finish her off (Seneca *Controversiae* 1.3).

[50] Greek mime was a realistic dramatic performance in speech, song, gesture and dance, in popular language and often farcical, generally setting out a situation from everyday life but with little sustained plot. The form grew from entertainments based on mimetic dancing, and there were mimes throughout Greek history. Sophron developed the genre in Sicily in the 5th century, and there are specimens from the Alexandrian period by Herodas and Theocritus (2, 15—literary versions hardly intended for performance). Others appear on papyri of the imperial period: *e.g.*, the Charition-mime, which seems to parody Euripides' *Iphigeneia in Tauris*—a Greek girl is rescued from imprisonment in a barbarian land by her brother and a comic slave, who make her captors drunk and escape with her (see D. L. Page, *Greek Literary Papyri* [London, 1950] [Loeb], no. 76, 336–49). Like early romance, mime was considered sub-literary, and little remains of it; it has been partially disinterred in modern times by papyrologists. We cannot point with any confidence to any specific influence of mime on ideal romance, although Petronius certainly drew heavily on the form. There is however a general similarity between the Charition situation (the adventures of Greeks abroad) and episodes in some Greek romances, especially that of Xenophon's *Ephesiaca* (3.11 notably). There is also similarity in fictional content and in the representation of ordinary people. Mime, however, was more realistic in subject and treatment. The form reached Rome some time before Cicero's day; he criticizes its crudity (see D. F. Sutton, "Cicero on Minor Dramatic Forms," *Symbolas Osloenses* 59 [1984], 29–36). Roman mime seems to have been even coarser in tone; real copulation and even real crucifixion are reported, the latter in the "Laureolus" mime; see Martial, *Epigrammaton* (or *Spectaculorum*) *Liber* 7. I am indebted for this reference to D. F. Sutton; see now his *Seneca on the Stage* (Leiden, 1986), Appendix 1, "Artificial Blood on the Roman Stage." See too Lesky, *History*, 746–49. The unsatisfactory monograph of H. Reich, *Der Mimus* (Berlin, 1903), has not yet been replaced. There was also a related form of dramatic entertainment that became popular in the early Empire and is generally known as "pantomime," although that term really applies to its main performer, a solo dancer who performed what would nowadays be called "mime" (of the Marcel Marceau variety); it included also speaking and musical performers, and represented mythological stories. See Lucian, *The Dance* (the Atticizing word for *pantomimos* is *orchestēs*, "dancer"). Aristides also wrote a treatise on the topic, now lost but known through a reply by

peatedly refers to his own story as a drama, and it is Greek drama that he too recalls, or "imitates."

No doubt the matter is not completely simple. There seems to have been some community of matter between Greek and Roman mime, for instance. It has been suggested that there are after all some reflections of Virgil in Chariton.[51] It seems possible that there are reflections of Roman elegy in Longus, who may have been a Roman, and Latin-speaking; but the Latin elegists are themselves deeply indebted to their Alexandrian predecessors. In other genres also there were available contemporary models in Latin literature: the historiography of Tacitus, the biography of Suetonius, come to mind at once; rhetorical theory received at Quintilian's hands its most systematic treatment. It could be mildly profitable to pursue further the question of the romance writers' indebtedness to Latin literature; but there would be no very spectacular conclusions.

To turn from specific genres to more general reflections, in the novel, of the preoccupations of the age, among several important contemporary cultural themes we may pick out three: the archaizing trend, the dominance of rhetoric, and the impulse towards religion, or religiosity. For the first, the allegiance of romantic writers to classical literature and tradition, and in some cases to classical history, is itself one of the ways in which they actually reflect the contemporary world. For the second, the hand of rhetoric is as visible in romance as anywhere else. Finally, romance authors and other writers alike are often imbued with religious sentiment, in different ways. The credulous and pious Aelian probably read Xenophon more avidly than he read more intelligent writers—theirs for their style I'll read, his for his love, of tuppence-coloured miracles—but all the romances contain a distinct element of paradoxography, and the point of paradoxography is generally that the more marvellous are the phenomena of this world, the more clearly do they show forth the gods.[52] All the romances represent dreams as an expression of divine interest in

Libanius; see Boulanger, *Aelius Aristide*, 247–49. See now on the whole topic Jones, *Culture and Society*, 69–75.

[51] Q. Cataudella, "Riflessi virgiliani nel romanzo di Caritone," *Athenaeum* 5 (1927), 302–12; see Hunter, *Daphnis and Chloe*, 76–77.

[52] This is explicit in the *Physiologus*, a collection of several dozen essays, of which a version may date (like many other such works) to the 2nd century; the wonderful properties of animals, plants, and minerals are interpreted as evidence of divine power (in a Christian sense in this case).

human affairs.[53] If Heliodorus seized on the *Life of Apollonius*, that may be in part because he was in tune with Philostratus's somewhat wry interest in cults and religious practices. Even Chariton, less disposed than his fellows to call upon the gods to carry the weight of his human story, nevertheless knows that the kind of all-triumphant love he celebrates should be credited to the account of Aphrodite, or Eros, or somebody like that.

That is not a one-way street. Romance absorbs such influences, but romance itself spreads outwards and invades the field of religious belief. Just as rhetorical prose affects Christian apologetic in the second century (Tatian is as much a sophist in his expression as any of his unenlightened pagan contemporaries), so we find in the period an increasing number of Christian and para-Christian narratives of adventure. They can hardly be narratives of love and adventure in the full sense, for ordinary human love is suspect (to say the least) and the erotic content of such stories is very tightly circumscribed, sometimes totally eliminated. Nonetheless, they are what Christian ideology could make of the romance form. Such narratives are essentially *acta*, accounts of the doings and achievements of those who carried and dispensed the faith. No "model" was needed, certainly, for adherents of the Christian religion to use this method of capturing their tradition. The biographical gospels, one supposes, would have been composed whatever course Greek literature might have taken; so would the account of Paul's missionary journeys, which already includes wanderings in distant lands. What is perhaps most interesting here is that in some texts there is an intrigue in which the religious activities of the principal characters are complicated by a love interest, although little comes of it. Thus, in the *Pseudo-Clementine Recognitions*, the initial impulse is given to the adventures by the fact that the mother of the hero (who is St. Clement) leaves Rome to avoid the advances of her brother-in-law; this entails the dispersal of her family, who wander extensively in a series of episodes before being reunited. At the same time, the burden of the story consists of Christian religious instruction. In the *Acts of Thomas* the romance element is more fully developed. Thomas, in India for missionary purpose, enters into contact with a royal family and there succeeds in converting a number of people. In some cases it is a married or be-

---

[53] The *Dreambook* (*Onirocritica*) of Artemidorus is dated in this period. It offers a somewhat more scientific approach than the *Physiologus*, but still degenerates into paradoxography at times.

trothed couple who are converted; and such is the encratist zeal of this excessive Christian hero that the couple become committed to total abstinence from sexual relations—which leads to problems.[54]

A short way to solve the troubles of the world. This is of course flying in the face of what pagan romance proposes, for its authors and their heroes are all very ready to accept the natural conclusion of their stories, once the appropriate circumstances have been achieved; Xenophon and Longus are quite explicit about that conclusion. But the point is that the theme of human love has been in some degree faced by the author of the *Acts of Thomas*, and not just set aside totally. Of course, this is still a long way from being a story based on love. Like the pseudo-Clementine text, it is based on ideological doctrine and edifying incident. In that, as in other respects (its framework of wandering, miracle-working "hero"), it too recalls the *Life of Apollonius*, as does the *Ethiopica*. Philostratus's text sets the pattern, in fact, for much of the subsequent history, in the Byzantine age, of adventure-narrative. Greek romance did not altogether die; it merely faded away, into hagiography. Romance, as a description of the situation of man-in-life, is in a broad sense a "religious" form. In that, it fits its period.

To sum up: romance is clearly in quite extensive contact with the cultural life of the early Roman Empire, but it is too new and too major to have its course affected, in any very substantial way by other kinds of literature, which by now are too restricted in scope or too traditional in manner to exert a strong influence. For all that, or perhaps *because* it was unchallenged, it made quite rapid progress; there is a big difference between *Ninus* and Longus. That difference seems to be sufficiently explained by the general strength of the form and, in particular, the need to solve major structural problems in it, analyzed in earlier chapters. Here, however, it would be foolish to try to draw the literary-historical map in much detail, for the state of our knowledge of the form does not permit that. It is certainly a more complex matter than we know, and there were probably several gradations, several levels of writing, in addition to linear progress. This caveat becomes more important with each new fragment published. Some recent publications (*Iolaus, Tinouphis*) even tempt us to wonder

---

[54] For religious narrative literature of this period see now Richard I. Pervo, *Profit with Delight: the Literary Framework of the Acts of the Apostles* (Philadelphia, 1987).

whether some aspects of the history of the form, and its complexities, may not go back earlier than the later Hellenistic age, even to the third century B.C.[55]

As envoi to this chapter we should consider briefly the shadow cast by romance on a later age. Although the present study deals mainly with love-romance, it should be emphasized here that ancient fiction is not confined to love-romance. From the second or third century A.D. society is faced with increasing pressure for fundamental change, and once more produces what it wants—or rather, what it is allowed to have.[56] In the following period the appetite for fiction remains, but the particular form of it that evokes erotica is held in check, as it has been in other societies. Popular fiction, such as *Ninus* and the *Ephesiaca*, appears to die out by the third century (with the possible exception of the *Ethiopica*); the sophistic trio appear to be the latest examples of the genre.[57] But at this point another form of popular fiction takes the place of Xenophon and his like. That form is hagiography.

Typically, the hagiographical romance is the largely fictitious biography of a saint. Material was plentiful; all that was really needed was the saint's name and a tradition of his or her martyrdom, and both existed in profusion in the Byzantine period. Legends or familiar stories of course readily attached themselves to such figures. Between his birth and death, as has been pointed out,[58] a saint could be expected to suffer the usual human vicissitudes and to display the approved virtues. Accordingly, there seemed no harm in inventing the details if, as was generally the case, they were not actually known; and martyrdom offered an exciting end. Such "lives" offered an excellent, generously receptive vehicle for light reading that would be both ideologically acceptable, even edifying, and entertain-

---

[55] See Chapter 2, n. 35.

[56] Well put by Hägg, *Novel in Antiquity*, 161: "The history of the birth of the novel was repeated once again: a new historical situation, with new demands, gave rise to a new literary form, which borrowed freely from predecessors and contemporaries. The novel was perhaps the main source for borrowings, and no doubt its popularity was deliberately used to propagate the new faith."

[57] Hägg, *Novel in Antiquity*, 161. Although no more romances of the "popular" pagan type (in the sense of the word used here) appear to have been *written* later than the 2nd century, or at the very latest the early 3rd century, they continued to be *read*; the Theban codex of Chariton was of the 6th–7th century, and contained, as it would seem, other similar texts (such as *Chione*).

[58] H. G. Beck, "Marginalien zum byzantinischen Roman," in H. G. Beck *et al.*, eds., *Kyklos* (Festschrift Keydell) (Berlin, 1978), 116–28, 122–23.

ing; no doubt both motives were present in their writing. These works are *literary* creations, it should be observed, written often by people of high position. They are not folktale, although, like the ancient romances, they could readily accept and develop folktale. Furthermore, from perhaps the seventh or eighth century the pagan romances were no longer linguistically accessible (given the development of the language) to less educated readers, and so for some hundreds of years such stories constituted the only acceptable popular literary entertainment available.[59] The line of descent from very much earlier "hagiographies"—of Cyrus the Great, Alexander, Apollonius—is clear; the appetite for such stories is perennial.

This, then, is one direction the romance instinct can take in an ideologically oriented society. It will find its way through the cracks in the system, so to speak, and reappear where it is perhaps least expected. But the further development of romance in the Byzantine world is a separate topic.[60] Here we shall close our examination of the form of romance in antiquity, and turn finally to some broader considerations of the general interpretation of the form.

[59] Beck, "Marginalien," 124–25.
[60] See in general Hägg, *Novel in Antiquity*, chapters 2 (Byzantine) and 5 (Alexander-Romance).

The Pattern of Romance

THE MAIN AIM of this study has been to analyze the genre of Greek romance, to examine the elements from which it is put together, how they are articulated, how the form works in its various instantiations. But what is it all about in the first place? In this final chapter I shall return briefly to interpretation of the form.

The religious narratives that figured at the end of the last chapter—Christian and para-Christian romance, hagiography—will recall once more Frye's remark that "there are close connections between the imaginative universe of romance and of Christianity."[1] In the imperial period Christianity is not the only imaginative world of its kind. It will be pertinent now to call attention to some other contemporary models of existence, so to speak, that bear a family resemblance to Christianity and are of manifest relevance to the practice and also the theory of romance, in its ancient and perhaps its modern manifestations.

First, Gnosticism, the cousin of Christianity. The exuberant mythology of Gnosticism, revealed by the discoveries of Nag-Hammadi and Qumrân in much fuller form than was known previously, cannot be strait-jacketed into a doctrine. That was the trouble with it, as Christian intellectuals saw: it offers an indescribably complex range of matter, of different versions—no two Gnostics say the same thing, observed Irenaeus.[2] It offers also what might be called romance matter, raw material for literature (some *Acts* are Gnostic in one sense or another), and for that reason should be credited to the imagination of the period, and set alongside the "mythology" expressed in ro-

---

[1] *Secular Scripture*, 92; cf. Chapter 2 at note 11.

[2] *Against Heretics* 1.11.11. Henry Chadwick describes Gnosticism as a "diabolical Doppelgänger" of Christianity (*Oxford Classical Dictionary*, 2nd ed. [Oxford, 1970], s.v. "Gnosticism"). Besides Christian elements, Gnosticism contained elements of religious thought from Plato (especially the Creatory of the *Timaeus*), Judaism, and Oriental sources (Mithraism, Zoroastrianism). For an account see H. Chadwick, *The Early Church* (Harmondsworth, 1967) (Penguin), 33–41; John Ferguson, *The Religions of the Roman Empire* (London, 1970), adds some details of the imagery of the Valentinian system which may be of special interest in the present context.

mance. For the Gnostic, human life is an attempt to regain the place on high that humanity lost at the fall. That place is with God, who is eternal, transcendent, and above all unknown: knowledge of God, *gnōsis*, is the essential condition of salvation. The world is not the creation of God, for the Gnostic; rather, it is a prison, created by God's creatures in ambitious revolt against Him; the "fall" is embodied in the figure of the "divine female," who may appear symbolically in the shape of a prostitute, or Helen of Troy. God has, however, endowed man with a divine spark which enables him to conceive the aim of deliverance from the world, and his true destiny is to achieve deliverance despite the opposition of evil spirits. A general resemblance to the plot of romance is at once visible. Clearly, the notion is in the air that human life involves trials, struggle, descent, salvation.

Secondly, we may consider the relationship of the romance to non-Christian religious systems. The concept of "aretalogy"—the listing of the benefactions of a deity—has already been mentioned in connection with the *Hymns* of Aelius Aristides. In romance the salvation of the heroes is often attributed in part to just such divine intervention. In pursuit of such thoughts Karl Kerényi, in 1927, advanced the suggestion that all of the Greek romances display a pattern found in the Egyptian mystery cult of Isis and Osiris, which in the Hellenistic period and the early centuries of the Roman empire was widespread in the Mediterranean world, and beyond.[3] The myth of Isis is itself a story of trials, struggle, descent and salvation: the tribulations of Osiris, the efforts of his consort Isis to counter the evil influence that has engulfed him, his triumphant resuscitation. Isis is the Egyptian fertility goddess who was equated with numerous similar figures throughout the ancient world; Osiris is the river Nile, which sinks only to rise again and fertilize the land. The skeleton of the story recounts how Osiris falls under the attack of Seth, the god of evil; his body is dismembered and the parts scattered around the world. Isis, lamenting, wanders in search of her consort, gathers together the limbs, reconstitutes the body, and by breathing on it brings it back to life. Horus, her son, seeks out and defeats Seth; and the resuscitated Osiris returns to his temple, triumphant over death, to reign eter-

---

[3] K. Kerényi, *Die griechisch-orientalische Romanliteratur in religionsgeschichtlicher Beleuchtung* (Tübingen, 1927 [Darmstadt, 1973]). For Isis-worship see especially Witt, *Isis in the Graeco-Roman World*.

nally as king of the dead. Osiris is thus the prototype of suffering humanity, who with God's help comes through tribulation to salvation.

This was offered as an interpretation, not always very clear, of the basic matter of Greek romance. More recently, a stricter version of it has seen in mystery ritual an answer to the question of the actual origins of the literary form of romance: it sprang from aretalogies composed in recognition of the benefactions of various deities—not just Isis, but others too.[4] Subsequently these "stories" were the subject of literary elaboration, with a proselytizing purpose, and the texts now extant are the ultimate result of such a process. Extensive resemblances can be found in them to the detail of the various mysteries, all of which demonstrate a general similarity to the mysteries of Isis; more specifically, the works of Xenophon, Achilles Tatius and Apuleius are Isis-texts, that of Heliodorus a Helius-text, Longus's a Dionysus-romance, and Iamblichus's *Babyloniaca* is based on the mysteries of Mithras.[5] There is no need here to discuss these theories in detail. They were unfavorably received, particularly the more recent version: the general criticism was that they are too ready to twist the smallest detail in such a way as to make everything fit a predetermined pattern, when simpler and more obvious explanation lies to hand.[6] Even in Kerényi's earlier exposition it is often difficult to see the wood for the trees. For all the excessive rigidity of such schematic interpretations, however, they do seem to look in the right direction.

[4] R. Merkelbach, *Roman und Mysterium.*

[5] There is one exception: in the last paragraphs of a long book (339–40) Merkelbach admits that the action of *Chaereas and Callirhoe* does not represent any mystery-pattern. He concludes that this is because Chariton did not understand that romances were really religious texts; he had read a number of them and had the idea of writing one himself, but as he did not understand the real reason why the plots progressed as they did, he simply followed what he took to be the general pattern but constructed his own plot "as the economy of the story demanded." This resulted in a better-constructed story, which is, however, "irritating" to the reader who knows what is supposed to happen in such a story. It is of course necessary to this view that Chariton be dated later than at least some other romance writers. That is the task undertaken by R. Petri (see Chapter 2, n. 3—as observed there, he does not succeed). The exception must throw doubt on the whole theory. There is an extension of the general theory in Merkelbach's *Die Hirten des Dionysos*, which uses *Daphnis and Chloe* in an attempt to reconstruct the mysteries of Dionysus in the form they had assumed by the time of the Empire (a much tamer form than the rites portrayed in Euripides' *Bacchae*).

[6] The fullest commentary appeared in R. Turcan, "Le roman 'initiatique': à propos d'un livre récent," *Revue d'Histoire des Religions* 163 (1963), 149–99.

Like Gnostic mythology, mystery-religion is romance matter. In this perspective romance, as a description of the situation of man-in-life, is a religious construct.

Let us return to the interpretation of ancient romance I have offered earlier in this study. It is closely related to Perry's description of romance as "the open form *par excellence* for the open society":

> In the vastly expanded world of Hellenistic and Roman times, the individual lost nearly all his quondam importance and representative significance, having become too tiny to be tragic, or heroic, or poetic, or symbolical of anything more than himself or a particular segment of contemporary society. . . . The bigger the world the smaller the man. Faced with the immensity of things and his own helplessness before them, the spirit of Hellenistic man became passive in a way that it had never been before, and he regarded himself instinctively as the plaything of Fortune. All this is conspicuous from first to last in the Greek romance.[7]

Worked out as systematic analysis of a narrative pattern, this leads, I have suggested, to the following kind of characterization.[8] A story like Chariton's is a fable, representing a specific social reality, the large world of Hellenistic and early imperial times. The private individual is lost in a world too big for him, isolated by involuntary travels from the society of his own people, and assailed by the dangers inherent in travel—to the point, even, of suffering apparent death; but he is recovered and sustained by love of, and fidelity to, his partner and his god, ultimately to find therein his salvation, his private happiness, and his very identity.

That is to say, this is a social interpretation of the pattern of romance. The stories I have been considering are in the first place reflections of their own times, of the physical and cultural conditions which evoked them. That is not necessarily all they are. They may, and in my view they do, embody experience, human experience, that transcends particular conditions: in that respect I see a good deal of merit in Kerényi's theory. With this qualification, however: romance is not *born* of Isis-ritual, is not its descendant. Rather, the narrative patterns of romance and of Isis-ritual are both products of the same imagination; they interpret, ultimately, human progress through life, but proximately the more specific experience of people in a large and

[7] *Ancient Romances*, 47, 48.
[8] See Chapter 2 and n. 12.

impersonal society. In other words, the two narrative patterns go back to a common source; the relationship is lateral, they are siblings or cousins, not parent and child.[9] In the same way, other romances would reflect *their* worlds; the *Odyssey*, for instance, would reflect the world of early Greek colonization.

Let us move, at this point, beyond the world of ancient romance, to a more universal pattern, and to a familiar interpretation of romance that is central enough in critical thought to serve as an exemplar of theory in the matter: that of Northrop Frye, which has been touched on in passing here and there in earlier chapters. Frye offers it as being of general validity, as applying to romance throughout the ages. The simplest and clearest way for the present purpose will be to abstract its main lines, for the most part in Frye's own words. For Frye, romance constructs a dream world, which replaces normal experience. "The normal form of romance is the quest story that reflects . . . cyclical movemement" (*Secular Scripture*, 186), and that movement is composed of ascent and descent: "the narrative movement keeps rising into wish fulfillment or sinking into anxiety and nightmare" (53). Ascent might be symbolized by, for instance, the achievement of marriage (152); descent by a search for a lost object (121). In terms of the stories we have been discussing, the reunion of Chaereas and Callirhoe would mark ascent; the apparent death of Callirhoe in Syracuse, or the enslavement of Chaereas near Miletus, would mark descent. The movement may frequently be spiral, "an open circle where the end is the beginning transformed and renewed by the heroic quest" (174). The realization of the lovers' initial impulse in the marriage that usually concludes the ancient love-romance would illustrate this pattern.

Experience, then, consists of movement between an idyllic world and a demonic world. These worlds are not the states of reality and illusion (respectively); rather, they are worlds characterized by the presence or absence (respectively) of *identity*: "reality for romance is an order of existence most readily associated with the word identity" (54). Identity is existence without circumstance, a state "in which there is nothing to write about" (54); circumstance is what happens to romance characters, and "the return to identity is a release from the tyranny of these circumstances" (54). So that, in summary, "illu-

[9] Cf. H.H.O. Chalk's review of Merkelbach's book in *Classical Review* 13 (1963), 162: "Any dramatic story presumably springs from the same psychic faculty as the drama of the mysteries."

sion for romance . . . is an order of existence that is best called alienation. Most romances end happily, with a return to the state of identity, and begin with a departure from it" (54).

This, then, offers a paradigm of interpretation, a view of the pattern of romance in general: it is a pattern of ascent and descent, of alternate triumph and tragedy, danger and salvation. How far do the ancient texts fit such a paradigm? Some similarities, some points of contact, will already have become visible, at various points in the discussion so far. Can they be joined up, stitched together, so as to form a coherent picture of the form of ancient romance?

The three schemes of interpretation that have been presented—Frye, Perry/Reardon, Kerényi/Merkelbach—are similar in outline; since they are all products of twentieth-century thought, a family resemblance is not surprising. The similarities can be brought out by a diagrammatic representation, as follows; it will be noted that remarkably little adjustment is needed to establish its terms.

	Setting	Initial Condition	Activity	Experience	Final Condition
Frye	dream world	alienation	quest	circumstance brings descent and ascent	identity
Perry/ Reardon	big world	isolation	travel	adventure brings trials, love sustains	salvation
Kerényi/ Merkelbach	life	?vulnerability	search	evil forces bring death, resuscitation	eternal life

There is manifestly one overall pattern here. The general setting in which the hero finds himself gives rise to his initial condition; that involves him in activities which bring experience and ultimately issue in a final condition similar to, but more profound than, his original state. That is, he has undergone a change that takes him to a higher spiritual level; to use the language of institutional religion, the hero is confirmed, in his condition of human being.[10]

The sequence of situations and events set out here is a different

[10] In the case of the Greek love-romance the generalizing masculine pronoun is somewhat inappropriate; the heroine is likely to be if anything more deeply affected by "circumstance" than the hero (who is sometimes a consort rather than an equal partner).

174

kind of description of the events of a narrative romance from our earlier analysis in terms of problem, conflict, development and solution; a different expression, that is, of Aristotle's analysis of literary *mimēsis*, the representation of human activities. But the terms correspond. The setting and initial condition (vulnerable individual in an alien world) constitute an initial problem; an activity (quest, adventure) gives rise to conflict (*agōn*, usually involving *hamartia* of some kind); experience (circumstance, hostile forces) leads to development (with *peripeteia, anagnōrisis, pathos* = suffering); and the final condition (salvation, identity) represents solution (happy/unhappy ending, with *metabolē*—represented in romance by the deepened spiritual condition of the hero, the top of the spiral, where the beginning is transformed and renewed). Which is to say that Aristotle is using philosophical language to say what the other analyses say in other kinds of language: Frye's is psychologically-based, Perry's culturally-based, Kerényi's religiously-based. We will choose among these analyses according to our predilection for one or another language. Frye himself sometimes uses the language of religion: "Most of what goes on in the night world of romance is cruelty and horror, yet what is essential is not cruelty as such but the presence of some kind of ritual"; sometimes even the language of mystery-religion: "at the bottom of the mythological universe is a death and rebirth process . . . at the top is the individual's regained identity" (*Secular Scripture*, 113, 183).

It would not be difficult, if it were the province of this book, to extend such a scheme to forms that romance has taken in our own day: for instance, the Harlequin romance (nurse and doctor), the national romance (*Gone With The Wind*), the Western, science fiction, Tolkien's creation. It could even be applied to forms that at first sight are less obviously romance forms, because more realistic in manner: the spy/detective/James Bond story. Or to myth-romance: Joyce, Kafka. Romance is strong and durable; versatile, receptive, capacious.

To return to Frye, a further step is taken when he transmutes a psychological explanation into a literary pattern that is self-sufficient, needing no other frame of reference (such as psychological behavior patterns, or social conditions).[11] Aristotle himself expressed this story-formula as a literary pattern; but for Aristotle, literature is mimetic, a *mimēsis* of a *praxis*, a generalized representation of an action

[11] For the following theory see *Anatomy of Criticism*, final chapter ("Tentative Conclusion"), 350ff., where Frye offers the following "admittedly speculative suggestion."

in the real world. For Frye, literature constitutes its own world, its own thought-world or conceptual framework, as does mathematics. From being a reflection of an objective world, it becomes an autonomous language. For the pure theorist of mathematics, things are number. For the pure theorist of literature, things are, similarly, words; words, word patterns, literate structures; "pure literature, like pure mathematics, contains its own meaning." Thus, three bricks exist; but so does the concept "three," detached from the bricks. Intellectual constructs can be erected on that premiss. Mathematics constitutes a self-sufficient order of things: one can think about "three," do things with it—multiply it, divide it—without asking "three what?" In the same way literature can exist in and for itself, without reference to a phenomenal world. Thus, in the present case, romance—like other kinds of writing—would exist as a pattern valid in itself, governed or shaped by its own laws, its own behavior, and not dependent for its existence, or for its interest, on (for instance) a common pattern in human existence. In that case, what has appeared as a psychological basis for the normal pattern of romance is not really a psychological basis. Terms like "dream," "alienation," "quest," "identity" are really only metaphors borrowed from psychology. The fundamental language of romance has no reference to psychology or to any other frame of human experience, any more than a mathematical equation refers to an external frame of experience. Literature, in short, is a language; like not only mathematics—an easily comprehensible analogy—but also music, painting, mythology; all of which *can* function mimetically but do not do so essentially. It is valid in itself; and it is the function of criticism to decipher it.

That is to say, this interpretation of literature is, as it were, a systematic generalization of its activity; literature is detached altogether from circumstance. Romance—to turn to our immediate brief—would be a particular case of this general theory, a dialect of the language of literature. In that case, clearly, no "field theory" of romance would be valid that fell short of such general theory. In particular, any mimetic theory such as Perry's—romance as the open form for the open society—would have no real cogency; it would not elucidate the language (or dialect) of romance, but at best only one of its utterances. On the other hand, it may be that in such a scheme Rohde's purely literary account of the genesis of romance—as the product of love-elegy and travel-story—would again begin to seem valid.[12]

[12] In this perspective Bowie's own "purely literary" account of the origins of the

One may ask whether an analogy really can be drawn between literature and mathematics. The matter is raised here not in order to embark on any general theory of aesthetics but with a specific purpose. One question raised by ancient romance is whether the romance genre is in principle an open-society form. The circumstances of its occurrence in antiquity, and its manifestations in the modern world, do strongly suggest that it is. This explanation would be related to the commonly advanced explanation of the rise of the novel in modern Europe, namely that it was due to social developments in the eighteenth century, in particular the rise of the middle classes. A further, associated question is, why did antiquity not develop prose fiction as modern Europe has done? Why, in particular, did the ideal romance not become the realistic novel? To put the matter more bluntly, "Why, despite its immensely rich literary inheritance, is the Greek novel so second-rate?"[13]

Possibly there is not really a problem to solve: "The failure of the Graeco-Roman world to produce a work like *Middlemarch*," the same

---

genre (*CHCL* 684; see Chapter 2, n. 12 above) will seem the more cogent: if (as may well be the case) the romance can be confined within the period (say) A.D. 50–250 (instead of spreading over ca. 100 B.C.–A.D. 400), "The novels' rise would reflect merely the avid reading and prolific writing of the age, their demise the decline of a peaceful and cosmopolitan Greek world," and there is no call to interpret it as a myth for its time, or as anything other than an event within its own self-contained framework of literary activity. In that case one should ask (a) if the demise of romance is a reflection of the decline of a peaceful and cosmopolitan Greek world, why is the birth of romance not equally a reflection of the rise of a peaceful and cosmopolitan Greek world?; and (b) why was it prose fiction (and not, say, epic or comedy) that was adopted by the early Empire as its principal form of creative literature? I find it hard to think that this manifestation of a perennial form of literature was born in a library. But propositions such as Frye's and Rohde's—and Bowie's—clearly have some affinity with other modern theories of the non-mimetic nature of literature. Scholars have begun to pursue the topic of ancient romance systematically through other modern theory. See, as one example, Consuelo Ruiz Montero, *La estructura de la novela griega*, Salamanca, 1988 (cf. *ead.*, "The Structural Pattern of the Ancient Greek Romances and the *Morphology of the Folk-Tale* of V. Propp," *Fabula* 22 [1981], 228–38). There is also the essay of M. M. Bakhtin on Greek romance in "Forms of Time and of the Chronotope in the Novel," in *The Dialogic Imagination: Four Essays by M. M. Bakhtin*, ed. Michael Holquist, trans. Caryl Emerson and Michael Holquist (Austin, 1981), 86–110; it was written over 50 years ago and is outdated, but does represent the views on the form of a very influential theorist. At a recent international conference ("The Ancient Novel: Classical Paradigms and Modern Perspectives") organized at Dartmouth, N.H. by James Tatum in July 1989, a number of papers addressed issues in modern theory; see the *Acta* of the conference: James Tatum and Gail M. Vernazza, eds., *The Ancient Novel: Classical Paradigms and Modern Perspectives* (Hanover, N.H.: Dartmouth College, 1990); and a volume of selected papers from it to be published by Johns Hopkins University Press.

[13] S. R. West, *Classical Review* 34 (1984), 201–203 (review of Hägg, *Novel in Antiquity*).

writer continues, answering her own question, "may seem to some no more remarkable than its failure to invent the bicycle." Certainly the elements were all there; but they were never put together in the appropriate way. Why not? To take another analogy, steam power was actually known in antiquity, but the idea of putting it to use was never pursued seriously; it remained a toy.[14] What was missing was, perhaps, quite simply the notion that it could be useful. Perhaps it was not needed, in the sense that work was already being done perfectly well by human (including slave) labor. Why did the eighteenth century need, and why did antiquity apparently not need, the developed novel? We are tempted to think that in both cases, steam engine and novel, all that was needed was an act of imagination.

These questions are clearly relevant to the present study. To discuss them fully, however, would be to embark on a rather different kind of book. Briefly, my own view is that romance does reflect primarily a condition of society, though the reflection is not necessarily a direct one, and will evolve with that society. Writers will certainly prey upon one another, as it were, but ultimately they are governed by the world they live in. That in itself supplies the essential answer to the question of why the romance did not develop into the novel in antiquity: it might well have done so—there are signs that the process had begun—if the open condition of society had not changed to a closed condition, the condition of institutionalized Christianity, with ideological imperatives that determined literary activities among others. Writers had more important things to do than describe people as they really were, as they have had in modern closed worlds; of course, that may not be by their own choice.[15]

[14] It is described in the *Pneumatica* of Heron of Alexandria (ca. A.D. 100); see *RE* VIII 1, 1041, 1047. According to J. G. Landels, *Engineering in the Ancient World* (London, Berkeley and Los Angeles, 1980), 28–31, a device of Heron's based on steam power ("a ball which spins round on a pivot when a cauldron is boiled") was itself too inefficient mechanically to be used as a power source; but in Heron's work can be found all the elements of a practical steam engine. Landels suggests that although there were technical obstacles to their combination (notably the lack of a high-quality fuel), it was probably economic and social causes that really stood in the way of the steam engine. The apparent stagnation of romance may offer an analogy.

[15] It should however be noted in passing that there seems to have been little if any positive censorship exercised in the Byzantine period on existing classical texts; they were in fact used very extensively, in their original form (allowing for the hazards of transmission), for the greater part of the standard Byzantine educational program—and this is a principal reason for their survival. See on this topic N. G. Wilson, *Scholars of Byzantium* (London and Baltimore, 1983), 8–27. But the writing of *new* texts of the same kind, especially stories glorifying secular passion, is a different matter.

178

A monitory coda. For all the similarity of the various romance schemes set out in this chapter, two different kinds of approach underlie them. The diagram on page 174 may seem to imply that a historical approach results in a Frye-like scheme of romance, but that is not altogether the case. The historical approach does suggest a provisional pattern, but given that our knowledge of the history of the form is fragmentary, the pattern is not an indispensable adjunct of it; whereas in Frye's theoretical formulation the pattern is the basis of the whole approach. Are the two approaches in conflict? Or are they reconcilable and complementary?

Frye is not primarily interested in fictionality, which he takes for granted; or, consequently, in historicity, in romance as social history.[16] In his kind of scheme, literary antecedents are (at least ideally) subsumed in an overarching "map" of literature as a total entity. Modes of literary expression will mutate and—so to speak—extrude literary history: myth, romance, mimesis, irony. The other approach would start from the other end, build literary history into a social scheme, see "the form romance in historical perspective" (it is the title of one of Perry's chapters). In this kind of scheme, literary forms will mutate with society: epic, drama, romance; with this mutation, the advent of fiction is a major turning point. In both schemes we can speak of an age of epic, an age of romance; so far, the two may meet. The problem strikes when literature is elevated to the condition of autonomous language. The business of criticism is to decipher that language. The business of scholarship is to establish its elements. The two aims are not opposed, but they are not identical.

In the case of ancient romance, the elements of the language are far from easy to establish. For historical reasons some very important elements—texts themselves, chronology—have been seriously misread, and wrongly assigned. To attempt both to determine and to decipher the fraction of the language of literature that is constituted by ancient romance is a somewhat hazardous undertaking, like try-

---

[16] Cf. the observations of David Martin reviewing Frye's more recent book, *The Great Code: The Bible and Literature* (London, 1982) in the *Times Higher Education Supplement*, July 23, 1982, 12: for Frye, "The Bible presents a *model* of exemplary history, not a succession of events . . . Professor Frye . . . has only the most incidental curiosity as to whether any of these events [sc. the events set out in the Bible] ever happened at all. . . . Professor Frye is not so much concerned with history and almost chides Christians and other critics for their concern with what did or didn't happen." It is not clear, in Frye's exegesis, just what the relationship between literature and society is, if there is a relationship; that question is not central to Frye's thought.

ing to solve an equation with too many unknowns, and this book will have failed if it has suggested an altogether simple resolution of the question of the nature of that form. For all the progress made since Rohde, both scholarship and criticism need to tread carefully. But it is a primary condition of any progress at all that what is known should be known generally. That has hardly been the case, so far; and these pages are offered not as an answer to the question of what ancient romance has to offer, but rather as a contribution to the anterior question itself, of what we should look for.

❋ *Bibliography* ❋

THIS BIBLIOGRAPHY contains all works appearing in the notes (with a few minor exceptions), along with a selection of editions and translations. It can be supplemented from those in T. Hägg, *The Novel in Antiquity*, 235–56, and the *Cambridge History of Classical Literature*, 877–86.

Abbreviations: for the abbreviations *CHCL, LSJ*, and *RE*, see p. xiii.

The Bibliography is arranged as follows:

A. *Texts and Translations*

    1. Novels: (a) collections
                  (b) individual authors

    2. Critical Works: (a) collections
                        (b) individual authors

B. *General*

A. TEXTS AND TRANSLATIONS

1. NOVELS

(a) Collections
The contents of the following vary slightly, but all contain most of the primary texts discussed in the present study.

Cataudella, Q., ed. *Il romanzo classico*. Florence, 1973 (1st ed., 1958).
Grimal, P. *Romans grecs et latins*. Paris, 1958 (does not contain Xenophon of Ephesus).
Kytzler, B., ed. *Im Reiche des Eros*. 2 vols. Munich, 1983.
Reardon, B. P., ed. *Collected Ancient Greek Novels*. Berkeley and Los Angeles, 1989.

(b) Individual Authors
Only the principal authors and texts are listed here.

Achilles Tatius.   *Leucippe and Clitophon*. Ed. S. Gaselee. Loeb Classical Library, text and trans. 2d ed., revised by E. H. Warmington (1st ed., 1917). Cambridge, Mass. and London, 1969.

———. Ed. E. Vilborg. Text and commentary. 2 vols. Stockholm, 1955/1962.

Leukippe und Kleitophon. Trans. K. Plepelits. Stuttgart, 1980.

Anon. *Chion of Heraclea: A Novel in Letters.* Ed. I. Düring. Göteborg, 1951.

Apuleius. *Metamorphoses (The Golden Ass).* Ed. S. Gaselee. Loeb Classical Library, text and Adlington's 1566 trans. (revised). London and Cambridge, Mass., 1915.

Les Métamorphoses. Eds. D. S. Robertson and P. Vallette. Budé, text and trans. 3 vols. Paris, 1940–1945.

The Golden Ass. Trans. Robert Graves. Penguin Books. Harmondsworth, 1950.

The Golden Ass. Trans. Jack Lindsay. Bloomington, 1962.

Chariton. *Chaereas and Callirhoe.* Ed. W. E. Blake. Text. Oxford, 1938.

Le roman de Chairéas et Callirhoé. Ed. G. Molinié. Budé, text and trans. 2d ed., revised by A. Billault (1st ed., 1979). Paris, 1989.

Chaereas and Callirhoe. Trans. W. E. Blake. Ann Arbor and London, 1939.

Kallirhoe. Trans. K. Plepelits. Stuttgart, 1976.

Quéreas y Calírroe. Trans. Julia Mendoza. Madrid, 1979.

Chion (See under *Anon.*)

Heliodorus. *Les Ethiopiques.* Eds. R. M. Rattenbury and T. W. Lumb. Budé, text and trans. 3 vols. Paris 1935–1943.

Aethiopica. Ed. A. Colonna. Text. Rome, 1938.

An Ethiopian Romance. Trans. M. Hadas. Ann Arbor, 1957.

Ethiopian Story. Trans. Sir Walter Lamb. Everyman. London, 1961.

Las Etiópicas. Trans. E. Crespo Güemes. Madrid, 1979.

Historia Apollonii Regis Tyri (The Story of Apollonius King of Tyre).

Ed. G.A.A. Kortekaas. Text and commentary. Groningen, 1984.

Longus. *Daphnis and Chloe.* Ed. J. M. Edmonds. Loeb Classical Library, text and Thornley's 1657 trans. (revised). London and New York, 1916.

Pastorales. Ed. G. Dalmeyda. Budé, text and trans. Paris, 1934.

Hirtengeschichten. Ed. O. Schönberger. Text, trans., commentary. 2d ed. (1st ed., 1960). Berlin, 1973.

Petronius.

Xenophon Ephesius.

Daphnis et Chloe. Ed. M. D. Reeve. Teubner; text. 2d ed. (1st ed., 1982). Leipzig, 1986.

Pastorales. Ed. J.-R. Vieillefond. Budé, text and trans. Paris, 1987.

Daphnis and Chloe. Trans. M. Hadas. In *Three Greek Romances*. New York, 1953.

Daphnis and Chloe. Trans. Paul Turner. Penguin Books. 3rd ed. (1st ed., 1956). Harmondsworth, 1989.

Satyricon. Ed. M. Heseltine. Loeb Classical Library, text and trans. 2d ed., revised by E. H. Warmington (1st ed., 1913). London and New York, 1969.

Le Satyricon. Ed. A. Ernout. Budé, text and trans. Paris, 1950.

Satyrica. Ed. K. Müller. Text. 3d ed., trans. by W. Ehlers (1st ed., 1961). Munich, 1983.

Satyricon. Trans. J. P. Sullivan. Penguin Books (1st ed., 1965). Harmondsworth, 1986.

Les Ephésiaques. Ed. G. Dalmeyda. Budé, text and trans. Paris, 1926.

Ephesiacorum Libri V. Ed. A. D. Papanikolaou. Teubner, text. Leipzig, 1973.

The Ephesian Tale. Trans. M. Hadas. In *Three Greek Romances*. New York, 1953.

Efesíacas. Trans. Julia Mendoza. With Chariton (see above). Madrid, 1979.

Fragments and Summaries

Translations of the principal fragments, and of texts existing only in summaries (Antonius Diogenes, *The Wonders beyond Thule*; Iamblichus, *The Babylonian Story*), will be found in the collections edited by Cataudella, Kytzler, and Reardon, and in the Spanish volume containing translations (Julia Mendoza) of Chariton and Xenophon Ephesius, all listed above. A new edition of the fragments is currently in press: S. A. Stephens and J. J. Winkler, eds. *Ancient Greek Novels: The Fragments*. Introduction, text, translation, and commentary. Princeton.

2. CRITICAL WORKS

Many editions and translations are available of the major texts. The following is a brief selection of convenient and reliable modern works, in which further bibliographical guidance may also be found.

(a) Collections

Russell, D. A., and Winterbottom, M., eds. *Ancient Literary Criticism: the Principal Texts in New Translations*. Oxford, 1972.

Russell, D. A. *Criticism in Antiquity*, Appendix, 173–208. Supplement to the texts in *Ancient Literary Criticism* (see preceding entry). London, Berkeley and Los Angeles, 1981.

(b) Individual Authors

Aristotle. *Poetics* Ed. D. W. Lucas. Text, introduction, commentary. Oxford, 1968.

———. *The Poetics of Aristotle*. Trans. Stephen Halliwell. Trans. and commentary. London, 1987.

———. *Poetics*. Trans. Richard Janko. Trans. and commentary; includes *Tractatus Coislinianus*, with a hypothetical reconstruction of *Poetics II*. Indianapolis and Cambridge, 1987.

———. *Rhetoric*. Ed. R. Kassel. Text. Berlin and New York, 1976.

———. *"Art" of Rhetoric*. Ed. J. H. Freese. Loeb Classical Library, text and trans. Cambridge, Mass. and London, 1926.

Hermogenes. *Hermogenes' On Types of Style*. Trans. Cecil W. Wooten. Chapel Hill and London, 1987.

'Longinus.' *'Longinus' On the Sublime*. Ed. D. A. Russell. Text and commentary. Oxford, 1964.

Menander Rhetor. *On Epideictic Oratory*. Eds. D. A. Russell and N. G. Wilson. Text, trans., commentary. Oxford, 1983.

B. GENERAL

Anderson, Graham. *Eros Sophistes: Ancient Novelists at Play*. American Philological Association, American Classical Studies Series, 9. Chico, Calif., 1982.

———. *Philostratus*. London, 1986.

Bakhtin, M. M. "Forms of Time and the Chronotope in the Novel." In *The Dialogic Imagination: Four Essays by M. M. Bakhtin*, Ed. Michael Holquist and trans. Caryl Emerson and Michael Holquist, 86–110. Austin, 1981.

Bartsch, Shadi. *Decoding the Ancient Novel: The Reader and the Role of Description in Heliodorus and Achilles Tatius*. Princeton, 1989.

Beck, H.-G. "Marginalien zum byzantinischen Roman." In *Kyklos* (Festschrift Keydell), ed. H.-G. Beck, 116–28. Berlin, 1978.

Beer, Gillian. *The Romance*. London, 1970.

Behr, C. A. *Aelius Aristides and the Sacred Tales*. Amsterdam, 1968.

Beye, C. R. *Epic and Romance in the* Argonautica *of Apollonius*. Carbondale and Edwardsville, 1982.

Bompaire, J. *Lucien écrivain*. Paris, 1958.

Booth, Wayne. *The Rhetoric of Fiction*. Chicago, 1961.

Bossuyt, I. "Maurice Ravel (1875–1937) en het ballet 'Daphnis et Chloe' (1909–1912)." *Kleio* 13 (1983), 199–211.

Boulanger, A. *Aelius Aristide et la sophistique dans la province d'Asie au IIe siècle de notre ère*. Paris, 1923.

Bowersock, G. W. *Greek Sophists in the Roman Empire*. Oxford, 1969.

———. "Philostratus." In *CHCL*, 655–58.

Bowie, E.L. "Greeks and their Past in the Second Sophistic." *Past and Present* 46 (1970), 3–41.

———. "The Novels and the Real World." In *Erotica Antiqua*, ed. B. P. Reardon, 91–96. Bangor, Wales, 1977.

———. "Apollonius of Tyana: Tradition and Reality." In *Aufstieg und Niedergang der römischen Welt*, eds. H. Temporini and W. Haase, II.16.2, 1652–99. Berlin, 1978.

———. "The Importance of Sophists." *Yale Classical Studies* 27 (1982), 29–59.

———. "The Greek Novel." In *CHCL*, 683–99.

———. "Theocritus' Seventh *Idyll*, Philetas and Longus." *Classical Quarterly* 35 (1985), 67–91.

Burnett, Anne Pippin. *Catastrophe Survived*. Oxford, 1971.

Cambridge History of Classical Literature, vol. 1: *Greek Literature*, eds. P. E. Easterling and B.M.W. Knox ("CHCL"). Cambridge, 1985.

Cancik, H. "Erwin Rohde, ein Philologe der Bismarckzeit." In *Semper Apertus: Sechshundert Jahre Ruprecht-Karls-Universität Heidelberg 1386–1986*, ed. W. Doerr, 436–505. Berlin and Heidelberg, 1986.

Cataudella, Q. "Riflessi virgiliani nel romanzo di Caritone." *Athenaeum* 5 (1927), 302–12.

Chadwick, H. *The Early Church*. Penguin Books. Harmondsworth, 1967.

Chalk, H.H.O. "Eros and the Lesbian Pastorals of Longos." *Journal of Hellenic Studies* 80 (1960), 32–51.

———. Review of R. Merkelbach, *Roman und Mysterium in der Antike* (Munich and Berlin, 1962). *Classical Review* 13 (1963), 161–63.

Cresci, L. R. "Il romanzo di Longo Sofista e la tradizione bucolica." *Atene e Roma* 26 (1981), 1–25.

Desideri, P. *Dione di Prusa: un intellettuale greco nell' impero romano*. Messina and Florence, 1978.

Dihle, A. "Zur Datierung des Metiochos-Romans." *Würzburger Jahrbücher für die Altertumswissenschaft* NF 4 (1978), 47–55.

Dodds, E. R. *Pagan and Christian in an Age of Anxiety*. Cambridge, 1965.

Durham, D. B. "Parody in Achilles Tatius." *Classical Philology* 33 (1938), 1–19.

Easterling, P.E., and Knox, B.M.W., eds. *The Cambridge History of Classical Literature*, vol. 1 (Greek). Cambridge, 1985.

Effe, B. "Longos: zur Funktionsgeschichte der Bukolik in der römischen Kaiserzeit." *Hermes* 110 (1982), 65–84.

Ferguson, John. *The Religions of the Roman Empire*. London, 1970.

Festugière, A. J. *Personal Religion Among the Greeks*. Berkeley and Los Angeles, 1954.

185

Festugière, A. J. Aelius Aristide, *Discours Sacrés: rêve, religion, médecine au IIe siècle après J.-C.* Paris, 1986.

Frye, Northrop. *Anatomy of Criticism.* Princeton, 1957.

———. *The Secular Scripture: A Study of the Structure of Romance.* Cambridge, Mass., 1976.

———. *The Great Code: The Bible and Literature.* London, 1982.

Gärtner, H. "Xenophon von Ephesos." *RE* 9A.2 (1967) 2055–89.

Gerschmann, K.-H. *Chariton-Interpretationen.* Diss., University of Münster, 1974.

Giangrande, G. Review of A. D. Papanikolaou, *Chariton-Studien* (Göttingen, 1973). *Journal of Hellenic Studies* 94 (1974), 197–98.

Gill, Christopher. "Plato's Atlantis Story and the Birth of Fiction." *Philosophy and Literature* 3 (1979), 64–78.

———. "Plato and Politics: the *Critias* and the *Politicus.*" *Phronesis* 24 (1979), 148–67.

Gronewald, M. "Ein neues Fragment zu einem Roman." *Zeitschrift für Papyrologie und Epigraphik* 35 (1979), 15–20.

Grube, G.M.A. *The Greek and Roman Critics.* London, 1955.

Hägg, Tomas. "Die Ephesiaka des Xenophon Ephesios—Original oder Epitome?" *Classica et Mediaevalia* 37 (1966), 118–61.

———. *Narrative Technique in Ancient Greek Romances.* Stockholm, 1971.

———. Review of G. Molinié, ed. *Chariton: le roman de Chairéas et Callirhoé* (Paris, 1979). *Gnomon* 53 (1981), 698–700.

———. *Den Antika Romanen.* Uppsala, 1980.

———. *The Novel in Antiquity.* Oxford, Berkeley and Los Angeles, 1983.

———. "The Parthenope Romance Decapitated?" *Symbolae Osloenses* 59 (1984), 61–92.

Halliwell, S. *Aristotle's Poetics.* London, 1986.

Harriott, Rosemary. *Poetry and Criticism before Plato.* London, 1969.

Haslam, M. W. "Narrative about Tinouphis in Prosimetrum." In *Papyri Greek and Egyptian . . . in Honour of E. G. Turner*, 35–45. Egypt Exploration Society. London, 1981.

Hefti, V. *Zur Erzählungstechnik in Heliodors Aethiopica.* Vienna, 1950.

Heiserman, A. "Aphrodisian Chastity." *Critical Inquiry* 2 (1975), 281–96.

———. *The Novel before the Novel.* Chicago and London, 1977.

Helm, R. *Der antike Roman.* Göttingen, 1948.

Helms, J. *Character Portrayal in the Romance of Chariton.* The Hague and Paris, 1966.

Holzberg, N. *Der antike Roman.* Munich and Zurich, 1986.

Hunter, R. L. *A Study of* Daphnis and Chloe. Cambridge, 1983.

Janko, R. *Aristotle on Comedy.* Berkeley, 1984.

Jones, C. P. *The Roman World of Dio Chrysostom.* Cambridge, Mass., and London, 1978.

————. *Culture and Society in Lucian*. Cambridge, Mass., and London, 1986.

Jüttner, H. *De Polemonis vita operibus arte*. Breslau, 1898. Reprint. Hildesheim, 1967.

Kennedy, G. A. *The Art of Persuasion in Greece*. London, 1962.

Kerényi, K. *Die griechisch-orientalische Romanliteratur in religions-geschichtlicher Beleuchtung*. Tübingen, 1927. 3rd ed. Darmstadt, 1973.

Knox, B.M.W. "Books and Readers in the Greek World." In *CHCL*, 1–41.

Kuch, H., ed. *Der antike Roman: Untersuchungen zur literarischen Kommunikation und Gattungsgeschichte*. Berlin, DDR, 1989.

Landels, J. G. *Engineering in the Ancient World*. London, Berkeley and Los Angeles, 1980.

Lavagnini, B. *Studi sul romanzo greco*. Messina and Florence, 1950.

Lesky, A. *A History of Greek Literature*, trans. J. Willis and C. de Heer. London, 1966; Berne (German original), 1957/1958.

Lightfoot, C. S. "Facts and Fiction—The Third Siege of Nisibis (A.D. 350)." *Historia* 37 (1988), 105–25.

Ludvíkovský, J. *Řecký Román Dobrodružný (Le roman grec d'aventures)*. Prague, 1925.

McCulloh, W. E. *Longus*. Twayne's World Authors Series. New York, 1970.

Marincola, J. "The Sources of Herodotus." *Arethusa* 20 (1987), 26–40.

McKeon, M. *The Origins of the English Novel*. Baltimore and London, 1987.

Maróth, M. "Le siège de Nisibe en 350 ap. J.-Ch. d'après des sources syriennes." *Acta Antiqua Academiae Scientiarum Hungaricae* 27 (1979), 239–43.

Marrou, H.-I. *Histoire de l'éducation dans l'antiquité*. 6th ed. (1st ed., 1948; English trans. G. Lamb, London, 1956). Paris, 1965.

Martin, David. Review of Northrop Frye, *The Great Code: The Bible and Literature* (London, 1982). *Times Higher Education Supplement*, July 23, 1982, 12.

Merkelbach, R. *Roman und Mysterium in der Antike*. Munich, 1962.

————. *Die Hirten des Dionysos: die Dionysos-mysterien der römischen Kaiserzeit und der bukolische Roman des Longus*. Stuttgart, 1988.

Michenaud, G. and Dierkens, J. *Les rêves dans les "Discours Sacrés" d'Aelius Aristide: essai d'analyse psychologique*. Brussels, 1972.

Millar, F. *A Study of Cassius Dio*. Oxford, 1964.

Moles, J. P. "The Career and Conversion of Dio Chrysostom." *Journal of Hellenic Studies* 98 (1978), 79–100.

Momigliano, A. *The Development of Greek Biography*. Cambridge, Mass., 1971.

Morgan, J. R. *A Commentary on the Ninth and Tenth Books of the Aithiopica of Heliodoros*. D.Phil. diss., University of Oxford, 1978.

————. "History, Romance and Realism in the *Aithiopika* of Heliodoros." *Classical Antiquity* 1 (1982), 221–65.

Müller, C.-W. "Chariton von Aphrodisias und die Theorie des Romans in der Antike." *Antike und Abendland* 22 (1976), 115–36.

Nilsson, M. P. *The Dionysiac Mysteries of the Hellenistic and Roman Age.* Lund, 1957. Reprint. New York, 1975.

Norden, E. *Die antike Kunstprosa.* Stuttgart, 1898. 5th ed. 1958.

Oliver, J. H. "Xenophon of Ephesus and the Antithesis Historia-Philosophia." In *Arktouros: Hellenic Studies Presented to B.M.W. Knox,* eds. G. W. Bowersock *et al.,* 401–406. Berlin, 1979.

Papanikolaou, A. D. *Chariton-Studien.* Göttingen, 1973.

Parsons, P. J. "Narrative about Iolaus." *Oxyrhynchus Papyri* 42 (1974), 34–41 (No. 3010).

Pernot, L. *Les discours siciliens d'Aelius Aristide.* New York, 1981.

Perry, B. E. "Chariton and his Romance from a Literary-Historical Point of View." *American Journal of Philology* 51 (1930), 93–134.

———. *The Ancient Romances.* Berkeley and Los Angeles, 1967.

Pervo, R. I. *Profit with Delight: The Literary Framework of the Acts of the Apostles.* Philadelphia, 1987.

Petri, R. *Über den Roman des Chariton.* Meisenheim am Glan, 1963.

Pouilloux, J. "Delphes dans les *Ethiopiques* d'Héliodore: la réalité dans la fiction." *Journal des Savants* 1983, 259–86.

Rattenbury, R. M. "Traces of Lost Greek Romances." In *New Chapters in the History of Greek Literature,* ed. J. U. Powell, III, 211–57. Oxford, 1933.

Reardon, B. P. "The Greek Novel." *Phoenix* 23 (1969), 291–309.

———. *Courants littéraires grecs des IIe et IIIe siècles après J.-C.* Paris, 1971.

———. "Aspects of the Greek Novel." *Greece and Rome* 33 (1976), 118–31.

———. Review of A. D. Papanikolaou, *Chariton-Studien* (Göttingen, 1973). *Classical Review* 26 (1976), 21–23.

———, ed. *Erotica Antiqua: ICAN 1976. Acta of the International Conference on the Ancient Novel.* Bangor, Wales, 1977.

———. "Theme, Structure and Narrative in Chariton." *Yale Classical Studies* 27 (1982), 1–27.

———. Review of G. Molinié, ed. *Chariton: le roman de Chairéas et Callirhoé* (Paris, 1979). *Revue des Etudes Grecques* 95 (1982), 157–73.

Reich, H. *Der Mimus.* Berlin, 1903.

Reitzenstein, R. *Hellenistische Wundererzählungen.* Leipzig, 1906. Reprint. Stuttgart, 1963.

Rohde, E. *Der griechische Roman und seine Vorläufer.* Leipzig, 1876. 3rd ed., ed. W. Schmid, Leipzig, 1914. 4th ed. (reprint of 3rd), with foreword by K. Kerényi, Hildesheim, 1960. 5th ed. (reprint of 4th), Hildesheim, 1974.

Ruiz Montero, C. "Una observación para la cronologia de Caritón de Afrodisias." *Estudios Clásicos* 24 (1980), 63–69.

———. "The Structural Pattern of the Ancient Greek Romances and the *Morphology of the Folk-Tale* of V. Propp." *Fabula* 22 (1981), 228–38.

———. *La estructura de la novela griega.* Salamanca, 1988.

Russell, D. A. "Rhetoric and Criticism." *Greece and Rome* 14 (1967), 130–44.

————. *Plutarch*. London, 1972.

————. *Criticism in Antiquity*. London, Berkeley, and Los Angeles, 1981.

————. "Longinus Revisited." *Mnemosyne* 34 (1981), 72–86.

————. *Greek Declamation*. Cambridge, 1983.

Sandy, Gerald N. *Heliodorus*. Twayne's World Authors Series. New York, 1982.

Schmeling, Gareth L. *Chariton*. Twayne's World Authors Series. New York, 1974.

————. *Xenophon of Ephesus*. Twayne's World Authors Series. Boston, 1980.

Schmid, W. "Chariton." *RE* 3.2 (1899) 2168–71.

Schwartz, E. *Fünf Vorträge über den griechischen Roman*. Berlin, 1943 (1st ed., 1896).

Segal, Charles. "The Two Worlds of Euripides' *Helen*." *Transactions of the American Philological Association* 102 (1971), 553–614.

Stadter, Philip. *Arrian of Nicomedia*. Chapel Hill, N.C. 1980.

Stinton, T.C.W. "*Hamartia* in Aristotle and Greek Tragedy." *Classical Quarterly* 25 (1979), 221–54.

Sutton, Dana Ferrin. "Cicero on Minor Dramatic Forms." *Symbolae Osloenses* 59 (1984), 29–36.

————. *Seneca on the Stage*. Leiden, 1986.

Szepessy, T. "Le siège de Nisibe et la chronologie d'Héliodore." *Acta Antiqua Academiae Scientiarum Hungaricae* 24 (1976), 247–76.

Tatum, James. *Apuleius and* The Golden Ass. Ithaca and London, 1979.

————. *Xenophon's Imperial Fiction: On* The Education of Cyrus. Princeton, 1989.

Tatum, James and Vernazza, Gail M. *The Ancient Novel: Classical Paradigms and Modern Perspectives*. Hanover, N.H.: Dartmouth College, 1990 (*Acta of the International Conference on the Ancient Novel 1989*).

Trenkner, Sophie. *The Greek Novella in the Classical Period*. Cambridge, 1958.

Treu, K. "Der antike Roman und seine Publikum." In *Der antike Roman: Untersuchungen zur literarischen Kommunikation und Gattungsgeschichte*, ed. H. Kuch, 178–97. Berlin, DDR, 1989.

Turcan, R. "Le roman 'initiatique'; à propos d'un livre récent." *Revue de l'Histoire des Religions* 163 (1963), 149–99.

Turner, P. "Novels, Ancient and Modern." *Novel* 2 (1968–1969), 15–24.

Vidal-Naquet, P. "Flavius Arrien entre deux mondes." In *Arrien: Histoire d'Alexandre*, trans. P. Savinel, 309–94. Paris, 1984.

Walden, J.W.H. "Stage Terms in Heliodorus's Aethiopica." *Harvard Studies in Classical Philology* 5 (1894), 1–43.

Walsh, P. G. *The Roman Novel*. Cambridge, 1970.

Wardman, Alan. *Plutarch's Lives*. London, 1974.

Watt, Ian. *The Rise of the Novel*. London, 1957.

Weinreich, O. *Der griechische Liebesroman*. Zurich, 1962 (originally published in *Heliodors Aithiopika*, trans. R. Reymer, [Zurich, 1950], 323–45).

West, S. R. Review of T. Hägg, *The Novel in Antiquity* (Oxford, Berkeley, and Los Angeles, 1983). *Classical Review* 34 (1984), 201–203.

Wijer, B. van de. "Enkele picturale voorstellingen van Daphnis en Chloe." *Kleio* 13 (1983), 212–20.

Wilamowitz-Moellendorff, U. von. "Der Rhetor Aristeides." *Sitzungsberichte der Preussischen Akademie der Wissenschaften*, 5 November, 1925, 333–53.

Wilcken, U. "Ein neuer griechischer Roman." *Hermes* 28 (1893), 161–93.

Wilson, N. G. *Scholars of Byzantium*. London and Baltimore, 1983.

Winkler, J. J. "The Mendacity of Kalasiris and the Narrative Strategy of Heliodoros' *Aithiopika*." *Yale Classical Studies* 27 (1982), 93–158.

Witt, R. E. *Isis in the Graeco-Roman World*. London, 1971.

Wolff, S. L. *The Greek Romances in Elizabethan Prose Fiction*. New York, 1912.

* Index *

Only a selection of modern scholars is included in this index. See the Bibliography for others cited in the notes.

THE LONG RETREAT

The Calamitous American Defense of New Jersey 1776

*The sick and half naked veterans
of the long retreat streamed past.*
—Attributed to Charles Willson Peale, watching the
American retreat across the Delaware River, 1776

*I shall not now attempt to give all the particulars
of our retreat to the Delaware; suffice it for the present
to say, that both officers and men, though greatly harassed
and fatigued, frequently without rest, covering, or provision,
the inevitable consequences of a long retreat,
bore it with a manly and a martial spirit.*
—Thomas Paine, *The American Crisis—Number One*

THE LONG RETREAT

The Calamitous American Defense of New Jersey 1776

ARTHUR S. LEFKOWITZ

The UPLAND PRESS
Metuchen, New Jersey

Suggested cataloguing information
Lefkowitz, Arthur S.
    The long retreat : the calamitous American defense of New Jersey, 1776 / Arthur
S. Lefkowitz. — Metuchen, N.J. : Upland Press, 1998.
        xxvi, 162 p. : ill. ; 24 cm.
        Includes bibliographical references (p. 151-157) and index.
        ISBN 0-9642916-7-3

        1. Trenton, Battle of, 1776.   2. Fort Washington (New York, N.Y.)--Capture,
        1776.   3. Princeton, Battle of, 1777.   4. New Jersey--History--Revolution, 1775-
        1783.   5. United States--History--Revolution, 1775-1783--Campaigns.   6. United
        States. Continental Army--History. I. Title.
        E241 .T7 L493 1998

Printed in the United States of America

For my wife, Susan

CONTENTS

PREFACE

General Washington's whole army followed that night, and made a grand but dreadful appearance. All the shores where lighted up with large fires. The Boats continually passing and repassing full of men, Horses, artilery, and camp Equipage. The Hollowing of hundreds of men in their difficulties . . . made it rather the appearance of Hell than any earthly scene.[1]

--Charles Willson Peale on the escape of the rebel army
across the Delaware River, December 1776

"These are the times that try men's souls." That opening line of Thomas Paine's initial essay of *The Crisis* is one of the most famous in American literature. "The Summer soldier and the sunshine patriot," Paine went on, "will, in this crisis, shrink from the service of their country: but he that stands it now, deserves the love and thanks of man and woman."[2] When he conceived the words, Paine was trudging along the muddy roads of New Jersey with George Washington's bedraggled army. He began to write the essay when the retreating force stopped briefly at Newark, and tradition has it that a drum head served as his desk. It was a gloomy November 1776, and the pursuing British seemed within reach of overtaking Washington and crushing the Revolution in its infancy.

---

[1]Charles Willson Peale, "Autobiography," undated entry, manuscript volume, American Philosophical Society, Philadelphia.

[2]Thomas Paine, "The American Crisis # 1 [1776]," *Collected Writings* (New York: Library of America, 1995), 91-99.

Paine's ringing call to duty helped awaken the rebel consciousness and galvanize popular support for the faltering rebellion. But if the words were legendary, their source of inspiration has been less understood. The retreat of Washington's army through New Jersey, while clearly a significant episode, has remained relatively obscure, hidden under the smoke and thunder of the Revolution's more storied events.

In fact, the three-week retreat of the American army across New Jersey was a remarkable saga, an event marked by blunders and bravery, politics and treachery, desperation and resourcefulness. It began when the British invaded New Jersey on the night of November 19th, 1776 and continued until Washington escaped with his battered command across the Delaware River into Pennsylvania on December 4th. The troops involved never forgot those traumatic days. Years later, artist Charles Willson Peale, then on active duty, vividly recalled watching as "the sick and half naked veterans of the long retreat streamed past."[1] The retreat marked the military low point of the war; it was arguably the closest the British came to winning the eight-year conflict.

Yet for all of its importance, historians have devoted scant attention to the 1776 retreat. The classic general history of New Jersey in the Revolution is Leonard Lundin's *Cockpit of the American Revolution* (1940), which offers the most comprehensive view of military operations during the eventful weeks of November and December. Beyond Lundin's book, however, there are only a handful of studies dealing with the retreat in any detail.[2]

Thus, the present book is the first to focus exclusively on the retreat across New Jersey and to trace the story of the rebel ordeal in all of its dramatic detail. Relating the story in a single narrative is an important task in itself, for the tale has never had a full telling. A comprehensive view of the retreat certainly adds another dimension to our understanding of what happened prior to the critical Battles of Trenton and Princeton. In fact, as I

---

[1]This quote has long been attributed to Peale, although it does not appear in any of his published or unpublished works. Yet the sentiments are similar to Peale's other observations on the retreat found in his unpublished "Autobiography."

[2]Leonard Lundin, *Cockpit of the Revolution* (Princeton: Princeton University Press, 1940). There also are accounts of the retreat in William Stryker's's *The Battles of Trenton and Princeton* (Boston: Riverside Press, 1898); Samuel Smith's *The Battle of Trenton* (Monmouth Beach, NJ: Philip Freneau Press, 1965); *The Battle of Princeton* (Monmouth Beach, NJ: Philip Freneau Press, 1967); and William Dwyer's *The Day is Ours!* (New York: Viking Press, 1983).

will argue, the bitter retreat is best interpreted as an integral part of the events that saw the fortunes of war swing back toward the Americans in the stunning campaign of late 1776 and early 1777. To see this clearly, however, we need to concentrate on the course and nature of the retreat itself.

This view is at some variance with most accounts of the patriot crisis of late 1776. Most studies, and even many contemporary accounts, have depicted an American army on the verge of final defeat, and an exhausted Washington reduced to indecisiveness. Yet less than three weeks after fleeing across the Delaware, this same rebel army and general rebounded to sting the British at Trenton and Princeton; with a stroke, the ragged army restored flagging patriot morale. It was one of the most stunning feats in the history of American arms.

But was it really the story of a beaten army rising from the near-dead? In reality, this traditional view, however satisfying, is probably inconsistent with the facts. There were no dramatic circumstances or events which changed the American situation between the time Washington was chased out of New Jersey and his Christmas night counterattack at Trenton. If anything, Washington's situation had deteriorated after he reached Pennsylvania and he certainly had no chance to take a rest from the war.

In fact, historians have tended to overdramatize aspects of the New Jersey retreat. Intentionally or not, the effect has been to make accounts of Washington's Trenton-Princeton campaign more electrifying. In turn, this has obscured our ability to see in the retreat itself anything of the nature of the army and its operations, of Washington's maturing as a commander, or of other significant aspects of the patriot war effort. This account seeks a fuller and more balanced perspective on those three turbulent weeks in late 1776, and thus a better view of why the war ultimately developed as it did.

Over the years, balancing perspectives on the 1776 retreat has not been easy. The early American accounts tended to idolize the participants, emphasizing their tribulations and sacrifices. Almost uniformly, patriotic accounts told of stalwart soldiers, resolute in the face of redcoat bayonets and eager to follow Washington to the front. Only time tempered such views. With few exceptions, serious studies of the American Revolution emerged only in this century. It took 150 years for the participants and their direct descendants to die-off and for emotions to calm down enough for authors to look at the Revolution at least a bit more dispassionately.

My conclusion is that the era of the American Revolution, and especially those days of the retreat across New Jersey, was very much like our own. As today, we saw the full spectrum of human behavior, from dedication and sacrifice to avarice and deceit. In this account, I have tried to present a balanced narrative of men serving under terrible stress, with some rising to the occasion and others sinking beneath its weight. And, admittedly, something of the old aura of respect for the rebels remains. It is justified: readers will find much here to make them proud of those who marched west with General Washington in late 1776.

Researching the retreat, like any other major event in the American Revolution, presented special challenges. One problem lay in the fact that only a relative handful of common soldier's diaries have survived from the Revolutionary era.[1] Such diaries and journals have offered some of the most telling perspectives on everyday military life and great battles. Unfortunately, many common soldiers were illiterate, and often it was just too much trouble for a soldier to carry a journal. In any case, first-hand accounts of the "long retreat" as seen from the ranks are rare.

Troop strength presented another problem. The issue is critical to understanding the events of November and December 1776, but records are confusing, making it difficult to evaluate the most alarming accounts of the state of the rebel army as the retreat gathered momentum. In fact, things were probably as bad as many contemporary stories indicated, a conclusion I have drawn from the troop returns tabulated in Charles H. Lesser's *The Sinews of Independence* (1976). Lesser has gathered all of the known returns of the army, shedding a great deal of light on the size and composition of the American forces for each month of the Revolution. Based on a review of Lesser's data, my account presents the rebels as a quite debilitated force. Yet however badly off, the patriot military was still a force to reckon with, a fact the British forgot at their peril.

Then there was the problem of General Charles Lee. Lee was an eccentric former British officer and Washington's senior lieutenant during the New Jersey retreat. Understanding Lee is crucial to understanding the events of late 1776. He died before the end of the Revolution and never wrote an autobiography. A biography of him appeared in London as early as 1792 and the New York Historical Society published his correspondence from 1871 to 1874. The *Lee Papers* are the foundation of our knowledge about the man. In 1951, John Aden wrote the only modern biography of this complex general,

---

[1]For a listing of extant published diaries and similar accounts by enlisted men, see Howard Peckham, ed., *Memoirs of the Life of John Adlum in the Revolutionary War* (Chicago: The Caxton Club, 1968).

Charles Lee, Traitor or Patriot? Aden was a good historian, but Lee was such a complicated person that Aden was unsure what to make of him. Certainly he was not a traitor, although some historians (albeit not most professional historians) have claimed as much. But without finding him disloyal, my research has led me to think worse of Lee's conduct and character than have Alden and many other writers. Indeed, I believe his actions during the New Jersey retreat flirted with outright mutiny.

In addition to many other revealing accounts of the action in New Jersey, I was able to take advantage of a number of sources unavailable to previous historians of the retreat. Perhaps most helpful in this regard was the diary of Hessian Captain Johann Ewald, who served in America from 1776 to 1783. Ewald was in New Jersey in late 1776 and an active participant in the British efforts to catch-up with Washington's army.

Historians knew a little about Ewald's diary and snippets of it had been published during the nineteenth century. However, no one knew that Ewald's diary was intact until a German nobleman, ruined by World War II, offered to sell it to Major Joseph Tustin, a U.S. Air Force historian stationed in Germany at the end of the Second World War. Tustin, who was fluent in German, recognized the significance of the Ewald diary and purchased it. He spent the next twenty years tracking down a missing volume and translating and annotating the complete diary for publication. Ewald's *Diary of the American War* was published in 1979 by Yale University Press; it proved an essential source in the writing of *The Long Retreat*.

In quoting from portions of the Ewald diary, as well as other primary sources, I have followed modern convention and retained original grammar and spelling. In addition, I have extensively footnoted my text. The narrative is written so that anyone with a basic understanding of the American Revolution can follow the story; the footnotes are designed to give technical information and make my sources available to more serious students of the War for Independence.

A number of historians contributed their expertise and time to help me write this book. Several people were especially helpful and I am pleased to acknowledge their generous assistance. First is Lieutenant Colonel Donald Londahl-Smidt, a retired U.S. Air Force officer and expert on the role of the Hessians in the Revolution. Donald has me almost convinced that the Hessians who fought in America were British allies and not hired mercenaries. George Woodbridge, another outstanding historian and valued friend helped me with information about uniforms, flags and the military organization of the Revolutionary War armies. George did the cover art for this book, which is an example of his fine artistic and historical skills. Todd Braisted, who may know more about the Loyalists than anyone since Governor William Franklin, is another researcher who generously shared his knowledge with me. Finally, I want to give special thanks to Bergen County historian John Spring. John generously shared with me his considerable knowledge about the British army's entry into and march through Bergen County, and especially the legend of Polly Wyckoff.

I also want to acknowledge and thank William McMillen from Richmondtown Restoration, Staten Island. Bill helped me understand the road and ferry system in New York and New Jersey during the colonial period. John Muller, curator of the Fort Lee Museum, provided invaluable information about the British invasion of New Jersey; Kevin Wright, curator of the Stueben House in Bergen County, shared his knowledge of the Crown forces' assault on New Bridge; and Richard L. Porter, a cultural resource specialist with The RBA Group (a firm of engineers, architects and planners), generously briefed me on the events associated with Raritan Landing. John Mills, curator of the Thomas Clarke House at Princeton Battlefield State Park, shared his keen understanding of the campaigning in late 1776 and early 1777.

Another valued contributor was Charles Cummings, Assistant Director of the Newark Public Library and the official historian of Newark, New Jersey. I also wish to acknowledge help from Eric Olsen, chief historian at Morristown National Historic Park; William E. Davidson, Commanding Officer of a Revolutionary War reenactment group portraying Captain Alexander Hamilton's New York Artillery Company; John Rees, whose interests are the Revolutionary War exploits of General William Maxwell and Colonel Israel Shreve; Edward Ayres, historian at the Yorktown Victory Center in Yorktown, Virginia, who helped with information about Virginia troops in New Jersey in 1776. Mark Thompson, from the University of North Carolina, corresponded with me concerning Colonel Henry Knox. Also free with their valuable time and advice were Philander Chase, senior associate editor of the Revolutionary War Series of *The Papers of George Washington*; Harry Kels Swann, at Washington Crossing State Historic Park, New Jersey; Revolutionary War scholar Kemble Widmer; and the late Mrs. Chaire Tholl, a great lady and a fine Bergen County historian.

Research for this book was done at several libraries and I want to acknowledge their help and the wonderful service of their librarians: the Rutgers University Library Rare Book Collection; the Firestone Library at Princeton University; David Flowler and the David Library of the American Revolution at Washington Crossing, Pennsylvania; Ms. Joni Rowe, museum specialist at Morristown National Historical Park; Don Wilcox and David Bosse from the William L. Clements Library at the University of Michigan; Ms. Mariam Touba at the New York Historical Society; and, finally, the Library Company of Philadelphia, a grand institution for people like myself who suffer from bibliomania.

I am especially grateful to my wife, Susan, who patiently read chapter drafts and made valuable suggestions, and to whom I have dedicated this book.

Arthur S. Lefkowitz
Piscataway, New Jersey, 1998

ILLUSTRATIONS

1. Portrait of George Washington (1776), by Charles Willson Peale.

2. Title page from Roger Stevenson's *Military Instructions for Officers* on partisan warfare (1775).

3. *Forcing Hudson River Passage* (1779), by Dominic Serres.

4. *A View of the Attack against Fort Washington and Rebel Redoubts near New York on the 16 November 1776,* by Captain Thomas Davies.

5. Detail from *A Topographical Map of the North Part of New York Island* (1777), by Claude Joseph Sauthier.

6-7. *Landing of the British Forces in the Jerseys on the 20th of November 1776,* by Captain Thomas Davies.

8-9. *Map of the New Jersey Campaign, 1776,* by George C. Woodbridge.

10. Disputed Washington letter of November 30, 1776, from William S. Stryker's *The Battle of Trenton and Princeton.*

11. Page from General Sir Henry Clinton's copy of Charles Stedman's *History of the Origin, Progress, and Termination of the American War* (1794).

12-13. Projected 1776-1777 winter quarters for the British in New Jersey, map by Captain John Montresor.

14-15. Illustration of a pontoon bridge built by British army engineers, from the Henry Clinton Papers.

16. Spy map of Princeton.

Illustrations appear as a group following page 68.

INTRODUCTION

The 1776 campaign was every bit the perilous enterprise rooted in popular legend. Even the most scholarly accounts characterize the month between late November and late December 1776 as one of the most chaotic and desperate periods of the War for Independence. The shock of the debacle at Fort Washington was still fresh when Cornwallis struck on the New Jersey side of the Hudson River. The tactical surprise at Fort Lee, a near disaster in itself with major losses in stores, arms and equipment, threw the rebels almost completely off balance. Disorganized and unsure of the extent of the British thrust, and certainly unaware of its intentions, Washington's units had no alternative but to fall back into the interior of the state. The "long retreat," as soldier-artist Charles Willson Peale reportedly called it, was underway, and the fate of the Revolution itself was in the balance. The army traveled roads that led from Fort Lee and, finally, across the Delaware River near Trenton on December 7. Every step of the way, patriots in ranks, in Congress, and in state and local government worked frantically to keep Washington's army alive. Seldom, if ever, has the survival of the republic depended so directly on the fortunes of war and on the outcome of a single campaign.

If the story of the retreat was grim, however, it was also interesting. *In The Long Retreat,* Arthur Lefkowitz has offered a fresh and richly detailed new narrative of the rebel plight in all of its confusion and drama. But in looking below the familiar story of patriot despair and British prowess, Lefkowitz has made some telling new observations and added a number of helpful and novel perspectives on the winter campaign of late 1776. What emerges from the pages of *The Long Retreat* is an American war effort that, if no less battered and desperate than previous historians have had it, was arguably more resilient and resourceful than most earlier scholarship has allowed. As bad as things were, the rebel army always remained operational.

Perspective is the key to this book. Surprisingly, it is the first major study devoted solely to the 1776 retreat, and telling the story whole presents certain advantages. Among these were chances to set the record straight on a number of points, some of them basic. Matters such as American and British troop movements, for example, have been contentious issues for as long as historians have written about the retreat, and here receive a fresh and thorough review. Questions of which units went where, by exactly which routes, when, and why, are critical to understanding the campaign. Lefkowitz has sorted through the available evidence, much of it conflicting, and it appears that he has come as close as we will ever get to establishing a definitive itinerary for both armies over the months of November and December. This alone is a valuable contribution.

Troop movements, however, concerned more than just the comings and goings of the armies. The details were revealing. For example, in tracking the routes of Washington's men and the pursuing columns under Lord Cornwallis, Lefkowitz finally dispels any lingering questions over the pace of the retreat. It was no race to the Delaware. After the tactical surprise at Fort Lee, Washington was able to regroup and fall back in a more-or-less organized fashion. Cornwallis came after him, but only deliberately. The only *coup de main* came at For Lee itself, an operation that fully demonstrated the British capability to strike hard and fast when they wanted to. In fact, there was no repetition, or even an attempted repetition, of the dramatic opening blow at Hackensack, Newark, New Brunswick, or anywhere else along the route to Trenton. Why not? Why, and how, did the retreating patriot forces not only get away, but how did they do so in such a condition that they were able to counterattack within weeks after having abandoned New Jersey?

The heart of *The Long Retreat* is the author's attempt to answer these and similar questions.

Many of the explanations lay with operations of the British army. Indeed, Lefkowitz strenuously faults the British for allowing Washington to escape. He is at pains to note that Howe's initial plan did not envision a knock-out blow at Fort Lee, or even in its immediate aftermath somewhere in the New Jersey interior. The British general had wanted simply to fully secure the Hudson River; and if this limited objective was short on imagination, it was perhaps justified by Howe's scant knowledge of the situation west of the Hudson. But Howe showed little dash even after patriot distress became clear. When Cornwallis and other more aggressive officers urged a bolder course, the royal Commander-in-Chief finally agreed to push further into the state. Still, however, he warned his subordinates to avoid any unnecessary risks. There is no doubt that had Howe ordered it, Cornwallis could have caught Washington somewhere along the line of retreat. But the general, fully appraised of Washington's difficulties, never gave the order.

Nor did Howe bring his entire force to bear. Rather, in December he sent a major expedition against Rhode Island to secure Newport as a naval base. Some of his senior officers, including Henry Clinton, who commanded the six-thousand-man Newport operation, thought the move ill-advised. That many men, they pointed out, might have struck another blow through central New Jersey and linked up with Cornwallis in the interior. A move with any celerity at all could well have trapped Washington somewhere in the New Brunswick area. But Howe was not interested. He no longer saw the ragtag patriot army as a serious threat. Instead, he was content to let Cornwallis push the rebels toward the Delaware while he sought to encourage loyalist activity in the growing zone of British occupation. As a decisive military solution to the rebellion, the New Jersey campaign was an opportunity lost.

Subsequent events would reveal the folly of not making the destruction of Washington's army the primary objective in New Jersey. But British errors explained only part of the campaign. If Howe and other senior British commanders made mistakes, the same was true of the Americans. In fact, patriots frequently hurt themselves badly. Lefkowitz makes it clear that Washington and other patriot officers were guilty of miscues serious enough to invite their own destruction.

Like many previous authors, for example, Lefkowitz is highly critical of Washington's decisions regarding the defense of Fort Washington. After the loss of New York City, any post on the east bank of the Hudson was of dubious value to the rebel army. Washington could not readily support it from New Jersey, and its garrison, while still relatively large and well equipped, was not strong enough to pose an offensive threat to the British. It was only an inviting target, clearly at risk, and the rebels should have pulled out when they had the chance. Instead, at Washington's orders, they stayed.

In one of the better narratives of the affair, Lefkowitz carefully traces the Commander-in-Chief's efforts to deal with events leading up to the climactic action at Fort Washington on November 16. There is a cogent explanation of the initial decision to hang onto the tenuous fortification and then, at last, when it was too late, to evacuate the embattled garrison. Indeed, the description of the final debacle, as seen from Fort Lee on the New Jersey side of the Hudson River, is quite poignant. The author gives due notice to the often poor advice Washington received from other officers over the days leading up to the fiasco, but finds it impossible to acquit the general of virtually full responsibility for the result. It is a familiar story, but Lefkowitz's account, and his judgment, is stinging and very convincing.

The Fort Washington affair was in every sense a monumental blunder. The loss of over twenty-eight hundred troops and all of their weapons and equipment was grievous; the men and material would have come in handy in New Jersey. In addition, the defeat was a shattering blow to patriot morale, and planning for operations in New Jersey, from the very start, labored beneath an ominous and unpromising cloud. Crisis permeated the counsels of the rebel command. The door to Fort Lee and the interior of the state was open, and Washington seemed at a genuine loss as to how to respond. The crushing defeat on the east bank of the Hudson had bequeathed a problematic beginning to the defense of the west side of the river.

Fort Washington was not the Commander-in-Chief's only failure. Lefkowitz is equally critical of the general's handling of his principal subordinate, Major General Charles Lee. The author is honestly exasperated by Washington's Hamlet-like relationship with his second-in-command. The Commander-in-Chief had placed high hopes on Lee's ability to react promptly and forcefully in the event of a British invasion of New Jersey. This faith may have been misplaced. Any of Washington's initial expectations that Lee would quickly stem or substantially slow the invasion were unrealistic. Even so, Lee showed little inclination to move against Cornwallis or to join forces with his chief in the crucial first few days after the American debacle at Fort Lee. Granting allowances for prudence after the British assault, Lee still showed little subsequent inclination to join forces with the main rebel army under Washington. In Lefkowitz's view this dilatory conduct became increasingly questionable. Yet if Lee was balky, Washington was equally remiss in dealing with him.

The Commander-in-Chief never effectively asserted his control over Lee. Desperate for reinforcements, and wanting to consolidate his remaining forces, Washington was anxious for Lee to link up with the Grand Army as it moved toward Pennsylvania. He repeatedly sent couriers to Lee's column, imploring Lee to hasten his march. In return, he received evasive answers and excuses. The recalcitrant general evidently believed that he could do more for the rebel cause with an independent command, and perhaps find an opening against the British rear as they moved farther into the New Jersey interior. Or perhaps he wanted as little as possible to do with a commander whose abilities he now questioned and whose fortunes seemed to be in eclipse. At some point, however, it should have become clear that, whatever his motives, Lee was not about to comply with pleas to join the rest of the army with any degree of energy or approval. Still, Washington never issued a preemptory order to force the issue; nor, apparently, did he ever consider relieving Lee in favor of a more obedient officer.

It is impossible to fully explain the situation. Lefkowitz has done as much as anyone to review the available evidence, and ends up wondering whether the Commander-in-Chief remained, in spite of everything, a bit awed by Lee's experience and reputation as a soldier. Perhaps. An alternative view might hold that Washington simply had problems enough just holding his army together; forcing the issue with Lee, and certainly relieving him, would have brought additional turmoil to the patriot command at the worst conceivable time. Whatever the source of his hesitancy, however, the daring British capture of Lee took Washington off the hook. John Sullivan, who succeeded to Lee's command, moved quickly to join the main army, and an embarrassing and possibly dangerous situation became moot. Even so, it reflected poorly on Washington's performance as a commander.

It also spoke poorly of Lee. While never raising the hoary old questions about treachery or Lee's actual loyalty to Washington or the Revolution, Lefkowitz has little patience with the man. He concedes that Lee was an extraordinary fellow. Brave, intelligent, energetic, experienced, and undeniably talented, he served the rebel cause well in the early months of the war. Yet he was also possessed of a high opinion of himself and a penchant for intrigue and sarcasm, and these character flaws ultimately limited his value as a senior officer. In the crisis of 1776, the human element mattered; to function effectively in adversity, the rebel commanding officers needed to see eye-to-eye. Yet relations between the two senior patriot officers frayed badly, and Lefkowitz lays the blame squarely on General Lee. The author clearly implies that his capture was no loss to the rebels (even if many of them saw things differently at the time); and, harsh as it may be, it is a reasonable assessment of the Lee affair.

Other patriot failings were not the fault of the Commander-in-Chief, but they were nevertheless important and had a grave impact on the rebel war effort. The lack of experienced staff officers, for example, told heavily on the Americans.   The details of moving an army made extended marches demanding exercises under the best of circumstances, and the 1776 retreat was anything but that: there were ammunition to distribute, reinforcements to rally, wagons and horses to arrange, food and forage to bring to the troops and their draft animals, and all manner of supplies to secure. Washington and his senior subordinates generally did the work themselves, and they kept the army supplied and moving. Yet they could not match the logistical skills of their British counterparts, and, at least in Washington's case, performed these functions only at the expense of operational concerns. The retreat was a grim test of the ingenuity and staying power of the young army; and in the pinch, frantic improvisation substituted for professional skills. But the very ability of the rebel army to get by in such fashion was a constant reminder of its amateur military status.

The Long Retreat, however, is at its best when looking beyond the mistakes of generals, British or American, or the shortcomings of Washington's young army. The rebels survived the campaign, and were in a position to counterattack, Lefkowitz argues, not only because of British blunders, but also because of steps taken on their own behalf. More than most other writers, the author credits patriots with orchestrating their own revival as 1776 drew to a close.

The first point to make in this regard was the state of the rebel army during the New Jersey campaign. It was in sorry condition: enlistments were running out, desertions increased, equipment losses were serious, and the enemy had the initiative. Yet the patriot ranks never broke. Washington and others called on every available resource, and in the end, they did so effectively. There was always just enough transport, ammunition, food, forage, and weapons; there remained an effective artillery arm; and, after the initial shock of invasion had worn off, a small but steady stream of reinforcements moved toward the retreating column. Units remained intact, even if thin. In short, patriot efforts kept their battered force operational. It was a retreating army, not a fleeing mob.

Washington also kept in touch with events beyond his immediate front. Even as he struggled to keep the main army alive, for instance, he acted prudently and decisively in providing command arrangements for patriot forces in Morris County (which would pay huge dividends in early 1777). He also maintained communications with Congress, state political leaders, and local officials, which gave him a fairly realistic view of popular opinion, militia activities, and intelligence on areas from which he could draw logistical support and reinforcements. With the exception of Lee, he worked reasonably well with his senior officers in efforts to concentrate scattered rebel troop formations and to rebuild the semblance of an effective Grand Army. In all of this, the Commander-in-Chief drove himself and his subordinates hard, but he produced results.

Significantly, Washington's aim was not purely defensive. Lefkowitz makes clear the general's desire to stabilize his own forces, and then find an opening for a counterattack. Certainly by the time he reached New Brunswick (November 29) he was looking for a chance to hit back, if only in some limited way. A success, no matter how small, would buy time for patriot forces to resupply and reinforce, keep Howe and Cornwallis off balance, and restore rebel morale. Still in retreat, Washington would fight if he could.

For those who looked carefully, there were signs that the battered rebels still had some fight left in them. At New Brunswick, Alexander Hamilton's artillery duelled gamely with the British across the Raritan River. Shortly thereafter, having marched through Princeton and on to Trenton, the Commander-in-Chief secured the safety of his baggage on the west bank of the Delaware and received encouraging word of reinforcements mobilizing in Pennsylvania. It was enough to tempt him to turn and fight. On December 6, he marched back to Princeton with some twelve hundred men, hoping to find an opportunity. He returned to Trenton and crossed to Pennsylvania only after learning that Cornwallis was moving from New Brunswick with a superior force. Frustrated for the moment, and understanding the seriousness of his army's condition, Washington's outlook nevertheless was not that of a beaten man.

When it came, the patriot counterattack at Trenton was a direct extension of the same impulse to strike back. The army that fought the Trenton-Princeton campaign, as Lefkowitz is at pains to point out, was not appreciably stronger than the force that had retreated across the Delaware. Bruised and staggered, it still had survived its ordeal in such condition as to allow a quick recovery. The period of rest, reinforcement, and reorganization in Pennsylvania was enough to allow Washington to seize the initiative; he struck the limited but telling blow he had sought to deliver at least since his brief stay in New Brunswick.

The results were all he could have wanted: Howe was profoundly embarrassed and the illusion of his army's invincibility shattered; subsequent British winter deployments returned most of central New Jersey to rebel hands; and the impact on patriot morale was electric. Really no more than minor fights--Trenton was a raid and Princeton a meeting engagement--the affrays of late 1776 and early 1777 yielded truly strategic rewards.

The author's assessment of the entire business seems sensible indeed. The retreat had been a rout only briefly. Washington's successful efforts to restore order and get his army across New Jersey spoke well of his ability to function under extreme pressure and to get the most out of his depleted resources. In the end, it is difficult to argue with Lefkowitz's conclusion that Washington did better with the men and material available to him than General

Howe did with his vastly superior resources.   Howe also made the mistake of complacency, reflected so clearly in his faulty winter quarters deployments. Whatever mistakes Washington made, complacency was not among them, and throughout the retreat, carelessness never contributed to the woes of his army.

There was a final lesson in *The Long Retreat*: The wise general will ruthlessly finish off even the most seemingly enfeebled enemy.   Given a respite, competent leadership, and at least a minimal resource base, even a grievously wounded army can rise and fight again.   Washington understood the point and redeemed a campaign and a revolution; Howe missed it and lost a war and much of an empire.

Mark Edward Lender
Kean University, 1998

CHAPTER ONE

Prelude to Invasion

To place any dependance upon Militia, is, assuredly, resting upon a broken staff.
—George Washington to John Hancock,
September 24, 1776

In March 1776, patriot fortunes in the War for American Independence were at high tide. After sustaining a siege of almost a year, the British army hastily abandoned the city of Boston. On March 17, they boarded warships and transports in Boston harbor and set sail for the Royal Navy base at Halifax, Nova Scotia. The evacuation was a galling retreat for the King's troops, and the news sent patriots cheering into the streets of the rebellious Thirteen Colonies while British sympathizers drew their curtains and waited.

The amateur army under George Washington had effectively besieged Boston. Washington's adversary, General William Howe, fully understood that offensive operations against the well-entrenched rebels would be costly, if even possible, and that New England was a hot-bed of patriot support. If he was to regain the initiative, he needed to regroup and reinforce his army, and then resume the offensive and crush the upstart Americans on ground of his own choosing.

General Howe's departure from Boston left the colonies completely in rebel hands, and patriot optimists, some of whom had stayed on the lines since the fighting at Lexington and Concord the year before, could be excused for thinking that the War for Independence was in its final stages.

George Washington's assessment was more sober. He had reason enough to be pleased with the successful operations at Boston, but he fully understood that the British had retreated only to reorganize, await reinforcements, and counterattack on a new front. The patriot commander was even sure he knew where they would strike. It would be to the South, at New York City.

A British initiative at New York made solid military sense. With a population of 22,000, New York was the second largest city in America; only Philadelphia, with 34,000, was larger. The city had a history as a British military base by the outbreak of the American Revolution. The British used it as their headquarters during the French and Indian War, and it had remained so until the shift to Boston shortly before the start of the Revolution. New York had an excellent harbor, which was free of ice in the winter, and had ample docks, ship repair facilities, warehouses and buildings which could be commandeered for the use of the military if necessary. The city also had a strategic location. Its position on the Hudson River was the key to communications and trade with New England and Canada; land routes to the interior lay across the river in New Jersey; and shipping from New York had relatively easy routes to the south. In addition, New York was a pleasant, tolerant city. It offered many diversions and a lively social life for officers and soldiers alike. Certainly the occupation of New York would offer the British better prospects than any attempt to recapture Boston.

The importance of New York City to the British was obvious to Washington even before Howe's evacuation of Boston. Thus, as he fenced with the redcoats in Massachusetts, his thoughts turned south and to how he might keep the great port on the Hudson in rebel hands. Unable to leave the Boston front himself, Washington ordered the army's most experienced officer, Major General Charles Lee, to go to New York and to take a look at the situation. Lee faced an arduous task, but he was the best man for the job, and he would play a major role in the subsequent events of 1776. His mission was one of the first key American steps in preparing for what both sides saw as the crucial showdown of the war. The army that emerged victorious at New York could well claim the final victory.

The man of the hour was Major General Charles Lee. In fact, Lee was one of the most extraordinary officers in the American army. Born in England in 1732, he was the son of a British colonel. He was the youngest of seven children, but only he and a sister, to whom he remained closely attached, survived to adulthood. Commissioned into his father's regiment as early as eleven years old, he was carried on the army roster while attending school. His education was extensive for the day. He studied in Switzerland and probably in France, and he emerged a well-read young man fluent in French and conversant in German, Italian, and Latin. Books were his constant companion throughout his life, and he enjoyed lacing his witty and often engaging letters and conversations with quotations from the classics. By any measure, he was one of the best educated and most intellectually accomplished men in Washington's army.

He was also a considerable soldier. By 1750, when his father died, and when he was eighteen, Lee began his active-duty career. In 1755, he came to America when fighting broke out between Britain and France, and he served on the ill-fated Braddock Expedition. During the march into western Pennsylvania, Lee met George Washington, then a colonel of Virginia militia. Like Washington, he survived the disaster, which saw the French and their Indian allies decimate the British column in the vicinity of what is now Pittsburgh. He served with distinction through the rest of the French and Indian War, including some hard fighting in northern New York, and in 1760 returned, as a captain, to England. Promoted to major the following year, he fought with great credit in Portugal, where he served until the war ended in 1763. He then went on half-pay when his regiment disbanded. By that time, Major Lee was a hardened veteran.

Without prospects for further glory or advancement with the British, Lee became a soldier of fortune in the Polish army. Poland was dominated by Russia, and Empress Catherine the Great had installed her Polish lover, Stanislaus Poniatowski, as King of Poland. Lee became an intimate of the puppet king and eventually rose to major general. His adventures included accompanying a Turkish army to Constantinople in 1766, during which his health suffered, several years recovering while roaming through Europe, fighting duels, and serving with the Russian army. In 1770, Lee returned to England, and although promoted to lieutenant colonel in 1772, the small peacetime British army offered him little hope for further advancement. Bored, he devoted himself to horses, politics, and land speculation in America.

In fact, politics became a serious interest, as Lee had developed some radical sympathies. He had come to hate monarchies. Perhaps he had seen the common people of eastern Europe suffering at the hands of tyrannical kings. But Lee especially came to despise George III, who had failed to fulfill promises to advance his career. As early as 1766, when the American colonies resisted the Stamp Act, Lee's anger was evident. "May God prosper the Americans in their resolutions," he wrote to his sister from Constantinople, "that there may be one Asylum at least on the earth for men, who prefer their natural rights to the fantastical prerogative of a foolish, perverted head because it wears a Crown."[1]

The growing political unrest in America suited Charles Lee's restless temperament and radical politics perfectly. In 1773, Lee returned to America after an absence of twelve years. Although his stated intention was to advance his land speculations, he promptly leaped into colonial politics, and his broad knowledge and military reputation gained him introduction to the most powerful men in America. Many of them, including his fellow survivor from the Braddock Expedition of 1755, Colonel George Washington, were spellbound by Lee's stories of his military adventures. Lee had lived the dashing military life that Washington had dreamed of as a boy. Citing the example of the Polish partisans, who waged *"la petite guerre"* against conventional European armies, Lee endlessly argued that the American colonists could defeat British regulars.[2] He became known in America as a military expert and a true friend of liberty.

Lee's first years back in America, from 1773 to 1775, were probably the happiest years of his life. Well regarded by a wide circle of acquaintances, reactions to him varied. At forty-three years old, few thought he was much to look at, for Lee was tall and skinny, with a large nose and small hands and feet. He was unmarried, although he had taken a Mohawk mistress during the

---

[1]Lee to Sidney Lee, March 1, 1766, *The Lee Papers* (New York: The New York Historical Society, 1871), I: 42-43.

[2]Guerrilla warfare was not an eighteenth-century term; irregular operations were called *"partisan warfare"* or *"petite-guerre"* at the time of the American Revolution. A military dictionary published in London in 1779 defined the terms: "Petite-Guerre, is carried on by a light party, commanded by an expert partisan, and which should be from 1000 to 2000 men; separated from the army, to secure the camp or a march; to reconnoitre the enemy or the country, to seize their posts, convoys, and escorts; to plant ambuscades, and to put in practice every stratagem for surprising or disturbing the enemy." George Smith, *An Universal Military Dictionary* (London: J. Milian, 1779), 202, reprint by Museum Restoration Service (Ottawa, Canada, 1969). Smith defined a partisan as "a person dexterous in commanding a party, who, knowing the country well, is employed in getting intelligence, or surprising the enemy's convoy, &c. The word also means an officer sent out upon a party, with the command of a body of light troops, generally under the appellation of the partisan's corps" (*An Universal Military Dictionary*, 199). Call it guerrilla warfare, petite-guerre or partisan warfare, it existed during the colonial wars and during the War for American Independence, with Lee as one of its exponents.

French & Indian War, with whom he had twin boys. Lee left her when his regiment moved on and he never saw her or his children again. He seemed incapable of a sustained romance with any woman, although some later thought him a libertine, and there are some hints in his correspondence that he may have been homosexual.[1] He had a moderate income from inheritances and was a man of modest tastes. Over the years his manners deteriorated, and although he could be a perfect gentlemen when he wanted, he was more commonly vulgar, sloppy and rude. He developed a strange passion for dogs and a troop of them followed him everywhere; Lee once quipped that he preferred the company of dogs to that of men. He was an egotist, a man of extreme moods and tempers. His new intimate in America, Colonel George Washington, politely called him "fickle," although others were less diplomatic. The powerful William Schuyler of New York thought Lee a sloppy and unwashed eccentric. John Adams, with no small ego himself, thought Lee the only man in America who knew more than he did about military affairs. He described him privately as "a queer creature. But you must love his dogs if you love him and forgive a thousand whims for the sake of the soldier and the scholar."[2] The perceptive Mercy Otis Warren, one of the most acute observers of the American scene, found Lee "plain in his person even to ugliness, and careless in his manners to a degree of rudeness. He possessed a bold genius and an unconquerable spirit: his voice was rough, his garb ordinary, his deportment morose. . .he was frequently agreeable in narration, and judicious and entertaining in observation."[3] Yet however they found him, Americans

---

[1]John W. Shy, "Charles Lee: The Soldier as Radical," in George Billias, ed., *George Washington's Generals* (New York: William Morrow and Company, 1964), 23.

[2]Billias, ed., *George Washington's Generals*, 23; James Flexner, *George Washington in the American Revolution* (New York: Little, Brown & Co., 1967), 23; Adams quoted in John Alden, *General Charles Lee* (Baton Rouge: Louisiana State University Press, 1955), 77.

[3]Mercy Otis Warren, *The History of the Rise, Progress and Termination of the American Revolution* (Boston, 1805), I: 292. Warren was the wife of the Governor of Massachusetts during the war; her history of the American Revolution was one of the first books to be authored by an American woman. Even earlier, however, another woman, Hannah Adams, dealt with the Revolution in her *A Summary History of New England. . .Comprehending a General Sketch of the American War* (Dedham, MA: H. Mann and J.H. Adams, 1799). Clergyman and historian Jeremy Belknap also left a vivid description of Charles Lee. Belknap found Lee, "a perfect original, a good scholar and soldier, and an odd genius; full of fire and passion, and but little good manners; a great sloven, wretchedly profane, and a great admirer of dogs." Quoted in Richard Ketchum, *The Winter Soldiers* (Garden City, NY:

thought more of Charles Lee than the British ever did. Certainly the more radical members of the Continental Congress, including John Adams and Benjamin Rush, admired him immensely.

At the outbreak of the Revolution, Lee's reputation was such that some Americans seriously considered him for Commander-in-Chief of the rebel army. But his English birth and the need to make political appointments precluded any chance he had for the top spot. The command went to Washington, the well-known and distinguished Virginian, while Artemus Ward of Massachusetts became second in command. Ward was elderly for a soldier, and few had much confidence in his military skills, but he was popular with patriots in New England and his appointment gave the army a necessary political balance. Lee, with the rank of major general, became the third highest ranking officer in the rebel army; it was a post of real significance, and as one of the few American officers with extensive military experience, patriots expected much of him.

Following his appointment to the Continental Army, Lee resigned his commission in the British army. He also insisted on a large compensation from the rebel Congress for the inevitable confiscation of his property in England where he would be declared a traitor. He then accompanied General Washington from Philadelphia to the seige at Boston. Washington was happy to have his eccentric but brilliant English friend at his side; as the war progressed, the commanding general was confirmed in his belief that Lee was an exceptional officer.

Ordered by Washington to prepare a defense of New York City, Lee left Boston in mid-January 1776. He arrived on February 14, bringing with him some zealous Connecticut militia recruited en route to help deal with New York Loyalists. Lee realized that the area around the city, with its waterways and islands, offered an almost endless combination of sea approaches and landing places. "What to do with the city puzzles me," he quickly wrote to Washington. "It is so encircled with deep navigable water that whoever commands the sea must command the town."[1] Lee expected a powerful Royal naval squadron to support any British invasion; but the Americans had no navy and faced the dangerous prospect of having to mount a static defense against an enemy which enjoyed every advantage. Yet Washington's determination to defend New York City was fixed; it was as much a political

---

Doubleday & Co., 1973), 200.

[1]*Lee Papers*, I: 309.

as a military decision. The Continental Congress wanted the city held and Washington felt obliged to carry out the wishes of his fellow delegates.

Lee began fortifying New York in late February, but within a few weeks he received a new assignment. The Continental Congress ordered him to go to South Carolina to help organize the defense of Charleston. Because of its milder winters, Charleston was under more immediate threat of attack than New York. Lee would do yeoman work in the South—in fact, he was instrumental in turning back a strong British assault in the spring of 1776—and his influence left its mark on New York's defenses. Soon after the British evacuated Boston, Washington started for New York with the rebel army. He arrived with the vanguard on April 13 and quickly put his soldiers to work on Lee's defensive plan. Lee's scheme called for extensive fortifications on the western tip of Long Island (modern Brooklyn) and Manhattan plus a gun battery on the New Jersey side of the Hudson River at Paulus Hook (today's Jersey City). Work went forward quickly, and the patriots had acted not a moment too soon.

In the midst of American preparations, the first British warships appeared in the waters off New York on June 25. Additional men-of-war and transports arrived and anchored off Staten Island in such numbers that, to some American defenders, their masts looked like a floating forest. On July 2, General William Howe landed his army unopposed on Staten Island.

The appearance of 25,000 British and Hessian troops among a Staten Island civilian population of 3,000 fueled Loyalists sentiments. On July 6, Howe gathered the local population to sign an oath of allegiance to the crown. A few days later, the Staten Island militia assembled at Richmondtown and were reviewed by Howe. They were estimated at 200 men and commanded by Colonel Christopher Billop, the island's largest landowner. The militia offered their services to General Howe who gratefully accepted. Throughout the summer of 1776, Howe continued to assemble his army on Staten Island. He proved to be a cautious and meticulous planner, and the unexpected lull was a blessing for the rebels, giving them additional time to prepare their defenses.[1]

---

[1] "Loyalist" or "Tory" were the terms used during the Revolution to describe Americans who remained loyal to England. Washington denounced them as "Unhappy wretches! Deluded mortals!" The Loyalists were as patriotic as the rebels, they just happened to be on the losing side. A popular rebel definition of a Loyalist (Tory) was "a thing whose head is in England, and its body in America, and its neck ought to be stretched." The Loyalist movement was widespread, and their numbers may have been up to one-third of the 2.2 million

In fact, Washington needed all of the time he could get. By the end of July, he had assembled an army of 12,333 officers and men to defend New York City and Brooklyn. An additional 3,677 rebel troops were stationed nearby in New Jersey under the command of General Hugh Mercer.[1] The number looked impressive, but the Army of the United Colonies consisted of untested Continentals and short term militia.[2] They were poorly armed and equipped, lacked cavalry, had no naval support, and were led by officers still learning their business.

Fortunately, some of the rebel officers displayed exceptional talent. In addition to Lee, there was Colonel Henry Knox, the talented and self-taught chief of artillery, as well as General Nathanael Greene. Only thirty-four when the war began, Greene was the son of a prominent Rhode Island family. Ambitious and headstrong, he was heavily built with graying hair and walked with a limp caused by a stiff right knee. Without previous military experience,

---

population of America, making the American Revolution as much a civil war as it was a war for independence. Probably some 50,000 Americans bore arms for the King during the Revolution as Loyalist militia, Provincials, or in the regular British army and navy.

[1]Charles H. Lesser, ed., *The Sinews of Independence, Monthly Strength Reports of the Continental Army* (Chicago, The University of Chicago Press: 1976), 26-28. The figures used are the "Present Fit for Duty & On Duty" and exclude the "Rank and File Sick, On Forlough, etc."   There were other American forces in addition to those in and around New York City.   There were 3,155 officers and men in South Carolina and 8,071 at Fort Ticonderoga and Skenesborough (present Whitehall), New York. The troops in upstate New York, "The Northern Department," were commanded at the time by General Horatio Gates.

[2]The term "American Army" at the time of the Revolution is a term of convenience. In reality, the rebels fought with a force composed of Continentals, State Troops, or militia. In June 1775, the Continental Congress authorized 60 regiments to be raised at the expense of the states. These regiments were known as the Continental Army (or Continental Line), which became the backbone of the rebel forces. Troops of the Continental Line initially agreed to serve for one year. The Continentals were under Washington's command, but from time to time, either Washington or the Congress ordered Continental regiments to support other American operations beyond Washington's direct control. In addition to raising Continental regiments, each state could enlist State Troops or "State Regiments." Such troops were under the control of the state governments and were generally raised for three to six months and used for home defense. They were often recruited from the militia, but were legally distinct. The militia were composed, in principle, of all eligible able-bodied men who were organized into local companies for emergency or limited service. The troops under General Washington's immediate command, be they Continentals, State Troops, or militia (and there was usually a combination of forces) were sometimes identified as "the Grand Army."

Greene nevertheless was a splendid organizer whose talents soon brought him to Washington's attention. By August 1776, the Rhode Islander was a major general and one of the Commander-in-Chief's closest advisors. But a few capable men could not substitute for a veteran staff or competent support services, a fact that bitter experience would soon drive home.[1]

Just how unready the Americans were quickly became apparent. On August 21, the patriot *Constitutional Gazette* of New York reported that "for some days past, the British army on Staten Island, have been embarking on board the transports; so that we expect their whole force before this city every tide. We hope to give them a reception, worthy of the free born sons of America, and may every freeman of America make this his Toast, That New York is now an asylum for American Liberty."   It was not to be.

The following day British troops landed unopposed on the western tip of Long Island (modern Brooklyn), and a few days later Howe ordered a column of Hessians down the Flatbush Road to probe the American defenses. The move was only a feint. While the Hessians occupied the Americans at the Flatbush Road, a second column composed of British troops marched undetected further onto Long Island during the night of August 26-27 and outflanked the American defenses. Washington had no cavalry to patrol his exposed right, and British flanking troops got behind the American defenders in Brooklyn. Upon hearing the sound of gunfire to their right, the Hessians at the Flatbush Pass pressed their attack. The ensuing Battle of Long Island was

---

[1]Washington had no cavalry at this stage of the Revolution. Historians have pointed out that a company of horsemen from Connecticut arrived in the American camp during the spring of 1776, but Washington turned them away. Some historians claim that Washington refused the services of cavalry because he had no experience in how to use them. But Washington actually turned the horsemen away because they were more trouble than they were worth. According to Alexander Graydon, who witnessed the incident, the Commander-in-Chief had no real choice in the matter. "Among the military phenomena of this campaign," he recalled, "the Connecticut light horse ought not to be forgotten.   These consisted of a considerable number of old fashioned men, probably farmers and heads of families, as they were generally middle aged, and many of them apparently beyond the meridian of life. They were truly irregulars; and whether their clothing, their equipments or caparisons were regarded, it would have been difficult to have discovered any circumstance of uniformity....Instead of carbines and sabers, they generally carried fowling pieces ; some of them very long, and such as in Pennsylvania, are used for shooting ducks. Here and there, one, 'his youthful garments, well saved,' appeared in a dingy regimental of scarlet, with a triangular, tarnished, laced hat." Graydon says that one of these horsemen was captured by the British, and "on being asked, what had been his duty in the rebel army, he answered, that it was to flank a little and carry tidings."   John Stockton Littell, ed., *Memoirs of His Own Time...by Alexander Graydon* (Philadelphia: Lindsay & Blakiston, 1846, orig. 1811), 155-156.

a disaster for Washington, who was lucky to get his beaten command across the East River to Manhattan Island.

New York City was in chaos as frightened civilians fled the city in the midst of frantic military activity to defend the place. An English traveler who arrived in New York in the turmoil left a vivid account of conditions there: "Landed in New York about nine o'clock," he recalled, "when one Collins, an Irish merchant, and myself rambled about the town till three in the afternoon before we could get anything for breakfast." They finally got "a little Dutch tippling house" to serve them an almost unpalatable stew, but in general there was "nothing to be got here. All the inhabitants are moved out. The town is full of soldiers."[1]

The British were elated with their victory on Long Island, and many of them wanted to strike again quickly before Washington could regain his balance. But Howe waited almost a month following the battle before taking further offensive action against the rebels, probably hoping to bring them to terms without further combat. The general and his older brother, Admiral Lord Richard Howe, had been empowered as peace commissioners by the British government, with the authority to offer the colonists most of what they wanted short of independence.[2] The Howes were sympathetic towards the colonists and may have hoped to end the war through negotiation and return to England as heroes. Congress was willing to talk, but negotiations ultimately broke down in mid-September over the issue of independence.

Meanwhile, the unexpected but welcomed lull in the fighting gave George Washington valuable time to reorganize and decide what to do next. Realizing that any further defense of New York City was doomed, the rebel chief used the time to move his sick and wounded out of harm's way, along with some of the army's baggage, in preparation for abandoning the city. But until they could get everything away, Washington had to continue to defend New York City and the rest of Manhattan Island. Consequently, he divided his army into three parts. He ordered General William Heath with 9,000 men to Harlem Heights, on the rugged northern end of the island, to dig fortifications; these would serve as a fall-back position should the rest of the

---

[1]*The Journal of Nicholas Cresswell* (New York: Dial Press, 1924), 158.

[2]In addition to his role as a peace commissioner, and his tactical command in and around New York, Howe commanded all forces in the British colonies lying along the Atlantic Ocean from Nova Scotia to East Florida, with the exception of Crown forces in Quebec.

army have to evacuate positions further south. General Israel Putnam was posted with 5,000 men to defend the city itself. Between Putnam's and Heath's corps, Washington placed General Nathanael Greene with 5,000 men to protect the center of the island. The result was an American army of three isolated corps, strewn over a 13-mile area: a situation fraught with risk.

The extent of the risk soon became all too clear. On September 15, Howe made his move to capture New York. From his new bases on Long Island, the British commander bypassed Putnam's relatively strong defenses on lower Manhattan and launched an amphibious attack against Greene. Howe picked Kip's Bay Cove on the East River (presently East 34th Street) for his landing. The location was ideal for an amphibious assault: a somewhat rocky shore behind which lay a long flat meadow with few natural defenses. The attack was textbook perfect. The inexperienced militia defending Kip's Bay were quickly routed by bayonet-wielding infantry. Other American troops soon joined the terrified militia in their flight, all running as fast as they could towards the safety of Heath's fortifications at Harlem Heights. The enemy were close behind, mockingly sounding horns and bugles as if on a fox chase. As the British army pushed across Manhattan Island, Putnam's troops in New York City narrowly escaped capture by retreating up the Greenwich Road, on the Hudson River side of the island, to the safety of Heath's lines. For the Americans, the Kip's Bay affair was a fiasco.

Washington arrived in mid-Manhattan in the midst of the turmoil. He was shocked and furious as he watched the panic-stricken defenders of Kip's Bay throwing away their muskets and running and shoving their way towards the safety of Harlem Heights. The general rode among the frightened militia, screaming at them to form behind nearby farm fences and stone walls, but he was unable to stop them. According to one American officer who witnessed the scene, Washington became so angry that he flew into an uncontrollable rage and began striking the militiamen with his riding crop. "The General was so exasperated that he struck several officers in their flight, three times dashed his hatt on the ground, and at last exclaimed, 'Good God, have I got such troops as those!' It was with difficulty his friends could get him to quit the field, so great was his emotions."[1]

---

[1]Henry Steele Commager and Richard B. Morris, eds., *The Spirit of Seventy-Six* (New York: Harper & Row, 1976), 467. The letter quoted was written on September 20 by General George Weedon to John Page, President of the Virginia Council. Washington wrote his own account of what happened in a letter to his brother, John Augustine Washington, dated September 22: "I rode with all possible expedition towards the place of Landing, and

Appalled at the conduct of the militia at Kip's Bay, Washington wrote a lengthy letter to John Hancock, the President of the Continental Congress. He renewed his appeal for a "new model army" of professional soldiers instead of continued dependence on one-year enlistments and militia. "To place any dependance upon Militia," he told Hancock, "is assuredly, resting upon a broken staff. Men just dragged from the tender Scenes of domestick life, unaccustomed to the din of Arms; totally unacquainted with every kind of Military skill, which being followed by a want of confidence in themselves, when opposed to Troops regularly trained, disciplined, and appointed, superior in knowledge, and superior in Arms, make them timid, and ready to fly from their own Shadows." Aware of Congressional fears of a professional army, the Commander-in-Chief insisted that "the Jealousies of a standing Army, and the Evils to be apprehended from one, are remote; and in my judgment, situated and circumstanced as we are, not at all to be dreaded; but the consequence of wanting one, according to my Ideas, formed from the present view of things, is certain, and inevitable Ruin; for if I was called upon to declare upon Oath, whether the Militia have been most serviceable or hurtful upon the whole, I should subscribe to the latter."[1]

Ironically, the Continental Congress had already voted to raise eighty-eight regiments of Continentals in a series of resolutions in mid-September. Hancock wrote Washington from Philadelphia on September 24, giving the Commander-in-Chief the news. Hancock explained that Congress agreed to "engage the Troops to serve during the Continuance of the War." In addition, they voted to offer bounties of money and land to induce men to enlist in the army. The Congress also adopted new Articles of War to tighten discipline.[2] Washington was given a blueprint for his "respectable army," but

---

where Breast Works had been thrown up to secure our Men, & found the Troops that had been posted there to my great surprise & Mortification, and those ordered to their Support (consisting of Eight Regiments) notwithstanding the exertions of their Generals to form them, running away in the most Shameful and disgraceful manner." Dorothy Twohig, ed., *The Papers of George Washington* (Charlottesville and London: University Press of Virginia, 1994), Revolutionary War Series, VI: 373.

[1]*Ibid.*, 393-400. This letter was written on September 25, 1776 from "Colo. Morris's" (still standing today and known as the Morris-Jumel Mansion) in Harlem.

[2]The death of General Richard Montgomery was one reason the Continental Congress agreed to heed Washington's advice and raise an army for the duration of the war. Richard Montgomery was a popular and able former British army officer who remained in America following the French and Indian War. Commanding the American troops besieging

the reorganization was months away. Meanwhile, he had to struggle on until the end of the year dependent upon his one-year Continentals and militia.

Following the Battle of Kip's Bay, the war fell silent again.[1] Washington commanded a force of 20,435, most of whom were manning the defensive lines at Harlem Heights.[2] The Americans had built two forts on the Hudson River during the spring and summer of 1776 to prevent the British from sailing their warships up the Hudson. Fort Washington stood perched on one of the highest points on Manhattan Island. Almost directly across the Hudson River from Fort Washington was its sister fortification, Fort Lee. Fort Lee stood atop the Hudson Palisades.[3] The seemingly powerful Fort Washington-Fort Lee defensive line, with its big guns, was a comfort to the jittery American army in their makeshift defenses at Harlem Heights.

The rebels had built the forts largely to protect the Hudson River. Of the major rivers in America, the Hudson was the most important during the War for Independence. The Hudson or "North River," as it was also called by the colonists, was navigable by ocean-going ships for 150 miles from its mouth at New York City to Albany. Along its banks lived tens of thousands

---

Quebec late in 1775, he was forced to prematurely attack the city on New Year's Eve, 1775 because the enlistments of many of his troops would expire the following day. He was killed and the assault was a failure. In his letter to Washington of September 24, 1776, Hancock said that "the untimely Death of General Montgomery alone, independent of other Arguments, is a striking Proof of the Danger and Impropriety of sending Troops into the Field, under any Restriction as to the Time of their Service."

[1]Following the Battle of Kip's Bay, the British established a defensive position across Manhattan at about the site of present 91st Street. The Americans facing them at Harlem Heights occupied positions corresponding to the ground from modern 147th to 161st Streets. On September 16th, the day following the British landing at Kip's Bay, there was some fighting between the two armies which ended in a draw, but at least the Americans acted with courage. This incident is known as the Battle of Harlem Heights.

[2]Lesser, ed., *The Sinews of Independence*, 32-33. This figure was the total American strength in the New York City area and includes approximately 3,500 officers and men in New Jersey under Nathanael Greene.

[3]The volcanically-formed cliffs which soar upward from the banks of the Hudson River were known simply as the "Steep Rocks" at the time of the American Revolution. The cliffs north of Tenefly, New Jersey were called Closter Mountain. These cliffs began to be called "The Palisades" about 50 years after the end of the Revolution. However, for ease of identification, I will use the modern term Palisades to describe these cliffs.

of people cultivating rich farmlands. The Hudson provided easy access into the heart of New York and New England.[1]

The defense of the Hudson became problematic when Washington realized that British warships could sail up river and land troops behind the American lines. Equally threatening was the fear that a British naval force on the Hudson would encourage the numerous New York State Loyalists, who were only waiting for leadership and arms from the British, to rise up against the rebels. British ships on the Hudson also could block vital rebel supply routes, especially troop reinforcements and food coming to New York City from patriot strongholds in New England.

There was another reason to defend the lower Hudson River. The Continental Congress had authorized the construction of eleven frigates, and the largest of these warships, *Congress* and *General Montgomery*, were under construction at Poughkeepsie, New York. The infant men-of-war had to be protected against efforts by the British to destroy them before they could get to sea.

The only American naval force available to defend New York City consisted of some lightly armed converted merchant ships and boats mounting a few cannons. This scratch force was no match for the British, who had the most powerful navy in the world. Unable to match the British at sea, the rebels had to depend on forts and gun batteries to defend New York harbor and the Hudson River.

Only a few places along the Hudson River's 150 mile length offered an opportunity for defense. One excellent defensive position was 45 miles north of New York City where the river took a bend, forcing sailing ships to slow down and making them easy targets for shore-based artillery. The American fortress at that location eventually was named West Point. The

---

[1]At the time of the Revolution, there were two great water routes that led from the Hudson River to the interior of North America: New York City to Lake Ontario, which took travellers north on the Hudson River to a point just below Albany, where the Mohawk River meets the Hudson; then west along the Mohawk River and across a carrying place protected by Fort Stanwix (modern Rome, New York), to the headwaters of the Oswego River; then north on the Oswego River to the Great Lakes and the interior of the North American continent. The second critical route connected New York City with Montreal: north on the Hudson from New York City beyond Albany to a 60 mile carrying point where there was a road. The carry was protected by the British outposts of Fort Anne and Fort Edward, New York. The 60 mile carry ended at the southern shore of Lake George, protected by the British post of Fort William Henry; then the route continued north on Lake George and into Lake Champlain, past the old French Fort of Crown Point and onto the Richelieu River; next past French-built Fort Chambly and onto the St. Lawrence River near Montreal.

other good defensive position lay at a point where the river squeezed between the rocky northern end of Manhattan Island and the cliffs of the New Jersey Palisades. With the defense of the lower Hudson River in mind, Washington reconnoitered the rugged, forested terrain on the uninhabited northern tip of Manhattan Island on June 12, 1776, accompanied by Colonel Rufus Putnam, the chief engineer of the American army. They found a hill which dominated the island's densely wooded northern tip and which butted against the Hudson, affording an excellent position to defend the waterway 220 feet below. The hilltop was christened Mount Washington.

Rebel troops were soon busy fortifying the postion. "In the course of some weeks, wrote Captain Alexander Graydon, "our labours had produced immense mounds of earth, assuming a pentagonal form, and finally issuing in a fort of five bastions." Graydon thought little of Rufus Putnam, whom he saw as "a self-educated man with want of experience."[1]   Nevertheless, Putnam was one of the few men available at the outbreak of the Revolution who knew anything about military engineering.[2]

The patriots labored away on their defenses in and around New York City during the summer of 1776 while the British army and navy continued to strengthen their forces on Staten Island. The first test of the American's Hudson River defenses came on Friday afternoon, July 12, 1776, the anniversary of James Wolfe's victory over the French at Quebec in 1761 and a day which the British army liked to celebrate. In addition, General William Howe's older brother, Admiral Lord Richard Howe was expected to enter New

---

[1]Rufus Putnam, a Massachsetts native, served as a colonial officer with the British during the French and Indian War and as Deputy Surveyor of West Florida (1773). In 1775, Putnam was commissioned a lieutenant colonel in the American army, and became an engineer quite casually. "Some of my acquaintance," he recalled, "mentioned me as having been imployed in that line in the Late war against Canada." He told Washington that "I had never read a word on the Subject of Fortification, that it was true that I had ben imployed on Some under British Engineers, but pretended to no knowledge of Laying works." Nevertheless, the Commander-in-Chief gave him the job (with the rank of colonel), and Putnam said that he finally got to read a book about engineering during the winter of 1776. Rowena Buell, *The Memories of Rufus Putnam and Certain Official Papers and Correspondence* (New York: Houghton, Mifflin and Company, 1903), 55-57.

[2]In November 1776, Putnam resigned his post as Chief Engineer to command an infantry regiment. He served as an infantry officer for the balance of the Revolution. The Americans got some competent military engineers when several French engineers arrived in 1777 as "volunteers." The British had established an engineering school at Woolwich, England in 1757 and they had skillful engineers serving with their army. The French had a similar school at St. Etienne.

York harbor that day with a fleet bringing additional troops from England. The rebels expected the British to salute this important day, and the British did, but in an unexpected manner.

At 3:30 in the afternoon, the stillness of the summer day was broken when two British frigates suddenly came alive, hoisted their sails, ran out their cannons and started racing across New York harbor for the mouth of the Hudson River. The two warships were the 44-gun *Phoenix* and the 24-gun *Rose*. They were accompanied by a schooner and two supply tenders. On board the five craft were about four hundred men, including a complement of Royal Marines. Rebel sentinels saw the frigates and sounded alarm cannons; church bells rang and the beat of drums called men to arms throughout the city. Artillerymen ran to their posts; this was the moment they had been waiting for.[1]

A number of witnesses recorded the action. Stephen Kemble, a New Jersey Loyalist, saw the affair as it developed from aboard a British warship at anchor near Staten Island. "About half after 3 in the Afternoon," he wrote, "His Majesty's Ship Phenix, Commanded by Capt. Parker, and the Rose, by Capt. Wallace, with the Tryal Schooner and two Tenders, got under Sail to pass the Town of New York; in about forty minutes they got abreast of Paulus's Hook [now Jersey City, New Jersey], before which time they did not fire a Shot, tho' they received the whole of the Rebels fire from Red Hook [part of modern Brooklyn], Governors Island, the Battery [today's Battery Park in lower Manhatten] and from some Guns in the Town." Kemble counted 196 shots fired at the squadron.[2] When the frigates got within range of the American batteries at Paulus Hook, they returned fire and drove the rebels from their guns. The warships also fired thundering broadsides into New York City, causing general consteration. "When they came this side of Trinity Church, they began to fire smartly," one civilan remembered. "The balls and bullets went through several houses between here and Greenwich [Greenwich Village]....The smoke of the firing drew over our street like a cloud, and the air was filled with the smell of powder. This affair caused a great fright in the

---

[1]The British fleet of transports and warships that eventually gathered in the waters around Staten Island was the largest concentration of warships up to that time in history. It was only exceeded in numbers by the Allied fleet which was assembled for the invasion of Normandy in 1944.

[2]*Journals of Lieut.-Col. Stephen Kemble* (New York: New York Historical Society, 1883), I: 80.

city. Women and children and some with their bundles came from the lower parts, and walked to the Bowery, which was lined with people."[1]

The Americans never did stop the men-of-war. Patriot artillery performed miserably. Some of their old cannons blew up under the pressure of live ammunition, killing or wounding their crews. A number of the casualities belonged to the New York State Provincial Company of Artillery commanded by Captain Alexander Hamilton, a student from Kings College (now Columbia University). Farther up river, the frigates ran past the guns of Fort Washington. The ships returned "our fire in great style," Graydon reported. "We were too high for their guns to be brought to bear upon us with any certainty; though one ball was thrown into the fort. Our elevated situation was nearly as unfavorable to the success of our fire upon them."[2] Carried by a favorable wind, the British squadron sailed majestically north, some thirty miles above the American defense lines before coming to anchor in the Tappan Zee region. It was a dazzling exploit to celebrate the anniversary of Wolfe's great victory at Quebec!

The sudden appearance of two powerful British warships on the Hudson River fulfilled Washington's worst fears of an enemy squadron operating on the river above New York City. The ships lingered deep in rebel territory for over a month, always a threat to patriots ashore and on the river, as well as to American ferry and other riverine interests and communications. Washington went to extraordinary lengths to trap or drive them away. For a month, he worked heatedly to block enemy navigation with various river obstructions, and even attempted an attack with fire rafts.[3] Nothing worked, and the enemy flotilla sailed home in mid-August unscathed but for a few lucky cannon hits.

---

[1]*Diary of the Reverend Mr. Shewkirk,* in Henry Steel Commanger and Richard B. Morris, eds., *The Spirit of Seventy-Six* (New York: Harper & Row, 1975), 422.

[2]John Stockton Littell, ed., Alexander Graydon, *Memoirs of His Own Time* (Philadelphia: Lindsay & Blakiston, 1846), 152.

[3]For the various schemes, see Fitzpatrick, ed., *Writings of Washington,* 5: 344; Edward Tatum, ed., *The American Journal of Ambrose Serle* (San Marino, CA: The Huntington Library, 1940), 54. Henry Duncan, Captain of H.M.S. *Eagle,* anchored off Staten Island, reported in his journal that "during the time we have been here, we have observed the rebels very busy in erecting batteries, fitting out row galleys, and making large and high buildings of wood to sink in the river to destroy the navigation above the town." What Duncan saw were river obstructions called *chevaux-de-frise.*

The passage of the two British frigates up the Hudson made it apparent that Fort Washington alone could not stop warships. Washington hoped that if he could mount gun batteries across the Hudson from Fort Washington, British ships would be caught in a murderous crossfire. There was an ideal site in New Jersey for such a battery. The ground was a little south of Fort Washington above a breach in the New Jersey Palisades. A narrow road ran through the opening from the crest of the Palisades to the Hudson River where Burdett's Ferry carried passengers and freight between New Jersey and Manhattan Island. By mid-July, Washington had his army hard at work on the project, and patriot guns on the Palisades subsequently blazed away (however ineffectually) at *Phoenix* and *Rose* when they returned south in August.

Despite their poor initial performance against the enemy ships, Washington appreciated the importance of the Palisades battery to the defense of New Jersey, and he ordered an expansion of the position above Burdett's Ferry. He gave the assignment to General Hugh Mercer, the rebel commander in New Jersey, who had a strong build-up underway by late September.[1] In mid-October, the growing fortification at Burdett's Ferry was renamed Fort Lee, in honor of General Charles Lee, now second in command of the Continental army.

While its name was impressive, Fort Lee was not a great citadel. It was really a fortified camp to support the gun batteries mounted on the crest of the Palisades. Thomas Paine, the author of *Common Sense* and civilian aide to General Nathanael Greene during November 1776, recalled Fort Lee as a "field fort," which was eighteenth-century nomenclature for a temporary earthen fortification. The post was a four-sided work about 2,500 feet square located on a flat tableland about a quarter mile behind the batteries on the

---

[1]The diary of soldier John Adlum has an entry for August 28th, 1776 which supports the belief that there were no major defenses at the Burdett's Ferry site during the early summer of 1776. Adlum said that he was at Paulus Hook and "in a few days after, we re-marched to the ground where Fort Lee was afterwards erected." Howard Peckham, ed., *Memoirs of The Life of John Adlum in The Revolutionary War* (Chicago: The Caxton Club, 1968), 19. Despite the many places in New Jersey named in honor of Hugh Mercer (1725-1777), he was a Scotsman by birth who emigrated to Virginia. In Scotland, Mercer was a physician and a supporter of Prince Charles Edward Stuart, remembered in history as "Bonnie Prince Charlie." Mercer supported the Jacobite uprising and participated in the Battle of Culloden in 1745 in which the English defeated the Scots and ended the rebellion. Many of the Highlanders, including Mercer, came to America following their defeat and sided with the rebels during the Revolution.   Mercer was mortally wounded at the Battle of Princeton on January 3, 1777.

Palisades. Over 300 huts arranged in a regular street pattern surrounded the fort, housing some 3,000 American soldiers. If the fort were in existence today, it would sit within the center of the modern town of Fort Lee, New Jersey. Just to the east were the guns on the crest of the Palisades, well placed in a natural defensive position 300 feet above the Hudson and protected by rudimentary earthworks. The gorge, which descended from the crest of the Palisades to the river, separated the fort from the batteries. There were no fortifications on the river shore. The earthen fort, the streets of huts, and the gun batteries on the Hudson were collectively called Fort Lee.

The guns at Fort Lee were already in operation when Washington and his army arrived at Harlem Heights on September 15, the same day they lost the Battle of Kip's Bay. On October 9, the troops watched from across the river as Fort Lee engaged a second foray by British shipping up the Hudson. Again the warships sailed passed the rebel river defenses "without any kind of damage or interruption." Colonel Thomas Ewing, an American officer who watched the incident, reported that the rebel gunfire was so ineffective that he could see a gentleman walking the deck of one of the frigates, seemingly in command, as if nothing was the matter. Ewing could see no damage being done to the British vessels.[1]

The dispatch of three warships to control the Hudson above the rebel army at Harlem Heights was ominous. Three days later, on October 12, General Howe further revealed his hand when he landed troops on Throgs Neck, a narrow peninsula jutting out from the Bronx into Long Island Sound. From Throgs Neck, Howe moved inland to outflank the rebels and cut off their retreat from Harlem Heights into Westchester County. In addition, more Royal Navy ships sailed above the Fort Washington-Fort Lee line to block any American move across the Hudson into New Jersey.

Faced with the threat of being surrounded, on October 16 Washington called his senior officers together for a council of war. There was much excitment at the council because General Charles Lee was present. Lee had

---

[1]The three British warships that ran past the American batteries were *Phoenix, Roebuck* and *Tartar*. The squadron was commanded by Captain Parker of *Phoenix*. The Americans watching from Harlem Heights, Fort Lee and Fort Washington may not have seen it, but the three ships had casualties as they passed the rebel batteries. Captain Parker reported a total of nine killed and eighteen wounded aboard the three ships. Force, ed., *American Archives*, Fifth Series, III: 818.

returned triumphantly from Charleston, South Carolina, where he had commanded Southern troops in a brilliant defense of Charleston in June 1776.[1] The generals debated whether to await attack in their position at Harlem Heights or to retreat to open country while there was still time. Lee favored retreat, scoffing at the idea of a position being good merely because its approaches were difficult. Further, he pointed out that there was only one escape route open to them from Harlem Heights, and that was via the Kings Bridge which connected Manhattan Island with the Bronx. "For my part," said Lee, "I would have nothing to do with the islands [Long Island and Manhattan] to which you have been clinging so pertinaciously."[2] Influenced by Lee's arguments, Washington decided to move while he had the chance.

On October 21, Washington abandoned Harlem Heights and crossed to the Bronx. His goal was the village of White Plains in Westchester County. However, at the insistence of the Continental Congress, and with the unanimous approval of his senior officers, he left a sizable garrison at Fort Washington with orders that the post " be retained as long as possible."[3]

General Howe and his army pursued Washington to White Plains with a splendid army of 20,000. The stand-off Battle of White Plains was fought on October 28, and the British then began positioning artillery for a renewed action. They planned another attack for October 31, but a heavy rainstorm canceled their assault. Washington used this rain shower to conceal the evacuation of his army from White Plains, and the rebels retreated north into rugged country on the Croton River in North Castle, New York, where they constructed a strong defense. Watching from a respectful distance, Howe's reconnaissance parties mistook piled-up cornstalks, with dirt still attached to their roots, for sturdy redoubts. The British general decided not to attack.

------

[1]In his memoirs, Sergeant Roger Lamb of the British army wrote that "During this attack [on Charleston] general Lee exposed himself to great danger; as the balls whistled about he observed one of his aid-de-camps shrink every now and then, and by the motion of his body seemed to evade the shot. 'Death sir,' cried Lee, 'what do you mean, do you doge? Do you know that the king of Prussia lost above an hundred aid-de-camps in one campaign.' "'So I understand, sir,' replied the officer, 'But I did not think you could spare so many.'" Roger Lamb, *Journal of Occurrences During the Late American War* (Dublin, Ireland: Wilkinson & Courtney, 1809), 99.

[2]Lee's comment was reported in Washington Irving, *The Life of George Washington* (New York: G.P. Putnam and Co.,, 1855), II: 381.

[3]Proceedings of a Council of General Officers, October 16, 1776, Force, ed., *American Archives*, Fifth Series, II: 1117-1118. Alden, *General Charles Lee*, 144.

The unbroken string of defeats and retreats had its effects on the American army. Many of the soldiers were demoralized and, with winter approaching, desertions ran higher than ever. Patriots had counted 18,730 fit for duty on September 28, 1776; but by the end of October, the number had dropped to 16,969.[1] The enlistments of the Massachusetts militia would expire on November 17 and they were determined to go home. Almost all the Continental regiments were eligible to disband on November 30 or December 31; few fresh troops were arriving to take their place. Enlistments were slow, which was no surprise since the Americans had lost every major engagement in the New York campaign and were on the run. Washington was aware that his army was diminishing with each passing day and wrote Congress to say "how essential it is to keep up some shew of force and shadow of an Army."[2]

Logistics added to Washington's problems. Food and equipment were in short supply, and the rebels had lost many of their blankets and tents during the months of fighting. By late October, the troops were sleeping unprotected on the frozen ground. Some men were losing heart and silently questioning whether George Washington was the right man to command the patriot army.

Washington's chief problem, however, remained General Howe. Over November 5 and 6, the British commander shifted his army from White Plains to Dobb's Ferry on the Hudson, where the Navy had supplies waiting.[3] These ships had successfully run past the rebel gun batteries at Forts Washington and Lee the previous day.

Unsure what Howe was up to, Washington again called a council of war. Some officers believed the British were finished campaigning for the year and heading for winter quarters in New York City. Others felt that Howe would try to penetrate deeper into New England or move north on the Hudson River towards Albany. Washington's assessment of the situation was that Howe definitely planned to continue to campaign before going into winter quarters. The Virginian believed that his opponent would use a part of his army to attack Fort Washington and another part to invade the rich farmlands

---

[1]Lesser, *The Sinews of Independence*, 32-36.

[2]Washington to the President of Congress, November 6, 1776, Fitzpatrick, ed., *Writings of Washington*, 6: 250.

[3]Kemble, *Journals*, I: 97-98. Kemble reported that the the march of the troops to Dobbs Ferry was "marked by the Licentiousness of the Troops, who committed every species of Rapine and plunder."

of New Jersey. After discussing the situation, the officers unanimously agreed to "throw a body of troops into the Jerseys immediately" and to detach 3,000 troops for the defense of the Hudson Highlands.[1]

On November 7, the day following his decision to send part of the army to New Jersey, George Washington wrote to inform Governor William Livingston of the situation. He gave the New Jersey leader the latest war news and warned that Howe was not finished for the year. The Commander-in-Chief thought it probable that the British general would press into New Jersey with at least part of his force, if only to affirm his reputation. He assured Livingston that if this occurred, he would at once "throw over a body of our Troops, with the utmost expedition, to assist in checking their progress."[2]

Such a move, however, would not be easy. Washington faced the problem of deciding how to split his little army to defend New Jersey and still protect the Hudson River and New England. His solution went against all established military doctrine: he decided to divide his small army in the face of a superior enemy. The plan called for splitting the army into three unequal pieces. Believing that New Jersey would become the focus of the war, Washington decided that he would personally lead all the troops whose homes were south of the Hudson River to New Jersey to help defend that state.[3] They totalled about 5,000 men. This force was too small to defend New Jersey. However, Washington calculated that he could add to this number the 2,146 men under Greene's command at Fort Lee, as well as the 1,500 Pennsylvania troops garrisoning Fort Washington.[4]

---

[1]Force, ed., *American Archives*, Fifth Series, III: 543-544.

[2]Fitzpatrick, ed., *Writings of Washington*, 6: 255-256. In this same letter Washington recommended that the New Jersey governor alert the state's militia, make any necessary repairs to the barracks in Elizabethtown, Perth Amboy and New Brunswick, and to remove all "Stock, Grain, Effects and Carriages" from the the seacoast to the safety of the interior of the state.

[3]On November 7, Washington wrote Greene from North Castle: "If you have not already sent my Boxes with Camp Tables and Chairs, be so good as to let them remain with you, as I do not know but I shall move with the Troops designed for the Jersey's, persuaded as I am of their having turned their Views that Way." Fitzpatrick, ed., *Writings of Washington*, 6: 254-255.

[4]On October 26, Greene reported to Washington that he had 2,146 officers and men present and fit for duty. Force, ed., *American Archives*, Fifth Series, II: 1250. A few weeks later, on November 14, Greene reported 2,667 troops under his command . Greene's

As agreed at the November 6 council of war, 3,000 troops would be headquartered at Peekskill, New York, and assigned to defend the Hudson Highlands. Washington gave this command to the unimaginative but reliable General William Heath. The third and largest portion of the army, consisting of 7,500 soldiers, would remain at North Castle under the command of General Charles Lee. Lee's mission was to deter any British thrust into New England and to wait as a reserve until General Howe's intentions became clearer.

At the same time, some decision was necessary regarding the future of the Fort Washington garrison on northern Manhattan. Preoccupied with defending the Hudson Highlands and New Jersey, Washington at first gave relatively little thought to the fort. Yet there was not much trepidation within the walls of the post. The officers in command felt confident that their sturdy fortress could withstand a siege for a considerable time. Greene assured the Commander-in-Chief that if Fort Washington was threatened, the men could be ferried across the Hudson River to the safety of rebel-held New Jersey. For the time being, then, the fort and its considerable garrison seemed safe enough.

Washington began his troop movements on November 8. The reports of spies and the sudden movement of enemy boats around Dobbs Ferry convinced him that an invasion of New Jersey was imminent.[1] He ordered part of his army across the Hudson River to New Jersey, and the Virginia, Delaware and Pennsylvania troops commanded by General William Alexander, better known as Lord Stirling, were quickly on their way. Once across the Hudson, Sterling's Brigade provided protection for 2,700 additional soldiers who made the crossing the followng day. Stirling reached Hackensack, New Jersey, with his brigade on November 12. Washington followed, leaving North Castle early on the morning of November 10, making various stops along the way to inspect fortifications and to consult with senior

---

force was spread out on or near the Hudson River from Sneeden's Landing opposite Dobbs Ferry to Clinton Point, which lay opposite Spuyten Duyvil. Greene mentioned other American strong points at Bergen, Hoboken, Bull's Ferry (present day West New York, New Jersey), and Hackensack. However, this figure is misleading because it included 1,510 who were sent by Greene from New Jersey to reinforce Fort Washington. Thus it is difficult to determine the exact number of American troops in New Jersey in mid-November, 1776. Adrian C. Leiby, *The Revolutionary War in the Hackensack Valley* (New Brunswick, NJ: Rutgers University Press, 1962), 58.

[1]Washington to Greene, November 8, 1776, Fitzpatrick, ed., *Writings of Washington*, 6: 257-258.

commanders.[1] By this time, the Commander-in-Chief was more concerned with the situation at Fort Washington and with the security of vital supplies at Fort Lee. He reached Fort Lee on November 13, consulted at length with General Greene, and rode on to Hackensack, a farming village six miles west of Fort Lee, where he established his headquarters at the Zabriskie Mansion.[2]

Having arrived in New Jersey, Washington now had to await events. In effect, the rebel commander had placed his faith in a plan that left his army divided in the face of a concentrated enemy who held the initiative. When the anticipated assault came, he had to trust that his subordinates, especially Lee, could quickly discern enemy intentions and react accordingly. Such a strategy was inherently risky even when undertaken by well-equipped and experienced armies, and Washington's was neither. But it was a gamble the general felt he had to take.

In the patriot commander's view, success depended chiefly on a quick response by Lee if the British launched a major invasion of New Jersey. He was counting on just such a reaction. If Howe moved, the general wrote one American officer, he was positive "that the troops under General Lee, will also cross Hudson's River, if it should be necessary in consequence of the Enemy's throwing their force over." Washington further emphasized his thinking on this point in his instructions to Lee dated November 10: "If the enemy should remove the whole, or the greatest part of their force, to the West side of Hudson's River, I have no doubt of your following with all possible dispatch."[3]   At least that was the plan.

---

[1]Fitzpatrick, ed., *Writings of Washington*, 6: 272, and Heath's *Memoirs*, 95.

[2]Fitzpatrick, ed., *Writings of Washington*, 6: 279.

[3]Fitzpatrick, ed., *Writings of Washington*, 6: 266. There are other references to Washington's dependence on Lee if General Howe invaded New Jersey. Washington ended a letter to Colonel (later General) Henry Knox, dated November 10, 1776, "It is unnecessary to add, that if the Army of the Enemy should wholly or pretty generally throw themselves across the North River, that General Lee is to follow." *Ibid.*, 6: 267.

CHAPTER TWO

Fort Washington

The Importance of the North River, and the sanguine wishes
of all to prevent the enemy from possessing it, have been
the causes of this unhappy catastrophe.
—Washington to Governor Jonathan Trumbull,
November 17, 1776

Washington had lost all direct contact with Fort Washington from the moment he left Harlem Heights on October 21. Until he arrived at Fort Lee on November 13, when he was able to discuss Fort Washington with General Greene, he had received only a few letters about affairs on the Manhattan side of the Hudson, and they were not reassuring. While he was still at Harlem Heights, Washington had witnessed the failure of the batteries at Forts Washington and Lee to prevent the Royal Navy from sailing up the river. The incident, which took place on October 9, had deeply disturbed the general, and he was hardly pleased to learn that similar events had recurred. How much faith could he place in the ability of his forts to defend the vital Hudson River?

Washington had not seen the next tests of the river forts. The first came on October 27, when the general and the Grand Army were at White

Plains. Two British frigates brazenly stopped below Forts Washington and Lee as part of a probe of the American defenses. The two frigates engaged the rebel batteries in an intense cannon duel and took a terrible beating for several hours; but neither was sunk, and they returned safely down river. On November 5, as Howe was moving towards Dobbs Ferry, three additional British ships successfully ran the Fort Washington-Fort Lee defensive line. The journal of H.M.S. *Pearl,* one of the ships involved, recorded a brisk fire from the Americans, which the British returned. "We recd a number of shot in our Hull & several between Wind & Water," the log noted, and "had the Major part of our running Rigging & and a great part of our lower Cut to pieces. found Wm Brown, Seaman Kill'd & several wounded. The Sails much torn our Mizen & Mizen top-mast shatter'd & and Boats much damaged." The British were under fire for about an hour and a half and, as *Pearl* candidly admitted, suffered battle damage and casualties; but the American batteries failed to sink any of the enemy ships or force them back down river. Once more, the rebel guns had come off second best.[1]

General Greene brushed off this latest failure of his river forts to stop enemy shipping on the Hudson River.[2] But when Washington received a report on the incident, he questioned the value of maintaining Fort Washington when it was unable to stop the enemy from sailing up and down the Hudson River at will. "The late passage of the 3 Vessels up the North River," he wrote to Greene on November 8, "is so plain a Proof of the Inefficacy of all the Obstructions we have thrown into it" "If we cannot prevent Vessels passing up, and the Enemy are possessed of the surrounding Country, what valuable purpose can it answer to attempt to hold a Post from which the expected Benefit cannot be had."[3] In fact, Washington had a point, and had he pushed it further he might have spared the army, and himself, some real pain.

Greene, however, had a seemingly plausible explanation. He fired back a detailed reply, dated November 9, in which he assured Washington

---

[1]The engagements, including *Pearl's* journal, are noted in William James Morgan, ed., *Naval Documents of the American Revolution*(Washington, DC: Naval History Division, Navy Dept., 1972), VI: 1428-29. Another account of the incident on November 5 is in *The Diary of Frederick Mackenzie*, I: 98.

[2]In fact, Greene mistakenly reported to Washington that fire from the forts seriously damaged the British ships; see Showman, ed., *Papers of Nathanael Greene*, I: 337-38.

[3]Fitzpatrick, ed., *Writings of Washington*, 6: 257-258.

that the fort was safe from being overrun and should not be abandoned. Greene insisted that the garrison at Fort Washington was in no danger because they could be quickly evacuated across the Hudson River to Fort Lee. Further, the fort was holding down a large number of enemy troops who had surrounded it. Even though the British were getting ready to besiege the fort, he promised Washington that it would take the enemy until the end of December to capture the post.[1] In short, there was no reason for undue concern. Washington's instinct still was to evacuate Fort Washington; but he had no first hand knowledge of the situation and he instead chose to rely on Greene's assurances.

General Greene, inexperienced with military engineering and lacking trained engineers to advise him, was mistaken about Fort Washington. It looked impressive because of its excellent natural defensive location, a hilltop which dominated the surrounding countryside. The American defensive works were a mile long. Well-placed outer works defended the fortifications from all land approaches and rugged cliffs rendered it unassailable from the Hudson River side. But Fort Washington was constructed of earth and wood and lacked most of the features necessary to resist siege or attack; there were no ditches, casements, palisades, or barracks, and the outer works were weak. The post lacked food, fuel and water to sustain a siege. Water had to be carried to the fort from the river, 280 feet below, and the British could easily sever this source if they attacked. Much of the garrison of Fort Washington was spread out in positions outside the earthen walls and the fort was too small to hold the entire command if the outer works were overrun.[2]

Fort Washington was essentially a Pennsylvania garrison. The commander was Colonel Robert Magaw, a thirty-five year old lawyer and patriot from Carlisle, Pennsylvania, who commanded the Fifth Pennsylvania regiment. Magaw's second-in-command was Lieutenant Colonel Lambert Cadwalader from Philadelphia. The regimental staff included yet another Pennsylvanian, William Demont, the adjutant. Unfortunately, he was also a traitor.

Demont was an Englishman by birth, and he deserted to the enemy on

---

[1]Showman, ed., *Greene Papers*, I: 344.

[2]Historians Douglas Marshall and Howard Peckham said that some American officers realized the shortcomings of Fort Washington, but their qualms were never effectively communicated to Greene. Douglas Marshall and Howard Peckham, *Campaigns of the American Revolution* (Ann Arbor: University of Michigan Press, 1976), 26.

the night of November 2, carrying with him a plan of Fort Washington, including the positions of its critical outer works. Demont passed safely between the lines and reached the British army where he turned over his valuable plans to Earl Percy who eagerly passed them on to Howe. Howe probably received Demont's plan from Percy on November 3 or 4. For Howe, it was a lucky stroke. Although the British general was planning an attack on Fort Washington, possession of Demont's plans gave him an incentive to accelerate his timetable for the assault. In fact, getting the plan of Fort Washington may have accounted for Howe suddenly breaking contact with the rebel army near White Plains on the night of November 5.[1]

At noon, on November 6, Howe arrived at Dobbs Ferry. To the south, the Hessian General Wilhelm von Knyphausen had already driven in the American outposts near Fort Washington.[2] This meant that the only escape route open to the garrison was to climb down the high cliffs to the west and to cross the Hudson River to Fort Lee. Howe proceeded to move against his prey. From Dobbs Ferry, the general marched southward while Cornwallis moved his corps to the east bank of the Harlem River.[3] Lord Percy brought up troops from New York City to a position below Fort Washington on the Harlem Plains. Fort Washington was now cut off and the garrison's only escape was across the Hudson River to Fort Lee.

In response to Howe's maneuvers, Greene sent Magaw additional troops from Fort Lee. It was a substantial reinforcement, which brought the

---

[1]Historian David Ramsey pointed out that Howe realized that Washington's army could not come to the aid of Fort Washington. "The Americans having retired (to North Castle)," he wrote, "Sir William Howe determined to improve the opportunity of their absence, for the reduction of Fort Washington." David Ramsey, *History of the American Revolution* (Philadelphia, 1793). Mackenzie reported in his diary on November 2 that a man named Diamond, "who says he was Ensign and Adjutant" deserted from Fort Washington. It is extraordinary, but Mackenzie appears to have interviewed Demont on November 2, and reported that Demont said that there was much disagreement and dissension at Fort Washington, "everybody finding fault with the mode of proceeding, and the inferior officers, even Ensigns, insisting that, in such a cause, every man has a right to assist in Council, and to give his opinion." *Mackenzie Diary,* I: 95.

[2]General von Knyphausen had recently arrived in America with a large number of Hessians to reinforce Howe's army. He was 60 years old at the time and a professional soldier of great personal courage although he is best remembered in the American Revolution as the German officer who buttered his bread with his thumb.

[3]In the eighteenth century, the term "brigade" or "corps" meant a minimum of three regiments which usually operated together under the command of a brigadier general.

Fort Washington garrison to some 2,900 men. But the odds were still grim: facing them were twelve British and fifteen Hessian regiments, totaling about 13,000 men. Colonel Magaw dispersed his troops into a wide arc of outer works in an area about four miles long and three-quarters of a mile wide between the Hudson and the Harlem Rivers and waited.[1]

Washington had arrived at Fort Lee with his staff on November 13, staying at Greene's headquarters in a farmhouse a few miles from the fort itself.[2] Again reassured by Greene that Fort Washington could withstand an assault, the Commander-in-Chief went to his headquarters in Hackensack and turned his attention to defending the interior of New Jersey against a possible British attack. Apparently, he planned to push on to Perth Amboy the next day.

But unknown to Washington, the situation at Fort Washington was changing rapidly for the worse. In fact, a crisis was in the making. On November 15, Colonel James Patterson, Howe's adjutant-general, approached Fort Washington accompanied by a drummer beating the parley.[3] Patterson was carrying a white flag and called upon Magaw to surrender the fort or suffer death by the sword. Magaw gave Patterson a written refusal and the parley ended.

Washington received word of the British ultimatum and quickly determined to go to Fort Washington and talk personally with Magaw. That night, he mounted his horse and rode hard from his headquarters in Hackensack to Fort Lee. Upon arriving at the fort, junior officers told him that Generals Greene and Putnam were across the river conferring with Colonel Magaw. Washington followed his generals and was in the middle of the Hudson River in a boat when he was met by Greene and Putnam returning

---

[1]Christopher L. Ward, *The Delaware Continentals* (Wilmington: Historical Society of Delaware, 1941), 92. Showman, ed., *Greene Papers*, 1: 358. Four battalions from the Flying Camp are identified as having been dispatched from Fort Lee by Greene to reinforce Fort Washington. They were all Pennsylvania units: Swope's, Watts', Montgomery's and Baxter's Bucks County Militia. Bradley's Connecticut Regiment, half of John Durkee's 20th Continentals (Connecticut) and 250 Maryland and Virginia riflemen commanded by Colonel Moses Rawlings are also identified as being sent to reinforce Fort Washington. Douglas Southall Freeman, *George Washington* (New York: Charles Scribner's Sons), IV: 248, note 111; Fitzpatrick,ed., *Writings of Washington*, VI: 285, 293.

[2]Leiby, *Revolutionary War in the Hackensack Valley*, 64.

[3]Beating the parley was a drum call designed to inform one's enemy that you wished to talk. The term is derived from the French word "parle": to converse.

from Fort Washington in their rowboat. The generals sat bobbing and talking with each other as the oarsmen held the boats together. Greene and Putnam said they had just come from a conference with Magaw who insisted that he could repel an attack. They assured Washington that everything possible had been done. Washington returned to Fort Lee, determined to see Magaw himself the following morning and make a final decision on whether the fort should be defended or abandoned. [1]

At sunrise, Washington was again in a boat with Generals Putnam, Greene, and Mercer. Just as they were about to pull away from the New Jersey shore, the generals heard the sounds of cannon fire from across the river. Washington ordered the boat to pull hard for the Manhattan shore; the British assault on Fort Washington had begun. As soon as their boat bumped the shoreline, the generals were out and climbing toward the crest. They found Magaw, and after conferring with him decided that the attack was the opening round of a long siege. Everything seemed well-managed by Magaw, and Washington was urged to return to the safety of Fort Lee. Washington saw that nothing more that could be done and he returned with his entourage to New Jersey. Once back, the generals quickly got to the crest of the Palisades to get a clear view of the action across the river. They were about to become spectators to one of the greatest defeats in American military history.

The morning of November 16 passed with the sound of intense gunfire from across the river. Much of the battle was hidden from view by the rugged hills and forests surrounding Fort Washington. But everyone at Fort Lee could hear the constant reports of artillery and small arms, and could see a great cloud of smoke above the tree line.

Through his telescope, Washington had an unobstructed view of the open terrain south of Fort Washington, and he could see clearly the noble defense of the fort's outer works by Colonel Lambert Cadwalader and his 800 Pennsylvanians. They fought well against imposing odds. Unknown to either Cadwalader or Washington, the patriots were under assault by a force over double their strength, commanded by Lord Percy. Washington could see Percy's troops advancing and Cadwalader's men being cut down. The British advance was inexorable. According to historian Washington Irving, the sight was almost too much for the patriot general: "It is said so completely to have

---

[1] General Israel Putnam (1718-1790) from Connecticut was technically in charge of the American defenses on northern Manhattan Island. See Fitzpatrick, ed., *Writings of Washington*, 6: 206. But Washington thought little of Putnam and worked with Greene on any serious matters, including the defense of Fort Washington.

overcome him, that he wept, with the tenderness of a child."[1] Perhaps. But whatever his emotional state, it was clear to the general that he was not watching a siege; Howe was assaulting Fort Washington from every side with 8,000 British and German troops. The British were moving in for the kill.

By mid-day, after hard fighting north of the fort, Crown forces had broken through the critical outer works, forcing the remaining 2,400 American defenders to retreat to the small earthen fort on the top of the hill. Fort Washington became a trap. It had been built to hold 1,000 men and it was now holding over twice that number. "A single shell," General Heath observed, "dropping among them, must have made dreadful havoc."[2]

As the battlefield fell silent, and Washington thought that the fighting had stopped so that the British could reiterate their surrender demand. At this point, the general sought to take advantage of the lull in the action to contact Magaw. An officer at Fort Lee, Captain John Gooch, volunteered to carry a message to Magaw. It was a promise of help. Washington told Magaw that if he could hold out until nighttime, some way would be found to evacuate his men.[3] In this version of a Revolutionary War marathon, the intrepid and obviously fit Gooch ran down to the Hudson River, jumped into a small boat, rowed himself across, raced up the steep cliff and through the enemy lines to Fort Washington. He found the fort so crowded that it was difficult to pass through. But Gooch found Magaw and delivered Washington's message.

The daring Gooch got a reply, and again braved enemy bullets and bayonets as he ran back through the enemy positions to his boat and rowed back to Fort Lee. He delivered Magaw's message to Washington: It was too late. Fighting on was impossible, and the surrender negotiations were too far advanced for Magaw to break them off. The gallant but distressed colonel

---

[1]Irving, *Life of Washington*, II: 424.

[2]William Heath, *Memoirs of Major-General Heath* (Boston: I. Thomas and E.T. Andrews, 1798), 97.

[3]Heath said that Gooch was a "brave and daring man" and identified him as being from Boston. *Ibid.*, 97. But Freeman says he was a Rhode Islander, a captain in the Ninth Continental Infantry, and cites Heitman. Freeman, *George Washington*, IV: 251, footnote 4; and Frances Heitman, *Historical Register of Officers of the Continental Army* (Washington, DC: Rare Book Shop Publishing Company, 1914), 251. The problem is that the Ninth Continental Infantry was with Charles Lee in Westchester, New York at the time of the British assault on Fort Washington. Lessor, *Sinews of Independence*, 41. It is probable that Gooch, who was Greene's friend, was on detached duty from his regiment and was present at Fort Lee on November 16, 1776.

had no real choice but to proceed with the capitulation, and even as Gooch had reached him, he was about to surrender the fort and its entire garrison. As Gooch returned to the New Jersey side of the Hudson, enemy regiments already were forming to receive the formal surrender. The defeat was total.[1]

The enduring silence at Fort Washington soon made clear the reality of surrender. Shocked rebel troops at Fort Lee, who saw quickly the gravity of the moment, ceased their frantic preparations to bring the men from Fort Washington across the river. Washington and his senior officers, including Greene, Putnam and Mercer, stood silently on the crest of the Palisades as they watched the American standard being lowered from the flagpole at Fort Washington.[2] They were a grim and bewildered audience. A patriot soldier

---

[1]Alexander Graydon was captured at Fort Washington. He noticed that the enemy seemed to have a perfect knowledge of the terrain and the American positions during their assault. Graydon wrote, "In the affair of Fort Washington, he [General Howe] must have had a perfect knowledge of the ground we occupied. This he might have acquired from hundreds in New York; but he might have been more thoroughly informed of every thing desirable to be known, from one Dement, an officer of Magaw's battalion, who was intelligent in points of duty, and deserted to the enemy, about a week before the assault." John Littell, ed., *Alexander Graydon, Memoirs of His Own Time* (Philadelphia: Lindsay & Blakiston, 1846), 215. In 1792, sixteen years after he deserted from Fort Washington, William Demont asked for compensation from the British government. His request stated his service to the British: "On the 2d of Nov 1776 I Sacrificed all I was Worth in the World to the Service of my King & Country and Joined the then Lord Percy brought in with [me] the Plans of Fort Washington by which Plans that Fortress was taken by his Majestys Troops the 16 instant, Together with 2700 Prisoners and Stores & Ammunition to the amount of 1800 Pound, at the same time I may with Justice Affirm from my Knowledge of the Works I saved the Lives of Many of his Majestys Subjects." Edward Floyd de Lancey, ed., Thomas Jones, *History of the New York During The Revolutionary War* (New York: New York Historical Society, 1879), 630. The story of John Gooch's exploit is from Force, ed., *American Archives*, Fifth Ser., III: 741, and Heath, *Memoirs of the American War*, 97.

[2]While marine artist Dominic Serres shows a red and white striped flag flying over Fort Washington, the Continental Army probably did not have a national flag at this point in the Revolution. More likely, since the fort was mostly garrisoned by Pennsylvania troops, a Pennsylvania regimental flag probably flew over it. The British recorded capturing two Pennsylvania rifle regiment standards ("2 Standards with a Rifleman on") and Colonel Magaw's purple standard. Edward Richardson, *Standards and Colors of the American Revolution* (Philadelphia: University of Pennsylvania Press, 1982), 113. There is also the possibility that the fort fought under a red standard with the motto "LIBERTY." Eleven such flags were captured at the Battle of Long Island. A red damask flag with the motto "LIBERTY OR DEATH" is reported to have been captured from the Americans at the Battle of White Plains, less than a month before the surrender of Fort Washington. *Ibid*, 105-106.

standing near the solemn generals recalled the seriousness of the occasion. Washington, he related, "seemed in any agony when he saw the fort surrendered."[1] Only a moment later, the King's colors rose to replace the rebel ensign. The victors savored the moment. The sound of wild cheering drifted across the river along with the music of the combined British and German military bands. The bitter Americans took no pleasure in the celebration.

The disaster was complete. The captured garrison of Fort Washington was marched off to makeshift prisons in New York City. Conditions for many of the prisoners were deplorable. A few of the lucky ones would be exchanged, but over time, most of the unfortunates would die from disease and mistreatment.[2] For all other rebels, the defeat only drove home the seeming invincibility of Howe's army.

While most patriots were still reeling, Charles Lee lost no time in distancing himself from the catastrophic events at Fort Washington. In fact, he used the disaster to enhance his own reputation with other patriot leaders. Lee wrote Doctor Benjamin Rush, his friend and influential member of the Continental Congress, shortly after the surrender: "The affair at Fort Washington cannot surprise you at Philadelphia more than it amazed and stunned me. I must entreat that you will keep what I say to yourself; but I foresaw, predicted, all that has happened; and urged the necessity of abandoning it." Even if the post had managed to hold out, he told Rush, it was useless to the patriots. On the other hand, Lee was not willing to broadcast his opinion of the disaster. Still, he wanted Rush to understand that Washington

---

[1]Joseph White, *A Narrative of Events... Charlestown, Mass., 1833*, reprinted in *American Heritage* 4 (June 1956): 74-79.

[2]Howe reported capturing 2,818 Americans at Fort Washington. British army casualties were stated at 460 men killed or wounded, the majority of whom were Germans. Blanco, ed., *The American Revolution: An Encyclopedia*, I: 578. There were some hard feelings over the surrender among the Americans, with at least one prominent New Englander remarking on the garrison's Pennsylvania origins. Joseph Trumbull, Commissary General of the Continental Army and influential son of Governor Jonathan Trumbull of Connecticut, remarked on this fact in a letter to a friend dated November 18, 1776. Trumbull's letter was intercepted by the British and published in a New York City newspaper. "It is said Mount Washington has surrendered," he wrote. "We don't yet hear particulars. I am glad a Southern officer [Magaw from Pennsylvania] commanded. The story is not told to his advantage here; be it as it may, we should not have heard the last of it from Reed [Joseph Reed from Pennsylvania] and some others of his stamp, if a New-England man had commanded." Joseph Trumbull to William Williams, November 18, 1776, and published in the *New York Gazette*, December 9, 1776; Force, ed., *American Archives*, Fifth Ser., III: 1498. New Englanders sometimes referred to people from New Jersey or Pennsylvania as "Southerners."

had clung to the post against his advice. "Let these few lines be thrown into the fire," he cautioned, "and in your conversation only acquit me of any share of the misfortune—for my last words to the General were—draw off the garrison, or they will be lost."[1]

Some 2,700 American troops were killed, wounded or captured at Fort Washington. It was an appalling defeat for the patriot cause, by far the worst they had suffered so far in the war.[2] Nathanael Greene's inexperience had led to his mistaken belief that Fort Washington was invincible. But the real blame for the catastrophe falls on Washington's shoulders; the crisis stemmed directly from his hesitation in ordering the fort to be abandoned while there was still time. For weeks before the British assault, Washington instinctively knew that trying to hold Fort Washington was folly. Its capture was one of the biggest mistakes Washington made during the entire course of the Revolution (if not *the* biggest mistake). The debacle was a sharp military setback for the rebellion and seriously damaged Washington's personal prestige.

Indeed, events had wounded the Commander-in-Chief to an extent he may not have immediately understood. Some critics saw the loss of Fort Washington and the gravity of the patriot difficulties that followed it as evidence that Washington was losing his grip; he had become too mentally and physically exhausted to make effective decisions. In the Continental Congress, some members bluntly said that Washington had made a mess of things. Maryland delegate Samuel Chase, after learning the details of the staggering losses at Fort Washington, sent a report back home which bitterly recorded that "2,200 of our Troops are prisoners. The fort was victualed for three Months & amply supplied with Cannon and all military stores. If this account be true, we have again blundered."[3] The account was true enough, and so was the blunder.

---

[1]Charles Lee to Benjamin Rush, November 20, 1776, *Lee Papers*, II: 288. Lee claimed that he had argued that Fort Washington should be evacuated, but that his proposal had been ignored. James Flexner, *George Washington in the American Revolution* (Boston: Little, Brown, 1967), 145.

[2]Only the surrender of almost 5,500 American troops at Charleston, South Carolina, in May 1780 surpassed the losses sustained at Fort Washington.

[3]Samuel Chase to the Maryland Council of Safety, November 21, 1776, Paul H. Smith, ed., *Letters of Delegates to Congress, 1774-1789* (Washington, DC: Library of Congress, 1976-): 5: 525.

CHAPTER THREE

Fort Lee

Gen. Howe must exert every nerve to effect something more than he has yet done with a land and marine force that all Europe had been taught to believe would in one Campaign crush America.
— Richard Henry Lee, November 1776

Despite the intense military activity at Fort Lee in the autumn of 1776, there was little else in the surrounding New Jersey countryside to indicate a state of war. Traveling west, beyond Fort Lee, the narrow farm roads quickly left the war behind as they passed considerable salt meadows and tidal marshes, then opened onto the rich and broad farmlands of the Hackensack Valley. This flat, abundantly watered valley was populated by prosperous farmers descended from the original settlers of New Netherland. From all accounts, the Hackensack Valley was delightful and prized farm country with handsome houses, active mills, and barns and yards brimming with livestock and grain.

The center of activity in the valley was the village of Hackensack, which lay along the Hackensack River five miles west of Fort Lee. This peaceful hamlet surrounded a village green. On the north side of the green was a church with a short white steeple, and next to it was a small stone building which served as the Bergen County courthouse. Near the courthouse was a tavern kept by Archibald Campbell. Also clustered around the green were a few small buildings that housed tradesmen including a blacksmith and a tanner.

The largest and most elegant building in Hackensack was the home of Peter Zabriskie, a local judge and wealthy landowner.[1] The Zabriskie Mansion, as it was called locally, was built of stone three feet thick and stood on the north side of the village green near the church. The road extending north from the village along the Hackensack River was dotted with pleasant farmhouses. Two miles along this road was a bridge across the Hackensack River. Built in 1745, it was called "New Bridge." It was also possible to cross the Hackensack on one of the several mill dams that had been constructed across the river. Enterprising farmers living along the river ferried passengers across the river for a fee. Three miles to the south of the village was a ferry called "Little Ferry" (today the town of Little Ferry).

A few miles to the west of the Hackensack River lay a meandering river named the Passaic, that could be traced to its source in the Great Swamp around Basking Ridge, New Jersey. A dilapidated bridge crossed the Passaic on the road from Hackensack, leading to another village named Acquackanonk (modern Passaic). There were other small farming communities spread over the countryside of northern New Jersey with quaint Indian and Dutch names like Totowa, Teaneck, Pascack and Paramus. From all accounts, the Hackensack Valley had some of the best farmland in all of the original Thirteen Colonies.

The majority of the people living in the Hackensack Valley were neither townsmen nor great landowners. They were independent farmers, usually owning seventy-five or a hundred acres of land from which they derived a comfortable existence. A fair number of the farms used slave labor.

People of Dutch ancestry were numerous in the Hackensack Valley. They doggedly spoke Dutch in their homes and churches and kept their Old World customs even though Holland had finally surrendered New Netherland to the English a century prior to the American Revolution. As the earliest settlers to arrive in New Jersey, the Dutch were among the largest land-owners in Bergen County, and they also owned the rich land along the banks of the Raritan and Millstone Rivers in the central part of New Jersey.

---

[1]This account is drawn from Adrian C. Leiby, *The Revolutionary War in The Hackensack Valley* (New Brunswick: Rutgers University Press, 1962), 7.

At the outbreak of the Revolution, New Jersey was a quiet, comfortable agricultural colony with no great commercial centers or seaports. The land was bountiful and New Jersey was known in the eighteenth century as the Garden of America. Produce from New Jersey's farms moved along country roads to the colony's river ports for shipment to nearby cities. In the eastern part of New Jersey, the roads led to the river ports of Perth Amboy, New Brunswick, Raritan Landing, Newark, and Elizabethtown. These port towns sent the bulk of their boats to New York City. In the western part of New Jersey, produce was sent to Philadelphia from the Delaware River port towns of Burlington, Salem, Bordentown, and Trenton.[1]

New Jersey's population had been steadily increasing in the years prior to the Revolution. In 1745, it was estimated at 61,000. By 1754 it had risen to 80,000 and reached approximately 115,000 by 1772.[2] On the eve of the American Revolution, Elizabethtown (present- day Elizabeth) had grown to between 200 and 300 houses, making it the largest and most important town in New Jersey. Trenton, Perth Amboy and New Brunswick had about a hundred houses each. Newark and Princeton were smaller but growing.

People of Dutch ancestry made up over one-sixth of the population of New Jersey. The vast majority belonged to the Dutch Reformed Church. The Scotch, Scotch-Irish, and Germans followed the Dutch to New Jersey and settled in the interior of the province, especially in Somerset and Hunterdon Counties.[3] The Scotch and Scotch-Irish were Presbyterians and the Germans were Lutherans. There were also Quakers who settled in the western part of New Jersey, along the Delaware River in Burlington County. People of Puritan stock had emigrated from New England to New Jersey, establishing themselves in Essex and Morris Counties with their commercial centers at Newark, Elizabethtown, and Morristown. There were also some 10,000 blacks in New Jersey in 1775, most of whom were slaves.

Like many of her sister colonies, New Jersey had moved slowly from

---

[1]Wheaton Lane, *From Indian Trail to Iron Horse* (Princeton: Princeton University Press, 1939), 50.

[2]Carl Woodward, *Ploughs and Politicks* (New Brunswick: Rutgers University Press, 1941), 146.

[3]The term Scotch-Irish referred mostly to refugees from Scotland who were forcibly removed to Ireland by the British government following the Scottish uprising of 1745. These people preferred to call themselves "Ulstermen," the county in Northern Ireland where they lived before coming to America.

protest to rebellion. Much of the support for the rebellion came from the poorest and least educated people in the colony; the Scotch-Irish farmers in the hilly regions of Morris County and those living on the borders of the great swamps and marshlands. Looking at each county in the colony, there was some support for the rebellion in Somerset and Hunterdon Counties. Bergen and Monmouth Counties were two of the biggest Loyalist centers in New Jersey. Less populated Sussex County also held many Loyalists. Middlesex County was generally for the rebellion as were Essex, Salem, and Cumberland Counties. Cape May County had too few people to matter. On balance, New Jersey was a largely patriot state, but with enough support for the King to make for bitter civil strife during the war.

New Jersey was slow to respond to the outbreak of the Revolution. However, within six months after the start of the war, the colony had raised three regiments which marched off to fight in Canada. By 1776, however, with these regiments gone, New Jersey had only a weak, poorly organized militia at home for regional defense. In June 1776, to help defend the state, the Continental Congress voted to raise militia companies from Maryland, Delaware, and Pennsylvania to form a mobile reserve named the Flying Camp. General Hugh Mercer was appointed commander of the Flying Camp and militia were recruited to serve until December 1 or December 30, 1776. The Flying Camp was, in theory, to rush to any point along New Jersey's shoreline where the enemy might attempt an invasion.

George Washington was desperate for manpower during the New York campaign and he depleted the Flying Camp to fill the ranks of the Grand Army. By November 14, the remaining poorly trained and equipped militia regiments of the Flying Camp had moved to Fort Lee or were guarding the Hudson River.[1] In the days following the loss of Fort Washington, General Washington came to the grim realization that these poorly disciplined and dispirited troops represented a significant portion of the men still available to him. It was not a comforting prospect.

It rained in northern New Jersey on the night of November 19, 1776. Major General Nathanael Greene was sleeping soundly at Fort Lee, knowing that five hundred American soldiers were patrolling the New Jersey side of the Hudson. The patrols ran from opposite Spuyten Duyvil to Sneden's Landing watching for a surprise attack.

Five miles away, in Hackensack, Washington was also sleeping. Before retiring, he had finally completed a private letter which he had started

---

[1]Force, ed., *American Archives*, Fifth Ser., 3: 663.

two weeks earlier to his confidant and brother, John Augustine. In this revealing letter (dated Hackensack, November 19), Washington wrote about what had happened since his arrival at White Plains in October. He was especially bitter at the loss of Fort Washington, writing that when he learned that a British squadron had sailed safely past the rebel gun batteries on the Hudson River on November 5, he had wanted to abandon the position. It was held contrary to his "wishes and opinion," he wrote, and he constantly faced "perplexities and mortifications." These included, he painfully reported, the poor quality of the officers in his army. "The different States," the general complained, commissioned men "without regard to the merits or qualifications of any officer, quarreling about the appointments, and nominating such as are not fit to be shoe blacks." Washington closed his letter with a passage that would later become famous. "I am wearied almost to death with the retrograde motions of things," he told John, and "solemnly" protested that a reward of twenty thousand pounds a year "would not induce me to undergo what I do." He wished his brother "all health and happiness," adding that "nothing in this world would contribute so much to mine as to be once more fixed among you in the peaceable enjoyment of my own vine and fig tree."[1] It was one of the general's most heartfelt letters of the war.

Since the dreadful surrender of Fort Washington, the morale of the Grand Army had reached a new low. There was whispered criticism of Washington's generalship from the officer corps and among politicians, all of which was a heavy burden for the sensitive Virginian to bear. Those closest to him knew that he felt himself wronged by such criticism. "We were in a fair way of finishing the campaign with credit to ourselves," wrote Tench Tilghman, one of the general's young aides, "and I think to the disgrace of Mr. Howe, and had the General [Washington] followed his own opinion, the [Fort Washington] garrison would have been withdrawn immediately upon the enemy's falling down from Dobb's Ferry. But General Greene was positive," Tilghman explained, "that our forces might at any time be drawn off under the guns of Fort Lee. Fatal experience has evinced the contrary."[2]

---

[1]Fitzpatrick, ed., *Writings of Washington*, 6: 242-247.

[2]Tench Tilghman wrote Robert R. Livingston from Hackensack on November 17, the day after the loss of Fort Washington. Force, ed., *American Archives*, Fifth Ser., III: 740. Tilghman (1744-1786) was a successful Philadelphia businessman, the son of a prosperous Maryland tobacco grower. He was a graduate of what today is the University of Pennsylvania, was an active patriot, and joined the American army at the start of the rebellion. Tilghman was an officer in the Flying Camp in the summer of 1776 and joined

The Commander-in-Chief did not hesitate to take decisive action following the loss of Fort Washington. Wisely, he did not seriously consider a stand at Fort Lee. Rather, he ordered all the equipment and stores at Fort Lee removed as quickly as possible in preparation for abandoning that post and retreating deeper into New Jersey. But a lack of transportation frustrated his efforts to move the vast amounts of equipment and foodstuffs to the safety of the interior of the state. The delay was frustrating and potentially dangerous. Still, the general worked energetically.

But the patriots had run out of time. On the morning of November 20, after a rainy night, Washington was up early and again working with his staff to get the Fort Lee stores away. At 10:00 a.m., he was absorbed in his work when a rider came galloping up to the Zabriskie Mansion from Orange-Town, New York, with urgent news: Howe's army had crossed the Hudson. The invasion of New Jersey had begun.[1]

The moment Washington finished reading the communication he immediately swung into action. He jumped to his feet and gave instructions for troops from his skeleton force at Hackensack to secure the strategic points between the crossroads of Liberty Pole (modern Englewood) and Fort Lee, especially the New Bridge. The Commander-in-Chief then mounted his horse

---

Washington's staff as an aide on August 8, 1776. He was an aide to Washington until the end of the Revolution, and Washington allowed him the honor of having him bring the news of Cornwallis's defeat at Yorktown (1781) to the Continental Congress. He was one of thirty-two men who served on Washington's military staff during the Revolution, and he served the longest, seven years. Many of Tilghman's staff colleagues were talented officers, but the rebels never developed a fully organized or effective staff during the war.

[1]The time of the arrival of the courier is mentioned in a letter from Robert H. Harrison to General Schuyler, dated Hackensack, November 20, 1776, Force, ed. *American Archives*, Fifth Ser., III: 781. Harrison's comments offer the most detailed account of how General Washington learned about the British invasion of New Jersey. Orange-Town, New York (modern Orangetown), is near the New Jersey border and close to the Hudson River. At the time, Orange-Town was probably an American outpost. Colonel Harrison's comments demonstrate that news of the invasion did not come from General Greene at Fort Lee, as some historians have believed; e.g., Freeman, *George Washington*, IV: 256. Having learned of the attack, Washington did not ride all the way to Fort Lee. He only went as far as the strategic crossroads of Liberty Pole to await the arrival of Greene with the Fort Lee garrison. Greene must have learned independently that the British army had landed. We can also speculate that upon receiving the news of the invasion, Washington sent an urgent dispatch to Greene with orders to abandon Fort Lee. This would account for Greene's noting, a few days later, that "His Excellency ordered a retreat immediately." Nathanael Greene to Governor Nicholas Cooke, December 4, 1776, Showman, ed., *Greene Papers*, 1: 360.

and, accompanied by Major General Israel Putnam and two of his aides (William Grayson and Robert Hanson Harrison), he rode east to the Hackensack River. He crossed using either one of the boats held there for the use of the army or by riding over one of the mill dams, and then galloped with his party down the road towards Fort Lee.

At the same time that Washington received the fearful news, an American officer arrived at Fort Lee with the same intelligence. A large British force, he said, had landed at dawn seven or eight miles above the fort.[1] General Greene could only conclude that they were coming hard, and he immediately began preparing to evacuate Fort Lee.

The Commander-in-Chief, who had questioned Greene's judgment in the aftermath of Fort Washington, now was in full accord. As Washington raced his horse eastward towards the Hudson River and Fort Lee, he knew that the post was nothing more than an incomplete earthen work garrisoned by a small, untrained force. Defense was folly. The Fort Lee garrison must be evacuated across the Hackensack River, but Washington knew that such a large number of men could only cross the river on the New Bridge. If the British seized the bridge before he could get the retreating troops across, or if the enemy gained control of the strategic crossroads at Liberty Pole, the Fort Lee garrison would be trapped. It would be a debacle that could easily finish the rebel army.

General Howe's hopes for the operation were probably not as high. But he wanted to do real damage at Fort Lee, and then to press the invasion of the New Jersey interior. Howe's units had moved the night before, under cover

---

[1]There was never any lack of opinion on how the warning of the attack reached Fort Lee. Thomas Paine, an aide to General Greene, recorded the time of the American officer's arrival at the fort, and Paine was there at the time. Eric Foner, ed., *Thomas Paine, Collected Writings* (New York: Literary Classics of the United States, Inc., 1995), *The American Crisis*, I: 93. The diary of Ensign Thomas Glyn contradicts Paine regarding the warning, saying that it came from a "Countryman" (a farmer). But Glyn is a less reliable source than Paine, who was actually at Fort Lee. Charles Stedman, who also witnessed events from the British side, told yet another version. He said that a British deserter warned Fort Lee. "Lord Cornwallis began his march with great secrecy and dispatch," Stedman wrote. "In all probability he would have surprised the fort and made the enemy prisoners of war, had not a deserter informed them of his approach." Charles Stedman, *History of the American War* (London, 1794), I: 219. There is also a legend that a slave girl later given the name Polly Wyckoff gave the first alarm. She supposedly was working in the kitchen of the Matthew Bogert farm when she looked out the window and saw British soldiers. Running into the living quarters where the family was seated, she exclaimed "Bogert's fields are full of Red Coats!" The story is in T. Earle Thompson, *An Elementary History of New Jersey* (New York, Hinds, Hayden & Eldredge, 1924), 56.

of the rainstorm. By dawn of November 20, a division of the British task force had landed and secured a landing at Closter, New Jersey. As Washington rode towards Fort Lee, the entire British invasion force of 5,000 had landed safely in New Jersey.

Historians do not know exactly when Howe decided to invade New Jersey. However, the operation seemed the logical next step after the fall of Fort Washington. This much was clear even to junior officers. As early as November 15, Captain Frederick Mackenzie wrote in his diary that "from the general appearance of matters, it is probable, that the moment Fort Washington is taken, General Howe will land a body of troops in Jersey from the right of his Army, and after taking Fort Constitution [Fort Lee] penetrate into that Province towards Philadelphia."[1]

The first evidence of Howe's intentions came in his order calling for fifty flatboats to move up the Hudson River from New York City. These boats would ferry the invasion force to New Jersey. Some of the boats floated undetected past the sentries at Fort Lee and were moored out of site of rebel observers at Spuyten Duyvil.[2] In a general order dated November 19, 1776, General Howe actually put the invasion of New Jersey into motion under the command of General Charles Earl Cornwallis, an aggressive career officer.[3]

---

[1]Mackenzie, *Diary*, 1: 105.

[2]On November 23, 1776, Vice Admiral Lord Richard Howe reported to the Admiralty that "Thirty flat boats were ordered up to Kingsbridge by the North River the Night of the 14th." Boats crews came from Navy transports. Twenty additional boats made the trip, "undiscovered" by rebel batteries, on the night of November 18. Donald M. Londahl-Smidt, "British and Hessian Accounts of the Invasion of Bergen County," *Bergen County History*, 1976 Annual, 45-47. The original letter is in Great Britain, Public Record Office, Admiralty, Class 1, vol. 487. The barges used by the British for their invasion of New Jersey were depicted in a watercolor by Captain Thomas Davies of the Royal Artillery. They had one mast and were manned by British sailors. Built in England, specially-modified transports brought them to America. There were also smaller boats in the British New Jersey invasion flotilla; called "batteau," they were long, light, flat-bottomed boats with a sharply pointed bow and stern.

[3]The general order, dated Nov. 19, which started the British invasion of New Jersey read as follows: "The following Corps are to Strike their Tents Load their Waggons & be in reddiness to March with their Blanketts & Provision this Night at Nine O'Clock. Two Compy Chassuiers 1st & 2d Lt. Infantry 1st & 2d Grenadiers 33d Regt 42 Regt. 3 Battns Hessian Grenadiers---2 Battn of Guards 100 Men of Roger's Corps without Arms two Engineers with twelve Carpenters & three Guides. They will receive their Orders from Lt. Gl. Ld. Cornwallis." Orderly book of the 1st battalion, detachment of the Brigade of

Lord Cornwallis, Sixth Earl of Eyre, and a member of the House of Lords, was a good choice to command the critical New Jersey mission. He was an ambitious and experienced officer, a man who had wanted to be a soldier from childhood. Just prior to his eighteenth birthday, his rich and indulgent father bought him an ensign's commission in the prestigious First Regiment of Foot Guards. But instead of joining his regiment, Cornwallis toured Europe with a Prussian officer and attended a military academy in Italy. When the Seven Years War broke out in 1757, Cornwallis abandoned his studies and rushed to join the fighting. He proved to be a bold and enterprising young officer who was beloved by his men. His youthful experience was the opening chapter in an illustrious military career.

At the time of the New Jersey invasion, Cornwallis was a seasoned veteran. He had seen plenty of combat during the Seven Years War, and his courage and intelligence were undoubted. Thirty-eight years old in his American command, he was described as short and thick set, his hair somewhat gray, his face pleasant, and his manner easy. He also had a cast in one eye, the result of a sports injury inflicted on him by a fellow classmate while in school at Eton. Cornwallis was married and deeply devoted to his wife, who had begged him not to leave her for the war in America. (Perhaps he should have listened to her. But in 1776, who would have predicted his fate at Yorktown in 1781?)

Under Cornwallis' command, the five thousand-man amphibious assault of New Jersey commenced at 11:00 p.m. on the night of November 19. The secretly-gathered boats emerged from Spuyten Duyvil onto the Hudson River, concealed under a driving rainstorm and a heavy fog, which was common along the Palisades.[1] The boats quietly ferried the first division, consisting of half of Cornwallis' force, to a point in New Jersey about five miles north of Spuyten Duyvil.

A variety of contemporary sources revealed the composition of the British invasion force. Lord Cornwallis commanded elite troops, mostly veteran infantry units. The force was composed of the First and Second Battalions of Light Infantry, the Forty-second (or Royal Highland) Regiment of Foot (better known as the "Black Watch"), and two companies of Hessian

---

Guards, August 2, 1776 to January 28, 1777, Manuscripts Division, New York Historical Society, New York.

[1]The exact number of soldiers taking part in the invasion varies from source to source, but 5,000 men is the generally accepted figure.

Jaegers.[1] In addition, Cornwallis was assigned his own Thirty-third Regiment of Foot, "The Detachment of the Brigade of Guards," three battalions of Hessian grenadiers commanded by Colonel Carl Emilius von Donop, and a hundred men from Lieutenant Colonel Robert Rogers' provincial Queen's American Rangers.[2]

Also important to the mission were three Bergen County loyalists. They were probably John Aldington, who owned a farm and brewery in English Neighborhood (now Leonia), John Ackerson, a Closter farmer, and William Bayard, who operated the Hoboken ferry. Traveling with Cornwallis, they led his men to a remote and unguarded landing site. There, the King's troops found a pitching place with a narrow path leading from the river's edge to the crest of the Palisades and onto the farm country of Tenafly, New Jersey.[3]

---

[1]The English translation of jaeger is hunter. In 1775, the British needed rifle units of their own to counter the dangerous patriot riflemen, most of whom came from the frontier counties of Pennsylvania, Maryland, and Virginia and carried the long, light and often skillfully made Pennsylvania long rifle. The jaegers were recruited from forest wardens and game keepers, wore green uniforms, and carried a short, accurate rifle with a large bore and an octagonal barrel of about 28 inches. George Neumann, *The History of Weapons of the American Revolution* (New York: Harper & Row, 1967), 134. The jaegers were fine marksmen as well as skilled and motivated soldiers. The two companies arrived in America in 1776, and if later outfits were not always up to the quality of the initial companies, they generally proved to be excellent troops. They were often used as scouts and frequently they provided marching columns with flank, rear, or advance security. The presence of the two jaeger companies with Cornwallis was further evidence of the high quality of soldiers who assaulted New Jersey on November 20.

[2]Donald M. Londahl-Smidt, "British and Hessian Accounts of the Invasion of Bergen County, 1776," 37 -38. Londahl-Smidt's extensive research has yielded a detailed list of the troops that comprised the Cornwallis expedition. Rogers, who commanded an elite corps of provincial scouts called Rogers Rangers during the French and Indian War, remained loyal to the King during the Revolution and raised the Queen's American Rangers. In the British army, the First, Second (also called the Coldstream Guards), and Third Regiments of Foot comprised the Brigade of Foot Guards. In February 1776, fifteen men were selected from each of the companies of the three regiments for service in America. The 1,101 officers and men were commanded by acting Brigadier General Edward Mathew and were known as The Detachment of the Brigade of Guards.

[3]"Pitching places" were used to throw logs down to the shore, where boats took them to New York. Historian Richard P. McCormick was the first to speculate on Aldington's role as a guide, but there is no definitive proof connecting any specfic Tory to the invasion force. Any number of local residents knew the terrain and could have helped the British. See "John Aldington," *Bergen County History*, 1970 Annual; John Spring, "The 1776 British Landing at Closter," *Bergen County History*, 1975 Annual.

Cornwallis's landing place has confused historians for over two hundred years. At the time, no one recorded the name of the exact site, and during the first decades of this century, historians decided the British came ashore at Upper Closter Landing (also known as Old Closter Dock Landing), which is seven and a half miles north of Fort Lee. However, compelling evidence now shows that the British army actually landed at Lower Closter Landing (later called Huyler's Landing) which is a one and a half miles closer to Fort Lee.[1]

The British next faced the arduous task of getting themselves and their artillery up the narrow and steep path from the river to the crest of the Palisades. Lieutenant Henry Stirke of the Light Infantry was one of the first men ashore. He looked up to see a "Precipice, above a half mile in length" and

---

[1]In 1898, William S. Stryker published his classic account of the Battles of Trenton and Princeton. Stryker briefly described the New Jersey retreat of 1776, and without supporting documentation placed the landing site at Old Closter Dock. William Stryker, *The Battles of Trenton and Princeton* (Boston and New York: Houghton, Mifflin and Company, 1898), 2. Later historians assumed the accuracy of Stryker's account, thus perpetuating the story.

The distance of these two landing sites from Fort Lee was important, but so was the road system that extended from the landings into the interior of New Jersey. In 1776, it was three miles longer to Fort Lee from Upper Closter Landing than from Lower Closter Landing. Based on the time of the British landing and their arrival at Fort Lee, it seems likely that Cornwallis came ashore at Lower Closter Landing. Historian John Spring explained that a fault in the Palisades at Lower Closter Landing created a steep but passable natural path from the shoreline of the Hudson to the crest. General Anthony Wayne surveyed the path in 1780 and reported that it was approximately four feet wide. This path is clearly shown in Captain Thomas Davies's watercolor painting. A local landowner and businessman named George Huyler widened and graded the path in 1840, which erased the original track. Other development along the Hudson Palisades in the last century altered the terrain and confused historians even further.

Historian Kevin Wright suggests that guides with Cornwallis may have overshot Lower Closter Landing on the night of Nov. 19 and arrived at Upper Closter Landing instead. Realizing their mistake, they brought the boats to Lower Closter Landing. This could account for the story that Cornwallis stopped at the Blackledge-Kearny House at Upper Closter Landing on the morning of Nov. 20. The house, built in 1750, is still standing at the water's edge.

Another theory is that the guides first brought Cornwallis to Lower Closter Landing, which he initially rejected as unsuitable. Looking at other landing sites, including Upper Closter Landing where he went ashore briefly, Cornwallis then returned to Lower Closter Landing where his troops landed and scaled the Palisades. The diary of Ensign Thomas Glyn, who took part in the operation, gives a tempting bit of information about the confusion over the landing site. The site was, he wrote, "beyond the usual landing place and considered inaccessible for any body of men." Thomas Glyn, "Ensign Glyn's Journal on the American Service with the Detachment of 1,000 Men of the Guards Commanded by Brigadier General Mathew in 1776," Nov. 20, 1776, unpublished manuscript, Princeton University Library, Special Collections, Princeton, NJ.

"impassable for Horses." Stirke said that his company, with another, was ordered to, "push up the hill, with as much expedition as possible to take post; and maintain it, till sustain'd."[1] The path that the light infantry companies struggled to climb was scarcely four feet wide, but that was enough. When they reached the top, the Light Infantry and German Jaegers secured a semi-circular defensive perimeter while other units made the climb. A Hessian officer, after ascending the rocky height, felt that the British were lucky to have landed unopposed. "Our disembarkation appeared terrible and impracticable as we landed at the foot of a rocky height and had to go up a very steep and narrow path. Fifty men," he said, " would have sufficed to hold back the entire corps if they had only hurled stones down on us."[2]

There were not enough boats to carry the five thousand British across the Hudson at one time. Thus Cornwallis had to split his invasion force into two divisions. The second division waited for the boats to return from New Jersey at the Philipse Farm, a vast tract in Westchester County directly across the Hudson from the New Jersey landing site. The farm was only a part of Philipsburg Manor, the seat of the influential Philipse family. The manor encompassed all the land along the eastern shore of the Hudson River from Spuyten Duyvil to the Croton River. The farm itself stretched along the Hudson River from Spuyten Duyvil to Yonkers, and the British used the Philipse dock, which reached three hundred feet across the river. (A large section of the Philipse Farm is located in the center of modern Yonkers.)

Waiting to embark in the second wave was Hessian Colonel Karl von Donop. An officer with many years of service, he found the crossing a time-consuming operation. Von Donop had started with his brigade from camp at Westchester County at 9:00 p.m. on November 19, proceeding to "Colonel Courtland's house" where he met the English Guards detachment. This combined force left the Courtland House at 3:00 a.m. and marched to the Philipse Farm, which they reached about two hours later. "It was only at 8 o'clock that we could be embarked." wrote Von Donop, "as the boats, which took over 2 battalions of light infantry, two Batt'ns of English Grenaders and

---

[1]Henry Strike, "A British Officer's Revolutionary War Journal," ed. S. Sydney Bradford, *Maryland Historical Magazine* 56, No. 2 (June 1961): 165.

[2]Translation of original manuscript, Military Reports and Narrations of the Hessian Corps in America, Item Z, Lidgerwood Collection, Morristown National Historical Park. The letter was from Lieutenant Johann Emanuel Wagner to Lieutenant General Wilhelm von Dittfurth, and dated, "In Camp at [English] Neighbourhood below Fort Lee, in the Province of Jersey, November 22nd, 1776."

the 33rd and 42nd Regiments to the New Jersey Coast opposite to Philips house, did not get back before that time." Most of the expedition's artillery was with the second division as well, which meant that the British had to avoid heavy fighting until the entire force was across the Hudson.[1]

Ensign Thomas Glyn provided another eye-witness account of the invasion. Glyn, who served in the Detachment of the Brigade of Guards, also crossed to New Jersey with Cornwallis's second division. He said the first division landed in New Jersey at daybreak, and, "as soon as the boats could return, the 2nd Division embarked at Philipses Farm and the whole Corps made to the crest of the Palisades good their landing without any opposition."[2]

The lack of opposition was fortunate, because the troops had a hard time getting up the Palisades. Both Glyn and von Donop recalled the climb with evident distaste. The Hessian complained that the landing place "appeared horrible and impracticable," and that the troops had to climb up a very steep path which was hardly four feet wide. "The rebels," he said, "must have considered it an impossible landing place, for they had no sentries posted at the place; for 50 men would have been sufficient to check our whole corps." Glyn made very similar observations. The Palisades, he wrote, had "a very perpendicular bank of rock 80 feet high to ascend," which made reaching the top very difficult; it was a poor "landing place and considered as unacceptable for any body of troops."[3]

---

[1]Donop to Lt. Gen. Baron von Heister, November 19, 1776, translation of original manuscript, Lidgerwood Collection of Hessian Manuscripts, Letter A, Morristown National Historical Park, 12-14. The best evidence shows that the Cornwallis's entire force gathered on the night of November 19 at Spuyten Duyvil where the first division embarked. The troops of the second division marched up the east side of the Hudson River six miles to the Ludlow area of Philipse's Farm. See Howe to Lord Germain, November 30, 1776: "The 1st Division for Embarkation landed next Day at 8 o'Clock in the Morning about seven Miles above the Fort, while the 2d. Division marched up the East Side of the River, by which Movement the whole Corps, were landed with their Cannon by 10 o'Clock under the Command of Lieutenant General Earl Cornwallis." Quoted in Donald M. Londahl-Smidt, "British and Hessian Accounts of the Invasion of Bergen County, 1776," *Bergen County History*, 1976 Annual, 47- 48. Lieutenant Strike's journal noted that "The Guards, with ye British, and Hessian Grenadiers; *and the Cannon succeeded us*." S. Sydney Bradford, "A British Officer's Revolutionary War Journal, 1776-1778," *Maryland Historical Magazine* 56, No. 2 (June 1961): 164.

[2]Thomas Glyn, "Ensign Glyn's Journal on the American Service with the Detachment of 1,000 Men of the Guards Commanded by Brigadier General Mathew in 1776." Unpublished manuscript, Princeton University Library, Special Collections, 28.

[3]Donop to von Heister, Nov. 19, 1776, Lidgerwood Collection; Glyn, "Journal," 28.

The soldiers also had to drag the artillery up the Palisades. There were eight pieces of artillery with the expedition: two light six-pounders, two howitzers, and four English three-pounders, all of which were manhandled to the crest of the Palisades by troops and sailors. It took until nearly 1:00 p.m. to get the cannons up the steep, narrow path from the river.[1]

As the last of his troops reached the top of the Palisades, Cornwallis wasted no time in starting toward Fort Lee. Ensign Glyn recalled that "Lord Cornwallis immediately formed his corps in two columns" and began "a very rapid march." The rebels, the young officer noted with satisfaction, "were completely surprised." But Glyn's claim that the advance was "immediate" may have been a charitable account of events. Von Donop timed the march from the top of the Palisades at about 2:00 p.m., which may indicate that the British had a hard time getting reorganized after their difficult climb.

Donop's account may have been closer to reality. The journal of another Hessian officer, Captain Johann Ewald of the Second Jaeger Company, also recorded a cautious initial advance. The amphibious landing in New Jersey was heavily covered by the Royal Navy, he recalled, and he noted that the first deployments in New Jersey were defensive. "At the top [of the Palisades]," Ewald wrote, the jaegers and light infantry moved to farms in Tenafly where they formed "in a semicircle behind the stone walls and posted sentries by platoon at distances of three hundred paces." There they stayed for the time being, with Fort Lee "two hours away from us on the left."[2] This was not a description of a hard-driving assault column.

The early British delays were providential for the Americans. Once clear of the cliffs, Cornwallis moved quickly, but by then word of his advance had spread. Warned that the British had landed, Washington rode to Liberty Pole, where he learned that the enemy had temporarily halted after advancing to a hill about two miles north of the village. He decided to stay at Liberty Pole to meet the retreating garrison from Fort Lee and lead them to Hackensack.

While waiting at Liberty Pole, Washington tried to inform General Lee of the developing situation. He instructed one of his aides, Lieutenant Colonel William Grayson, to return to Hackensack and send a dispatch to Lee

---

[1]Glyn, "Journal," 28; von Donop to von Heister, November 19, 1776, Lidgerwood Collection; "Journal of Lieutenant General von Heister's Corps, January 1776 to June 1777," Letter H, Lidgerwood Collection.

[2]Joseph P. Tustin, trans. and ed., *Diary of the American War: Diary of Captain Johann Ewald* (New Haven and London: Yale University Press, 1979),. 17. Ewald had no political stake in the war, and his opinions were generally impartial and honest.

with details of the British invasion. Washington told Grayson to have Lee move his corps across the Hudson River. The Commander-in-Chief assumed that Lee would quickly respond, for such was the plan Washington had adopted before leaving North Castle.[1]

After being warned of the British advance, the first reaction of the garrison was, incredibly, to eat a hasty breakfast. Then, with growing disorder fueled by rumors, they streamed off, abandoning their fort and moving westward down Fort Lee Road (a military road built by the army). They passed quickly over Red Hill Road and through English Neighborhood to the Kings Highway (modern Grand Avenue, Leonia), where they turned north. Their route then took them west towards the crossroads of Liberty Pole where Washington, Putnam, and a few aides anxiously awaited them.

The retreating Fort Lee garrison was composed mostly of the poorly trained troops of the Flying Camp. They amounted to about two thousand officers and men.[2] Even with Washington in command, they were no match for the pursuing enemy column.

Washington led the retreat west from Liberty Pole along Liberty Road to New Bridge Road, and then over the Hackensack River at the New Bridge. The retreat became tumultuous. As news of the enemy advance spread, the poorly disciplined Fort Lee garrison came close to panic. Some of the retreating Americans broke away from the main column and went south through English Neighborhood and modern Ridgefield. This group crossed the Hackensack River at Little Ferry and made their way to Hackensack along

---

[1]Grayson's dispatch to Lee, dated Hackensack, Nov. 20, was detailed and alarming. It reached Lee only a few hours after Cornwallis came ashore. "They landed this morning between Dobbs's Ferry and Fort Lee," Grayson wrote, "as it is imagined, at a place called Closter Dock, nearly opposite to Philips's house, and (as the General has been informed) in great numbers, and an advanced party of them have proceeded as far as a hill two miles above the liberty pole, about a mile and an half above General Greene's quarters where I left his Excellency." The roads to the interior of New Jersey were still open, he noted, and retreat was still possible. British intentions were unclear, "but it is imagined the getting possession of Fort Lee is one part of their design; however, it is possible, and perhaps probable, they may have other and more capital views." Grayson then conveyed Washington's advice to move his command to the New Jersey side of the Hudson and "there wait for further orders." Force, ed., *American Archives*, Fifth Ser., III: 780.

[2]There is no reliable count of the troops at Fort Lee. A return of November 13, 1776 listed 2,667 officers and men "fit for duty"; but after the dispatch of last-minute reinforcements to Fort Washington, the Fort Lee garrison on Nov. 20 was probably about 2,000. "Return of the Forces encamped on the Jersey Shore, commanded by Major-General Greene, November 13, 1776," Force, ed., *American Archives*, Fifth Ser., III: 663-664.

what is now Hudson Street. Discipline was no better in the main body. The men abandoned artillery on the road and littered the retreat route with equipment and provisions as they hastened toward the safety of New Bridge.[1] Some six miles separated Fort Lee from New Bridge, no small distance when running from a vastly superior army.

In the commotion, some of the men broke into the liquor supply of the camp sutlers and got drunk. General Greene rode back to Fort Lee two hours after the evacuation and collected several hundred of these drunken stragglers, but he estimated that nearly a hundred more remained hidden in the woods.[2]

Despite Washington's trepidation, Lord Cornwallis made no attempt to seize New Bridge. Nor did his corps chase the retreating garrison.[3] Once

---

[1]Force, ed., *American Archives*, Fifth Ser., III: 1058.

[2]Force, ed., *American Archives*, Fifth Ser., III:., 1071. The British took over a hundred prisoners in the vicinity of Fort Lee, some of whom were probably among the drunken stragglers. See Donald Londahl-Smidt, "British and Hessian Accounts of the Invasion of Bergen County, 1776," *Bergen County History*, 1976 Annual, 50. Captain Johann Ewald also made contact with the column of troops that Greene had gone back to recover. He skirmished with them and called for reinforcements; instead, Ewald received orders from Lord Cornwallis to withdraw. "Let them go, my dear Ewald," Cornwallis told him, "and stay here. We do not want to lose any men. One jager is worth more than ten rebels." Tustin, ed., *Ewald Diary*, 18.

[3]The myth of a race between the Americans and the British for New Bridge can be attributed in part to George Washington's own belief at the time that the British were headed for the bridge. Writing to Governor William Livingston the day after the retreat from Fort Lee, he noted that "Their intent evidently was to form a line across, from the place of their landing to Hackensack Bridge, and thereby hem in the whole Garrison between the North and Hackensack Rivers. However, we were lucky enough to gain the Bridge before them; by which means we saved all our men." Fitzpatrick, ed., *Writings of Washington*, 6: 302. Another source for the story was General Heath, who later wrote that an express rider arrived from Hackensack "with a most alarming account of what he had seen with his own eyes, viz. that the Americans were rapidly retreating, and the British as rapidly pursuing." Heath, *Memoirs*, 88.

It is possible that Cornwallis did not know the New Jersey terrain; and local opinion often attributed the British failure to seize New Bridge to ignorance of the countryside. Some historians have agreed, pointing to an inaccurate map (a hand-drawn chart by British cartographer Claude Joseph Sauthier) which shows New Bridge south of Hackensack. See, for example, Douglas W. Marshall and Howard H. Peckham, *Campaigns of the American Revolution* (Ann Arbor: University of Michigan Press, 1976), 27. But this argument is flawed, as the Sauthier map was drawn after the New Jersey invasion. The fact is that Cornwallis was clearly led by Loyalists who were very familiar with the area. How else did he find a remote and unguarded landing site along the Palisades? Cornwallis knew the terrain well enough, but his objective was to seize Fort Lee and not Washington's army.

Cornwallis had assembled his force on the crest of the Palisades, he advanced deliberately into the interior on a farm road bordering the property of John Ackerson. Ackerson was a Loyalist and may have been one of Cornwallis's guides.[1] As the Crown forces moved inland, they found themselves marching through beautiful farm country. The Germans, in particular, were impressed. One Hessian officer wrote home that "I prefer this province to any other I have seen in America so far. It is not very mountainous; the coast is [not] high and steep except near the North River. It is well cultivated and I find excellent fruits everywhere and very many cattle."[2] It was war; but for some of the confident attacking army, it was also a walk in the country.

The first British troops descended on Fort Lee at dusk. As one British officer recalled, the rebels left a mess behind them. "They have left some poor pork," he wrote, "a few greasy proclamations and some of that scoundrel Common Sense man's letters."[3] The fellow obviously took a dim view of Thomas Paine. However, the Americans had left much more than "greasy proclamations" in their hasty retreat. In and around the post, the royal troops swept all of the former garrison's artillery, a huge supply of forage, and a stockpile of provisions. Every rebel entrenching tool and stacks of tents also fell into British hands. The booty included a herd of over two thousand cattle. Von Donop was amazed at the extent of the haul. "At the foot of the mountain was an important storehouse for corn," he reported, "and in almost every house there were stored large quantities of provisions. At the summit of the forts themselves were huts and tents for more than 6,000 men and quantities of all sorts of provisions and a large amount of ammunition." The Hessian colonel also noted the capture of the gun batteries on the Hudson River, where the

---

In this regard, Bergen County historian Kevin Wright has offered another interesting theory. Wright points out that the Americans had defended Fort Washington just a few days earlier instead of abandoning it. In fact, they had reinforced Fort Washington just before the British assault. Cornwallis may have believed that the Fort Lee garrison would make a similar stand, and he could not have accurately predicted or planned on their hasty retreat.

[1] John Ackerson's land was confiscated in 1784 and purchased by Captain John Huyler. The modern Palisades Parkway, the Greenbrook Nature Sanctuary, and Tammy Brook Country Club have eliminated all traces of the farm road that Cornwallis traveled from the crest of the Palisades.

[2] Item Z, Lidgerwood Collection.

[3] Quoted in Frank Moore, *The Diary of the Revolution* (Hartford: J.R. Burr Publishing Co., 1875), 350.

delighted British found "several 32 pounders together with 2 middle sized and one extraordinarily heavy iron mortar."[1] That night, Cornwallis and his men feasted on the captured food and then slept in the tents of the rebel garrison.[2]

General Charles Cornwallis had performed well, but not brilliantly. He reached New Jersey without detection, but his corps took too long to form on the crest of the Palisades and lost the element of surprise. His landing place was too far from Fort Lee to reach it without the rebels having some warning. Perhaps, as historian Kevin Wright believes, Cornwallis was convinced that the Fort Lee garrison would defend their post, and surprise was not his real concern. In any event, Cornwallis took the fort but missed the rebel army.

That army was in a sorry state. The night of November 20 found the

---

[1]Item A, Lidgerwood Collection. An undated report by Samuel Cleaveland, Brigadier-General, Royal Artillery, "Return of Ordnance and Stores taken by his Majesty's Troops in the Redoubts and Lines of the Enemy, from their landing at Frog-Neck, West-Chester County, from the 8th of October to the 20th of November, 1776," offered a more detailed list of ordnance captured at Fort Lee. The list was extensive: "Fort Lee: The Rock, Redoubt, and Batteries in the Jerseys: Iron Ordnance: 5 thirty-two pounders, 3 twenty-four ditto, 2 six ditto, 2 three ditto, 1 thirteen-inch brass mortar, 1 ten-inch ditto; 2 thirteen-inch iron mortars, 1 ten-inch ditto, 1 eight-inch ditto." Force, ed., *American Archives*, Fifth Ser., III: 1058. The brass mortar on Cleavland's list had an interesting history. It was part of the cargo of the British ordnance brig *Nancy,* captured at the entrance to Boston harbor in 1775. The Americans named the mortar "Congress" and used it in the siege of Boston. Ward, *War of the Revolution*, 1: 114. Legend says that to celebrate the British evacuation of Boston in March 1776, the rebels filled "Congress" with liquor and used it as a giant punch bowl. The mortar was moved from Boston to a gun battery in New York City in 1776 and later to Fort Lee, where it was recaptured. In his narrative of the New Jersey operation, Captain Andrew Snape Hamond, of HMS *Roebuck*, claimed that the mortar was the same piece of ordnance taken by the Americans from *Nancy*. William James Morgan, ed., *Naval Documents of the American Revolution* (Washington: Government Printing Office, 1976), 7: 266.

[2]Francis, Lord Rawdon, wrote to Robert Auchmuty on November 25, 1776 and recorded some wonderful, but perhaps questionable, details on the capture of Fort Lee. Rawdon did not participate in the attack and his information was second-hand. But his letter has the ring of truth and generally agrees with the fully-confirmed accounts of other British witnesses. "His Lordship [Cornwallis] immediately marched to attack" Fort Lee, Rawdon said, but upon reaching it found that the rebels had fled "so precipitately that the pots were left absolutely boiling on the fire, and the tables spread for dinner of some of their officers. In the fort they found but twelve men, who were all dead drunk. There were forty or fifty pieces of cannon found loaded, with two large iron sea mortars and one brass one, with a vast quantity of ammunition, provision and stores, with all their tents standing." Quoted in Henry Steele Commager and Richard B. Morris, eds., *The Spirit of Seventy-Six* (New York: Harper & Row, 1975), 496.

rebel troops, including the Fort Lee garrison, without tents and cramped into houses and barns along the main road from New Bridge to the Hackensack village green. The British sent patrols forward to the Hackensack River to observe the rebel-held town, but there was no action.

The night was illuminated by huge campfires which lit both sides of the Hackensack River. On the eastern shore, Cornwallis' justly happy men were celebrating their victory. During the night, British and Hessian soldiers plundered the local farms.[1] On the western shore, the dejected patriot army lay exhausted and solemnly inventoried its remaining materials. Depleted units were getting ready for what some believed would be the last gasps of the American Revolution. Under cover of darkness, scores of disheartened American soldiers silently deserted their posts and began the trek back to their homes.

---

[1]Ensign Thomas Glyn's "Journal" says that General Cornwallis issued an order on November 20 warning his troops not to plunder. Apparently, the order was ineffective. Captain Ewald noted that "during the night all the plantations in the vicinity were plundered, and whatever the soldiers found in the houses was declared booty." Tustin, ed., *Ewald Diary*, 18.

CHAPTER FOUR

Hackensack

I must leave a very fine Country open to their Ravages.
—Washington to Charles Lee, November 21, 1776

The fleeing remnants of the Continental establishment began stumbling into Hackensack at dusk on November 20. A village resident described the wretched scene: "The night was dark, cold and rainy, but I had a fair view of Greene's troops from the light of the windows as they passed on our side of the street. They marched two abreast, looked ragged, some without a shoe to their feet and most of them wrapped in their blankets."[1]

The troops found whatever shelter they could and lay down to sleep. As bad as things were, the men perhaps felt lucky that at least they did not share the fate of the troops of Fort Washington, who were imprisoned in New York. Washington could scarcely count four thousand men fit for duty.[2] The rebels' material losses were staggering. The garrison had managed to save only

---

[1]Quoted in Leiby, *Revolutionary War in the Hackensack Valley*, 72.

[2]William S. Stryker, *The Battles of Trenton and Princeton* (Boston: The Riverside Press, 1898), 3.

two field pieces; all other artillery at Fort Lee had been lost. Also, nine hundred tents and every entrenching tool the army owned had been abandoned. Only the narrow Hackensack River divided the two armies. The next morning, Washington faced the difficult task of informing the Congress of what had happened at Fort Lee. "The unhappy affair of the 16th," he began sadly, "has been succeeded by further misfortunes." He then proceeded to tell his civilian bosses of the new setbacks and his precarious situation at Hackensack.[1]

Looking back, Washington had predicted the British invasion of New Jersey for its bountiful food, wood for fuel, and feed for animals. But his good judgment in moving a portion of his army to New Jersey was forgotten in the desperate military situation that followed the loss of Fort Lee. Washington had marched into the state only those troops whose homes were south of New England—about three thousand men. He anticipated that this small force would be increased by the garrisons at Forts Lee and Washington, as well as by the Flying Camp and New Jersey militia. He was wrong on every count. Washington's first shock was the Fort Lee garrison. Arriving at Fort Lee on November 13, he was stunned to learn from Greene that the garrison consisted of untrained and poorly disciplined troops from the Flying Camp. They were far less numerous than expected, especially after Greene had clandestinely drawn many away at the last moment to help defend Fort Washington.[2] The Fort Washington garrison included some of the best troops in the Continental Army, all of which were lost in the staggering defeat of November 16.

Then there was the continuing disappointment of the New Jersey militia. The general usually was able to count on the short-term service of militia to augment his army, and had expected to do so in New Jersey.[3] But

---

[1]Fitzpatrick, ed., *Writings of Washington*, VI: 295-296.

[2]In a letter to Congress of Nov. 19, Washington identified the Fort Lee troops as the Maryland militia brigade of Brig. General Reazin Beall, the New Jersey militia with Brig. General Nathaniel Heard, and the Pennsylvania militia under Brig. General James Ewing. In this same letter, he named the only other American troops in New Jersey as "Hand's Hazlet's; the Regiments from Virginia." Fitzpatrick, ed., *Writings of Washington*, VI: 293-294. These brigades were all part of the Flying Camp commanded by General Hugh Mercer. Ernest Kipping and Samuel Stelle Smith, *At General Howe's Side* (Monmouth Beach, NJ: Philip Freneau Press, 1974), 56, fn 9.

[3]Washington calculated on adding at least 5,000 men to his army from the Flying Camp and New Jersey militia before he left North Castle for New Jersey. Washington to John Augustine Washington, Dec. 18, 1776, Fitzpatrick, ed., *Writings of Washington*, VI: 397.

the troops of the New Jersey militia failed to respond to orders or entreaties to turn out and defend their state. As the crisis built, the citizen-soldiers were reluctant to leave homes and families exposed, and they seldom rallied in appreciable numbers.

Washington also had to cope with other invasion threats. He knew that Howe's army might attack at virtually any point along the New Jersey coast. There were any number of good landing places, and Perth Amboy, Elizabethtown, and Woodbridge were particularly vulnerable because they were directly across from British-held Staten Island.[1] A landing at any one of these locations would put the British on a good road system, in easy communication with their base at New York City, and on the shortest route across the state to Philadelphia. Security on the New Jersey coast was a real problem.

Therefore, soon after he arrived in New Jersey Washington felt compelled to deal with the situation. He dispatched eight regiments from his already-meager force to protect the exposed coastline from Amboy to Elizabethtown Point. These were regiments the general could have used with the main army, but the Commander-in-Chief felt he had no choice in the matter. It was essential that he prevent a British strike into the New Jersey interior.

The detached troops served under the command of Lord Stirling, the popular New Jersey general. The soldiers had an ambitious assignment. Their deployment sought to protect as much of the coastal region as possible as well as the most important routes leading inland. On November 18, a few days before the British invaded the state, Stirling wrote Congress that he was at New Brunswick with five regiments, having left three en route to guard the coast near Rahway.[2] His troops were not models of discipline. Some of them found large stores of liquor at New Brunswick and proceeded to get drunk.[3] General Adam Stephen arrived from Virginia after a long march with three Virginia regiments, which were ordered to remain at Perth Amboy. Colonel

---

[1] As Douglas Freeman pointed out, the correspondence of most Americans failed to make distinctions between the place names of Amboy, Perth Amboy, or South Amboy. Most references to these names, unless very specific, usually meant the general area of Raritan Bay. Freeman, *George Washington*, IV: 303.

[2] Force, ed., *American Archives*, Fifth Series, III: 750.

[3] "Diary of Lieutenant James McMichael," *The Pennsylvania Magazine of History and Biography*, XVI, No. 2 (1892): 139.

Hand had an additional 1,200 troops stationed between Elizabethtown and Woodbridge to guard the coast.[1]

Washington's situation would have been much improved if he still had the 2,900 troops from Fort Washington. Why did he stick by Greene after the disaster at Fort Washington? The answer lies in Greene's gift for organization and administrative detail. Greene proved one of the most capable American officers in the Revolution. He was a good combat officer, but his real talent was for organization.[2] Greene displayed these skills on October 29, 1776, when he submitted a plan to Washington for establishing supply depots across New Jersey. He proposed moving valuable stores from coastal areas to more secure inland depots, which was only logical. If an invasion of New Jersey took place, Greene anticipated an American retreat into the interior, and perhaps all the way to Philadelphia. His plan was to deposit provisions in a prearranged retreat route: Hackensack, Acquackanonk, Elizabethtown, Newark, Springfield, Bound Brook, Princeton and Trenton. Greene's plan was entitled "An Estimate of the Magazines To Be Laid In At the Following Posts for the Subsistence of the Troops and for the Horses In Waggons and Artillery" and was put into action by early November.[3]

While the British captured a staggering amount of foodstuffs and

---

[1]Stephen's brigade was composed of the 4th, 5th and 6th Virginia regiments. These troops started north from Virginia to reinforce Washington in September, 1776. The brigade was in Princeton, New Jersey, on November 8 and Washington ordered it to Fort Lee. This order was countermanded, and the brigade went instead to Perth Amboy, where Stephen replaced General Mercer. John Sellers, *The Virginia Continental Line, 1775-1780* (Ph.D. diss., Tulane University, 1968), 181-182. On Hand's men, see Clement Biddle to the President of Congress, Nov. 17, 1776, Force, ed., *American Archives*, Fifth Series, III: 740.

[2]Historian Christopher Ward commented that "with inexplicable infatuation," Greene "made the grand mistake of his whole military career" in holding Fort Washington. *The Delaware Continentals*, 93.

[3]On November 7, Washington wrote Greene with the news that he was going to send part of his army to New Jersey. Washington was also thinking where to place military depots. He wrote Greene: "They can have no capital Object in view, unless it is Philadelphia...I am of Opinion, that if your Magazines at Princeton were increased and those in the vicinity of New York lessened, it would be better. We find great risque and inconvenience arising from having Stores near Navigation, perhaps a Magazine at Brunswick might not be amiss." George Washington to Nathanael Greene, White Plains, November 7, 1776. Fitzpatrick, ed., *Writings of Washington*, VI: 253-254. For Greene's plan for magazines in New Jersey, see Showman, ed., *Greene Papers*, 1: 327.

equipment at Fort Lee, still larger quantities had been removed to the interior of New Jersey before the attack. Ammunition, in particular, had been moved to safety. During their subsequent retreat through New Jersey, the rebels never faced critical shortages of ammunition or food. This can only be attributed to the genius of Greene in organizing depots and the good sense of Washington in looking beyond Greene's bad judgment at Fort Washington to recognize his great talent for organization.[1]

On November 21, the intentions of General Lee were paramount among Washington's concerns. Washington wrote to Lee describing the events of the day before, and again emphasized the need for Lee to bring his command across the Hudson River and into New Jersey. The letter was diplomatic: like many other colonials, Washington remained impressed by the former British colonel. "It must be painful to you as well as to us to have no news to send you," he wrote, "but of a melancholy nature." Washington related the British landing and advance, and the retreat of the Fort Lee garrison. "We have no Account of their movements this Morning," he continued somberly, but noted that the situation was grim. He had "not above 3,000 Men" with him, and material losses and shock had left them "broken and dispirited." Under the circumstances, an offensive was impossible. "I have resolved to avoid any Attack," he wrote, "tho' by so doing I must leave a very fine country open to their Ravages." New Jersey was crucial to patriot fortunes. It was a source of food and supplies, he observed, and thus he wanted Lee's corps in the state. But Washington's respect for Lee inhibited him from sending a direct or preemptory order. Instead, he was circumspect. "Upon the whole therefore, I am of Opinion, and the Gentlemen about me concur in it, that the publick Interest requires your coming over to this side, with the Continental Troops." The Commander-in-Chief explained that "My reasons for this measure and which I think must have weight with you, are, that the Enemy are evidently changing the Seat of the War to this side of the North River" and "It is therefore of the utmost Importance, that at least an

---

[1]Most accounts of the 1776 retreat did not mention food shortages, although the narrative of Sergeant Joseph White, of Colonel Henry Knox's artillery regiment, was an exception. "The privations and sufferings we endured," he wrote years later, "is beyond description--no tent to cover us at night--exposed to cold and rains day and night -- no food of any kind but a little raw flour." Other contemporary sources corroborated the lack of tents and the bad weather—hardly insignificant problems—but White's account stands alone regarding the lack of food. Perhaps this old and revered veteran exaggerated his sufferings to impress his young readers. Joseph White, *A Narrative of Events...* (Charlestown, MA, 1833). Reprinted in *American Heritage*, No. 4, June 1956.

Appearance of Force should be made, to keep this Province in the Connection with the others."[1]

The deference in Washington's letter was puzzling. The general may have felt humiliated by his repeated errors in judgment during 1776, including his mistake in trying to defend New York City and failing to abandon Fort Washington while there was still time. He apparently felt obligated to convince his second-in-command of the necessity for the action he advocated.

When Washington finished his letter to Lee, he called for an express rider to carry it to Lee's camp at North Castle. However, while Washington's back was turned, another letter to Lee was quietly slipped into the horseman's dispatch case. The second letter carried to General Lee was from the cultured and successful Philadelphia lawyer, Joseph Reed (1741-1785), who was the most important member of Washington's military circle at the time and the commander-in-chief's closest counselor.

Reed would play an interesting role in unfolding events. Washington delighted in having bright, educated, politically-connected men in his military family. They served as aides and secretaries, often composing or redrafting his correspondence, orders and other official documents. Washington had grown up in moderate wealth, but had little formal education. He spoke no foreign language and had never traveled to Europe. What he knew, he had learned from books and his association with educated people. He liked the company of rich, young men of education and social grace. Of all who served close to him throughout the Revolution, Washington most admired Reed. Reed was the son of a wealthy Trenton merchant. He had obtained a good education in London and returned to the colonies to pursue a successful career as a lawyer and businessman in Philadelphia. Reed was everything that Washington dreamed of being in his youth: intellectual, sophisticated, charming and rich. By the outbreak of the Revolution, Reed already had joined the rebel cause and served on several important committees.

Although he had no training or experience as a soldier, Reed agreed to join Washington's staff as an aide with the rank of lieutenant colonel. He proved temperamental, but was prized by Washington as a first-rate expediter and troubleshooter. As an attorney, Reed knew about law and public affairs. He was also a brilliant writer. By late 1776, Reed was the army's adjutant general (that is, its administrative head) and Washington's trusted friend.

Soon after joining the army, Reed came to despise the amateur

---

[2]Fitzpatrick, ed., *Writings of Washington*, VI: 297-300.

officers who then were Washington's favorites. He was particularly put off with Greene, the son of a Rhode Island blacksmith, and Henry Knox, the fat Boston bookseller and self-taught artillerist.   Reed blamed them for influencing Washington to defend New York City instead of burning it, and for holding Fort Washington when it should have been abandoned. Besides the actual loss of Fort Washington, Reed was angry because the fort was defended by many fellow Pennsylvanians, including some close friends, who now were dead or captive in New York. Reed was drawn to the cosmopolitan and intellectual Lee, whom he saw as a savior of the American cause.

Reed had his enemies. The influential Joseph Trumbull, who was commissary general of the Continental Army and the son of the Governor of Connecticut, had this to say about him: "he has done more to raise and keep up a jealousy between the New-England and other troops than all the men in the Army beside. Indeed, his stinking pride, as General George Clinton expresses it, has gone so far that I expect every day to hear he is called to account by some officer or other; indeed, he is universally hated and dispised; and it is high time he was displaced."[1]

It was Reed who quietly dropped a second letter into the pouch of the dispatch rider sent off to Lee. Reed knew the contents of Washington's letter, since the Commander-in-Chief had dictated it to him.[2] In his own letter, Reed concurred with Washington's appraisal of the situation, but added that "I have some additional reasons for wishing most earnestly to have you where the principal scene of action is laid. I do not mean to flatter or praise you at the expense of any other," he told Lee, "but I confess I do think it is entirely owing to you that this army, and the liberties of America, so far as they are dependent on it, are not totally cut off. You have decision, a quality often wanted in minds otherwise valuable," and he credited Lee with the survival of the army through the actions around New York and White Plains. He also thought that Lee might have prevented the disaster at Fort Washington. Officers and men looked to him with confidence, Reed insisted, and even the enemy worried about him and seemed "to be less confident when you are present."[3]

---

[1]Joseph Trumbull to William Williams, North Castle, New York, Nov. 18, 1776. Force, ed., *American Archives*, Fifth Ser., III: 1497-1498.

[2]The draft of Washington's letter to Lee was in Joseph Reed's handwriting.

[3]Reed to Lee, Nov. 21, 1776,   William B. Reed, *Life and Correspondence of Joseph Reed* (Philadelphia: Lindsay and Blakiston, 1847), I: 255-257.

Reed's flattering dispatch went on to blame Greene for influencing the Commander-in-Chief to hold Fort Washington. Thus Washington vacillated until, as Reed put it, "the blow was struck" and the fort was lost. "Oh! General," wrote Reed, "an indecisive mind is one of the greatest misfortunes that can befall an army; how often have I lamented it this campaign. All circumstances considered, we are in a very awful and alarming situation, one that requires the utmost wisdom and firmness of mind." As soon as events allowed, he wanted Lee and others of like mind to visit Congress and present a plan for the reform of the army. Reed concluded with a final assertion of Lee's importance to the cause.[1] It was an extraordinary letter, calculated to flatter the colossal ego of a general already the rallying point for critics of the Commander-in-Chief.

Reed's imprudent communication was not the limit of his mischief. According to Heath's memoirs, Reed also had sent Lee an earlier message, written on November 20. Heath recalled sending a cavalryman to Washington in Hackensack, who arrived at Washington's headquarters and learned that the British had landed in New Jersey and that the Fort Lee garrison was rapidly retreating towards Hackensack. "The Adjutant-General [Reed] wished to write to Gen. Lee," Heath recalled; "but he had neither pen, ink, nor paper with him." The messenger had "a rough piece of wrapping-paper in his pocket" and Reed had a pencil; but after writing to Lee that "we are flying before the British. I pray," the pencil broke. Reed "then told the light-horseman to carry the paper to Gen. Lee, and tell him that he was verbally ordered to add, after I pray, you to push and join us."[2] The rider returned to Heath, relating everything he had seen, and, although fatigued and wet, insisted on pushing on to Lee's headquarters to deliver Reed's message.

The village of Hackensack lay in level, open country between the Hackensack and Passaic Rivers. On the morning of November 21, the New Bridge across the Hackensack River was intact and defended by American skirmishers who had barricaded themselves into several buildings. The eastern approach to the bridge was well suited for defense; it was at the end of a long, narrow spit of land jutting out from the shoreline and surrounded by swamps. Hard by the bridge stood the sturdy, stone Hoogland Tavern, built in 1767. There were a few other buildings nearby, but the tavern was the best position from which to defend the bridge.

---

[1] Reed to Lee, Nov. 21, 1776, Reed, *Joseph Reed*, I: 255-257.

[2] Heath, *Memoirs of the American War*, 88.

On the morning of November 21, British light infantry, grenadiers, and a company of jaegers approached the New Bridge from the east under the command of Major General John Vaughan.[1] As Vaughan's force advanced, the rebel defenders set fire to their stores and some of the houses. "The Americans had occupied the houses on both sides of the bridge and defended themselves very well," Ewald noted, but "the post was forced and the greater part were killed, wounded or captured."[2] The British captured the bridge intact, although Cornwallis did not push on to Hackensack until the following morning. By the afternoon of November 22, one resident reported, "the church green was covered with Hessians, a horrid, frightful sight with their whiskers, brass caps and kettles or brass drums."[3] With Hackensack secured, New Jersey Loyalists emerged from their silent watching to congratulate Lord Cornwallis and offer their services. Probably no one was happier than Dr. Abraham Van Buskirk, whose elegant home stood near New Bridge. Van Buskirk, a surgeon, had been secretly raising a Loyalist regiment in anticipation of a British invasion. Now he openly enlisted men for his regiment, which was designated the 4th Battalion, New Jersey Volunteers.[4]

By the time the British reached Hackensack, Washington was gone. The general knew his position at Hackensack was untenable, and that he needed to retreat in order to consolidate his forces, rally the New Jersey militia, and await the arrival of Lee with the best part of the army. The Commander-in-Chief abandoned Hackensack on November 21, having already decided to

---

[1] Howe to Germain, Nov. 21, 1776, *Bergen County History*, 49.

[2] Stirke, *Bergen County History*, 54; Ewald, *Diary of the American War*, 18-19.

[3] Leiby, *The Revolutionary War in the Hackensack Valley*, 77.

[4] On July 1, 1776, Howe authorized the former Attorney General of the Province of New Jersey, Cortlandt Skinner (1728-1799) to raise a provincial regiment to be called the New Jersey Volunteers. On paper, the Volunteers had five battalions, each of 500 men. A sixth battalion was later authorized. Abraham Van Buskirk was secretly commissioned by Skinner as a colonel and commander of the 4th Battalion. Van Buskirk in turn, clandestinely recruited men for his regiment while Bergen County was still under control of the rebel army. William Bayard was another Loyalist suspected of recruiting for the Volunteers prior to the British invasion of New Jersey. Bayard operated the ferry that ran between New York City and Hoboken. The Volunteers, like other provincial regiments, were armed, paid, fed and clothed by the British government. Provincial troops were subject to the same discipline as regular British army troops and were obligated to serve anywhere they were ordered. Troops of the New Jersey Volunteers probably accompanied the Crown forces as they advanced through New Jersey in pursuit of Washington.

head for the town of New Brunswick on the western bank of the Raritan River. Washington retreated from Hackensack and marched his army west to the Passaic River and the little port village of Acquackanonk Landing (modern Passaic), on the river's west bank. The village had numerous wharves and landings to load shipments of local produce and lumber, which were sent down the Passaic to Newark, Perth Amboy, or New York City.[1]

Only one bridge crossed the Passaic, a frail wooden structure close to the village. Washington ordered it destroyed as soon as his army was safely across. He occupied the Blanchard House during his tense overnight stay in Acquackanonk.[2] Probably from there, Washington wrote Governor Livingston to call out the New Jersey militia. He believed its members surely would respond, now that their state had been invaded.

As Washington scurried out of Hackensack, General Howe journeyed from New York City to inspect Fort Lee and congratulate Cornwallis. Howe's invasion had limited objectives; he wanted Fort Lee in order to secure the Hudson River, and then to use this foothold as a "ready road to penetrate into Jersey." The British commander was heartened by reports that the road between Fort Lee and Hackensack was littered with rebel muskets and equipment; and British light infantry also found twelve pieces of abandoned American artillery.[3] The operation had done well.

The quick success of Cornwallis and the news that Washington's army was in tatters led Howe to authorize a deeper drive into New Jersey. However, the British commander was still thinking in limited terms: quarters and food for his army during the coming winter and using New Jersey as a base for an offensive against Philadelphia in the spring. It was more militant officers who talked about conquering New Jersey and pushing all the way to Philadelphia by the end of the year. And Cornwallis was just the tough

---

[1]Washington to William Livingston, Nov. 21, 1776, Fitzpatrick. ed., *Writings of Washington*, VI: 302. Washington wrote that he would link up with troops under Lord Stirling near New Brunswick. On Passaic, see Wheaton Lane, *From Indian Trail to Iron Horse*, (Princeton: Princeton University Press, 1939), 63.

[2]Albert H. Heusser, *In the Footsteps of Washington* (Paterson, NJ: privately printed, 1921), 260.

[3]General Sir William Howe to Lord George Germain, Nov. 30, 1776, Force, ed., *American Archives*, Fifth Ser., III: 925; "Return of Ordnance and Stores taken by his Majesty's Troops in the Redoubts and Lines of the Enemy, from their landing at Frog-Neck...to the 20th of November, 1776," *ibid.*, 1058.

combat officer to lead them. As one British officer wrote, Cornwallis's "face seems to be set towards Philadelphia."[1] As Cornwallis prepared to resume his attack, Howe quickly reinforced him with troops from New York, including the 16th Dragoons under the command of Colonel William Harcourt.[2] But the weather suddenly turned cold and rainy, and by the time Cornwallis got his army into motion Washington had fled Hackensack and crossed the Passaic River. Advanced elements of Cornwallis' army arrived at the Passaic to find the bridge destroyed and the rebels encamped on the far shore.

---

[1]Rawdon to Robert Auchmuty, Nov. 25, 1776, in Commager and Morris, ed., *The Spirit of 76*, 497.

[2]On November 21, Ensign Henry Stirke wrote in his diary that "This day a body of Light Dragoons landed and joined us." Light dragoons were elite troops who rode and fought on horseback. They were used for scouting and raids deep into enemy territory. The term "heavy horse" or simply "dragoons" specified men who used horses to get to a battle but fought on foot. Heavy horse and dragoons were more heavily armed and rode bigger horses than the light dragoons. Two British regiments of light dragoons participated in the American Revolution, the 16th and 17th. They were the only British cavalry to serve in the war. The Americans developed an equivalent to the light dragoons later in the Revolution, which they called "light horse."

CHAPTER FIVE

Newark

*It is difficult to determine how Washington's army could have been
saved, if General Howe had not limited Cornwallis by exact orders.*
—Historian Henry Carrington, 1877[1]

At dawn on Friday, November 22, Washington and his battered little
army pulled out of Acquackanonk and marched south along the narrow farm
road on the west bank of the winding Passaic River. The weather turned cold
and it started to rain, turning the roads to mud as the rebels retreated south.[2]
In late afternoon, the exhausted and sodden vanguard of the Grand Army
arrived in Newark. The rest of the army, under Washington, halted in the
village of Belleville that night and entered Newark in the morning. Many were

---

[1]Henry Carrington, *Battles of the American Revolution* (New York: A.S. Barnes
& Company, 1877), 258.

[2]Weather conditions in the New York area were noted in the *Journals of Lieut.-Col.
Stephen Kemble* (New York: New York Historical Society, 1883) I: 101; *Diary of Frederick
Mackenzie* (Cambridge: Harvard University Press, 1930) I: 114; and Edward Tatum Jr., ed.,
The American Journal of Ambrose Serle (San Marino, California: The Huntington Library,
1940), 145. The muddy roads were reported in the "Diary of Andrew Hunter," Nov. 21, 1776,
Firestone Library, Special Collections, Princeton University, Princeton, New Jersey.

sick; some were sent to Morristown and others were cared for in the town's churches, which were turned into makeshift hospitals. All of Lord Stirling's troops at New Brunswick began the march towards Newark to reinforce Washington's meager corps.[1]

Marching with Washington's army was the middle-aged Thomas Paine, who accompanied the column as a civilian. He had become famous as the author of the pamphlet *Common Sense*, even though it had been published anonymously in January 1776. Paine accepted a political appointment as General Greene's secretary and was with Greene at Fort Lee when the British attacked. Paine witnessed everything that had happened since the evacuation of Fort Lee and began to write about it when he got to Newark with the retreating American army. Legend says that Paine used the head of a drum as a desk when he began writing his justly famous *The American Crisis--Number One.* Paine's essay vividly captured the moment: the times were indeed such as to "try men's souls."[2]

---

[1]Sergeant Thomas McCarty was with Stirling's (Alexander's) brigade. His journal entry for Sunday, November 23, 1776 included orders "to march back to stop the enemy, as they were expected to be now marching towards Elizabethtown." He identified the regiments with him on the march as "the Delaware Battalion [Colonel Haslet's First Delaware Regiment] in front, the 3rd Virginia in the center, and the 1st Virginia Regiment in the rear." The riflemen followed the baggage. McCarty did not advance beyond Elizabethtown; nor did he say that any of Stirling's other regiments went further than Elizabethtown. From this account, it appears that Stirling had orders to bring up his brigade from the New Brunswick area to reinforce the Grand Army at Newark. However, he stopped at Elizabethtown, probably ordered to wait because Washington was planning to retreat to New Brunswick and would pick up Stirling's troops en route. Jared C. Lobdell, ed., "The Revolutionary War Journal of Sergeant Thomas McCarty," *Proceedings of the New Jersey Historical Society*, 82 (1964); guide to the Draper Manuscripts, Wisconsin Historical Society, Madison, Wisconsin. The start of the march on November 23 is noted in the "Diary of Lieutenant James McMichael," *Pennsylvania Magazine of History and Biography*, 16 (1892).

[2]Paine immigrated from England in 1774. He was one of the group of wandering misfits and idealists attracted to the unrest in America. (Charles Lee belonged to this same group.) In July 1776, following the publication of *Common Sense*, Paine marched to Perth Amboy with the newly formed Pennsylvania Flying Camp commanded by General Roberdeau. There was no provision for a secretary to Roberdeau, and Paine served as a volunteer, asking only that his expenses be paid. From Perth Amboy, Paine went to Fort Lee, and about September 19, General Greene appointed him an aide-de-camp. Historian Richard Ketchum believes that Paine wrote much of the first *Crisis* in Newark, added to it over the next few days, and then hastened to Philadelphia where the essay came out on Dec. 19, 1776 in the *Pennsylvania Journal*. Richard Ketchum, *The Winter Soldiers* (Garden City: Doubleday &

Without knowing it, a British officer fully corroborated Paine's observations of the American situation. Writing of the American army, he recorded his belief that "no nation ever saw such a set of tatterdemalions. There were but few coats among them but what are out...are mostly gone."[1] Samuel Blatchley Webb (1753-1807), an aide-de-camp and secretary to Washington, wrote from Newark on November 24 that "Fatal necessity has obliged us to give up to the Enemy much of a fine country, well Wooded, Watered & Stock'd; not only that, but our Cannon, Mortars, Ordinance Stores &c are mostly gone."[2]

The first rumors of the capture of Fort Lee reached members of the Continental Congress in Philadelphia on November 22. Confirmation of the disaster came a day later, when Washington's letter to President John Hancock, dated November 21, was read aloud to the delegates. Alarmed by this latest setback, Congress appointed a delegation of three members (John Witherspoon, William Paca, and George Ross) to immediately travel to New Jersey to consult with Washington. John Hancock informed the general of the

---

Co., 1973), 211.

[1] This quote is attributed to an "English Officer" (perhaps Major John Andre) and appears in T.N. Glover, *The Retreat of '76 Across Bergen County* [abstract of a paper read on Nov. 20, 1905] (Hackensack: Bergen County Historical Society, 1905), 22.

[2] Samuel Blatchley Webb, *Correspondence and Journals of Samuel Blachley Webb* (New York: Wickersham Press, 1893), I: 172. This quote is from a letter Webb wrote to his friend Joseph Trumbull (Commissary General of the Continental Army). Webb was a wealthy and educated young man serving in Washington's military family. While Webb's fiery comments seem too spirited for the circumstances, he made some valid points. Washington's weakened army was still a dangerous fighting force. To give "a true Account of our Situation," Webb wrote, was "next to Impossible." No troops, he assured Trumbull , were more active on a retreat; "Our Soldiers are the best fellows in the World at this Business." The entire army had numbered under two thousand men when the British struck, he noted, and a stand was impossible. But at Newark, the rebel army had regrouped; they were ready to fight, and the British knew it. It was "a sacred truth they never yet have ventured to Attack Us but with great Advantages; they pursue no faster than their heavy Artillery can be brought up. With this they Scour every piece of Wood, Stone Walls, &c, before they approach. If they come on soon we shall I trust give a good acct to our Country." They had to, as many rebel enlistments were up on Dec. 1, and Webb feared that much of the army would go home.

delegation in a November 24 letter, which also authorized Washington to order troops from the Northern Department to come to his aid.[1]

Washington wrote Congress soon after his arrival in Newark. "The situation of our Affairs is truly critical," he admitted, "and such as requires uncommon exertions on our part. From the movements of the Enemy and the information we have received, they certainly will make a push to possess themselves of this part of the Jerseys." Desperate for help, Washington wrote in the same letter that he was sending the influential General Mifflin back to his home city of Philadelphia to report to the Congress, "In order that you may be fully apprized of our Weakness and of the necessity there is of our obtaining early Succours."[2]

Looking everywhere for help, Washington dispatched the urbane Reed on a similar mission to Burlington to confer with Governor Livingston and the New Jersey legislature.[3] Of course, Washington had no idea that Reed had written Lee from Hackensack a few days earlier.

There is a sketch in David Ramsay's 1793 *The History of the American Revolution* in which Washington confers at Newark with his confidant, Reed. According to Ramsay, Washington asked Reed, "Should we retreat to the back parts of Pennsylvania, will the Pennsylvanians support us?" Reed replied, "[I]f the lower counties are subdued and give up, the back counties will do the same." The general said, "[W]e must retire to Augusta county, in Virginia. Numbers will be obliged to repair to us for safety, and we

---

[1]Smith, ed., *Letters of Delegates to Congress*, V: 528, 534. A few days following the staggering manpower losses at Fort Washington, the general was already looking towards the Northern Army as a source for badly needed reinforcements. On November 20, 1776, just four days after the fall of Fort Washington (and the same day the British attacked Fort Lee), he wrote to General Schuyler, commanding the Northern Army, asking Schuyler to send his Pennsylvania and New Jersey regiments. The enlistments of these regiments were expiring but Washngton hoped that they would continue to serve or reenlist. Robert Harrison to William Schuyler, Nov. 20, 1776, Force, ed., *American Archives*, Fifth Ser., III: 780-781.

[2]Fitzpatrick, ed., *The Writings of George Washington*, VI: 303.

[3]Reed's mission was to assist Livingston to raise four New Jersey regiments that would serve until April 1, 1777. Freeman, *George Washington*, IV: 267. The dispatch of these two competent officers is summed up in a postscript from Webb to Trumbull: "Mifflin gone for Philadelphia. Reed to Brunswick, Burlington &c." Webb, *Journals*, I: 173.

must try what we can do in carrying on a predatory war, and if overpowered, we must cross the Allegany mountains."[1]

In 1776, Newark was a farming center of three thousand people on the west bank of the Passaic River. An English traveler, passing through Newark in September, 1776, called it "Nothing more than a Village." It had about one hundred forty dwellings scattered irregularly over some two miles.[2] All accounts agree that the land around Newark was very fertile and the farms prosperous. Some inhabitants were fishermen, and the brackish Passaic River was known for its excellent clam and mussel beds.

Washington probably occupied the Eagle Tavern in Newark as his headquarters near the modern intersection of Broad and William Streets.[3] The village was too small to shelter much of the army, and the majority of the soldiers camped in open farmland behind the village.[4] Today this area is called High Street Ridge. The soldiers were in wretched condition; having lost all their tents in the flight from Fort Lee, they had to sleep on the ground and improvise protection from the wet and cold. Blankets were scarce and the

---

[1]David Ramsay, *The History of the American Revolution* (Philadephia, 1793), I: 291. This same story appears in Washington Irving's biography of Washington. In the Irving version, George Washington is conferring with General Hugh Mercer in early December 1776. ."What think you," said Irving's Washington, "if we should retreat to the back parts of Pennsylvania, would the Pennsylvanians support us?" "If the lower counties give up, the back counties will do the same," was the discouraging reply. "We must then retire to Augusta County in Virginia," said Washington. "Numbers will repair to us for safety, and we will try a predatory war. If overpowered, we must cross the Alleganies." Irving, *Life of Washington*, II: 448. There is a third variation of the story, which appears in William Gordon's *History of the Independence of the United States*, II, 141, in which Washington has his exchange with adjutant Reed and then passes his hand over his throat, and remarks, "My neck does not feel as though it was made for a halter. We must retire to Augusta county in Virginia."

[2]*The Journal of Nicholas Cressell* (New York: Dial Press, 1924), 157; Burnaby, *Travels Through America*, 105.

[3]In 1921, Albert H. Heusser privately published a Washington travelogue, *In the Footsteps of Washington* (Paterson: NJ). "Some historians maintain that Washington ate and slept at the ancient Eagle Tavern," he wrote, "while others insisted on alternate sites; but the evidence was too vague to substantiate any claim. Heusser identified present-day Military Park, in the center of modern Newark, as the site of the army's encampment. See pages 262-263.

[4]Frank J. UrQuhart, *History of The City of Newark* (Newark: Lewis Historical Publishing Co., 1913).

ground was freezing. It was as if a legion of beggars had descended on a gentle village of small farmers. The civilians in Newark were scared. According to diarist Andrew Hunter, they were "engaged in carrying off their goods to places of security."[1]

Washington knew that the narrow Passaic River was a minor obstacle and would only briefly delay Cornwallis. The rebels needed to retire to a defensive position where they could recover and recruit a new army. The village of Morristown was an ideal place for that purpose, and it was only a short journey west from Newark. Morristown sat on a fertile plateau surrounded by the rugged Newark Mountains (today called the Watchung Mountains). Few roads ran into Morristown, and each was easily defended, especially in the winter, when deep snow made the area difficult to penetrate. In addition, the local farmers were friendly to the rebellion. Washington was aware of the advantages of Morristown because the village had become the rallying point for the New Jersey militia. During a council of war held at Newark, several of his officers urged a move to Morristown.[2] But Washington was convinced the enemy's objective was the rebel capital of Philadelphia, and he felt duty-bound to keep his army, no matter how frail, between it and the Crown's forces. Under this strategy, Washington had no option but to march his army southwest from Newark, to the town of New Brunswick on the Raritan River.

New Brunswick lay in the middle of New Jersey and along the best road between New York and Philadelphia. At New Brunswick, the Americans would have the advantage of having the Raritan between them and the enemy. In addition, Washington had a supply depot at New Brunswick and hoped to find many New Jersey militiamen waiting for him there.

It is impossible to appreciate the danger of Washington's decision to retreat to New Brunswick instead of Morristown without analyzing the network of roads and navigable rivers in central New Jersey at the time of the Revolution. New York City and Philadelphia, the most important commercial

---

[1]Andrew Hunter, "Diary, 1776-1779," bound manuscript, Special Collections, Princeton University. This entry is dated Nov. 24, 1776, when Hunter was at Newark. Hunter was a Princeton graduate, Class of 1772, and a chaplain to the New Jersey troops.

[2]Washington Irving, *Life of George Washington* (New York: G.P. Putnam & Co., 1855-1859), II: 440.

centers of the colonies, were ninety miles apart and separated by New Jersey. It took at least one and a half days by fast stage to make the trip.[1] Although crude by European standards of the time, New Jersey had the best transportation system in the colonies. The early routes between New York and Philadelphia were by ferry to Staten Island and then across Staten Island to the old Blazing Star Ferry at Travis (modern Rossville) on the Arthur Kill. This ferry took freight wagons and coaches to Woodbridge, New Jersey, from which a road went to New Brunswick.[2] A variation of this route was across Staten Island to the ferry at Captain Billop's Landing to Perth Amboy, New Jersey, connected by road to New Brunswick. Still another alternate route: a boat to Bergen Point (modern Bayonne, New Jersey) and follow a decent road north along Bergen Neck to Newark. From Newark, there was a tolerable road southwest, which picked up traffic from the ferry crossings at Elizabethtown Point and Woodbridge and ran west to New Brunswick.

From New Brunswick, all traffic went through the college town of Princeton and into Trenton on the eastern bank of the Delaware River. At Trenton, an active river port, goods and passengers were transferred to boats for shipment downstream to Philadelphia. Two busy ferries at Trenton also took traffic across the river to Pennsylvania. On that side, a good road ran to Philadelphia via the town of Bristol.

---

[1]The stage wagon was a lightweight vehicle with a flat top, pulled by four or six horses, and had leather or woolen side curtains and large wheels set on crude springs. Luggage was stowed under the seats; heavier baggage was fastened on the rear. The passengers sat on four rows of seats; twelve people, including the driver, were considered a full load. In 1771, Abraham Skillman advertised that his stage would travel between New York and Philadelphia in a day and a half. More typically stage wagons made the journey in two days. John Mercereau advertised that his coach, the "Flying Machine," would run between Paulus Hook Ferry and the Indian Queen Tavern, Philadelphia, in two days' time. Passengers stayed overnight in Princeton, New Jersey, halfway between the two cities. In addition, there was the travel time by ferry between Paulus Hook, New Jersey and New York City. The advertisement for the "Flying Machine" noted that "As the Machines set off from Powles-hook early in the morning, passengers should cross the ferry the evening before." Patrick M'Robert, *A Tour Through Part of the North Provinces of America* (Edinburgh, 1776), 41. In the snow, sleighs or sledges replaced wheeled vehicles. More elaborate and costly coaches had come into use just prior to the Revolution.

[2]By the eve of the American Revolution, the New Blazing Star tavern and ferry crossing was in operation a few miles north of the original Blazing Star. The New Blazing Star ferry provided service from Staten Island to either Woodbridge or Elizabethtown Point. There was a second crossing from Staten Island to Bergen Neck, to the east of Decker's Ferry known as Ryerson's Ferry.

Another early route across New Jersey was the Old York Road. It followed a route from Elizabethtown, Scotch Plains, Bound Brook and Ringoes to a ferry across the Delaware River at Lambertville, New Jersey. The road continued on to Philadelphia. Then there was Lawrie's Road, running east-west across New Jersey from Perth Amboy to Burlington, unpopular because it passed through a "barren Country" and bypassed many of New Jersey's important commercial centers.[1] It also was possible to take an all-water route from New York harbor to the mouth of the Delaware River, then up the Delaware to Philadelphia.

Fast travel times were as big an obsession in colonial America as they are today. The New Jersey stage wagon was one way to reduce travel time between New York City and Philadelphia, but a big improvement arrived in 1764 with Cornelius Van Vorst's new ferry service from the bottom of Cortlandt Street in New York City to Paulus Hook Island, New Jersey.[2] From Paulus Hook Island, a new road and ferries brought passengers and freight across the wetlands and hills of Bergen County to Newark. There already was a good road between Newark and Philadelphia via Woodbridge, New Brunswick, Princeton and Trenton. The entire route was flat, making the trip faster. The new ferry and road connecting Paulus Hook to Newark were great successes, and caused a shift in New York City-Philadelphia traffic from the older routes. This made Newark an important commercial and travel center.

At the outbreak of the War for Independence, the New York-Newark-New Brunswick-Trenton-Philadelphia route was the most popular and busiest transportation system in America. From Elizabethtown south, it was originally named the Assanpink Trail, then the Old Dutch Road and the Upper Road by the time of the Revolution. A traveler took the busy New York-Paulus Hook ferry-Newark-Philadelphia route sometime during 1774-1775 and wrote down the distances from New York City in his journal, including: 9 miles to Newark; 15 miles to "Elizabeth-town"; 35 miles to Brunswick; 52 miles to "Prince-town"; 65 miles to Trenton; and 95 miles to Philadelphia.

---

[1]Lane, *From Indian Trail to Iron Horse*, 104.

[2]Paulus Hook was a low-lying point of sand protruding into the Hudson River, partially surrounded by a salt marsh. The Hook was two miles east of the village of Bergen. Both Paulus Hook and Bergen are now unidentifiable, and are parts of modern Jersey City.

The Revolutionary War armies used the Upper Road as they maneuvered south from Newark. The route played a central role in the campaign.[1]

Washington and his army arrived in Newark using the secondary roads that served northern New Jersey. Then, at Newark, he joined the road that bore the heavy traffic between New York and Philadelphia. The Upper Road would allow his army to move faster, but Loyalists told the British about this route and all the alternate roads across New Jersey. With this knowledge, the Crown's forces could outflank Washington's retreating army.

The general had much to ponder while his army was at Newark. His men faced the threat of the British outflanking them by landing troops at Perth Amboy and cutting off any retreat along the Upper Road to New Brunswick. The Americans would be caught on the flat, defenseless plains of central New Jersey, trapped between Cornwallis' six thousand men moving south from Hackensack and a second British force moving north from Perth Amboy. If this happened, the only direction open to Washington would be west towards Springfield and Morristown. This would save his army, but leave the Upper Road wide open to Philadelphia. Washington knew the possibility of a landing at Perth Amboy was real because spies in New York City had warned him of a British fleet of warships and transports with seven thousand troops, supposedly preparing to embark on a secret mission. This fleet could sail to Perth Amboy in a day.

Washington worried constantly about this British task force while he waited in Newark for the New Jersey militia and Lee to arrive. "The frequent advices," he informed Congress, "that the Enemy were embarking or about to embark another detachment for Staten Island, with a view of Landing at Amboy to co-operate with this, which seemed to be confirmed by the information of some persons who came from the [Staten] Island."[2] Another lethal scenario had Cornwallis maintaining pressure on Washington in New Jersey while British troops at New York sailed for the Delaware River, and

---

[1]M'Robert, *A Tour Through Part of the North Provinces of America*, 43. The Upper Road actually started at Elizabethtown Point, where there was a ferry from Staten Island. The Upper Road is today's New Jersey Highway 27 from Elizabeth to Princeton, and then New Jersey Highway 202 from Princeton to Trenton.

[2]Washington to the President of Congress, Nov. 30, 1776, Fitzpatrick, ed., *Writings of Washington*, VI: 314-315. Another warning of a landing at Perth Amboy came in a letter from Lee to Washington of Nov. 26. "Several deserters come out today," Lee wrote, "inform us that a considerable embarkation is made for Amboy." *Lee Papers*, II: 316.

then on to capture Philadelphia. This mystery fleet and its seven thousand troops were no subterfuge, and will enter into this narrative later.

The Commander-in-Chief faced other serious questions as well. Manpower problems were acute. On November 23, he reported to Congress that he had 5,410 troops with him in and near Newark. Of these, more than 2,000 had the right to leave on December 1, when their enlistments expired. An additional 1,000 men could leave on January 1.[1] In urgent need of reinforcements, Washington quickly acted on the wishes of Congress and instructed General Philip Schuyler, the commander of the Northern Department, to immediately send part of his force south to New Jersey. Schuyler's corps was in wretched shape at Fort Ticonderoga, New York, but Schuyler responded promptly and ordered eight regiments of New England troops, amounting to 1,200 men, to move south under the command of General Horatio Gates.[2] Washington gave New Brunswick as the probable meeting

---

[1]Force, ed., *American Archives*, Fifth Ser. III: 821-822.

[2]After an auspicious start in 1775, an effort to conquer British-held Canada ended disastrously in 1776. By December 1776, the Northern Army had retreated south to Fort Ticonderoga, where it reported having 5,000 men. But this was only on paper. Its actual numbers had been vastly reduced by expired enlistments, smallpox, malaria, dysentery, and desertions. A return of the forces at Fort Ticonderoga, dated November 29, 1776, noted only 1,413 men fit for duty. Force, ed., *American Archives*, Fifth Ser., III: 1589. An additional, and more detailed, return is in Charles H. Lesser, ed., *The Sinews of Independence*, (Chicago: The University of Chicago Press, 1976), 41.

Gates said that eight regiments were en route to Albany, where they would spend the winter or reinforce Washington; but Gates named only seven regiments: "Bond's, Porter's, Bedel's, Stark's, Poor's, Greaton's, and Patterson's." On Nov. 27, Schuyler ordered these regiments to Washington in New Jersey. Gates to the President of Congress, Nov. 27, 1776, Force, ed., *American Archives*, Fifth Ser., III: 874. The brigades sent as reinforcements from the Northern Department were Vose's, consisting of Greaton's 24th Continentals (Massachusetts)and Bond's 25th Continentals (Massachusetts), and Porter's Massachusetts regiment; a brigade commanded by General Gates; and brigades commanded by Reed (2nd Continental Regiment, formerly the 3rd, New Hampshire), Stark (5th Continental Regiment, formerly the 1st New Hampshire), Poor (8th Continental Regiment, formerly the 2nd New Hampshire), Paterson (15th Continentals, Massachusetts). See "State of Troops at Tyonderoga, 17 November, 1776," Force, ed., *American Archives*, Fifth Ser., III: 743-744; Lesser. ed., *The Sinews of Independence*, 38; regimental histories in Wright, *The Continental Army*, 197-199, 203, 205, 214, 219-220; and Stryker, *Battle of Trenton*, 354, which gives the lineage of Stark's, Poor's, Reed's and Paterson's regiments. Some 1,200 troops probably embarked from Albany to reinforce Washington.

Getting reinforcements from the Northern Department was a sound idea. Troops from the north quickly reached lower New York state by sailing down the Hudson River from Albany. Gates' regiments then sailed to the river town of Esopus (Kingston) New York.

place. Fort Ticonderoga was a long way from New Jersey and there was little hope that these reinforcements would arrive in time to make a difference.

Adding to Washington's problems was a Tory uprising in Monmouth County, New Jersey. Encouraged by the entry of the British army into New Jersey, pro-British factions in Monmouth were becoming more aggressive. Washington dispatched the New Jersey State Regiment, commanded by Colonel David Forman, to put down the uprising.[1]

Washington learned from scouts and parties of riflemen that Cornwallis was still near Hackensack and had not yet crossed the Passaic River. The Commander-in-Chief was desperate for reinforcements and risked stopping at Newark in hopes that the militia, called out by Livingston, would rally to him.[2] The Grand Army had to stay in one place long enough for the militia to learn where it was and march to its aid. But the militia never formed, save for a few hundred men who gathered at Morristown. However, Washington and his officers remained confident because Lee soon would be arriving with his seven thousand troops. After all, Washington's directive to Lee had been clear before he left Westchester: "If the Enemy should remove the whole, or the greatest part of their force, to the West side of Hudson's River, I have no doubt of your following, with all possible dispatch."[3]

This voyage took two days. *Diary of Chaplain David Avery*, microfilm edition of manuscript, Princeton Theological Seminary, Princeton, New Jersey.

After Schuyler dispatched reinforcements to Washington and allowed regiments whose enlistments had expired to march off, he was left with six regiments at Fort Ticonderoga, one of which was the 3rd New Jersey Regiment, commanded by Elias Dayton. Lesser, ed., *The Sinews of Independence*, 41.

[1]The New Jersey State Regiment was raised for limited service during the New York campaign and disbanded by the end of 1776. In early November 1776, the regiment reported 253 officers and enlisted men present and fit for duty. It was part of Colonel Nathaniel Heard's Flying Camp brigade. Lesser, *Sinews of Independence*, 37.

[2]On November 25, Livingston wrote General Matthias Williamson from Burlington: "By Intelligence just received of the Enemy's having made a Descent into this State who will doubtless take Encouragement from not meeting with the opposition which it is in our Power to give to ravage the Country I think it necessary that you should immediately call out the whole militia of this State & march them towards Newark as fast as they are raised taking their orders in their march from General Washington." Carl E. Prince, ed., *The Papers of William Livingston* (Trenton: The New Jersey Historical Commission), I: 188.

[3]Fitzpatrick, ed., *Writings of Washington*, VI: 266.

On November 21, Lee received the first appeal for help from Washington and got busy immediately. But instead of breaking his camp and marching to reinforce Washington in New Jersey, Lee used the news to write several letters, one of which was to James Bowdoin, the influential president of the Council of Massachusetts. In this letter, Lee suddenly created two American armies, "that on the east and that on the west side of North River," telling Bowdoin they should operate independently of each other and that the idea of reinforcing from one side to the other, on every motion of the enemy, was chimerical. Lee proceeded to play on the fears of the New Englanders by reminding them that even though the enemy had invaded New Jersey, a British attack north of New York was still possible; the enemy might "alter the present direction of their operations, and attempt to open the passage of the Highlands, or enter New England." Pressing his point, Lee told the fearful Massachusetts men that once his army was in New Jersey with Washington, there would be no chance of returning to defend New England. "We must depend on ourselves," Lee concluded.[1]

The same day Lee received Washington's "request" to cross the Hudson, he sent a letter to Major General William Heath. Heath commanded the four thousand troops Washington had left at Peekskill, New York, to guard the Hudson River. He was from Roxbury, Massachusetts, where he was active in politics and the local militia before the war. His high rank in the Continental Army was part of the price for Massachusetts' support of the Revolution. Enthusiastic and loyal, his talents were limited; commanding the small garrison at Peekskill was typical of the assignments Washington gave mediocre but politically important generals.

Yet Heath thought he knew Washington's mind in late November, and thus he was taken aback by Lee's letter. Lee told Heath that he had just received, "a recommendation, not a positive order, from the General, to move the corps under my command to the other side of the River." Lee gave excuses why he could not comply and told Heath to send two thousand men from his command across the Hudson. Lee promised he would replace Heath's detachment with troops from his own corps. Heath replied instantly (on the night of November 21), writing that he would not comply with Lee's request. He quoted his orders from Washington to stay at Peekskill with his corps and guard the Hudson River. Under the circumstances, Heath protested that it "would be very improper in me to order any of the troops from posts to which

---

[1]Lee to James Bowdoin, Nov. 21, 1776, *Lee Papers*, II: 291-292.

they are so expressly assigned, and from business which in his Excellency's view is so very important."[1]

But Heath was no literary match for Lee. Lee's response was a classic of superciliousness: "Sir, I perceive that you have formed an opinion to yourself that shou'd General Washington remove to the streights of Magellan, the instructions he left with you upon a particular occasion, have to all intents and purposes invested you with a command separate from and independent of any other superior. That General Heath and General Lee are merely two Major Generals, who perhaps ought to hold a friendly intercourse with each other, and when this humour or fancied Interests prompts, may afford mutual assistance; but that General Heath is by no means to consider himself obliged to obey any orders of the Second-in-Command--this Idea of yours, sir, may not only be prejudicial to yourself but to the Public." Lee concluded: "If any misfortune shou'd happen from this refusal, you must answer for it."[2]

Lee was distancing himself from the American defeats at Forts Washington and Lee and using them to advance his own career. However, he was still subordinate to Washington and had to respond to instructions to cross the Hudson. Luck had given Lee an independent command, the most powerful left to the rebels, and he would not throw away this opportunity by having his corps absorbed into Washington's retreating army. He apparently believed that if he could bring off some dramatic stroke, it would prove his military genius and his superiority to Washington as a commander.

But all of Lee's actions were unknown to Washington when an express rider rode into Newark on Sunday, November 24. The courier bore a letter from Lee, dated November 21 and addressed to Reed. Lee's dispatch was full of excuses, saying that he had no easy means of crossing the Hudson River and, "we cou'd not be there in time to answer any purpose--I have therefore order'd General Heath who is close to the only Ferry which can be pass'd, to detach two thousand men...a mode which I flatter myself will answer better what I conceive to be the spirit of the orders."[3]

Washington maintained his composure, but his response revealed his

---

[1]*Ibid.*, 291; Heath to Lee, Nov. 21, 1776, *ibid.*, 299.

[2]Lee to Heath, Nov. 26, 1776, *Lee Papers*, II: 313-314. Lee's response to Heath is included here to give this interesting confrontation continuity. There would be further efforts by Lee to pry troops from Heath.

[3]Lee to Reed, Nov. 21, 1776, *ibid.*, II: 301.

first signs of irritation with Lee. "You seem to have mistaken my views intirely in ordering Troops from Genl Heath to cross Hudson's River to this side," the general wrote. "The importance of the posts and passes thro' the High Lands, is so infinitely great, that I never thought there should be the least possible risk of loosing 'em." The Commander-in-Chief then came to the point. It is "your division I want to have over," he reminded Lee. Satisfied that his letter would eliminate any confusion and quickly bring Lee to New Jersey, Washington sent him a second dispatch later that day, warning that he had intelligence that the British were trying to intercept his march.[1]

But Lee's game continued. On the night of November 26, another dispatch arrived from Lee, who had not budged from North Castle. Washington fired back a reply the following morning, now clearly losing his patience and desperate for Lee's reinforcements. "My former Letters were so full and explicit, as to the necessity of your marching as early as possible, that it is unnecessary to add more on that Head. I confess I expected you would have been sooner in motion," he wrote.[2]

Dispatches continued to fly. Another note from General Lee arrived in Newark, this one dated November 26. He complained that Heath should have obeyed him and sent two thousand men across the Hudson, adding that he could not move his own units because of enemy activity in Westchester and the need to provide security for the area. Lee added that judging by the British activity in Westchester, "we conceived the numbers transported to the Jerseys not near so great as you were taught to think." Continuing his excuses, Lee said he had no shoes or blankets for his men, and was waiting for militia to arrive to take over the defense of Westchester County before he could cross the Hudson. He closed by saying that he would "take care to obey yr Excellency's orders in regard to my march as exactly as possible."[3]

---

[1]Fitzpatrick, ed., *Writings of Washington*, VI: 306. Douglas Southall Freeman feels that Washington thought Lee "merely had misunderstood or had misinterpreted orders"; *George Washington*, IV: 264-265.

[2]The letter arriving on November 26 was written by Lee the day before. Its contents have been lost; but we can surmise from Washington's reply that Lee said his men were unable to march. Washington's reply is in Twohig, ed., *The Papers of George Washington*, VII: 224. The editors of Washington's papers believe he may have been responding to Lee's letter of November 24, which he inadvertently referred to as having been dated November 25.

[3]*Lee Papers*, II: 315.

Washington remained in jeopardy, but if he had known what the British commanders were thinking and doing after their Fort Lee victory, he might not have been so worried. By failing to pursue the rebels quickly after capturing Fort Lee, the enemy lost a potentially decisive opportunity. The British, however, never seemed to have grasped this fact.

On November 21, the 16th Light Dragoons arrived in New Jersey to join Cornwallis, giving him the added advantage of cavalry. The next day, the dragoons and some light infantry "scoured the country as far as the Passaic River, and," as Howe reported, "found the enemy had abandoned all the intermediate country"[1] Only a few miles separated the two armies, but there was no movement from Cornwallis's corps; it remained incomprehensibly quiet in camps along the banks of the Hackensack River. American scouts and riflemen were operating in the no-man's-land between the armies. But they could have done little to stop Cornwallis if he made a lunge at Washington's battered troops.[2] The British never hinted at making any such movement.

In fact, Cornwallis was in no hurry. It rained heavily on the night of November 23, but the 24th and 25th were, "soft, warm days".[3] Lord Cornwallis did not take advantage of this fine weather to pursue the rebels further. His failure to quickly follow up on his victory at Fort Lee seems a mystery, especially with Cornwallis' aggressive reputation. But the British general's leisurely pursuit of Washington makes sense in light of a meeting he had with Howe at Fort Lee on November 22. Howe visited the fort two days after the British captured it.[4] Cornwallis and Howe surely discussed the military situation. The seizure of Fort Lee had been the purpose of the British assault on New Jersey. But success had emboldened Cornwallis. He asked his commander to let him advance further into New Jersey to try to catch

---

[1]*Diary of Lieutenant Stirke*, Nov. 21, 1776. Stirke, an officer in the light infantry company of the 10th Regiment of Foot, witnessed the arrival of the dragoons. Force, ed., *American Archives*, Fifth Ser., III: 925.

[2]Ewald, *Diary of the American War*, 20-21.

[3]*Diary of Frederick Mackenzie*, I: 114-115.

[4]*Kemble's Journal*, 101. Kemble's entry for November 22 noted that "the General went to Jersey; return'd about 11 at Night." Captain von Muenchhausen, an aide to Howe, corroborates Howe's presence at Fort Lee on November 22. "I had just arrived at the headquarters in New York," he wrote, "when my General departed for the Hudson River by a big detour, and from there crossed to Jersey with two of his aides." Muenchhausen, *Diary*, 5.

Washington's crippled army. Further operations seemed promising, he suggested, and cited Tory reports that the American forces were weak and demoralized. A vigorous push might finish the patriots.

Confronted with changing and apparently favorable circumstances, Howe assented. Still, he imposed limits on any new advance. He gave Cornwallis orders to move only as far as New Brunswick, which would give the British control of much of "east Jersey" and ample fertile country in which to find foodstuffs and towns for winter quarters. Then Howe said Cornwallis should have reinforcements before he advanced. It was the time lost in waiting for reinforcements that accounts for the delay in pursuing Washington's army.

The reinforcements arrived quickly as troops moved steadily across the Hudson. The English Brigade arrived at Fort Lee on November 25, followed the same day by the 2nd and 4th British brigades. By December 1, Cornwallis probably had a force of around ten thousand men in New Jersey. In anticipation of an advance, he had been sending out scouting parties and patrols; but with his new units ready, Cornwallis felt he could advance in strength. On November 26, he finally moved his reinforced corps out of Hackensack to capture rebel-held Acquackanonck on the Passaic.[1]

Unfortunately for the British, the dry weather of the past two days turned to rain. In poor conditions, Cornwallis moved cautiously, sending his right column across the Passaic about 4:00 a.m.; covering the move, British artillery fired into the opposite woods to "prevent ye lurking Scoundrels, from annoying us in Crossing."[2]   The left column, under Brigadier General Mathews, included the Brigade of Guards, the Hessian grenadiers and thirty jaegers. It was a strong force. These troops began their march an hour behind Cornwallis, moving along the main road to the decrepit bridge that crossed the Passaic. Once there, Ensign Glyn reported, they "found the Bridge demolished" and the rebels in sight "on the Heights above the Town."[3] But the

---

[1]Samuel Steele Smith, *The Battle of Trenton* (Monmouth Beach, N.J.: Philip Freneau Press, 1965), 5-6; Letter FZ, Lidgerwood Collection, Morristown National Historical Park, "Short Description of the Journey of the Hon. Hessian Troops from Bremerlehe to America under the Command of His Excellency Lieutenant-General Von Heister," Nov. 25, 1776; "Journal of Lieutenant General von Heister's Corps, January 1776 to June 1777," Lidgerwood Collection.

[2]*Diary of Lieutenant Stirke*, Nov. 26, 1776; "Glyn Diary," Nov. 26, 1776; *Mackenzie's Diary*, I: 115.

[3]"Glyn Diary," Nov. 26, 1776.

Americans retreated from Acquackanonk when Cornwallis's column suddenly appeared. Cornwallis had waded the Passaic a mile and a half upstream to surprise the patriots, and the maneuver had worked.

Having secured the village, the British seized a sloop to bring Mathews's corps over. This occurred without American opposition. That night, the successful but tired British camped at Acquackanonk, only nine miles from Newark.[1] Their day had gone very well indeed.

The following morning, November 27, the advance continued. Leading the way, the 16th Light Dragoons, and the 1st and 2nd Battalions of Light Infantry, reached to the village of Second River (modern Belleville) on the road to Newark. The rest of Cornwallis' men waited at Acquackanonk in what Baurmeister called a "day of rest." They had earned it. Other units, however, remained active. The 4th Brigade under General Grant moved up to join Cornwallis. The following day, three additional regiments of Hessians arrived from New York under the command of an arrogant officer with 35 years of soldiering, Colonel Johann Gottlieb Rall.[2]

On November 28, Cornwallis broke camp at Acquackanonk and advanced in two columns against Washington at Newark. The right column, commanded by von Donop, included the Hessian grenadiers, two British regiments, the two companies of jaegers, and two six-pound field pieces. This column advanced on the town from the west and "marched into quarters at a village to the right of Newark." Cornwallis commanded the left flank, and his column was solely British troops with the army's baggage. Cornwallis remained in close contact with his superiors in New York as he advanced.[3]

The British moved through prosperous farms, and looting became a serious problem among the troops. The general was unable to restrain them, wrote Kemble, and their plundering "carried to a most unjustifiable length."

---

[1]Baurmeister, *War in America*, 73; the entry for November 26 noted that "General Cornwallis forded the Passaic with his entire corps and remained during the night without tents near the village of Acquackanonk."

[2]"Glyn Diary," Nov. 27, 1776.

[3]Letter FZ, Lidgerwood Collection, Morristown Historical Park, "Short Description of the Journey of the Hon. Hessian Troops from Bremerlehe to America under the Command of His Excellency Lieutenant-General Von Heister," 40. The "Glyn Diary," Nov. 28, 1776, indicates that "the parish" was Mountain Meeting House, now Orange, New Jersey. Baurmeister, *War in America*," 73, called the area the "Newark Mountains." on page 73. Muenchhausen, *Diary*, 5; his entry for Nov. 28 recorded the arrival of two couriers from Cornwallis at New York headquarters.

Ewald wrote that the residents had fled, and their houses were robbed and destroyed by the troops.[1] Historian Leonard Lundin summed up the situation: "Upon crossing the Passaic River, the invaders found themselves in a promised land, where everything they could desire was theirs for the taking." The lists of depredations compiled after the war were astonishing. However briefly, the British officers lost control of their men, who simply took what they wanted and destroyed much of what they could not take.[2]

Cornwallis had expected Washington to stand and fight at Newark. However, the British arrived about 1:00 p.m. to find the village deserted.[3] The Americans, obviously well-informed of the British advance, easily slipped away during the morning and retreated further south towards Elizabethtown, Woodbridge, and New Brunswick.

A future president of the United States, James Monroe, was with Washington in Newark. Monroe was a young lieutenant in the 3rd Virginia Regiment. He drafted pieces of his autobiography from 1827 to 1830, after retiring from public life. But he was proud to have fought with the venerated Washington: "I saw him in my earliest youth," he recalled, "in the retreat through Jersey, at the head of a small band, or rather, in its rear, for he was always near the enemy, and his countenance and manner made an impression on me which time can never efface." While "on the rear guard at Newark," Monroe counted the troops who passed him, which he reckoned at "less than 3,000 men." Yet the general was unshaken. "A deportment so firm, so dignified, so exalted, but yet so modest and composed," the former lieutenant wrote, "I have never seen in any other person."[4] Monroe died on July 4, 1831.

The British never came close to capturing Washington's army at Newark. The belief among some historians in a narrow rebel escape is based

---

[1] *Kemble Papers*, 101-102; Ewald, *Diary*, 22. Ewald noted the army marching in only one column to Newark. However, every other eyewitness source is clear that there were two columns. Ewald would have been with von Donop in the column on the right flank. The Glyn diary, in particular, supports the idea that there were two columns advancing south from Acquackanonk.

[2] Leonard Lundin, *Cockpit of the Revolution* (Princeton: Princeton University Press, 1940), 173.

[3] Archibald Robertson, *His Diaries and Sketches in America* (New York: The New York Public Library, 1930), 114.

[4] *The Autobiography of James Monroe* (Syracuse, 1959), 24.

in large part on a letter Washington wrote to Congress on November 30. While in New Brunswick, the Commander-in-Chief informed the delegates that he quit Newark "as our force was by no means sufficient to make a stand against the Enemy, much superior in number, with the least probability of success, and whose advanced Guards were entering the Town by the time our Rear got out."[1] The vigilant rear guard of the American army was composed of riflemen and other combat-hardened troops, and the British never got close enough to press them. Washington's main army was safely gone by the time the vanguard of Cornwallis' army reached the outskirts of Newark. A few hours after arriving safely in New Brunswick, it was a somewhat relieved Washington who wrote to General Heath that all was well: "The Enemy gave us not the least Interruption upon our March."[2] The Americans had retreated again, but things could have been much worse.

---

[1]Twohig, ed., *Papers of George Washington*, VI: 232-233.

[2]Fitzpatrick, ed., *Writings of George Washington*, VI: 310-311. Benson Lossing referenced a similar story. "Often the music of the pursued and the pursuers," Lossing wrote, "would be heard by each other, yet no action occurred." Benson Lossing, *Pictorial Field Book of the Revolution* (New York: Harper & Brothers, 1855), II: 15. William Stryker fueled the myth of the near-capture of Washington's army at Newark when he wrote "the enemy's advance guard entered Newark, November 28th, as the American army left that city." Stryker, *Battles of Trenton and Princeton*, 9.

CHAPTER SIX

New Brunswick

This retreat into, and through New-Jersey, was attended with almost every circumstance that could occasion embarrassment, and depression of spirits.
—Historian David Ramsay, 1789[1]

New Brunswick, wrote traveler Peter Kalm, was "a pretty little town in the province of New Jersey, in a valley on the west side of the river Rareton." The houses had small front porches with benches, "on which the people sat in the evening, in order to enjoy the fresh air, and to have the pleasure of viewing those who passed by." Another visitor described New Brunswick as "a small trading town, situated on Rareaton River, which is navigable to the town for small craft." Yet another thought that the town, along with Philadelphia, had "the handsomest women that I saw in America."[2]

---

[1]David Ramsay, *The History of the American Revolution* (Philadelphia: R. Aitken, 1789), I: 398.

[2]Peter Kalm, *Travels into North America* (Barre, MA: Imprint Society, 1972), 120; *The Journal of Nicholas Cresswell* (New York: The Dial Press, 1924); 157. Andrew Burnaby, *Travels Through The Middle Settlements in North America* (London, 1798), 104.

John Adams passed through New Brunswick in 1774 and said the town had about one hundred fifty houses, three churches and several paved streets. The beauty of the Raritan River impressed him, as did the number of boats there, in front of the town.

By the eve of the Revolution, New Brunswick carried on a brisk trade with New York City. Warehouses and storehouses lined the waterfront. Every day, sloops loaded corn, flour, bread, linseed, meat, and timber for sale in New York. Occasionally, a ship would sail from New Brunswick for the West Indies or England. The town was a popular stop on the Upper Road, and profited from the many travelers who stopped at its numerous taverns and inns. The three best-known taverns were the White Hart, Sign of the Ship, and Indian Queen.[1] New Brunswick's days of peace were numbered, however, for it was about to become a seat of war.

On November 28, 1776, the patriot Grand Army evacuated Newark and retreated south to Elizabethtown, described at the time as "very pleasantly situated" with "about four hundred houses, most very neat brick buildings."[2] Washington passed quickly through Elizabethtown and made no effort to defend it. His destination was New Brunswick. The road from Elizabethtown to New Brunswick, called the Upper Road, or sometimes the Old Dutch Road, passed through Rahway, Woodbridge and Piscataway. Near Woodbridge, it was joined by a road from Perth Amboy on the seacoast.

The vanguard of Cornwallis's force entered Newark from the north as Washington's rear guard abandoned it to the south. Stories already circulated about looting and rape by the Hessians. Some civilians from Newark and Elizabethtown fled west to safety in the rugged Morris County terrain around the villages of Chatham and Morristown. Other frightened refugees loaded families and belongings into wagons, and jammed the rough, rain-soaked road south of Newark along with Washington's ragtag soldiers.

The delegation sent from the Continental Congress found Washington at Elizabethtown. Having taken the Upper Road from Trenton, they saw the terrible condition of their army as they passed the sick and wounded moving ahead of the main force. Congressman George Ross was shocked. "The distress of our Soldiers," he wrote to a friend, "who I have met almost naked and hardly able to walk or rather wade through the mud has given infinite pain

---

[1]Kalm, *Travels into North America*, 121; Lane, *From Indian Trail*, 61, 109.

[2]Patrick M'Robert, *A Tour Through Part of the North Provinces of America* (Edinburgh, Scotland, 1776), 33.

but I shudder to tell you that they fall dead on the road with their packs on their backs or are found accidentally, perishing in hay lofts."[1] The scene was of hurry and confusion as the congressmen reached Washington. The tall Virginian took the delegates out of the stream of humanity and spoke calmly with them by the side of the road. Those close to the general said that the loss of Fort Washington, less than two weeks earlier, had toughened him. It was the sturdy Washington, frontier Indian fighter who had saved the shattered remnants of Braddock's army on the Pennsylvania frontier, who retreated with his soldiers through New Jersey.

Washington told the delegation that he would try to form a defense line at New Brunswick, and said he was convinced that the Royal army meant to push all the way to Philadelphia. Ross stood by the roadside and counted only two thousand dirty and poorly clothed American soldiers. He learned that a second column, of less than two thousand, followed half an hour behind. It shook Ross to see how small and shabby Washington's army was, and to learn that the enlistments of half would expire within days. Meanwhile, they were being pursued by a reported eight thousand enemy soldiers.[2] It was dangerous for the three rebel congressmen to remain so close to the enemy. Having seen enough, they turned back towards Philadelphia to report to the Continental Congress. Washington continued his retreat towards New Brunswick.

The following morning, a tired and mud-spattered post rider with a letter from Lee found Washington nearing New Brunswick. Surrounded by aides and protected by his heavily-armed Life Guard, Washington eagerly tore it open.[3] Here, finally, thought Washington and his staff, was the news that Lee had crossed the Hudson! Lee's letter was dated November 26. Washington was discouraged to find it addressed from "Philipsbourg," New

---

[1]Paul H. Smith, ed., *Letters of Delegates to Congress 1774-1789* (Washington, D.C.: Library of Congress, 1979), V: 547.

[2]George Ross to James Wilson, Nov. 28, 1776, Smith, ed., *Letters of Delegates to Congress*, V: 449-550.

[3]Washington was protected at the time by a bodyguard force of about 50 enlisted men. Carlos Godfrey, *The Commander-In-Chief's Guard* (Washington, D.C.: Stevenson-Smith Company, 1904), 37. The official name of Washington's guard force was "The Commander-in-Chiefs Guard." It was also known popularly by the soldiers during the Revolution as "Washington's Life Guard." The unit was formed in March, 1776, while the American army was still at Cambridge, Massachusetts, and was commanded throughout the war by Captain Caleb Gibbs (1748-1821) of Massachusetts. Little is known about the Guard during 1776 since all the records for the year were destroyed in a fire at the Charlestown Navy Yard in 1815.

York. Lee had not even moved from his camp. Lee began his letter by complaining that Heath would not release his two thousand men to reinforce Washington: "the want of Carriages and this disappointment with respect to Heath...have still detained me here" and, again, he claimed that the British were very active in his district. He enumerated other problems: lack of transportation, bad roads, no militia to defend New York if his army moved out, no blankets, no shoes no money. But the letter ended with the long hoped-for news that "I set out tomorrow."[1] Washington slowly folded the dispatch while he pondered the shock that it would be days before any reinforcements could reach him. Scouts reported that Cornwallis and his legion had stopped in Newark, but now were advancing and not far behind.

On the morning of November 29, the first ragged American soldiers crossed the Raritan River and entered New Brunswick.[2] They had marched 25 miles through continuous rain the previous day. Washington arrived later that day with the main body of the Grand Army. The Raritan River now separated Washington's little army from the Crown's forces. Cornwallis was finally moving fast. His main army left Newark at daybreak on November 29, but had to advance carefully because of the threat of rebel skirmishers and, more important, the corps of the cunning Charles Lee, whose position still was unknown to Cornwallis. Concerned about Lee, Cornwallis ordered Ewald's

---

[1]Lee to Washington, Nov. 26, 1776, *Lee Papers*, II: 315. "Philipsburg" implies anywhere in the large tract of territory in Westchester County, New York, owned by the Philips family.

[2]Stryker said that Washington's army marched in two columns from Newark to New Brunswick. One column reached New Brunswick by way of Elizabethtown and Woodbridge following the main road (the Upper Road) while the other went via Springfield, Scotch Plains, and Quibbletown (part of modern Piscataway). This column arrived at New Brunswick on the afternoon of Nov. 29. While Stryker gives no references for this information, it is probably correct, although the column which marched via Springfield may have been small. Stryker, *Battles of Trenton and Princeton*, 10. Stryker also states that a small body of troops commanded by General Lord Sterling were sent in advance of the main army to guard the Raritan River at New Brunswick. This information would support the story that the Grand Army arrived in New Brunswick to find some soldiers had found a supply of liquor in the town and had gotten drunk. There was no bridge across the Raritan River at New Brunswick in 1776. The first bridge to ford the Raritan at New Brunswick was opened in 1795. There was a ferry at New Brunswick across the Raritan called "Inian Ferry" (Inman Ferry) after John Inman, who started a ferry service there in 1686. The reference to a bridge at New Brunswick during Washington's retreat refers to the Landing Bridge (modern Landing Lane Bridge stands on the same location) at the village of Raritan Landing, which was two miles above New Brunswick.

Jaeger company to patrol towards Springfield.[1]   Arriving at Elizabethtown, Cornwallis ordered a halt for the night. The common soldiers and the women following the corps immediately began to plunder the town. The vanguard of Cornwallis's army, including a battalion of British light infantry and the lst Hessian Jaeger Company under the command of Captain Carl August von Wreden, advanced further along the upper road to Rahway, where they spent the night.[2] The next day, Saturday, November 30, Cornwallis' corps was up early and out of Elizabethtown. Some elite troops moved ahead of the main column and occupied Woodbridge and Perth Amboy, both of which they found deserted. The weather remained miserable: heavy rain and wind. The roads were a sea of mud, which slowed Cornwallis's advance.[3] Cornwallis continued to have serious problems preventing pillaging. Everywhere, British and Hessian soldiers, "women of the army," camp followers and children broke into the hastily evacuated houses and looted valuables.

"Women of the army," camp followers and children were characteristic of all eighteenth-century armies, including the American army during the Revolution. Women of the army were traditionally wives or other female relatives of common soldiers, and authorized to accompany their men wherever the army went. They commonly did laundry and sewing, and occasionally acted as nurses for meager pay. These women were a tough, hard-working lot. Camp followers, on the other hand, were considered "loose women," prostitutes who usually stayed with the sutlers. Some children were often part of this curious entourage behind an 18th Century army. A typical sight in central New Jersey at the time was a group of women of the army or camp followers at a roadside, guarding a hastily-assembled pile of household goods. British or Hessians would break into an empty house and carry out anything from furniture to frying pans. They would heap these by the road and

---

[1]Ewald, *Diary of the American War*, 22; Bernard Uhlendorf, ed. and trans., *Revolution in America*, (New Brunswick: Rutgers University Press, 1957), 73; "Glyn Diary." Ewald made his headquarters at Liberty Hall, the manor of Governor William Livingston, on the road between Elizabethtown and Springfield. Ewald said he did not permit Livingston's house to be looted, even though it was the home of "one of the first and most fiery rebels."

[2]Baurmeister, *Revolution in America*, 73.

[3]Mackenzie reported the weather on Nov. 30 from nearby New York City as "rain all night, and most part of this day, attended during the night, with a strong wind at N.E. The transports here cannot move until the wind and weather are more favorable." Mackenzie, *Diary*, I: 117.

leave women to guard the spoils until they could return to help carry them off.[1]

The morning of November 30, Ewald's Jaeger company was reinforced by thirty troops from the 16th Dragoons, and skirmished with some rebel militia. They were certain that Lee's corps was somewhere in the area. The night of November 30, Ewald linked up with the 2nd Battalion of Light Infantry, commanded by Major Maitland, at the village of Connecticut Farms Meeting (modern Union). Maitland's light infantry had been protecting Cornwallis' right flank for the past couple of days; now they did the same with Ewald's company as Cornwallis advanced. Ewald stopped in the Rahway area for the night, kept his men under arms, posted sentries and would not permit any campfires. Cornwallis spent the night of November 30 with his main army at Rahway while Maitland and Ewald protected his right flank from a surprise attack.

Various elements of Cornwallis' army were spread out along the Upper Road between Newark and Woodbridge. It appeared to be a dangerous situation for the Crown forces, partially caused by Cornwallis's now-determined pursuit of Washington's army. However, unknown to Cornwallis and his army, there was no strong body of American troops to attack their isolated columns. The next morning, December 1, Cornwallis resumed his advance towards New Brunswick. At the same time, Ewald and Maitland entered Rahway around noon and followed the Upper Road to join the main British army, which was approaching the Raritan River.[2]

---

[1]This scene is based on an eyewitness description of the looting of a house by Crown soldiers in Piscataway. Lundin, *Cockpit of the Revolution*, 174. For a fuller discussion of women in the army, see Evan Cornog, *Come all you Gallant Heroes* [exhibition catalog] (New York: Fraunces Tavern Museum, 1991), 17.

[2]Baurmeister, *Revolution in America*, 73; Ewald, *Diary*, 22-24; "Glyn Diary," Nov. 28, 1776. New Jersey historian Cornelius Vermeule made the intriguing statement that the Crown forces advanced in two divisions to the Raritan River. Vermeule said, "They had come down in two divisions; one by way of Elizabeth and Rahway , its progress marked by burning buildings and ravished homes; the other by way of Springfield and Scotch Plains, which did less damage, possibly because it was more exposed to attack by the militia." Vermeule, "Some Revolutionary Incidents in the Raritan Valley," *Proceedings of the New Jersey Historical Society*, New Series, Vl (1921), 76. Vermeule did not give his sources for this information. However, there is evidence that Colonel Carl Emilius von Donop's brigade of Hesse Cassel grenadiers advanced from Newark or Elizabethtown to the Raritan River via Springfield, Scotch Plains, and Quibbletown (part of modern Piscataway) at the same time that Cornwallis was advancing along the Upper Road. There are a few clues to indicate that von Donop marched to the Raritan via Springfield and Scotch Plains. One is a comment by Ensign Glyn, dated Newark, November 28: "Col. Donop will stop at Lord Cornwallis's Quarters where he will

Washington had a very different set of concerns during those days. He was up early on November 30, which some have called the worst day of the American Revolution. He faced a host of problems at his hastily-established headquarters in Cochrane's Tavern in New Brunswick.[1] To his mortification, the only reinforcements found at New Brunswick were some stragglers from the Flying Camp. Washington now confronted the reality that on December 1, the next day, the enlistments of two thousand soldiers representing almost half his army would expire. And the enemy was just hours away.

The Commander-in-Chief wrote Congress that day to explain his dreadful situation. He asked for help from the Pennsylvania militia, "the situation of our Affairs being truly alarming." His force was now very small, he warned, and the British were only four or five miles away and were reportedly landing fresh troops at Perth Amboy. He had also learned that a second enemy column of Hessians was moving against his right flank, having arrived at Springfield the night before. "I do not know how far their views extend, but I doubt not they mean to push every advantage resulting from the small number and State of our Troops." Stopping the enemy was unlikely, as his army was dwindling. The general wrote of the failure of the New Jersey militia to turn out in the face of the invasion, a circumstance he found vexing in the extreme. That was not all. "Added to this," he wrote, "I have no assurances, that more than a very few of the Troops composing the flying Camp will remain after the time of their engagement is out; so far from it, I am

receive his instructions." *Glyn Diary.* Perhaps von Donop was given a special assignment. Another is a reference by Washington to a second column of Hessian troops advancing towards the Raritan River via Springfield. Fitzpatrick, ed., *Writings of Washington,* VI: 315.

There is one piece of solid evidence that the Crown forces advanced from Newark to New Brunswick in a single column along the Upper Road. The evidence is from the diary of Archibald Robertson, a British engineer who marched with Cornwallis from Newark to New Brunswick. Robertson said that von Donop's corps was at Elizabethtown on November 29. His entry for November 30 includes "Donop's Corps to Woodbridge." Robertson, *His Diaries and Sketches,* 114. Looking at the military situation, it seems unlikely that a Crown forces column would have been ordered to march to the Raritan River through the rebel-held area around Springfield and Plainfield--especially since Cornwallis was convinced that General Charles Lee was somewhere in the area with his corps.

[1] Douglas Southall Freeman called Nov. 30, 1776 "that most miserable of his wretched days." *George Washington* (New York: Charles Scribner's Sons, 1951), IV: 271; Richard Durnin, *George Washington in Middlesex County, New Jersey* (North Brunswick: Middlesex County Cultural and Heritage Commission, 1989). Cochrane's Tavern was located at the southwest corner of present Neilson and Albany Streets.

told, that some of Genl Ewing's Brigade, who stand engaged to the lst of January, are now going away." As a rule, Washington's communications with Congress were circumspect, but he had pulled no punches in this letter.[1]

The general still had no idea where Lee was. He wrote Lee soon after arriving at New Brunswick on the 29th, patiently urging him to move, but, as in the past, failing to issue a direct order.[2] Washington felt compelled to downplay his anger at the sensitive Lee to preserve harmony and keep the Continental Congress from finding new reasons to meddle in army affairs. Amid all that, a courier arrived from Lee's camp with a letter addressed to Washington's aide, Reed. With Reed away on assignment, Washington eagerly took the sealed dispatch and tore it open, believing it contained public business and, he hoped, good news. Washington quickly realized that it was a personal communication, a reply to the letter Reed had sent Lee from Hackensack. In disbelief, Washington read:

> My Dr. Reed:
> I receiv'd your most obliging, flattering letter -- lament with you that fatal indecision of mind which in war is a much greater disqualification than stupidity or even want of personal courage -- Accident may put a decisive Blunderer in the right -- but eternal defeat and miscarriage must attend the man of the best parts if curs'd with indecision."[3]

Washington was stunned to discover that his dearest friend and confidant had engaged in a secret correspondence with his imperious senior lieutenant. Worse, Reed and Lee seemed to share a low opinion of Washington's leadership.[4] It was a harsh blow, but Washington had to overlook it, in the interest of unity, rather than confront Reed. He refolded the letter, put it back in its envelope and sent Reed an apologetic note. "The inclosed was

---

[1]Twohig, ed., *Papers of Washington*, VII: 232-233.

[2]Fitzpatrick, ed., *Writings of Washington*, VI: 311-312.

[3]*Lee Papers*, II: 305-306.

[4]Washington's high opinion of Joseph Reed is revealed in a letter Washington wrote Reed from New York City, dated Apr. 15, 1776. Reed had resigned his post as a temporary staff officer and Washington wrote him, "When, my good Sir, will you be with me? I fear I shall have a difficult card to play in this Government and could wish for your assistance and advice to manage it." Fitzpatrick, ed., *Writings of Washington*, IV: 483.

put into my hands by an Express from the White Plains," he wrote. "Having no Idea of its being a Private Letter, much less suspecting the tendency of the correspondence, I opened it, as I had done all other Letters to you, from the same place and Peekskill, upon the business of your Office, as I conceived and found them to be." This was the only reason, he assured Reed, that he had seen the contents of the letter. He then thanked the younger officer for his efforts on his recent mission, for which he wished success, and closed with a greeting for Mrs. Reed.[1] Washington, personally wounded, had reacted with stoic self-restraint.

The next day, the general paraded the troops whose enlistments were expiring and pleaded with them to stay. They were badly trained and equipped, but he needed every man. Washington and his senior officers exhorted and appealed in vain; on Sunday, December 1, some 2,060 troops gathered their belongings and walked off without an apology or backward glance. This was not the worst. The remaining soldiers of the Flying Camp, whose enlistments expired on January 1, also began deserting. Washington had to order units to patrol the roads leading towards Pennsylvania and the ferries across the Delaware River to apprehend them. Despite these efforts, losses to desertion were serious. No amount of patrolling could stop all of the men determined

---

[1]Force,ed., *American Archives*, Fifth Series, III: 921. Joseph Reed survived this nasty episode and his friendship with Washington continued until Reed's death (1785) at the age of 44.   Politically savvy, Reed realized his bad judgment in befriending the busybody Charles Lee. Reed apologized for his secret correspondence with Lee in a letter to Washington of Mar. 8, 1777. "My pressing him most earnestly to join you as soon as possible," he wrote, "led to expressions and an answer which must have been disapproved by you, and which I was far from expecting....No man in America, my dear General, more truly and ardently wishes your honour, happiness, and success, or would more exert himself to promote them." William Reed, *Life and Correspondence of Joseph Reed* (Philadelphia: Lindsay and Blakiston, 1847), I: 259. Reed mentioned the incident in another letter to Washington (June 4, 1777). He said that he understood "how difficult it is to regain lost friendship; but the consciousness of never having justly forfeited yours, and the hope that it may be in my power fully to convince you of it, are some consolation for an event which I never think of but with the greatest concern." Reed asked that Washington "judge of me by realities, not by appearances, and believe that I never entertained or expressed a sentiment incompatible with that regard I professed for your person and character, and which, whether I shall be so happy as to possess your future good opinion, or not, I shall carry to my grave with me." *Ibid.*, 259-260. This time Washington replied cooly (June 14, 1777). "I was hurt," he wrote, "not because I thought my judgement wronged by the expressions contain'd in it, but because the same sentiments were not communicated immediately to myself. The favorable manner in which your opinion, upon all occasions, had been received...entitled me, I thought, to your advice upon any point in which I appeared to be wanting." Fitzpatrick, ed., *Writings of Washington*, VIII: 247.

to go home. The rebel chief was left with only 3,400 effectives as scouts came into New Brunswick with the news that Crown forces were less than two hours away.[1] Rumors persisted that additional British reinforcements had landed at Perth Amboy. The shallow Raritan River, with numerous fords, would not delay the enemy long.

Washington resorted to minor trickery: He kept his little army in constant motion at New Brunswick to make the enemy believe he had a much bigger force. On December 1, he also wrote Lee again, this time practically begging him to bring his corps into New Jersey: "I must entreat you to hasten your march as much as possible, or your arrival may be too late to answer any valuable purpose."[2]

The Commander-in-Chief had no options except to retreat further into the New Jersey interior; the same logic then dictated that he might have to cross the Delaware River into Pennsylvania in the hope of forming a new defensive line. This, of course, required boats that he did not have.[3] Thus, even before abandoning New Brunswick, he took steps to assure his ability to reach Pennsylvania. He ordered Colonel Richard Humpton of the 11th Pennsylvania Regiment to go to the two Delaware ferries at Trenton and secure all the boats. Humpton also was ordered to gather all other boats he could find on the Delaware River and bring them to the Trenton ferries. Boats were not the only problem; there were also the army's supplies and equipment to worry about. In addition to finding all available watercraft, the rebel general

---

[1]Force, *American Archives*, Fifth Series, III: 822. A Newark return dated November 23 notes that the enlistments of the following brigades were to expire on December 1: General Beall's Maryland Brigade (1,200 men); General Heard's Brigade of Flying Camp men from New Jersey (800); and Colonel Bradly's (60). Fitzpatrick, ed., *Writings of Washington*, VI: 312. In a letter to Governor Livingston, Washington mentioned the names of the two large brigades that departed on December 1 and candidly admitted that he expected other losses to expired enlistments and desertions. Congressman George Read of Delaware wrote his wife on Dec. 6, 1776, that some of the members of the Flying Camp had arrived in Philadelphia, although he hoped that urgent appeals would induce some of them to reenlist, if only briefly. Read to Gertrude Read, Dec. 6, 1776, Smith, ed., *Letters of Delegates*, V: 582. John Marshall, *The Life of George Washington* (London: Printed for Richard Philips by J. Adlard, 1804) II: 597.

[2]*Ibid.*, 599; Fitzpatrick, ed., *Writings of Washington*, VI: 318.

[3]Washington had failed to make any preparations to get the garrison of Fort Washington across the Hudson River and he was determined not to repeat this mistake; he made sure that there were boats waiting to take his army across the Delaware River.

further instructed Humpton to get the army's baggage across the Delaware and to secure it in some safe place just beyond the river on the Pennsylvania side.[1] Humpton was a reliable officer whom Washington had already entrusted with important missions. A former British captain who had emigrated to Pennsylvania at the end of the French and Indian War, Humpton quit his 600-acre farm when the Revolution broke out and joined the rebellion. His military experience was welcomed. Washington sent General William Maxwell to join in Humpton's mission, and ordered General Israel Putnam to have rafts made from timber available at Trenton.[2]

Once Washington was satisfied with the Pennsylvania arrangements, he turned his attention to his problems in New Brunswick. At about 1:30 p.m. on December 1, the first British troops reached the banks of the Raritan River. They quickly brought up two field pieces and began an intense artillery duel with the few rebel batteries across the river. Two Americans were killed. The

---

[1]Twohig, ed., *The Papers of George Washington*, VII: 248. On Dec. 1, Washington ordered Colonel Richard Humpton to proceed to the Trenton area and "to see all the boats there put in the best Order with a sufficiency of Oars and poles and at the same time to Collect all the Additional Boats you [can] from both above and below and have them brought to those ferry's and Secured for the purpose of Carrying over the Troops and Baggage in most expeditious Manner." Quartermaster and other personnel were to render all possible assistance, and Humpton was to take special care to secure Durham boats. They were large and offered the best means of transporting the army and its baggage and stores. The Durham boat was a shallow-drafted vessel designed to go against the current of the Delaware River; depending upon conditions, could move by oars, poles, or sail, or it could float with the current. It was designed to transport iron made at the Durham furnace, located a little below the Delaware River port of Easton, Pennsylvania, to Philadelphia. It varied in length from 40 to 60 feet and was approximately 8 feet in width. Durham boats carried the bulk of the freight between Philadelphia and the upper Delaware River during the colonial period. They were also used on the Susquehenna and Mohawk Rivers.

[2]Humpton's whereabouts on Dec. 1 have been a matter of speculation; e.g., Stryker, *Battles of Trenton and Princeton*, 15, and Leonard Lundin, *Cockpit of the Revolution* (Princeton: Princeton University Press, 1940), 146. However, the wording in Washington's orders to Humpton and in related correspondence implies that the colonel was in New Brunswick with the Grand Army when he received his orders. Fitzpatrick, ed., *Writings of Washington*, VI: 318-319. Stryker, *Battles of Trenton and Princeton*, 15.

Americans had just five cannons at New Brunswick, all in Captain Alexander Hamilton's company of New York State Artillery.[1] They were lucky to have any artillery at all after the Fort Lee disaster. There is no record of whether Washington took note of young Hamilton, for whom American history had bigger plans. However, George Washington Parke Curtis, Washington's step-grandson, wrote in his *Recollections* that Washington had been "charmed by the brilliant courage and admirable skill" of Hamilton, who directed effective battery fire against the advancing British columns.[2] Surveying his weak position, Washington wrote a second letter to Congress, saying he had to retreat across the Delaware.

Meanwhile, the British were active on the opposite side of the Raritan. No bridge crossed at New Brunswick, but there was a bridge two miles up the river, Landing Bridge, at the village of Raritan Landing. Jaegers, guided by local Tories, hurried north on the Great Road Up Raritan, a roadway following the river on the Piscataway side, passing rich farmland and fine homes.[3] Upon reaching the village, they turned onto a causeway where they could see the bridge a short distance away. Advancing towards the bridge, even the dullest among them realized that its seizure would give the Crown forces an

---

[1]Robertson, *His Diaries and Sketches in America,* 114. Eight companies of artillery were authorized for the Continental army and commanded by Colonel Henry Knox. In addition, several states raised their own artillery companies. New York State raised two companies. In late 1776, one of the units was helping to defend the Hudson Highlands and the other, commanded by Captain Alexander Hamilton, accompanied Washington's army when it crossed the Hudson River to defend New Jersey. During the retreat, Hamilton's company was the only artillery Washington had with him. Robert Wright, Jr., *The Continental Army* (Washington D.C.: Government Printing Office, 1983), 62; and James Flexner, *The Young Hamilton* (Boston-Toronto: Little, Brown and Company, 1978), 122-123.

[2]James Thomas Flexner, *The Young Hamilton* (New York: Little, Brown & Company, 1978), 123.

[3]Burnaby, *Travels Through the Middle Settlements in North America,* 104. Burnaby traveled up the Raritan River from New Brunswick in 1759-1760. In his journal, Burnaby described the countryside along the Raritan River as "exceedingly rich and beautiful; and the banks of the river are covered with gentlemen's houses." The lower Raritan River could be crossed at a point about two miles above Raritan Landing. At this location, the river was shallow and had a firm, rocky bottom. A trail identified as "Vincent's path to Greenland's" crossed the Raritan at this point. C.C. Vermeule, "Raritan Landing That Was," *Proceedings of the New Jersey Historical Society,* 54 (1936): 87. There is no indication that the Crown forces went any further up the Raritan River than Raritan Landing at this point in the Revolution. The probable reason is that they feared operating too far from their main army.

opportunity to bag Washington's army at New Brunswick.

As the jaegers approached the bridge, they found it partially dismantled and defended by rebel riflemen whose marksmanship they had come to respect. The jaegers took cover in buildings on the Piscataway side of the river and started skirmishing with the rebels. Washington went through the motions of appearing to defend New Brunswick, but ordered his army to evacuate at dusk and to march on the Upper Road towards Princeton. The soldiers did not have enough wagons to remove all their baggage; some one hundred tents were burned to prevent the enemy from taking them.[1] As usual, a tenacious rear guard remained behind to delay the enemy.

Captain Fredrich Heinrich Lorey of the jaegers was posted at Raritan Landing. When darkness fell he realized that the rebels had abandoned their positions near the bridge and ordered his men across to form a defense perimeter on the New Brunswick side. He did not advance further for fear that American riflemen still lurked. About the same time, the jaegers captured two sloops below the bridge, loaded with stacks of clothing, shoes and wine.[2]

Any thoughts of advancing into New Brunswick that night were forsaken after a shocking incident at Landing Bridge at dusk. A young Hessian officer of the Block Grenadier Battalion, Captain Von Weitershausen, rode up to Raritan Landing, carrying orders from von Donop. He delivered his dispatch and turned his horse to ride away. Then a rifle shot rang out and Von Weitershausen dropped from his horse, mortally wounded through the breast and spine. That night, the Crown forces sat huddled around their campfires, loaded weapons nearby. They talked about the tragic shooting of Von Weitershausen and of how the rebels were purposely aiming at officers. The sentries were nervous of a surprise attack. Rumors said Lee had crossed the Hudson River from New York with ten thousand rebels and could be near.[3]

Washington stayed with the rear guard at New Brunswick until about 7:30 p.m., then retreated towards Princeton with the last of his comand. His army was already eight miles ahead of him. The next morning, Cornwallis

---

[1]Ewald, *Diary of the American War*, 24.; "Personal Recollections of Captain Enoch Anderson," *Papers of the Historical Society of Delaware*, XVL (1896), 27.

[2]Ewald, *Diary of the American War*, 24.

[3]Letter FZ, Lidgerwood Collection; 42; Letter K, ibid., 42-43. Captain von Weitsershausen died three days later and was buried at New Brunswick.

reconnoitered New Brunswick and occupied it with the Scottish Highlanders. The only rebels the British found were several sick or dead.[1] Cornwallis kept his army in defensive positions in the town and on the alert for a surprise attack, especially from Lee. The specter of Lee, if not the person, was proving an effective deterrent. Cornwallis posted light infantry beyond the town on the road to Princeton, but made no effort to chase Washington. Hessians occupied the houses along the Piscataway side of the Raritan River and British troops occupied the farmhouses further to the rear. On the night of December 1, Colonel Rall was at Newark with his Hessian brigade. He, too, worried about a rebel attack and ordered his pickets doubled when he was warned that rebels commanded by General Matthias Williamson were in the Newark area.[2]

If only Cornwallis had known Washington's actual situation! The American army almost ceased to exist as it retreated south from New Brunswick. Greene wrote shortly afterwards that "when we left Brunswick we had not 3000 men, a very pitiful army to trust the Liberties of America upon."[3] But Washington got his first good news in weeks: through the pleas and influence of General Mifflin, the Philadelphia Associators were en route to Trenton to reinforce the Grand Army.[4] The Commander-in-Chief could only hope that they would arrive in time, and that the addition of these amateur soldiers to the army would make a difference.

---

[1]Samuel Smith, *The Battle of Trenton* (Monmouth Beach, NJ: Philip Freneau Press, 1965), 5; Stirke, *A British Officer's Revolutionary War Journal*, 166.

[2]Letter K, Lidgerwood Collection, 43; Baurmeister, *Revolution in America*, 74.

[3]Greene to Governor Nicholas Cooke, Dec. 4, 1776; Showman, ed., *The Papers of General Nathanael Greene*, I: 362.

[4]In 1775, the militia of the City of Philadelphia consisted of five battalions and called themselves the "Associators of the City & Liberties of Philadelphia." Boatner, *Encyclopedia of the American Revolution*, 48.

CHAPTER SEVEN

Princeton and Trenton

As we go forward into the country the Rebels fly before us, & when we come back, they always follow us, 'tis almost impossible to catch them. They will neither fight, nor totally run away. but they Keep at such a distance that we are always above a days march from them. We seem to be playing at Bo peep.
-- Captain William Bamford, 40th Regiment of Foot[1]

News reached Philadelphia on December 2 that the forces of the Crown had crossed the Raritan River and captured New Brunswick; the town was the last American defense line in New Jersey. The road to Philadelphia was now open to the enemy. In days, it was rumored, the British and their Hessian hirelings would reach the city. Philadelphia panicked. Although some patriots strove for calm and worked to prepare a makeshift defense, many shops and schools closed; the roads out of the city were jammed with fleeing people and wagons.

Meanwhile, in New Jersey, Washington's skeleton of an army was in

---

[1]William Bamford, Diary, "The Revolutionary Diary of a British Officer," *Maryland Historical Magazine*, 28 (1933): 17-19.

flight towards the Delaware River. The troops had marched out of New Brunswick after nightfall on December 1, following the Upper Road towards Princeton, Trenton, and the hope of eventual security on the Pennsylvania side of the river. When the army was a safe distance out of New Brunswick, it camped for the night in the woods beside the road. It was a miserable bivouac. Soldiers had no tents or blankets to fight the cold; some suffered without shoes. In the morning, they broke camp and resumed the march towards Princeton through what one traveller had described before the war as "very fine country."[1] A farmer rising at dawn to tend his animals would have met a pitiful sight as the soldiers of the Grand Army passed, organized for fighting in hostile country.[2] First would have come pickets, isolated men on foot or mounted, scouting ahead of the army and alert for trouble. Next would be the advance party, composed of the remnants of Sheldon's Light Horse (Connecticut militia), and Maryland and Virginia riflemen, tough frontiersmen in long hunting shirts of various colors and carrying Pennsylvania rifles. The advance party also would have had some infantrymen, probably reliable veterans detached from the three Continental regiments Washington still had.

After the advance party were infantry regiments, marching according to their place in the order of battle. First was Sterling's brigade, consisting of Isaac Read's 1st Virginia Regiment followed by the remnants of Colonel John Haslet's 1st Delaware Regiment. Better known as "The Delaware Blues," Haslet's corps had formed on the Green in Dover, Delaware, in the summer of 1776, and marched off in high spirits to join Washington's army for the defense of New York City. The Delaware troops had suffered so many battle

---

[1]The details of the encampment of the army on the night of Dec. 1 are from "Personal Recollection of Captain Enoch Anderson," *Papers of the Historical Society of Delaware*, (1896): 27-28. Sergeant McCarty's journal for Monday, Dec. 2, implies that the army stopped for the night between New Brunswick and Princeton. His entry reads, "Day break we march on and came to Princetown," McCarty, 38. M'Robert, *A Tour of the Northern Provinces*, 33.

[2]Lesser, *Sinews of Independence*, 40-44. The order of the Grand Army on the road from New Brunswick to Princeton is based on the "General Return of the Army, December 1, 1776" and "Return of the Forces in the Service of the United States...Under the Command of his Excellency George Washington...December 22, 1776." At the time of the Revolution, the order in which regiments were listed in the returns was the same as the order in which the regiments lined up on a battlefield or their order of march when the army was on the move.

casualties and deaths from disease that by December 1776, they ceased to exist as a fighting unit.[1] Next came the 3rd Virginia (181 officers and men fit for duty) commanded by George Weedon, a former Fredericksburg innkeeper and pre-war acquaintance of Washington. Weedon was followed by the 6th Marylanders (199 officers and men), whose commanding officer, Otho Holland Williams, had been wounded and captured at Fort Washington.

Next came a newly organized brigade. The unit was scratched together from existing battalions, many of which had sustained heavy losses. The commander was General Hugh Mercer, a former Virginia doctor and apothecary shop owner. Mercer's brigade marched with the 232 officers and men of the 27th Massachusetts Continentals in the lead. Following them were 419 men with the 20th Connecticut Continental; then came the "shattered remnants" of Smallwood's Maryland Battalion. The proud Marylanders, after months of hard campaigning, were down to 262 officers and men. Counted among the missing was its commander, William Smallwood, seriously wounded at the Battle of White Plains in October.[2] Next in Mercer's brigade came the Connecticut State Regiment, with only 108 men. Many wore a mix of civilian and military clothing, dirty and threadbare from long campaigning. But no matter how ragged, every soldier had a clean musket and some type of cartridge box, filled with ammunition. At the end of Mercer's Brigade came the 105 remaining officers and men of Moses Rawlings' Maryland and Virginia Rifle Regiment.

Following Mercer on the tense march towards Princeton came the three Virginia regiments of General Adam Stephens. A traveler described one

---

[1]Blanco, *American Revolution, An Encyclopedia*, I, 452-453; and Dwyer, *The Day Is Ours*, 120. Haslet's Delawares had organized in the summer of 1776 with about 700 men. Some 550 of its men took part in the Battle of Long Island in August 1776. By late 1776, the regiment was down to six men. It was known as the Delaware Blues because its men were smartly dressed in blue coats with red facings. The light infantry company wore distinctive peaked black leather helmets with a tall plate on the front with the inscription, *"Liberty and Independence."* Their commander, Colonel John Haslet, was born in Ireland, where he had studied for the ministry and later medicine. He was a doctor and ardent patriot when the Revolution started. Haslet was killed on Jan. 3, 1777 at the Battle of Princeton.

[2]Fitzpatrick, *Writings of Washington*, VI: 346. Blanco, *American Revolution Encyclopedia*, II, 1538. The regiment was raised by Smallwood and Mordecai Gist in 1776 and was in the heaviest fighting at the Battles of Long Island and White Plains.

1. First Portrait of George Washington as Commander-in-Chief, by Charles Willson Peale. John Hancock was the President of the Continental Congress in the spring of 1776 when George Washington visited Philadelphia to confer with Congress. Hancock used the opportunity of Washington's visit to commission Charles Willson Peale to paint this three-quarter length portrait of the Commander-in-Chief. Washington sat for the portrait twice during his brief stay in Philadelphia. He is shown wearing a light blue silk sash, the badge of rank for the Commander-in-Chief. Peale completed the portrait sometime during the summer of 1776; however, he kept it on display in his studio until early December, 1776. Fearing that the Crown forces would overrun Philadelphia, Peale quickly delivered the portrait to Hancock on December 3rd, 1776 and was paid for his services. A few days later Peale marched off with his militia company to reinforce Washington's army in New Jersey. It is believed that Hancock quickly packed the portrait into a wagon and sent it to his Boston home for safe keeping. Courtesy of the Brooklyn Museum, Dick S. Ramsay Fund.

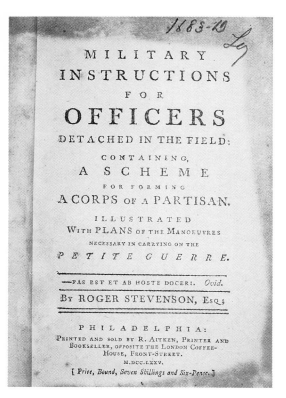

2. Title Page from a 1775 Manual on Partisan
Warfare. What we call today guerrilla warfare
was known as partisan warfare or petite guerre
(small war) at the time of the American
Revolution. This is the title page from a military
textbook on partisan warfare. The book includes
how to stage an ambush and fight using hit-and-
run tactics. It was first published in London in
1770 and republished in Philadelphia in 1775.

The publication of *A Manual on Partisan
Warfare* in America reflects the colonists interest
in possibly fighting a partisan war against the
British. Published with permission from The Library
Company of Philadelphia.

3. Forcing Hudson River Passage, by Dominic Serres. This painting depicts the action on October 9, 1776 of a British naval squadron running the American defenses on the lower Hudson River. It was painted in 1779 by marine artist Dominic Serres (1722-1793). The large ships depicted are (from left to right) the frigates *Tartar*, *Roebuck*, and *Phoenix*. They are escorted by three smaller vessels (to the left of *Tartar*), which were the schooner *Tryal* and two tenders which cannot be accurately identified. The painting was commissioned by Admiral Sir Hyde Parker, the father of Captain Hyde Parker who commanded the flotilla.

Serres probably executed a total of five copies of this painting. Other than the Hudson River being too narrow in the paintings, they are otherwise accurate. Serres was provided with eye witness descriptions of the action from which he based his work. In the picture, the British warships are sailing north and being briskly cannonaded by Fort Lee on the New Jersey side (left) and Fort Washington on upper Manhattan Island (right). The British warships are sailing close to the Manhattan side of the river. One explanation for this is that the British warships were being guided by an American deserter, described as being the brother of the ferryman at Burdett's Ferry, who knew that the passage through the chevaux-de-frise was close to the Manhattan side. However, it is more likely, that in the 18th Century, the natural channel at this point in the Hudson River was close the Manhattan side.

The flag defiantly flying atop rebel held Fort Washington has thirteen alternating red and white stripes and was referred to as the "Rebel Stripes." It was the first, unofficial American national standard. Courtesy U.S. Naval Academy Museum.

4. A View of the Attack against Fort Washington and Rebel Redoubts near New York on the 16 of November 1776, by Thomas Davies. This eyewitness portrayal of the assault on Fort Washington was made from a vantage point in the Bronx, looking across the Harlem River to upper Manhattan Island. Davies included a hand written note that a battery of twelve-pounders was commanded by, "your humble Servant." Published with permission from the I.N. Phelps Stokes Collection, Miriam and Ira D. Wallach Division of Art, Prints and Photographs, The New York Public Library, Astor, Lenox and Tilden Foundations.

5. Detail of the Map of Northern Manhattan Island. This detail is from a map entitled, *A Topographical Map of the North Part of New York Island,* by Claude Joseph Sauthier (printed in London by William Faden, 1777). It depicts the British assault on Fort Washington on November 16, 1776. The map shows the positions of Fort Washington and Fort Lee. Note that one British frigate, HMS *Pearl*, is shown on the Hudson River, above the Fort Washington-Fort Lee defense line. *Pearl* gave supporting fire to the Hessian assault against the northern defenses of Fort Washington. Author's collection.

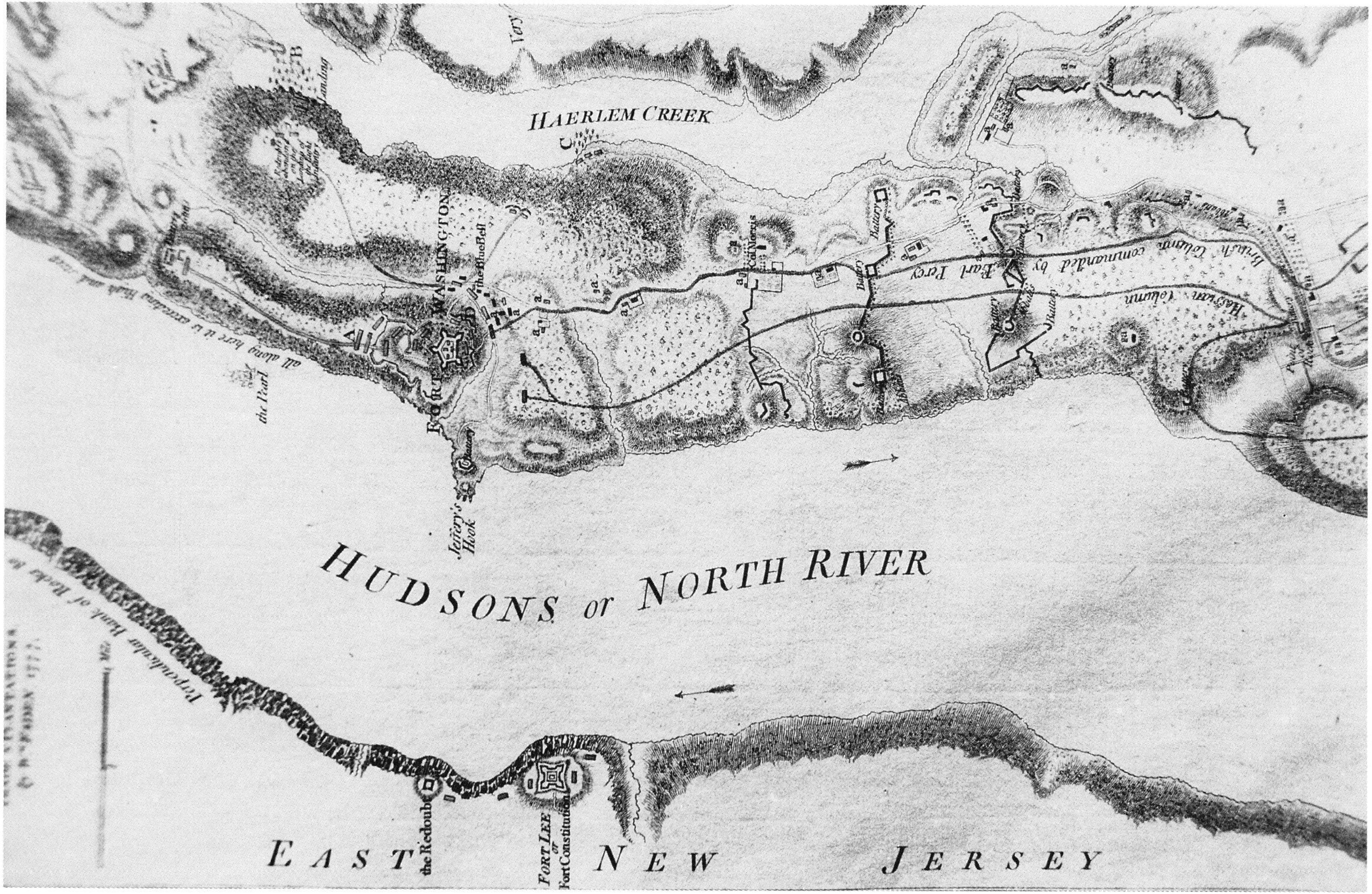

HAERLEM CREEK
FORT WASHINGTON
the Blue Bell
Col. Morris
Jeffery's Hook
Battery
the Pearl
all along here it is exceeding High and steep
Landing
Earl Percy
British Column commanded by
Hessian Column
HUDSONS or NORTH RIVER
Perpendicular Bank of Rocks
Mile
the Redoubt
FORT LEE or Fort Constitution
EAST NEW JERSEY

6-7. The Landing of the British Forces in the Jerseys on the morning of the 20th of November 1776, by Captain Thomas Davies. Despite the absence of professional combat artists, the American Revolution produced some outstanding illustrations made mainly by British artillery and engineer officers. These officers were trained to draw and paint, at least in water colors, as part of their curriculum at the Royal Military Academy at Woolwich, England. Among other duties, they were expected to be able to produce rapid and accurate sketches of ground, forts, buildings and landscapes for military evaluation purposes.

A dramatic example of combat art from the American Revolution is this watercolor showing the landing of Cornwallis' army in New Jersey. It was painted by Captain Thomas Davies (1737-1812), a British artillery officer who served in America during the Revolution. Inscribed below the watercolor, in pen and ink, is the caption *The Landing of the British Forces in the Jerseys on the 20th of November 1776 under the Command of the Rt Hon. Lieut Genl Earl Comwallis.*

Davies illustration of the Crown forces landing in New Jersey was probably begun on the scene. He commanded Cornwallis' artillery and was close to the action during the 1776

campaign. A close examination of the original watercolor reveals that Davies paid great attention to detail. The exclusion, in the watercolor, of the Blackledge-Keary House (built in 1750 and located at Upper Closter Dock Landing) is further evidence that Cornwallis landed at Lower Closter Dock Landing. See C.P. Stacey, *Thomas Davies* (Ottawa: The National Gallery of Canada, 1972).

This watercolor has sometimes been attributed to Lord Francis Rawdon, later 1st Marquess of Hastings (1754-1826), solely because Rawdon bought the picture from Davies soon after it was made. Most of Davies drawings were done to fulfill his military duties or to be sold to officers who collected, like Lord Rawdon.

Davies was appointed a gentleman cadet at the Royal Military Academy, Woolwich March, 1755. As a student, his natural aptitude for drawing was nurtured by Paul Sandby, Drawing Master at the Academy, who is considered by many today to be the father of English watercolor. Davies was a soldier for most of his adult life and lived in relative obscurity with his artwork hidden in private collections. Published with the permission of the Emmet Collection, Miriam and Ira D. Wallach Division of Art, Prints and Photographs, The New York Public Library, Astor, Lenox and Tilden Foundations.

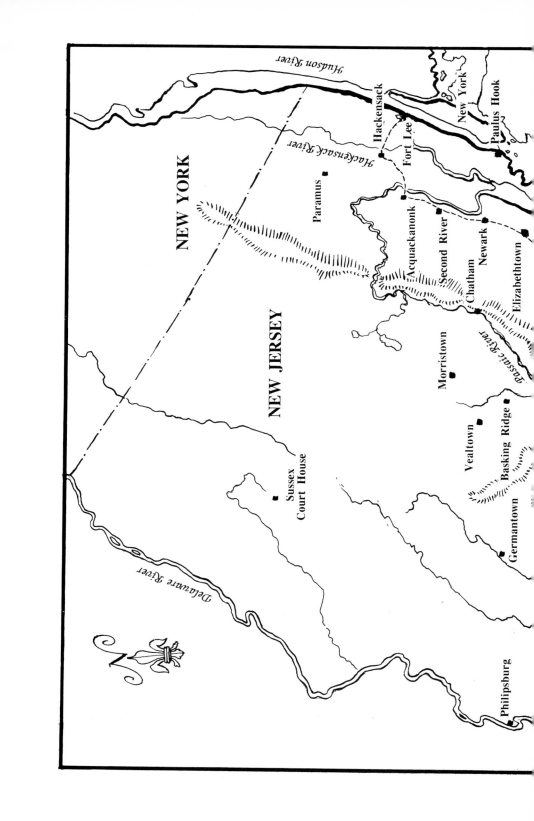

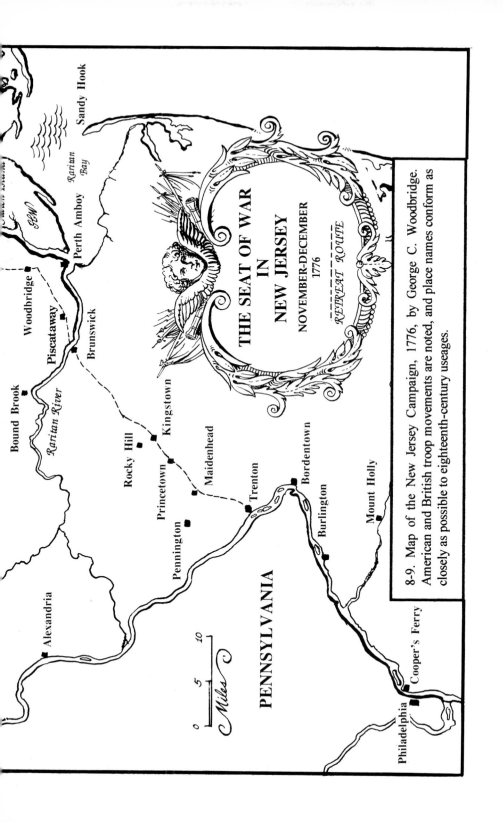

THE SEAT OF WAR
IN
NEW JERSEY
NOVEMBER-DECEMBER
1776

RETREAT ROUTE

Sandy Hook

Raritan
Bay

Perth Amboy

SEW

Woodbridge

Piscataway

Brunswick

Bound Brook

Raritan River

Kingstown

Rocky Hill

Maidenhead

Princetown

Trenton

Bordentown

Pennington

Burlington

Mount Holly

Alexandria

PENNSYLVANIA

0 5 10
Miles

Cooper's Ferry

Philadelphia

8-9. Map of the New Jersey Campaign, 1776, by George C. Woodbridge.
American and British troop movements are noted, and place names conform as
closely as possible to eighteenth-century useages.

10. Alleged Letter of George Washington to Charles Lee, November 30, 1776, from William S. Stryker's *The Battle of Trenton and Princeton*

Brunswick, 30th of November, 1776
The movements of the enemy are, since I wrote you from Newark, of such a nature, as things stand at present, sincerely to be wished for. I have feared that they would take Newark, Elizabeth Town and Amboy for their winter quarters in order to undertake from these places early in the spring an attack on Philadelphia and at the same time having a favourable season ahead that they would make a diversion on the Delaware river with their fleet. The advantages they have gained over us in the past have made them so proud and sure of success that they are determined to go to Philadelphia this winter. I have positive information that this a fact and because the term of service of the light troops of Jersey and Maryland are ended they anticipate the weakness of our army. Should they now really risk this undertaking then there is a great probability that they will pay dearly for it for I shall continue to retreat before them so as to lull them into security.

The authenticity of this letter is questionable because it is optimistic, in contrast to Washington's other communications during the New Jersey retreat. On the date this letter was allegedly written, Washington arrived at New Brunswick with what remained of the Grand Army. The British were close behind and Washington was desperate for reinforcements from General Lee. The letter's optimism seems inconceivable under the circumstances. The fact that this letter was intercepted by the Crown forces adds to the suspicion that it was a subterfuge, meant to fall into enemy hands.

The original letter was found among the archives at Marburg, Germany by William Stryker. It was first published in Stryker's, *The Battles of Trenton and Princeton* (Boston and New York: Houghton, Mifflin and Company, 1898), pages 326-327. The original letter supposedly is still in the Marburg Archives, to which access is complicated.

The editors of *The Papers of George Washington* agree that this letter was a forgery. "While I cannot prove that it was a hoax," Senior Associate Editor Philander D. Chase has written, "the language and the content of this letter persuades me that it is not a legitimate letter. I include it in a note in volume 7 in order to warn readers away from it, fearing that some of them will stumble across it in Stryker" or elsewhere "and not realize... that it is fraudulent." Personal communication, Chase to the author, May 18, 1995.

11. General Sir Henry Clinton's Copy of Stedman's *History*. Charles Stedman (1745-1812) was a Philadelphia Loyalist who served as a British army officer. Stedman saw extensive service during the American Revolution. He went into exile in England at the end of the war where he published one of the first histories of the Revolution in London in 1794. Stedman's *The History of the Origin, Progress, and Termination of the American War* was a scathing criticism of General William Howe's management of the war.

General Sir Henry Clinton owned a copy of Stedman's book. This is page 221 of Volume One from Clinton's copy of Stedman. Stedman is describing Clinton's efforts to get the Howe brothers to divert the Rhode Island task force to support Cornwallis by outflanking Washington's retreating army. Clinton added the following note to Stedman's text: "or be landed at Amboy to have Cooperated with L Cornwallis or embarked on board Ld Howes Fleet landed in Delaware and taken possession of Philadeiphia." Published with the permission of the William L. Clements Library.

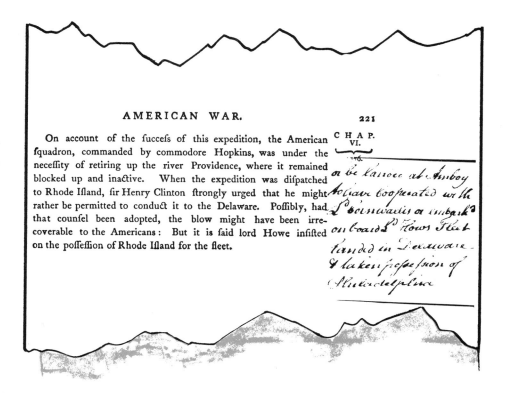

AMERICAN WAR.   221

On account of the fuccefs of this expedition, the American fquadron, commanded by commodore Hopkins, was under the neceffity of retiring up the river Providence, where it remained blocked up and inactive. When the expedition was difpatched to Rhode Ifland, fir Henry Clinton ftrongly urged that he might rather be permitted to conduct it to the Delaware. Poffibly, had that counfel been adopted, the blow might have been irrecoverable to the Americans : But it is faid lord Howe infifted on the poffeffion of Rhode Ifland for the fleet.

CHAP.
VI.

or be landed at Amboy to have Cooperated with L Cornwallis or embarkd on board Ld Howes Fleet landed in Delaware & taken possession of Philadelphia

	Colonel Donnop	BURLINGTON	42.d Reg.t 2. Battalions. Hessian Grenadiers, 1. Batt.n Detachment of Jagers
		Communication from BURLINGTON to BORDEN'S TOWN	Hessian Grenadiers, 1. Batt.n
		BORDEN'S TOWN	Hessian Grenadiers 2. Batt.ns Detachment of Jagers
	Colonel Raille	TRENTON	Rall's Brigade 20. Dragoons 50. Jagers
	Brig.r Gen.l Leslie	PRINCE TOWN	2.d Brigade Light Infantry 2. Batt.ns 3. Troops, 16. Dragoons
Major General Grant Commanding in New Jersey	B.r G.l Matthew	HILLSBOROUGH, &c.a	3. Batt.ns 4.th Brigade
		BRUNSWICK	British Grenad.rs 2. Batt.ns 3. Troops, 16. Dragoons
		LANDING	Guards.
		SPANKTOWN	46.th Reg.t 1. Troop. 17. Dragoons.
		AMBOY	33.th Reg.t
		ELIZABETH TOWN	Waldeck Reg.t 1. Troop, 17. Dragoons
		NEWARK	2. Batt.n 71. Reg.t
		AQUAKENUNK	1. Batt.n 71. Reg.t
		HACKINSACK	26.th Reg.t
		NEW BRIDGE	7.th Reg.t
		BERGEN	57.th Reg.t
		PAULUS'S HOOK	50. Men from the 57. Reg.t

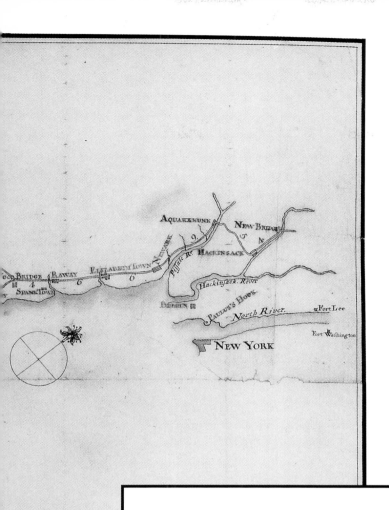

12-13. Projected 1776-1777 Winter Quarters for the Crown forces in New Jersey. This informative manuscript map was drawn by Captain John Montresor (1736-1799) about December 12th, 1776 to indicate projected winter quarters for the army in New Jersey. The map was probably prepared by Montresor for the British high command in America. Montresor was appointed chief engineer in America in December, 1775, and served throughout the New York campaign of 1776. The handwritten note on the upper left corner is in the handwriting of General Henry Clinton and reads, "Capt Montresor after the misfortune of Trenttown this gentlemen has forgot the Assompink [Assumpink] Creek which is however here put in." Assumpink Creek, which runs through Trenton, has been penned into the map. Published with the permission of the William L. Clements Library.

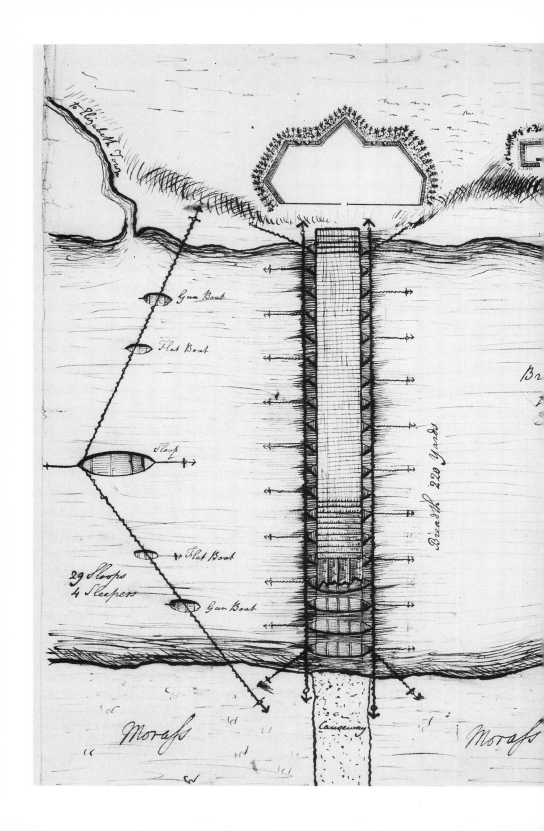

to Elizabeth Town

Gun Boat

Flat Boat

Sloop

Flat Boat

29 Sloops
4 Sleepers

Gun Boat

Breadth 220 Yards

Br

Morafs

Causeway

Morafs

from Staten Island

Jersies, by C. Laird's

ion.

14-15. Illustration of a Pontoon Bridge built by British Army Engineers, 1780. Following their retreat across the Delaware River, the Americans expected the Crown forces to bring up pontoons to ford the Delaware River. This pen and ink drawing, from the papers of Sir Henry Clinton, and shows a pontoon bridge that the British built in 1780 across the Arthur Kill, which separates Staten Island from New Jersey. In December 1776, the British had similar boats in New York City and Howe could have transported overland across New Jersey in the special wagons. Once in the water, the boats were fastened together and planking was laid to create a roadway. On the left side of the illustration, the engineers have constructed a barrier to prevent enemy fire ships or fire rafts from reaching the bridge, which also is defended by fortifications (depicted at the top of the illustration). Published with the permission of the William L. Clements Library.

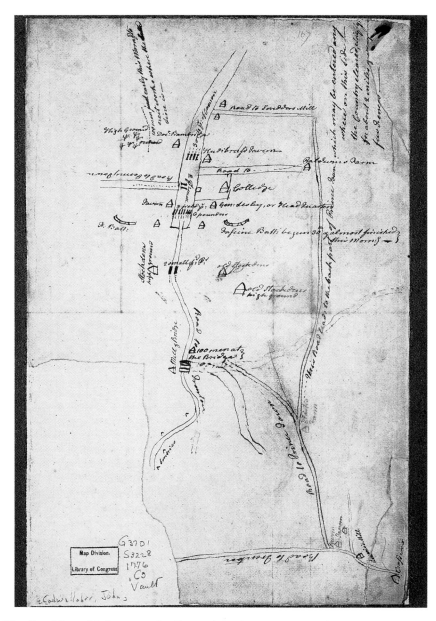

16. The Spy Map of Princeton. On December 31, 1776, Colonel John Cadwalader (1742-1786) wrote General Washington from Crosswicks, New Jersey with information about the enemy garrison at Princeton. Cadwalader included this crude map in his report.   The map was probably drawn by the spy whom Cadwalader had sent into Princeton the previous day. Cadwalader only identifies his spy in his letter to Washington as, "A very intelligent young Gentleman." The spy map includes the position of British headquarters and gun batteries at Princeton. Cadwalader apparently sent several spies into Princeton during late December and their information helped Washington execute his successful attack on Princeton on January 3rd, 1777. Library of Congress Collection.

of his regiments as "a set of dirty, ragged people, badly clothed, badly disciplined and badly armed."[1]

Flags probably were dispersed along the line. These were regimental or state flags, probably in tatters.[2] The Americans still had no national flag. Each regiment had a few fifers and drummers.

Moving with the column on horseback were Washington and his official staff. Washington probably wore a blue regimental coat faced with buff and, since it was now December, he also wore a warm black cloak or greatcoat over his regimentals. Even his clothing was somewhat threadbare from hard use. A gold epaulet sat on each shoulder. If Washington went into battle, he would don a distinguishing light-blue sash, symbol of the Commander-in-Chief. Washington's official family included Greene, who was deputy commander, and other high-level functionaries. Typically, these were the acting chief of artillery, Colonel Henry Knox, a quartermaster, a clothier, an adjutant, aides, and secretaries.[3] Washington's aides wore the uniform of their regiments. They rode horses and were armed with sword and, probably, a pair of saddle pistols. Paine, as Greene's secretary, would have ridden on horseback with the official family although he held no military rank and would not be uniformed.

Close to the Commander-in-Chief rode some heavily armed mounted troopers of Washington's Life Guards. Next in the column were the weary men of Ewing's and Hand's Pennsylvania Flying Camp, militia regiments with

---

[1]*Journal of Nicholas Cresswell*, 163-164. Cresswell saw the 6th Virginia as it passed through Leesburg, Virginia, on Oct. 10, 1776. Several months of marching and fighting must have added further to the distress and ragged appearance of the Virginia troops.

[2]Both armies had flags or "colors" at the time of the Revolution. Some colors were quite large in order to assist in unit identification in the field. British Captain George Smith, in his *An Universal Military Dictionary* (London: J. Millan, 1779), 65, specified "the size of the colours to be 6 feet 6 inches flying, and 6 feet deep on the pike." Regiments did not carry national flags and the American army probably never fought with one. It appears that the national flag was used by naval vessels, fortifications, towns, and possibly army headquarters.

[3]Knox's exact whereabouts during late November through early December are a mystery. From his correspondence we know he was with Lee's corps on Nov. 22, 1776. Knox wrote an expense report from Peekskill, New York, on Nov. 23. Sometime in between Knox made his way across northern New Jersey, probably with Lee's corps, because the next reliable information we have to trace his location is a letter he wrote to his wife Kitty dated "Trenton Ferry, December 8th, 1776."

no uniforms. The few cannons left to the army, probably a mix of three-, four- and six-pounders, were dispersed throughout the column, unloaded because of bouncing and jarring on the roadbed but with crews nearby for quick action. The artillery carriage side boxes or lockers, as they were called, carried some ammunition; but the bulk of their shot and powder was in the baggage train at the rear. Flankers were spread out on both sides of the column to warn of a surprise attack.

An early-to-rise New Jersey farmer also might have glimpsed Captain Alexander Hamilton, who commanded the Independent New York Artillery company. A young man, Hamilton already was a veteran with a growing reputation in the army. Long after the war, an officer who had marched on the retreat recalled the New Yorker. He was still "a youth, a mere stripling, small, slender, almost delicate in frame, marching beside a piece of artillery, with a cocked hat pulled down over his eyes, apparently lost in thought, with his hand resting on the cannon, and every now and them patting it as he mused, as if it were a favorite horse, or a pet playing."[1] Hamilton's company wore dark blue regimental coats with buff facings and breeches. They had seen hard service since the start of the New York campaign.

The army's wagons went behind the marching column, carrying all of the extra ammunition, food and animal fodder, the few tents that the army still possessed, kitchen equipment, bedding and spare clothing belonging to the enlisted men. There may have been a wagon with engineer's tools: shovels, axes, saws and picks and specialized implements. This support train was guarded by a small number of infantry walking alongside, as well as mounted men ready to respond to any alarm.[2]

---

[1]Washington Irving, *Life of Washington* (New York: G. P. Putnam, 1856), III: 88. Washington Irving does not say the incident occurred at Princeton, following the American withdrawal from New Brunswick. However, Nathan Schachner, one of Hamilton's biographers, repeats this story, stating that it took place at Princeton: "The Americans made a sorry spectacle as they straggled into Princeton. But Hamilton's long months of hard driving now showed their effect. His company drew all eyes by the disciplined appearance of its ranks and the brisk, soldierly stride of its men." *Alexander Hamilton* (New York: Appleton-Century Company, 1946), 54.

[2]Knowing the role of the support train of wagons is important to understanding how the American Revolution was fought. For example, the need for many wagon loads of equipment and supplies meant the armies had to stay on or near roads. Therefore, almost all of the fighting of the Revolution was fought near roads. It was impossible for an army to move cross-country. Sometimes, the military wagon trains that saw service in the American Revolution would stretch out for miles.

No matter how destitute the army, it had wagons to carry the officers' personal property. Any officer who could afford the expense also had his own personal wagon or wagons. Washington usually had two, for items such as tents and spare clothing. Following the baggage train came the rear guard riflemen and reliable infantrymen, continually checking behind them for trouble. Further back were a few mounted scouts watching the road from New Brunswick. These experienced men knew the difference between an enemy patrol and an advancing column, and at the first sign of real danger they rode forward to warn the army. Close to the rear of the army were sutler's wagons. These civilians sold necessities and luxuries, including liquor, to those soldiers who could afford them. There were probably few sutlers in the Grand Army at this point, because of the cold weather and the soldiers' poverty. Also at the rear were any women of the army, camp followers and children.

This column filed into Princeton sometime between 8:00 and 9:00 a.m. on the morning of December 2. Princeton was a neat village of only one street formed by the Upper Road. It had somewhere between sixty and eighty houses amid well-cultivated fields, the houses widely separated by gardens and pastures. At its center stood Nassau Hall, housing the College of New Jersey (modern Princeton University). The college building was visible from a considerable distance and dominated the village. A pre-war visitor, Patrick M'Robert, said the village was clean, healthy looking, and had a "fine extensive view of the country round."[1]

The American army found Princeton deserted. Residents had fled when they heard that the British and Hessians were near. The Delaware River ferry crossings to Pennsylvania were choked with frightened civilians, carrying whatever they could on their backs, and sick and wounded soldiers. A girl saw the scene as akin to the Day of Judgment.[2] Residents had to hide whatever belongings they could not carry into the woods or leave them behind; the American vanguard had already taken most of their wagons and horses.

---

[1]This description of Nassau Hall is based in part on the Marquis de Chastellux, who visited Princeton in 1780; *Travels in North America* (London, 1787), I: 160. M'Robert, *A Tour of the Northern Provinces*, 33.

[2]New Jersey had approximately fifty ferries in active use in the middle of the eighteenth century. Among the busiest were those at Lambertville, the two ferries at Trenton, and Cooper's Ferry (Camden). Wheaton Lane, *From Indian Trail to Iron Horse* (Princeton: Princeton University Press, 1939), 44. Lundin, *Cockpit of the Revolution*, 157-158.

The president of the college, John Witherspoon, was known to be "as high a son of liberty as any man in America."[1] Witherspoon, in fact, was one of the New Jersey signers of the Declaration of Independence. When the news came that the American army was retreating, Witherspoon realized the invaders might soon reach Princeton. Calling his students together on November 29, he told them "in a very affecting manner" that he had to disband the college; the students had to leave for their own safety.[2] Some of the students had come to study from as far as Virginia and South Carolina; but all realized they had to flee, and tumult soon filled Nassau Hall as they packed belongings and scoured the village for wagons. Some said goodbyes from room to room. As a signer of the Declaration, Witherspoon was marked as a traitor by the British. He fled Princeton with his family and whatever possessions they could quickly gather.[3]

Like Witherspoon, Princeton landowner and lawyer Richard Stockton had signed the Declaration. He also got away on November 29 after burying the family silver and other treasured objects in the garden of Morven, his large and handsome home. Stockton left his son Richard, 12, at Morven with a trusted servant and took the rest of his family. But instead of heading for the safety of Pennsylvania, Stockton rode south to the home of his friend, John Cowenhoven, in Monmouth County, where he thought he would be safe. However, a band of Tory militia captured Stockton and carried him off to brutal captivity in New York City. The Continental Congress protested his

---

[1]The comment was made by John Adams, who visited Princeton in August 1774. John Maclean, *History of the College of New Jersey* (Philadelphia: J.B. Lippincott & Co., 1877), I: 320.

[2]There is an account by an unknown student of the evacuation. "On the 29th of November, 1776," he wrote, "New Jersey College, long the peaceful seat of science and haunt of the Muses, was visited with the melancholy tidings of the approach of the enemy." Witherspoon, "deeply affected at this solemn scene, entered the [Nassau] Hall where the students were collected, and in a very affecting manner informed us of the improbability of continuing them longer in peace; and after giving us several suitable instructions and much good advice, very affectionately bade us farewell." John Hageman, *History of Princeton* (Philadelphia: J.B. Lippincott & Co., 1879), 124. Lundin, *Cockpit of the Revolution*, 157, also has an account of the closing of the College of New Jersey.

[3]Thomas Wertenbaker, *Princeton 1746-1896* (Princeton: Princeton University Press, 1946), 59. John Witherspoon's country home, "Tusculum," was later pillaged by the Crown forces. Mark Boatner, *Landmarks of the American Revolution* (Harrisburg: Stackpole Books, 1973), 211.

harsh treatment to no avail. Stockton finally succumbed to his tormentors and, to save his life, signed General Howe's pardon. His action marked him as a defector and he was never again active in politics. He died of cancer in 1781.[1]

Washington halted at Princeton only long enough to drop off two brigades under Stirling, then rushed on to Trenton. He told Stirling "to watch the Motions of the Enemy and give notice of their approach."[2] This was a bold move since the troops left at Princeton represented almost half his army.   But Washington made his intentions clear in a letter to Congress, saying he wanted to get his baggage and stores across the river and then "face about with such Troops as are here fit for Service and March back to Princeton and there govern myself by Circumstances and the movements of General Lee." Remarkably, Washington was full of fight and eager to strike some blow.[3] The rebel troops at Princeton promptly made themselves at home in the deserted college building and watched for an enemy advance. American spies continued to filter in and out of New Brunswick. Along the twelve miles from Princeton to Trenton, the troops who pushed on found a good road with many taverns and inns. "The country round about displays variety of agreeable prospects and rural scenes," said one traveller. "I observed many large fields of wheat, barley, and hemp." All around were fertile meadows and pastures. Many of the houses in view were built of rough stone.[4] Large barns with high roofs looked like small churches.

---

[1]Lundin, *Cockpit of the Revolution*, 160-161.

[2]The two brigades left at Princeton consisted of the five Virginia regiments and Haslet's Delawares, about 1,200 men. Fitzpatrick, ed., *Writings of Washington*, VI: 331. Legend has it that Washington stood on the porch of the Olden House, just outside Princeton, to watch his little army march past on their way to Trenton. Boatner, *Landmarks of the Revolution*, 210. Fitzpatrick, ed., *Writings of Washington*, VI: 325.

[3]Fitzpatrick, ed., *Writings of Washington*, VI: 331. On Dec. 5, Washington wrote Congress that "as nothing but necessity obliged me to retire before the Enemy, and leave so much of the Jerseys unprotected, I conceive it to be my duty, and it corresponds with my Inclination, to make head against them, so soon as there shall be the least probability of doing it with propriety." *Ibid.*, 330. Washington also decided to post a strong rear guard at Princeton to protect General Lee's corps if Lee made an attempt to link up with Washington's army in New Jersey.

[4]Wendy Martin, ed., "The Itinerarium of Dr. Alexander Hamilton," in *Colonial American Travel Narratives* (New York: Penguin Books, 1994), 200. Hamilton toured from Annapolis, Maryland, to Portsmouth, New Hampshire, in the summer of 1744.

Washington neared Trenton at noon with his little army. He had heard nothing from Lee for days. Perhaps he hoped that he would find Lee in Trenton, standing in front of his seven thousand veterans and greeting his commander. How splendid it would be to see General Nixon's steady New England brigade, McDougall's combat-tested New Yorkers and General John Glover's 14th Regiment of tough Massachusetts fishermen. It would be a great reunion for the Continental army, and Washington finally could take some offensive action. Instead, in Trenton Washington only found another deserted village, this one on the very edge of New Jersey. But, as Washington entered Trenton from the north, a detachment of twenty-six dragoons moved in from the south. These were the 1st Troop of Philadelphia City Cavalry, the first reinforcements to reach Washington since he left Hackensack. Their commander, Captain Samuel Morris, reported his troop had left Philadelphia on December 1 and brought the heartening news that 1,500 Philadelphia Associators had been mobilized and were marching towards Trenton in order to reinforce Washington.[1]

The boats waiting at Trenton told Washington that Colonel Humpton had done his job well.[2] Washington ordered that they be loaded immediately with all the army's military stores and baggage for ferrying across the Delaware. It took three days of constant crossing and recrossing with every available boat to move everything. Fortunately the enemy had not stirred from New Brunswick, reported Stirling from the rear guard at Princeton. Additional reinforcements from Philadelphia were now trickling into Trenton--410 men,

---

[1]One of the volunteer privates in the 1st Troop was Benjamin Randolph, a master cabinet-maker. The commander-in-chief was happy to see him because the General's wife, Martha, had lived in Randolph's Chestnut Street boarding house for several months. Martha Washington had last seen her husband during the summer when George visited Philadelphia to meet with Congress. When he returned to New York, he left her in the care of the Randolphs. Martha went back to Mount Vernon soon after, but returned to Philadelphia later in the summer in the hopes of joining her husband in New York. The military situation made journeying beyond Philadelphia dangerous, and she remained with Randolph and his family through the late summer and fall of 1776 before returning for a second time to Mount Vernon.

[2]Colonel Humpton cleared the Delaware River and its tributaries of anything that could float in a radius of 40 miles from Trenton. He did the job with the help of the galleys of the Pennsylvania Navy and the Hunterdon County, New Jersey militia. See John W. Jackson, *The Pennsylvania Navy* (New Brunswick: Rutgers University Press, 1974), 74-76.

part of the recently recruited regiment of Pennsylvania and Maryland Germans commanded by Colonel Nicholas Haussegger.[1] The Philadelphia Associators, roused in part through General Mifflin's efforts, were still on the way.

The troops arriving at Trenton were welcome but they were inexperienced. What Washington wanted was Lee with his veterans. He was desperate for news when a post rider finally galloped into Trenton on December 3 with a dispatch from Lee. It was dated November 30 and written at Peekskill, New York. The letter began, "Dear General: I received yours last night, dated the 27th, from New-ark. You complain of my not being in motion sooner, I do assure you that I have done all in my power, and shall explain my difficulties when we have both leisure." Lee wrote that he would enter the Province of Jersey "with four thousand firm and willing troops, who will make a very important diversion. Had I stirred sooner, I should have only led an inferior number of unwilling."[2]

Lee promised to cross the Hudson "the day after tomorrow" (December 2). Intially, Washington was relieved. Finally, he thought, Lee was on the move toward the main part of the army. But Lee quickly dashed his commander's hopes. He closed his letter by asking that Washington "bind me as little as possible, not from any opinion, I do assure you, of my own

---

[1] On Nov. 25, the Continental Congress called out the Associators of Philadelphia and the surrounding counties to serve for six weeks. The Congress also directed that the German Battalion (commanded by Colonel Haussegger) was to march immediately. Worthington Ford, *et al.*, eds.., *Journals of the Continental Congress, 1774-1789* (Washington D.C.: Government Printing Office, 1904-1937).

[2] *The Lee Papers* (New York: New York Historical Society, 1873), II: 322. Heath recalled that Lee arrived at his headquarters on Nov. 30, en route to New Jersey., and asked for a cup of tea. Lee's second request was for 2,000 men from Heath's command to march with him to New Jersey. Heath refused. Lee reduced his request to 1,000 men. Heath again refused, stating that not a single man would march because Heath had positive written instructions from Washington not to remove any of his troops from the defense of the Hudson River. The argument continued, with Lee claiming he was Heath's superior and would detach two of Heath's regiments. But Lee left Peekskill the following morning without taking anyone from Heath's command and crossed the Hudson on Dec. 2 and 3. Heath thought that Lee's men were as good as any in the army, but noted that "many of them were so destitute of shoes, that the blood left on the rugged frozen ground, in many places, marked the route they had taken; and a considerable number, unable to march, were left at Peekskill." William Heath, *Memoirs of Major-General Heath* (Boston: I. Thomas and E.T. Andrews, 1798), 94-96.

parts, but from a persuasion that detached Generals cannot have too great latitude, unless they are very incompetent indeed."[1] Washington read Lee's letter in disbelief. The commander-in-chief did not want Lee operating independently, but to reinforce the Grand Army. Surely, Washington reasoned, Lee had misinterpreted his instructions, and he dashed off a letter that same day imploring Lee to come: "You will readily agree that I have sufficient cause for my anxiety, and to wish for your arrival as early as possible."[2] Greene saw the situation differently, and politely warned Washington about Lee in a letter dated December 7. He stated bluntly that he did not think that Lee could be trusted with discretionary orders: "I think General Lee must be confined within the Lines of some General Plan, or else his operations will be independant of yours."[3]

Lee now had to move. He had run out of excuses for inaction, and he feared that continued recalcitrance would provoke the Continental Congress; thus he prepared to move his division across the Hudson River and into the New Jersey theater of operations.[4] But Lee's immense ego would not let him put himself under Washington's command any longer. Lee had decided he was a better soldier than Washington, and determined to maintain a separate command as long as possible. He began crossing the Hudson at Peekskill on December 2 with about 2,500 men.[5] He kept up his new game in a letter to

---

[1]*Lee Papers*, II: 322.

[2]Fitzpatrick, ed., *Writings of Washington*, VI: 326.

[3]Showman, ed., *The Papers of General Nathanael Greene*, I: 366.

[4]Whatever his opinion of Washington, Lee had to maintain the good will of Congress if he wanted to replace Washington. Congress wanted to know Lee's situation, and on Dec. 2 directed Washington "to send Colonel Stewart, or any other officer express to General Lee, to know where and in what situation he and the army with him are." Ford, ed., *Journals of the Continental Congress*, VI: 1000. Washington admitted that he had lost touch with Lee, although he had tried to contact him. He feared that his letters had failed to get through. Fitzpatrick, ed., *Writings of Washington*, VI: 324-325. The "Colonel Stewart" mentioned by Congress was Lt. Colonel Walter Stewart, an' aide-de-camp to General Gates. Francis Heitman, *Historical Register of Officers of the Continental Army* (Washington D.C.: Rare Book Shop Publishing Company, 1914) , 520-521; Fitzpatrick, ed., *Writings of Washington*, VI: 325n.

[5]When Lee crossed the Hudson on Dec. 2, he commanded a force of between 2,500 and 3,000. This small number seems implausible given the 7,500 men in Lee's division in early November. However, the numbers are correct and show the serious

Washington from Haverstraw, New York, on December 4, stating that the retreat from New Brunswick made it impossible for him to know where to rejoin the main army. Instead, Lee wanted to add the troops from the Northern Army, which were nearing Morristown, to his own force. This would give him a total of 5,000 men to startle the enemy, "hanging on their flanks or rear."[1]

Washington sent personal emissaries to apprise Lee of his situation. The first was the dependable Humpton, whom he dispatched on December 5 to find Lee and report back concerning his strength, condition, and route of march. In addition, Washington told Humpton to find out about the eight regiments under General Gates, as well as the militia attached to General Williamson. Two days later, without waiting for news from Humpton, Washington sent Major Robert Hoops to find Lee. Hoops carried a letter telling Lee that he could safely cross the Delaware at Alexandria (modern Frenchtown, New Jersey). Washington had secretly ordered boats and troops to wait for Lee at this point on the river, far above the enemy's positions.[2]

Lee, however, advanced through New Jersey at the proverbial snail's pace. He seized horses and wagons along his route of march. On December 6, Lee's division was at the Ringwood Iron Works. On December 8, the main column marched through the village of Pompton and the following day they went through Hanover and stopped for the night at Parsippany. Lee's troops were advancing cautiously because there were rumors that 7,000 or 8,000

---

problems which the American cause faced in late 1776. On Nov. 17, Lee lost three Massachusetts militia regiments (2,000 men) when their enlistments expired. Richard Ketchum, *The Winter Soldiers* (Garden City, NY: Doubleday & Company, Inc., 1973), 162; *Lee Papers*, II: 288; Freeman, *George Washington*, IV: 254. The British had accurate information about the strength of Lee's corps, estimating that he had about 2,500 men; Kemble, *Journal*, I: 102. Lee's command consisted of the brigades of Colonels John Glover, Paul Sargent, and Daniel Hitchcock. Hitchcock commanded a consolidated "New England Brigade" composed of units from Rhode Island, Massachusetts, and New Hampshire. Hitchcock, a Rhode Islander, was in the last stages of consumption, but insisted upon marching with Lee. He died at Morristown on Jan. 13, 1777. Herbert Wade and Robert Lively, *This Glorious Cause* (Princeton: Princeton University Press, 1958), 92-93. Desertions and sickness drastically reduced Lee's numbers further from mid-November, when he reported 5,589 fit for duty, plus 60 light horse and some artillery. Force, ed., *American Archives*, Series Five, III: 831-832.

[1]*Lee Papers*, II: 329-330.

[2]Fitzpatrick, ed., *Writings of George Washington*, VI: 329, 335-336; *Lee Papers*, II: 336-338. For information about the gathering of boats to take Lee's corps across the Delaware River, see Fitzpatrick, ed., *Writings of Washington*, VI: 337, 341.

Hessians and Tories had marched from New Brunswick to intercept them. Lee and his suite advanced ahead of his main column. He stopped at Morristown on December 8 and reached the village of Chatham, a few miles east of Morristown, later that day. He remained at Chatham to await his corps, which arrived on December 10.[1]

It was at Morristown on December 8 that Humpton, Washington's first emissary, found Lee. Although Humpton was sent to gather information, he also was to encourage Lee to quickly move to join Washington on the Delaware. Lee sent Humpton back to Washington with a letter stating that 1,000 New Jersey militia were expected to join his own corps of 2,700 at Morristown. Still secretly determined to maintain his independent command, Lee found reasons to remain in northern New Jersey. "If I was not taught to think that your army was considerably reinforced," he wrote, "I should immediately join you; but as I am assured you are very strong, I should imagine we can make a better impression by hanging on their rear." Lee said he would use Chatham as his base of operations. "It is at a happy distance from Newark, Elizabethtown, Woodbridge, and Boundbrook."[2]

Having sent Humpton off with this disingenuous missive, Lee moved his corps east from Morristown to Chatham on December 8 to get closer to the enemy while still having the protection of the rugged terrain of Morris County. Chatham was the gateway to Morris County. It sat on the west bank of the Passaic River, a strategic location, and astride an important road that ran from Elizabethtown to Morristown. Chatham had a bridge over the Passaic, which was fordable at only a few places as it snaked through central New Jersey. Lee probably made Day's Tavern his headquarters.[3] On the afternoon of December 8, Major Hoops arrived in the village. Responding to Hoops' dispatch, which reiterated Washington's pleas for Lee to hurry to the Delaware, Lee remained evasive. "I cannot persuade myself that Philadelphia is their

---

[1]Hay to Heath, Dec. 15, 1776, in Force, ed., *American Archives*, Fifth Series, III: 1236. Lee to Colonel Chester, Dec. 7, 1776, in Henry Johnson, *The Campaign of 1776 Around New York and Brooklyn* (Brooklyn: The Long Island Historical Society, 1878), 145. Louise Rau, ed., "Sergeant John Smith's Diary of 1776," *Mississippi Valley Historical Review*, 20: 263.

[2]Lee to Washington, Dec. 8, 1776, *Lee Papers*, II: 337.

[3]Donald White, *A Village at War* (Rutherford. NJ: Fairleigh Dickinson University Press, 1979), 73. Day's tavern was ideally located by the main road and the bridge; it soon after appeared on an American army map.

object at present," he wrote the commander-in-chief, adding that "it will be difficult, I am afraid, to join you; but cannot I do you more service by attacking their rear? I shall look about me tomorrow, and inform you further."[1]

This communication hardly reassured Washington of Lee's intentions, and dispatches between the two generals now flew back and forth at a frantic pace. Humpton returned to Washington's Delaware River headquarters on the night of December 9 with Lee's letter, and Washington shot back another reply the following day. The general almost begged Lee to move: "I cannot but request and entreat you and this too, by the advice of all the Genl. Officers with me, to march and join me with all your whole force, with all possible expedition."[2] On December 11, a worried and perplexed Washington wrote again. He wanted Lee to come on with all speed and warned "that Philadelphia, beyond all question," was the British objective. Loss of the *de facto* captial city, he was sure, would have "fatal consequences" for the embattled rebel cause.[3] (The recalcitrant Lee probably never got the chance to read this letter, but that comes later in the story.)

Yet Washington did much more in his first days at Trenton than try to communicate with the elusive Lee. From the moment the Continental commander reached Trenton, he knew that ultimately he would have to deal with the British on or near the Delaware. Thus he busily shipped his supplies across the Delaware and counted his reinforcements. He used every minute, while Cornwallis sat motionless with his impressive army in New Brunswick. Washington and his officers were baffled by the British army's inertia; the only explanation Washington could offer was the heavy rain.[4] Whatever the reason, the patriot general was glad of the respite.

At New Brunswick, Loyalists were arriving with reports that

---

[1]*Lee Papers*, II: 337.

[2]Washington to Lee, Dec. 10, 1776, Fitzpatrick, ed., *Writings of George Washington*, VI: 341-342. It is surprising that Washington never gave Lee a direct order to bring his corps to Pennsylvania. The commander-in-chief may have doubted himself after the loss of Fort Washington, or he may have wanted to avoid an open controversy within the officer corps in order to discourage any intervention by Congress. Certainly Washington never forcefully complained to Congress about Lee's dilatory march; e.g., Fitzpatrick, ed., *Writings of George Washington*, VI: 336.

[3]Fitzpatrick, ed., *Writings of Washington*, IV: 348.

[4]Washington to the President of Congress, Dec. 4, 1776, Force, ed., *American Archives*, Fifth Series, III: 1070.

Washington's army was in wretched shape. Cornwallis knew that an assault now would destroy or scatter Washington's army and open the road to Philadelphia, but Howe's orders pinned him at the Raritan River.[1] Cornwallis raced an aide back to Howe's headquarters in New York to seek permission to press the pursuit.[2] Howe replied that he would come to New Brunswick and make a decision on the spot. However, Howe and his older brother, Admiral Lord Richard Howe, were preparing a different kind of assault, which they hoped would end the American rebellion; Cornwallis would have to wait.

In accepting command of British forces in America, the Howe brothers also were named "the King's Commissioners for restoring peace to his Majesty's Colonies and Plantations in North America." They took this role seriously, and already had made several peace overtures to the Americans, notably a meeting with a delegation from the Continental Congress after their thrashing of Washington's army on Long Island in August, 1776. The Howes chose their moments well for conciliatory gestures.

On November 30, with British forces advancing unchecked across New Jersey and Washington's army seemingly in ruins, the Howes felt the time was right for another peace initiative. They announced a decision to offer a pardon to "all persons whatsoever, who are assembled together in arms against his Majesty's government, to disband themselves, and return to their dwellings, there to remain in a peaceable and quiet manner." The offer was comprehensive, and extended to rebels active in government and politics, including those in Congress. Anyone who appeared within sixty days before a representative of the British government, including a military officer, could receive a pardon by signing an oath of allegiance. They would then be free to go about their business. In the view of the Howes, the offer was not only

---

[1] A Parliamentary inquiry later asked Cornwallis if Howe had ordered him to halt at New Brunswick. "I understood it to be the General's directions," Cornwallis responded, "that I should halt at Brunswick, but had I seen that I could have struck a material stroke, by moving forward, I certainly should have taken it upon me to have done it." Cornwallis also claimed, rather improbably, that his men were worn out from their march and in no real condition to strike a quick blow at Washington. In part, he may have been covering for Howe, whose conduct of the New Jersey campaign had come in for serious criticism. Troyer Steele Anderson, *The Command of the Howe Brothers During the American Revolution* (New York: Oxford University Press, 1936), 201-203. Cornwallis would have pushed on against Washington immediately if he had not been ordered by Howe to halt at the Raritan River.

[2] Thomas Fleming, *1776, Year of Illusions* (New York: W.W. Norton & Company, Inc., 1975), 419-420.

politic, but generous, coming as it did in the wake of the dramatic British successes in the field.[1]

An immediate taker was Joseph Galloway (1731-1803). Galloway was a leading lawyer, former speaker of the Pennsylvania Assembly and a confidant of Benjamin Franklin. Prior to the Revolution, Galloway and Franklin had shared a vision of an imperial union between America and England. But, once the war began, Franklin abandoned the idea and warmed to the rebel cause. Not Galloway, who remained adamant in his beliefs. He was particularly unhappy with the democratic constitution that Pennsylvania adopted in September, 1776. Galloway became an outcast and sought refuge in his country home, Trevose. By late 1776 he was convinced that the rebellion would collapse. Galloway also feared for his life, left his wife to guard their home, and headed for the British army in New Jersey. He got to New Brunswick with a wagon-load of belongings and several British sympathizers from his neighborhood and swore an oath of loyalty to the King. Galloway was an important rebel defector, but he would quickly prove to be a nuisance to General Howe.[2]

Meanwhile, American spies drifted in and out of New Brunswick in early December, reporting back to Stirling at Princeton that the town was full of British troops. One spy reported that every house in New Brunswick was full of redcoats. He was told that the Hessians were at Bound Brook. Spy Abram Sleight reported about 8,000 enemy troops in and near New Brunswick and another 20,000 between New Brunswick and Elizabethtown. Sleight saw only two field pieces, but other spies saw more cannon across the Raritan in Piscataway. One told Betty Miller that an additional 8,000 British reinforcements were en route to Cornwallis, and the officers talked of winter quarters in Philadelphia.[3] On the morning of December 5, General Howe unexpectedly sailed from New York City to New Jersey. He landed at Elizabethtown Point, where he inspected the fortifications the Americans had built, then continued on to Perth Amboy, distributing copies of his proclamation along the way.

---

[1]Force, ed., *American Archives*, Fifth Series, III: 927-928. According to General Howe, more than 2,700 New Jersey men took the oath during the winter of 1776-1777. Lundin, *Cockpit of the Revolution*, 159.

[2]John Ferling, *The Loyalist Mind, Joseph Galloway and the American Revolution* (University Park: The Pennsylvania State University Press, 1977), 37.

[3]Force, ed., *American Archives*, Fifth Series, III: 892.

Howe cut an impressive figure as he rode through central New Jersey with his entourage. As a privileged aristocrat and commander-in-chief, he had a great many people with him. Howe was dressed for the field in a scarlet, gold-laced uniform coat. A falling collar of dark-blue velvet, and buttonholes set in threes, indicated his rank. Riding with him were his two most important administrators: his adjutant and his quartermaster-general, both in silver epaulets, laced buttonholes set in threes, and crimson waistsashes. Riding close by were Howe's aides-de-camp, representatives who carried out innumerable military and personal duties for the general, including carrying important dispatches and other privileged information. They sported red coats with blue facings, silver embroidery and two gold epaulets.[1]

One of Howe's aides at this time was a young German aristocrat, Captain Levin Friedrich Ernst von Muenchhausen of the Hesse-Kassel Leib Regiment. Von Muenchhausen was fluent in German, French and English. This was essential: Howe spoke only English, and General Leopold Philipp, Freiherr von Heister, commander of the Hesse Kassel forces in America, spoke only German and French. Von Muenchhausen translated British orders into German. He rode at Howe's side through the 1776 campaign.[2] Howe probably had his chief of artillery with him, General Samuel Cleaveland, and one or more engineers whose training as mapmakers was valuable at headquarters. As commander-in-chief, Howe also had at least one military secretary assigned to travel with him (possibly a civilian) who would be privy to everything at headquarters and attend high-level meetings. A military secretary would translate Howe's decisions into orders and draft important correspondence. The general's entourage also would have featured a cook and several servants to attend to his feeding, clothing and other personal needs.

Although the area around Elizabethtown and Perth Amboy was held by the British army, there were still the dangers of rebel skirmishers or, so the British still thought, a surprise attack from Lee's corps. Howe would have had guards, possibly elite Hessian grenadiers, in whom he had great confidence.

---

[1]Charles Lefferts, *Uniforms of the American, British, French, and German Armies* (New York: New York Historical Society, 1926), 148; and Philip Katcher, *Armies of the American Wars* (New York: Hastings House, 1975), 51; John Mollo and Malcolm McGregor, *Uniforms of the American Revolution* (New York: Blandford Press Ltd., 1975), 155.

[2]Ernst Kipping, trans., and Samuel Steele Smith, ed., *At General Howe's Side, 1776-1778* (Monmouth Beach, N.J.: Philip Freneau Press, 1974).

Included in Howe's group of personal bodyguards were probably members of the 16th Light Dragoons.[1] These mounted troops were distinctively dressed and equipped, with white breeches and red coats faced with blue. Their black-painted metal caps bore an elegant red horsehair crest, falling almost to the shoulder. The front plate of their caps bore a ribbon and cipher designating them as "The Queen's Light Dragoons." They were well-armed with a carbine, a pair of pistols in holsters on their saddles, and a sabre. Howe and his military family were on horses or in carriages, but moved along slowly to stay with the infantry assigned to protect them. Armies of the time tended to move slowly anyway because of their cumbersome supply wagons and artillery. Because he was on horseback, Howe could stop for a fine lunch, for example, while the infantry marched. He would catch up later.

Howe spent the night at Perth Amboy as the guest of General Grant, who commanded there. It was a comfortable evening. Grant's house was the largest and best in town, the Governor's Mansion. Perth Amboy sat on a neck of land that faced into New York Bay, and its port had once made it the commercial rival of New York. It was a particularly scenic place. When he first viewed it, William Penn supposedly exclaimed, "I have never seen such before in my life," and another traveler said that Perth Amboy had the best oysters in America. The next morning, Howe left Perth Amboy at 9:00 a.m. for New Brunswick; he took General Grant's 4th Brigade with him and left one regiment behind to guard the town.[2]

Howe and his column passed through a charming landscape, high in places but with valleys, all well-cultivated. The hills afforded views of houses, farms, gardens, cornfields, forests, lakes, islands, roads and pastures in central New Jersey. The weather for the last few days had turned surprisingly warm

---

[1]Kipping and Smith, eds., *At Howe's Side*, 8. On December 26, Captain Friedrich von Muenchhausen noted in his diary that he commanded 20 dragoons, "and deployed them all around the General, about a quarter of an hour's march from him, to search out any harm that might befall him." The light dragoons were the elite cavalry of the time. They prided themselves on their horsemanship and weapons handling. The 16th Light Dragoons, "The Queen's Own," were part of the Crown forces advancing across New Jersey in late 1776.

[2]Benson Lossing, *The Pictorial Field-Book of the Revolution* (New York: Harper & Brothers, 1855), II: 10. Alexander Hamilton, "Itinerarium," in Wendy Martin, ed., *Colonial American Travel Narratives* (New York: Penguin Books, 1994), 204. Grant's 4th Brigade consisted of the 17th, 46th, 55th and 40th regiments.

for early December, which must have added to Cornwallis' frustration as he awaited Howe's arrival in New Brunswick.[1]

At mid-day on December 6, Howe finally arrived in New Brunswick and immediately ordered Cornwallis to advance further into New Jersey. Why, after almost a week of inactivity, had Howe now authorized an advance beyond the Raritan River? Again, Howe had limited goals when he invaded New Jersey: foremost was to take Fort Lee and clear the lower Hudson of rebel fortifications; secondly, he needed New Jersey to provide winter quarters for a portion of his army. Howe had seemed content to halt his offensive at New Brunswick, having conquered much more of New Jersey than he could have hoped when the attack on Fort Lee began.[2] But he changed his mind when all news from New Jersey showed that an advance beyond New Brunswick might disperse the Grand Army and push on to Philadelphia.

In New York, Howe heard that three to four hundred people were coming into New Brunswick each day to take the oath of allegiance.[3] From New Brunswick, Captain Ewald wrote in his diary that "Several distinguished persons arrived from Pennsylvania, who implored the general [Cornwallis] to press General Washington as closely as possible." Such a course, they insisted, would bring the rebels to bay somewhere "in the vicinity of the Delaware, by which his retreat would be cut off. There we could surely destroy or capture his disheartened army." Tempers, Ewald noted, were frayed. One of the civilians, Joseph Galloway, the Hessian reported, was "so enraged over the delay of the English that he exclaimed, 'I see, they don't want to finish the war!'"[4] British spies intercepted a letter from Washington to the Board of War sometime after the Royal army invaded New Jersey, confirming the sorry state of the rebel Grand Army. The stolen letter revealed when the

---

[1]Kalm, *Travels Into North America*, 122; Serle, *Journal*, 155.

[2]*Diary of Frederick Mackenzie*, I: 113; Force, ed., *American Archives*, Fifth Series, III: 926, 1316.

[3]Freeman, *George Washington*, IV: 276n.

[4]Ewald, *Diary of the American War*, 25.

service of all the American troops would expire, and conveyed Washington's apprehensions that the men would not reenlist.[1]

Having taken his time to decide to advance beyond New Brunswick, Howe now moved quickly. He ordered von Donop's Corps and Jaegers to Bound Brook, which lay a few miles further up the Raritan River. Reports told of the rebels taking a strong position on a hill beyond the village, where they also had destroyed a bridge over the Raritan.[2] About 4:00 p.m., Howe advanced his army towards Princeton in two columns. Cornwallis commanded the column on the right, consisting of the Jaegers, Hessian grenadiers, the 42nd Regiment of Scottish Highlanders, and two troops of the 16th Regiment of Light Dragoons. It marched up the south branch of the Raritan to Van Veghten Bridge (in modern Finderne), where it bivouacked for the night. The column on the left, which consisted of the British infantry under General Leslie, made even less progress. They crossed the Raritan at Landing Bridge and bivouacked on the high ground near New Brunswick. Howe dined that evening with Cornwallis.[3]

The advance resumed the next morning. General Howe was with the British infantry on the Upper Road, in the vanguard, which dictated a slow advance because rebel skirmishers prowled the small woods and dense thickets. Howe's column moved steadily in a train with two battalions of light

---

[1]This incident is included in a report from the Committee of Foreign Affairs to the American representatives in France. The report, Dec. 21, 1776, noted that "about this time General Howe became possessed of a letter (by the agency of some wicked person, who contrived to get it from the express) written by General Washington to the Board of War, in which he had given an exact account when the time of service of all our battalions would expire, and his apprehensions that the men would not reenlist without first going home to see their families and friends." Force, ed., *American Archives*, Fifth Series, III: 1326. British spies also managed to steal other letters carried by Army express riders. Serle, *Journal*, 137.

[2]Robertson, *His Diaries and Sketches in America* (New York: New York Public Library, 1930), 115. Carl Emil Kurt von Donop (1740-1777) was a commander of grenadiers and Jaegers. Letter K, Lidgerwood Collection, 43. The hills to which the journal refers probably are the Watchung Mountains, which rise behind Bound Brook.

[3]Ewald, *Diary of the American War*, 25. Ewald's reference to Jaegers and Hessian grenadiers was probably to von Donop's corps, which had advanced to Bound Brook in advance of the Cornwallis column. Kipping and Smith, eds., *At Howe's Side*, 6.

infantry, two battalions of grenadiers, one hundred fifty mounted light dragoons and eight three-pounders marching in battle order.[1]

The pretty countryside was mostly flat. Near almost every farm was a spacious orchard of apple and peach trees. Cherry trees abounded along the road. But the British and Hessian soldiers were too concerned about their safety to enjoy the scenery.[2] Despite their caution, several British scouts were surrounded and killed by rebels in a thicket. Afterward, well over a hundred rebels were seen running away, but the pursuing Crown forces could not catch them. The rebels who harried the British advance probably were detachments from Stirling's two brigades left behind at Princeton.

Early in the morning, a British reconnaissance team commanded by General Erskine left Cornwallis' camp in the direction of Morristown to collect information on the whereabouts of Lee and his corps.[3] The two main British columns continued towards Princeton on their separate routes amid fences and farmhouses, orchards and wheatfields.[4] By this time, Washington had all his army's baggage safely across the Delaware and all the boats standing by on the river at Trenton. With everything ready for a retreat across the Delaware to Pennsylvania, and with no sign that the enemy was stirring at New Brunswick, Washington decided to march back towards Princeton with 1,200 men. Greene preceded Washington and arrived at Princeton on the afternoon of December 6 to assume command of Stirling's brigade. But Greene quickly learned that the British were advancing towards Princeton, and he sent Washington an express to this effect on December 7. When Washington

---

[1]Kipping & Smith, eds., *At Howe's Side*, 6.

[2]This description of the land between Trenton and New Brunswick is from Kalm, *Travels in North America*, 118.

[3]Ewald, *Diary of the American War*, 26-27. According to Ewald, Erskine took the Jaegers, a detachment of Scots and a hundred mounted troops; clearly Erskine considered Lee to be a dangerous enemy.

[4]Most accounts of Howe's advance towards Princeton mention two columns of troops. The exception is the diary of Archibald Robertson, who says there were three columns. Robertson was an army engineer. On Dec. 7, he noted a "Right Column consisting of Donops Corps march'd along the North West Side of the Millstone River By Hillsborough [today's Millstone] and Schencks Bridge, where we were joined by the Centre Column under General Grant consisting of the 4th Brigade. The Reserve and Guards with the General kept the highway." Robertson, *Diaries and Sketches in America*, 115.

received Greene's message, he immediately turned his troops back towards the Delaware.[1]

Howe's troops occupied a nearly deserted Princeton on the evening of December 7. His Hessian aide-de-camp, von Muenchhausen, admired the College of New Jersey. "Its main building," he wrote, "has 36 windows on its length and 24 on its width, and is four stories high. A remarkably excellent library has till now been spared by the war."[2] Howe posted his two Jaeger companies in the woods facing Trenton to prevent a surprise attack.

Stirling's rebel brigade had evacuated Princeton earlier in the day. To slow any pursuit, his troops tore apart the wooden bridge across Stony Brook, a stream a few miles south of the village. As they retreated towards Trenton, the troops skirmished with some of the British advance guards, killing at least one light dragoon. Stirling's brigade arrived at Trenton that night and started crossing the Delaware. However, some of his men must have stayed behind because Ewald wrote in his diary that rebels roamed around Princeton all night, and sporadic fighting continued.[3]

In Princeton, British and Hessian soldiers and their women plundered every building. A big, new house owned by patriot Jonathan Dickinson Sergeant mysteriously burned to the ground that night. Morven, Richard Stockton's magnificent home, was ransacked of everything of value, from furniture and clothing to cattle, horses, hogs, sheep, and grain. The college did not escape either. Valuable books from the library were stolen to be sold later, or thrown into blazing fires to warm the invaders.[4] The lone survivor of the

---

[1]Historian Samuel Smith commented that Washington ordered an immediate retreat back to Trenton when he learned that the enemy was advancing by different roads. Washington thought this might be an attempt by the enemy to get in the rear of his troops at Princeton. *The Battle of Trenton*, (Monmouth Beach, N.J.: Philip Freneau Press, 1965), 6.

[2]Quoted in Smith, *Battle of Trenton,* 6. The college building to which von Muenchhausen refers was Nassau Hall, although his window count was wrong.

[3]Varnum Lansing Collins, *A Brief Narrative of the Ravages of the British and Hessians* (Princeton: The University Library, 1906), 3; Ewald, *Diary of the American War*, 27.

[4]The present site of Sergeant's house is 6 Mercer Street; it was the only Princeton house burned during the Revolution. Boatner, *Landmarks of the American Revolution*, 209. Thomas Wertenbaker, *Princeton 1746-1896* (Princeton: Princeton University Press, 1946), 59. British and Hessian soldiers had plundered libraries in New York City as well;

pillaging at Nassau Hall was the orrery, a complicated scientific instrument built by David Rittenhouse to show the movements and positions of bodies in the solar system. The British intended to ship it back to England. The orrery, an apparatus of balls moved by wheelwork, was a sensation. John Adams saw it during a pre-war tour of the college and recalled that "It exhibits almost every motion in the Astronomical world: the motions of the sun and all the planets, with all their satellites, the eclipses of the moon, sun, &c."[1]

A regiment of soldiers crowded into Nassau Hall and slept in the classrooms, Prayer Hall, and the students' chambers. The basement became a stable. Nassau Hall also was turned into a temporary prison by the British; anyone suspected of being a rebel, or of aiding the rebels, was dragged off to confinement in the college building.[2]

As the Crown forces sacked Princeton, Washington's army was back at Trenton and hurriedly crossing the Delaware. By Sunday morning, December 8, Washington's entire army had been safely transported across the river. Washington had his troops tear down bridges on the New Jersey roads paralleling the Delaware, and every ferry crossing on the Pennsylvania side of the river was guarded.[3]

Among the Philadelphia Associators activated to join Washington at Trenton was a company of eighty-one men. Its second-in-command was a fragile-looking lieutenant named Charles Willson Peale. Peale was an unusual soldier: he was one of America's first professional artists. He studied in London and returned to America to pursue a career as a portrait painter. His clientele was exclusive; in 1772, he painted the earliest known portrait of Washington at Mount Vernon. Peale's militia company departed Philadelphia on the evening of December 5, moving up the Delaware by sailboat. The

---

see Jones, *History of New York During the Revolutionary War*, I: 136.

[1]Mark Boatner, *Landmarks of the American Revolution* (Harrisburg: Stackpole Books, 1973) 208. The Marquis de Chastellux saw the orrery when he visited the college later in the war; it was still a "very beautiful astronomical machine," but not working. Marquis de Chastellux, *Travels in North America* (London, 1787), I: 162-163. A second Rittenhouse orrery was housed at the University of Pennsylvania. The orrery was invented by an English scientific instrument maker named George Graham (1671-1751), who named his invention in honor of his patron, Charles Boyle, 4th Earl of Orrery. Silvio A. Bedini, *Thomas Jefferson: Statesman of Science* (New York: Macmillan Publishing, 1990), 114.

[2]Wertenbaker, *Princeton 1746-1896*, 59.

[3]Marshall, *Life of Washington*, II: 603.

troops linked up with other patriots in Trenton on the afternoon of the 7th, and expected duty in or around the town.[1] But shortly after arriving, they were ordered to join Washington in Pennsylvania. Peale watched the army crossing the Delaware late into the night of December 7. The entire army crossed that night, and the operation, he wrote, "made a grand but dreadful appearance. All the shores were lighted up with large fires," and the boats were jammed with men, equipment, weapons, and horses. "The Hollowing [howling] of hundreds of men in their difficulties of getting Horses and artilery out of the boats, made it rather the appearance of Hell than any earthly scene."[2] As "the sick and half-naked veterans of the long retreat streamed past," Peale thought he saw a familiar face. He looked closely at a ragged and debilitated man wrapped only in an old, dirty blanket. Shocked, Peale recognized his younger brother, James, who had been with Washington since the New York campaign.[3]

General Howe resumed his leisurely advance from Princeton towards the Delaware River the following morning. His vanguard reached the outskirts of Trenton at 2:00 p.m. on December 8.[4] They found Trenton a pleasant town, just off the river on a sandy plain. The houses were mostly two stories high and widely separated, giving Trenton a long, narrow appearance. Most homes had a garden, a well, and a cellar; and while some were stone, most were constructed of wooden planks.[5] Trenton was a busy place before the war. There were some local merchants, but it was mainly a transfer point for goods going between Philadelphia and New York City. Goods arrived at Trenton by boat from Philadelphia, then were loaded onto wagons to complete their

---

[1]Horace Wells Sellers, "Charles Willson Peale, Artist-Soldier," *The Pennsylvania Magazine of History and Biography*, 38 (1914): 271.

[2]Charles Willson Peale, Autobiography, undated manuscript, American Philosophical Society, Philadelphia.

[3]Kenneth Silverman, *A Cultural History of the American Revolution* (New York: Thomas Y. Crowell Company, 1976), 327; Blanco, *American Revolution Encyclopedia*, II: 1284; Charles Sellers, *Charles Willson Peale, Early Life* (Philadelphia: The American Philosophical Society, 1947), 140-141.

[4]Historian Henry Carrington commented on the slow advance of the Crown forces from New Brunswick to Trenton. Carrington calculated that Cornwallis delayed 17 hours at Princeton and took an entire day to march the 12 miles between Princeton and Trenton. Carrington, *Battles of the American Revolution*, 257-258.

[5]Kalm, *Travels in North America*, 117.

journey east. The process was reversed for goods bound from New York to Philadelphia. Travelers had the choice of going between Philadelphia and Trenton by boat on the Delaware, or making the complete Philadelphia-New York City trip by stage wagon or coach. There were two busy ferries. One, located about a mile south of town, was the Old Trenton Ferry, or Trent's Ferry, established in 1726. The second, in operation since 1773, lay a half-mile farther downstream and was known as the New Trenton Ferry. Inns and taverns were plentiful, and included the popular Eagle Tavern.

But Trenton was almost deserted when the Royal army arrived there on the afternoon of December 8. As the troops reached the outskirts of the town, von Muenchhausen recalled, "some inhabitant came running toward us, urging us to march through the town in a hurry so we could capture many of the enemy" who were still crossing the Delaware. But Howe suspected that Washington had artillery on the opposite shore, and did not want to move his main body into range. Instead, he sent only some light troops toward the river. Howe, Cornwallis, and some staff officers accompanied these men, and as they reached open ground near the Delaware, they came under heavy fire. Waiting rebel gunners "opened a terrific fire upon us with all their batteries," von Muenchhausen wrote, and "the light infantry and jaegers were forced to retreat in the greatest hurry to the valley at the left. On their way, in the blink of any eye, they lost 13 men."[1] Washington, the old Indian fighter, had not forgotten how to bait his enemies into an ambush.

While the Crown forces occupied Trenton, Washington deployed his meager force on the Pennsylvania side of the Delaware River, careful to stay away from the riverfront. On December 12 and 13, he divided a seventy-mile riverfront into command sections and spread his forces. Four brigades (Stirling, Mercer, Stephens and de Fermoy) were to guard the Delaware River from Yardley's Ferry (now Yardley, Pennsylvania) to Coryell's Ferry (modern New Hope, Pennsylvania). Individual units were posted within supporting distances.[2] Extending south from Yardley's Ferry to the ferry opposite Bordentown, New Jersey, were the remnants of the Pennsylvania Flying Camp, commanded by Ewing, and some New Jersey militiamen under General Dickinson.

Below them, more Pennsylvania militia extended the line farther south. Their commanding officer was Colonel John Cadwalader, an influential

---

[1]Kipping and Smith, eds., *At Howe's Side*, 6.

[2]Fitzpatrick, ed., *Writings of Washington*, VI: 364.

and active Philadelphia patriot. Cadwalader had established his headquarters at Bristol and his troops occupied positions as far down river as Dunk's Ferry (now Beverly, New Jersey).[1] The third battalion of Philadelphia Associators, under Colonel Nixon, guarded Dunk's Ferry, while galleys of the Pennsylvania Navy patrolled the river. Artillery was apportioned among the brigades, and small redoubts were thrown up at all possible fords. The troops had three days' rations, and every unit was assigned a rendezvous in case the enemy made a successful attack across the river.[2]

Washington's troops were in deplorable shape, and conditions were miserable for the men on the lines. "This night we lay amongst the leaves without tents or blankets, laying down with our feet to the fire," one veteran recalled. "It was very cold. We had meat, but no bread. We had nothing to cook with, but our ramrods, which we run through a piece of meat and roasted it over the fire, and to hungry soldiers, it tasted sweet. The next day we moved up the Delaware. In this way we lived, crouching among the bushes."[3] Times were hard, but the army remained operational.

At Trenton, General Howe was told there were boats at Coryell's Ferry, about fifteen miles up the Delaware. Howe wanted the boats, and ordered Cornwallis to take four regiments halted at Maidenhead (present day Lawrenceville, New Jersey) to go after them. At 1:00 a.m. on December 9, Cornwallis left Maidenhead with the Reserve and the 2nd Battalion of Light Infantry.[4] They passed through the small village of Penny Town (today's

---

[1]One hundred thirty United States Marines were attached to Cadwalader's command and helped to defend the western bank of the Delaware. They were part of four companies of Marines organized in mid-1776 in Philadelphia. There is no evidence that Marines participated earlier in the New Jersey campaign.

[2]Fitzpatrick, ed., *Writings of Washington*, VI: 360-364; Marshall, *Life of Washington*, II: 605; Henry Carrington, *Battles of the American Revolution* (New York: A.S. Barnes & Company, 1877), 264-265.

[3]"Personal Recollection of Captain Enoch Anderson," *Papers of the Historical Society of Delaware*, 16 (1896): 28.

[4]This ferry was also referred to as Corriell's Ferry; it ran between modern Lambertville, New Jersey, and New Hope, Pennsylvania. Sir William Howe to Lord George Germain, Force ed., *American Archives*, Fifth Series, III: 1316-1317. Some sources refer to four regiments being at Maidenhead; others specify that the Reserve and the 2nd Battalion of Light Infantry were there. The references probably confirm each other. The Battalion of Light Infantry equalled roughly one regiment and the Reserve was three

Pennington) and arrived at Coryell's Ferry to find that the rebels had removed or destroyed all the boats in the area. He also found rebel troops behind makeshift fortifications on the Pennsylvania side of the crossing. Taking no further action, Cornwallis returned to Penny Town at 2:00 p.m. that afternoon and bivouacked there.[1] Howe sent additional scouting parties up and down the river, but made no serious attempt to cross the Delaware.

Yet the British commander could have pursued Washington across the Delaware if he had wanted to. Galloway, the Pennsylvania Loyalist with Howe, noted 48,000 feet of boards at Trenton.[2] There were also John Rickey's hardware store and two blacksmith shops in Trenton, from which the British could have procured all the nails and iron necessary to build boats. Failing all else, the invaders could have torn down some of Trenton's one hundred wooden houses for lumber. But nothing was done to construct boats or rafts at Trenton. The British also had the equipment and engineers to quickly bring boats from New York City or New Brunswick to cross the Delaware or use their boats to build a pontoon bridge.

But Howe simply had no intentions of going beyond Trenton. The lack of boats was only later used as an excuse for failure. When Howe reached Trenton, he already had advanced much further into New Jersey than originally planned. In his view, the obstacle of the Delaware River and the approaching winter season were sufficient reasons to order an end to the offensive. Besides, the end of the war seemed almost at hand. On December 13, Howe announced that he was through campaigning for the season. He rode back to New Brunswick on the evening of the 15th and set out for New York on the 16th. It is only in retrospect that not pushing into Pennsylvania stands out as a mistake.

Howe left behind several winter cantonments in New Jersey. Two of the garrisons were placed at Bordentown and Trenton along the banks of the Delaware, eight miles apart. The posts (of greatest honor because they were closest to the enemy) were put under the command of von Donop. Fifteen hundred Hessians would winter at Bordentown under von Donop's immediate

---

regiments.

[1]Washington sent the 400-man regiment of Pennsylvania and Maryland Germans under Col. Nicholas Haussegger to Coryell's Ferry to check any attempt by the British to cross. On Cornwallis' march, see Robertson, *His Diaries and Sketches in America*, 116.

[2]Galloway cited in Stryker, *Battles of Trenton and Princeton*, 37.

command, and fourteen hundred others would stay at Trenton under Colonel Rall. The balance of the "chain of posts" in New Jersey were at Princeton, New Brunswick, Perth Amboy and Elizabethtown. Overall command in New Jersey fell to the tough and capable General James Grant, based at New Brunswick.[1] Howe returned to New York and settled in for the winter with his beautiful mistress and the good company of his fellow officers. A season of theater was already being planned by the talented young Major John Andre.

Rall was given the honor of commanding at Trenton, the most exposed point to the enemy, as a reward for his courage in the assault on Fort Washington. Rall was a good combat leader, but never should have been given command of the brigade assigned to winter at Trenton. His garrison was dangerously isolated, facing rebels across the river with no reinforcements nearby. Rall disdained the rebels. When a subordinate officer asked Rall's permission to erect redoubts to defend the town, he roared, "Lasst sie nur kommen! Keine Schanzen! Mit dem Bajonet wollen wir an sie!" ("Let them come! We want no trenches! We'll at them with the bayonet!")[2] Brave words, but foolish.

Howe adopted a dangerous scheme when he placed his troops in scattered cantonments. It left the individual garrisons isolated and open to rebel assault. But Howe felt he had no choice in the matter. Supplies were short, and spacing out his garrisons would enable the various detachments to live off the countryside.

There was also the question of manpower. The British lacked the strength to augment the size of the garrisons or to increase the number of posts, either of which would have made the entire chain more secure. This was Howe's fault. On November 27, only days after Cornwallis overran Fort Lee, Howe had dispatched some seven thousand troops to invade Rhode Island. The operation, mounted to secure the harbor of Newport for the fleet, succeeded. Howe thought that he could spare the detachment; but many other British officers questioned its wisdom. General Sir Henry Clinton was one of them. Clinton, who commanded the Rhode Island expedition, pointed out that

---

[1]Grant replaced Cornwallis, who had requested leave to winter in England. Grant was one of six general officers serving in America who were members of Parliament. He was famous for a speech he made in the House of Commons in February 1775, proclaiming "that the Americans could not fight, and that he would undertake to march from one end of the continent to the other with five thousand men." Quoted in Stryker, *Battles of Trenton and Princeton*, 48.

[2]*Ibid.*, 107.

a landing at Perth Amboy in late November, in support of a continuing advance by Cornwallis across central New Jersey, might trap Washington's retreating forces in a British pincers. If the redcoat and Hessian columns moved quickly, Clinton thought, the effort could place the rebels in an impossible situation and smash them once and for all.[1] But General and Admiral Howe were adamant, and the fleet sailed with Clinton's men. Their departure not only took pressure off Washington during the retreat, it also allowed Heath to conduct his December operations in New Jersey, and removed thousands of British soldiers from the decisive theater of war at a critical time.[2]

Howe would have to get through the winter with the troops on hand. He was confident that the army could handle any eventuality, but he admitted that his line of posts was thin. "The chain, I own, is rather too extensive," he wrote on December 20, "but I was induced to occupy Burlington to cover the County of Monmouth, in which there are many loyal inhabitants; and trusting to the almost general submission of the County to the southward of this chain, and to the strength of the corps placed in the advanced posts, I conclude the troops will be in perfect security."[3]

If only he had known. From across the Delaware, Washington, still looking for a fight, watched Rall and his Hessians at Trenton like a hungry fox eyeing a chicken coop.

---

[1]William B. Willcox, ed., *The American Rebellion: Sir Henry Clinton's Narrative of His Campaigns, 1775-1782* (New Haven: Yale University Press, 1954), 55.

[2]The decision of the Howe brothers to push ahead with the Rhode Island venture embittered many British and loyalists, who thought that the Howes had thrown away a chance to finish Washington in a link-up between Clinton and Cornwallis somewhere around New Brunswick, or perhaps further toward the Delaware. E.g., *Diary of Frederick Mackenzie* (Cambridge: Harvard University Press, 1930), 105, 113-114; Jones, *History of New York During the Revolutionary War*, I: 130-131. The British garrisoned Newport with about seven thousand men for three years; they gained nothing of strategic importance.

[3]Force, *American Archives*, Fifth Series, III: 1317. The British forces attempted to occupy the Delaware River town of Burlington, New Jersey, on Dec. 11, 1776, but were chased off by the Pennsylvania Navy.

CHAPTER EIGHT

Morristown

*To understand Lee in depth, a psychiatrist instead of a
historian is probably required.*
—Historian John W. Shy (1964)[1]

When General Washington was at Newark, he ordered General Philip
Schuyler to send him reinforcements from the Northern Department. These
reinforcements were commanded by Horatio Gates. Gates was 47 years old,
with the appearance of a kindly grandfather; but behind the soft facade was a
tough, experienced soldier.[2] Gates wasted no time in moving. On December
4, he arrived at Esopus (modern Kingston), New York, where his troops
disembarked from boats and began to march towards New Jersey. Gates
followed the Old Mine Road, which led through lower New York state to the

---

[1]George Athan Billias, ed., *George Washington's Generals* (New York: William
Morrow, 1964), 22.

[2]Gates was born in England in 1728. His parents lacked the means to buy him a
commission, but Gates had the backing of the Duke of Leeds, who employed his parents
and may have been his real father. Leed's bought him a lieutenancy in 1749, when he was
21. He immediately went to America, and eventually served on the ill-fated Braddock
Expedition in 1755 (on which he met Charles Lee, Thomas Gage, and George Washington).
He returned to England after the fighting ended in America, but his humble beginnings
impeded his military career. Returning to America, he purchased 600 acres in western
Virginia. His neighbor and friend was another former British officer, Lieutenant Colonel
Charles Lee. When the Revolution began, Gates offered his services to the rebels and was
quickly appointed a brigadier general. After serving as adjutant-general of the army, Gates
was appointed second-in-command of the Northern Department.

Delaware River near Port Jervis. With Gates, as his second-in-command, was General Benedict Arnold (1741-1801). While passing through the state, Gates appealed to fifteen hundred militiamen with General George Clinton to join him. To Gates' chagrin, they refused, unwilling to leave New York.

On December 11, Gates led the remnants of his force, numbering some six hundred men, along the Old Mine Road into northern New Jersey. [1] They spent the night in the village of Montague, about seven miles from the New York border.[2] The troops had suffered terribly during the journey from Albany. One diarist complained that "what I suffered on the march cannot be described. With no tents to shelter us from the snow and rain, we were obliged to get through it as well as we could."[3] Gates knew little about the military situation when he entered New Jersey. He knew only that Fort Washington had surrendered and Washington's army was retreating toward Pennsylvania. The next day, the column continued south to the hamlet of Walpack, New Jersey, near the Delaware River. It started to snow, which halted the march. Simultaneously, Gates learned that the enemy had occupied Trenton, and he sent an aide-de-camp, Major James Wilkinson, to find Washington and bring back news of the military situation.[4] Gates gave Wilkinson a letter for

---

[1]The Old Mine Road probably was the first wheeled-vehicle road in America. It was an old Indian trail that the early Dutch settlers developed into a wagon road to gain access to the copper and silver mines of northwestern New Jersey. C.G. Hine, *The Old Mine Road* (New Brunswick: Rutgers University Press, 1963, orig. 1909); Boatner, *Landmarks of the American Revolution*, 265; Nelson, *General Horatio Gates*, 74.

[2]Gates arrived in New Jersey with only four regiments from the Northern Department: Stark's, Poor's, Patterson's and Read's. According to the strength report from Fort Ticonderoga dated November 17, 1776, these regiments had 1,653 men. The loss in manpower can be attributed mostly to illness, and the lack of shoes and warm clothing to sustain the troops on their long journey to join Washington's army. "Diary of Chaplain David Avery," microfilm edition of manuscript, Princeton Theological Seminary Library, Princeton, New Jersey.

[3]John Greenwood, *A Young Patriot in the American Revolution, 1775-1783* (Westvaco, 1981), 79; originally published as *The Revolutionary Services of John Greenwood of Boston and New York, 1775-1783*, ed. Isaac J. Greenwood (New York: De Vinne, 1922).

[4]*Avery Diary*, Dec. 12, 1776. Gates occupied the Isaac Van Campen house, near Walpack. Hine, *The Old Mine Road*, opposite p. 147. Wilkinson (1757-1825) was from Maryland, went to Philadelphia in 1773 to study medicine, and enlisted as a private the outbreak of the Revolution. Promoted to captain in 1776, he served as aide-de-camp to Gates and others, and ended the war as a general. Gates' letter to Washington, sent with Wilkinson, is in Twohig, ed., *The Papers of George Washington*, VII: 308.

Washington, explaining Gates' situation and asking the commander-in-chief to give him a safe route to the Grand Army's camp. Then, increasingly anxious about the military situation and without waiting for Wilkinson to return, Gates marched his division away from the river to Sussex Courthouse (modern Newton) on December 13. Sometime during the day, Gates was told that the enemy had three divisions at Princeton, Trenton and Burlington, which further increased his uneasiness.[1] The enemy had obviously moved in force across the center of New Jersey, hardly good news.

Wilkinson's mission was eventful. He reached Sussex Courthouse on the first day of his ride, December 12, where he learned that Washington had crossed the Delaware to Pennsylvania a few days earlier and had removed all boats from the river. He also discovered that General Lee was nearby, at Morristown, with his division. With the enemy reported all along the Delaware, Wilkinson decided it was safer to get information from Lee's corps. The determined major took a guide and followed the muddy road toward Morristown and the camp of the greatly respected Lee.[2]

Lee had arrived at Morristown from Chatham on December 11, the same day that Gates crossed the border into New Jersey. Lee probably was heading for the Delaware to consolidate his force with Washington's Grand Army, per Washington's repeated requests, even though he would have preferred to stay in Chatham, where he was in a good position to cut enemy communications and raid the Crown's outposts at Elizabethtown, Rahway and Newark. On arriving in Morristown, Lee wrote Washington that he had sent out two reconnaissance officers that day, one to tell him where the Delaware could be crossed above Trenton and the other to examine the road to Burlington, a town on the Delaware south of Trenton.[3]

The dispatch of these officers, however, suggests that Lee had much in mind than a march to join Washington. There was no reason for him to

---

[1]See the "Avery Diary," Dec. 13, 1776: "We hear ye Enemy are in three grand divisions, at Princeton, Trenton & Burlington."

[2]James Wilkinson, *Memories of My Own Times,* 4 vols. (Philadelphia, 1816), I: 111.

[3]White, *A Village at War,* 77; Rau, ed., *Sergeant Smith's Diary,* 263. Charles Lee to George Washington, Morristown, December 11, 1776; *Lee Papers,* II: 345.

check where the Delaware could be crossed safely above Trenton, because he already knew from Major Hoops that boats were waiting to take his division across at Alexandria. His mention of sending an officer towards Burlington also is intriguing. If the general planned to ferry the Delaware at Burlington, his force would need to cross the Upper Road (Lee called it "the great Brunswick post road") somewhere along its route through central New Jersey. Lee had wagons with him and had to stay on the roads. This meant he would probably cross the Upper Road at Princeton, where there was a Crown forces garrison. A surprise raid on Princeton, which would have temporarily cut the enemy's communication and supply lines, followed by a successful crossing of the Delaware at Burlington, near Philadelphia, would have been a riveting demonstration of Lee's military skills.[1] Lee also could have been planning an attack on New Brunswick, but this was much less likely.[2] There is no way to tell for certain what was on his mind.

The last lines Lee wrote about his situation in New Jersey give no clue to his plans. "If I stay in this Province" he wrote to Gates, "I risk myself and Army and if I do not stay the Province is lost for ever --I have neither guides Cavalry Medicines Money Shoes or Stockings--I must act with the greatest circumspection."[3] Clearly, though, Lee had his doubts about a quick march out of the state. Lee issued four days' provisions to his troops on December 12 and prepared to move his division out of Morristown early the next morning. A snowfall that night delayed the departure, but by the late morning of the 13th all wagons and carts were loaded, and the division was ready to march to Vealtown (Bernardsville). The sick were left behind. The day became warmer and the melting snow made the road muddy. Many of the soldiers had no shoes and covered their feet with cowhide they had hastily laced together.[4] Sometime during the late afternoon or evening of the 13th, Lee left his division under the charge of his second-in-command, General John

---

[1]There is a second-hand account holding that Lee's secretary had said that "there would be warm Work before they joyned G. Wash." Franklin Dexter, ed., *The Literary Diary of Ezra Stiles* (New York: Charles Scribner's Sons, 1901), II: 105-107.

[2]John Alden, *General Charles Lee* (Baton Rouge: Louisiana State University Press, 1951), 155.

[3]Lee to Gates, Dec. 12/13, 1776, *Lee Papers*, II: 348.

[4]Louise Rau, ed., "Sergeant John Smith's Diary of 1776," *Mississippi Valley Historical Review*, 20 (1933-1934): 264.

Sullivan. Then, accompanied by Major William Bradford, Jr. (an aide-de-camp), two French volunteer officers and a squad of bodyguards, Lee rode to the Widow White's tavern in the village of Basking Ridge to spend the night. The tavern was only three miles from Vealtown, convenient for Lee to rejoin his corps the next morning.

While he could hardly have known it, Lee's decision to leave the security of his camp was one of the most controversial of his explosive career. It remains a mystery, although some historians have speculated that he was seeking the company of a woman.[1] Whatever his intentions (or hopes), events quickly took a dire turn.

At 4:00 a.m. on December 14, Wilkinson caught up with Lee at the tavern in Basking Ridge. The young officer found Lee lying in bed and informed him that his old comrade, Gates, was nearby with six hundred men from the Northern Department. Wilkinson then said he had a letter from Gates to Washington. Lee took the letter, broke the seal, and read it. Nothing more happened that night and the exhausted Wilkinson slept for a few hours.

He awoke later in the morning to find Lee sitting at a table in the tavern in his nightshirt. Lee had just finished breakfast and was completing a letter that he wanted Wilkinson to take back to Gates. Its content was dark. "The ingenious maneuver of Fort Washington," he sarcastically told his former British army comrade, "has unhing'd the goodly fabrick We had been building--there never was so damn'd a stroke--entre nous, a certain great man is most damnably deficient--He has thrown me into a situation where I have my choice of difficulties." While not stating it directly to Gates, Lee also may have wanted to add the Northern regiments to his own forces.[2] Pausing from his writing, Lee invited Wilkinson to have breakfast before returning to Gates' camp. Wilkinson had no need to go on to Washington's command for

---

[1]Historian James Thomas Flexner commented that "Lee had a propensity for sleeping in strange places (and with strange women)." James Flexner, *George Washington in the American Revolution* (Boston: Little, Brown, 1967), 167.

[2]*Lee Papers*, II: 348. Lee's letter to Gates may have been a proposition to encourage Gates to halt his march to Washington's camp and add his regiments to those of Lee. If so, historian Paul David Nelson has insisted that "Gates refused to be shaken from his resolution to obey his orders to join the commander in chief." Paul David Nelson, *General Horatio Gates* (Baton Rouge, 1976), 73-74. Lee mentioned his notion of putting the reinforcements from the Northern army under his command in a letter to Washington dated Dec. 4, 1776; in effect, he also proposed an independent command for himself in the Morristown area. *Lee Papers*, II: 329-330.

information, since Lee and his officers were informed of the Grand Army's situation on the Delaware River.

Breakfast ended dramatically. About 10:00 a.m., Wilkinson got up from the table and looked indifferently out the window. To his horror, he saw a party of British dragoons galloping up the lane towards the tavern with weapons drawn. Wilkinson bellowed a warning to Lee, who jumped up from his chair, saw the charging dragoons, and screamed, "Where is the guard-- damn the guard, why don't they fire?" In fact, the surprised guards had fled and the dragoons advanced with virtually no opposition.

How had British dragoons managed to learn Lee's whereabouts so deep in rebel-held territory? Following his occupation of Trenton, Cornwallis became alarmed about the location of Lee and his corps. Cornwallis knew only that Lee was somewhere in New jersey with a force estimated at 7,500 men. Having served with Lee in Portugal during the Seven Years War, Cornwallis knew him to be a clever and enterprising officer. He feared that Lee would launch raids against his isolated garrisons, which were strung out across New Jersey from Fort Lee to Trenton. He had to know where Lee was. On December 12, he dispatched a portion of the 16th Queen's Light Dragoons, consisting of its commander, Colonel William Harcourt (1743-1830), four subalterns, and twenty-five troopers, with orders to find Lee's position.[1]

It was a dangerous mission. Harcourt's party started from Penny Town (modern Pennington) and rode eighteen miles to the village of Hillsborough, where they camped for the night. The village was occupied by a British battalion. Beyond the hamlet lay rebel-held territory. During the night, the house in which the officers slept mysteriously caught fire and burned to the ground. The men escaped and spent the rest of the night in a barn. Next morning, Harcourt and his troopers resumed their mission and crossed the Raritan River on the bridge at Bound Brook. Every additional step took them deeper into enemy territory.

Yet Harcourt was not traveling blindly. At some point north of Bound

---

[1]Worthington Ford, *British Officers Serving in the American Revolution, 1774-1783* (Brooklyn, 1897), 67. Lieutenant Banastre Tarleton was also on the mission and wrote his mother an account of the exploit; Tarleton's letter (of Dec. 18, 1776) is the most reliable account of Lee's capture. Robert Blass, *The Green Dragon* (New York: Holt, 1957), 20-22.

Brook, a Tory guide evidently joined the scouting party. This was probably Richard V. Stockton.[1] With their guide, the dragoons proceeded north, on what today is King George Road, in the direction of Morristown. Probably from rebels they captured on the way, Harcourt learned that Lee was at a tavern in the remote village of Basking Ridge, protected only by a headquarters guard of thirty soldiers. It was a tempting opportunity, and Harcourt decided to lunge deeper into the interior and capture the rebel general.

Harcourt's dragoons reached Basking Ridge without detection. They found Widow White's tavern with woods on one side and an orchard on the other.[2] The troopers rushed the building from both sides and surprised and scattered the headquarters guards, who had stacked their arms and sought warmth by sunning themselves on the south side of a nearby house. Having chased off the guards, the British horsemen turned to the tavern and their prey. They surrounded the building and began firing into every window and door. Inside were Lee, Major Bradford, Wilkinson, the two French officers and some of Lee's guards. A heated exchange of gunfire went on for several minutes. One of the Frenchmen and some of Lee's guards were wounded.

Harcourt's men then threatened to burn down the building if Lee did not surrender. Several men tried to escape through a back door, but were cut down by the dragoons. The French colonel was captured trying to escape through this door. At almost the same moment Lee emerged from the front door, Wilkinson heard one of the dragoons yell from outside, "Here is the general. He has surrendered."[3] Lee emerged from the tavern dressed in his

---

[1]On the identity of Stockton, see John Alden, *General Charles Lee*, 332, note 21. William Robins, another New Jersey loyalist, also claimed he rode with Harcourt. Patriots always believed that Tories were involved in Lee's capture; one apocryphal account held that a Tory, angered over the loss of a horse to the rebel army, rode all the way to British-held New Brunswick to disclose Lee's location. Joseph Trumbull to Governor Jonathan Trumbull, Dec. 17, 1776. Force, ed., *American Archives*, Series Five, III: 1265.

[2]Dexter, ed., *Diary of Ezra Stiles*, II: 106.

[3]One of the French officers was Lt. Col. Sieur Gaiault de Boisbertrand. He was Lee's adjutant-general and captured along with Lee. Both Frenchmen were volunteers in the American Army. William Bradford, Lee's aide-de-camp at the time, said that a French colonel and a French captain were with Lee at the inn, and that the captain (Jean Louis de Virnejoux) had recently arrived from Paris, by way of Massachusetts, with dispatches for the Continental Congress. Dexter, ed., *Diary of Ezra Stiles*, II: 106; Bass, *The Green Dragoon*, 19.

usual slovenly style, this time in slippers and blanket coat, his collar open, and his shirt soiled from several days' use. There was no time to allow him to put on clothes. Lee was thrown on a horse which the British found saddled and ready. (The horse was Wilkinson's, just made ready to carry him back to Gates' camp.) One of Harcourt's dragoons sounded a trumpet, and the horsemen reassembled and rode off as quickly as they had arrived. It was ten to fifteen minutes from the time the dragoons were spotted racing toward the tavern until they rode off with Lee as their captive. The British horsemen avoided rebel patrols and safely returned to the British outpost at Hillsborough. Lee was sent first to Cornwallis' headquarters at Penny Town and then to New Brunswick.[1]

Bradford, who had narrowly escaped, raced with the news of Lee's capture to Sullivan, the former New Hampshire lawyer who was Lee's second-in-command. He found Sullivan at noon marching with the troops eight miles from Vealtown. Wilkinson, another escapee, also reported to Sullivan before riding back to Gates and delivering Lee's letter.[2] Sullivan tried to intercept Harcourt's dragoons but was too late. They had too great a lead and the rebels had no information on their route.[3]

---

[1]This account of Lee's capture is based on the eyewitness accounts of Banastre Tarleton, a dragoon officer who participated in the raid, and of Wilkinson, who was with Lee but got away. Both accounts are in Commager and Morris, *Spirit of 'Seventy-Six*, 501-504. Lieutenant Colonel William Harcourt received the thanks of Parliament and was made a king's aide-de-camp as a reward for his exploit.

[2]Wilkinson says he rode to Sullivan's column immediately following Lee's capture. He provided some interesting detail in his autobiography: "So soon as Lieutenant-colonel Harcourt retreated with his prize, I repaired to the stable, mounted the first horse I could find, and rode full speed to General Sullivan, whom I found under march toward Pluckamin [a village west of Vealtown]. I had not examined General Lee's letter [the letter Lee had written to Gates just before his capture] but believing a knowledge of the contents might be useful to General Sullivan, who succeeded him in command, I handed it to him, who after perusal, returned it with his thanks, and advised me to rejoin General Gates without delay, which I did the next morning at Sussex court-house, whither he had led the troops from Van Kempt's." James Wilkinson, *Memoirs of My Own Times* (Philadelphia: Abraham Small, 1816), I: 111.

[3]Sullivan had few horse available to attempt a rescue. A "Return of the Forces under the command of General Lee, November 24th, 1776" listed 102 light-horse present and fit for duty. Force, ed., *American Archives*, Fifth Series, III: 831. These troopers were part of the Connecticut Light Horse. Lesser, *Sinews of Independence*, 41. However, these troopers may not have accompanied Lee's division into New Jersey, and Sullivan probably organized a small scratch group of mounted soldiers, whom he sent unsuccessfully after Harcourt's seasoned dragoons.

Now in charge of Lee's brigade, Sullivan immediately ordered the troops to march to the Delaware. Sullivan was in a hurry to reach the relative safety of Pennsylvania as he feared enemy attack as they marched across New Jersey. The column spent the night of December 14 in Germantown, New Jersey (modern Oldwick), and December 15 at Potters Town (Potterstown). There was a scare in the camp the following morning as word circulated of a British attempt to surround the brigade. Sullivan's men quickly loaded up their wagons and marched off. In fact, the command never made contact with the enemy, but the troops were on edge for most of the march.

Moving toward the Delaware, officers knew that boats were waiting for them at Alexandria. But, probably fearing an enemy attack if he moved southwest toward there, Sullivan instead marched due west to the ferry at Philipsburg. His troops crossed the river on the night of December 16.[1]

As Sullivan took his brigade west, Wilkinson returned to Gates' camp and reported Lee's capture. "Major Wilkinson returned from Genl Lee's army," Chaplain David Avery wrote, and brought "tidings that yesterday morning about 70 of the light horse came upon Genl Lee and took him prisoner and a French Colonel."[2] Upon receiving the news, Gates resumed his march to reinforce the Grand Army. On December 15, his exhausted troops crossed the Delaware twenty miles above Easton; they then marched to the Moravian settlement at Bethlehem, Pennsylvania, where a military hospital had been established. There they rested a few days before resuming their trek. They were joined on December 18 at Bethlehem by what was left of Sullivan's division. Gates and his troops pushed on from Bethlehem on December 20 and arrived at Washington's camp on December 22. Elements of Sullivan's division staggered into camp on December 20, 21, and 22.[3] For all concerned, it had been a bitter and difficult trek.

Lieutenant Joseph Hodgkins marched across New Jersey with Lee's division. As he neared Washington's camp, he wrote his wife that "tho we are Very Much fatagued with a long march we have Ben [been] on the march ever since ye 29 of Last month and we are now within 10 or 12 miles of general

---

[1]Rau., ed., *Sergeant Smith's Diary*, 265.

[2]"Avery Diary," Dec. 14, 1776.

[3]Rau, ed., *Sergeant Smith's Diary*, 266; Dexter, ed., *Diary of Ezra Stiles*, 106; Washington to Robert Morris, Dec. 22, 1776, Fitzpatrick, ed., *Writings of Washington*, VI: 420-421.

Washingtons Army we Expect to Be there to night But how long we shall stay there I Cant tell neither Can I tell you much about the Enemy only that they are on one side of the Dilleway River and our army on the other about 20 miles from Philadelphia." He noted the troops crossing the river "Last Sunday 40 or 50 miles above head Quarters on account of the Enemys Trying to intercept our Crosing" and recalled the perilous times of the last several weeks. "We have Marched since we came from Phillips Manner about 200 miles the gratest Part of the way whas Dangrus By Reason of the Enemy being near & not only so But the Contry is full of them Cursed Creatures called Torys." He longed for home, but warned that travel would be difficult. The weather had turned bad, and he could only send his assurance that he remained her "most afectionate Companion Till Death."[1]

Having finished their long march, neither Gates nor Arnold took part in Washington's Christmas night raid on Trenton. Complaining of illness, Gates went to Philadelphia on December 23. Arnold was ordered by Washington to proceed to Rhode Island, to help organize defenses there. The reinforcements that Gates brought from the Northern Department were reorganized under the command of General Arthur St. Clair. Renamed St. Clair's Brigade, they took part in the Christmas night raid on Trenton. The unit had an effective strength of about five hundred men.[2]

What happened to Charles Lee? Following his capture near Basking Ridge, he was held prisoner in New York City. Despite initial threats that he would be tried as a traitor, eventually Lee was well-treated by his captors and exchanged for a British officer in the late spring of 1778. Back with the American army, Lee had few friends among intimates of the commander-in-chief. He also frowned on Washington's efforts to train the Continental Army on the professional European model. Still, Washington allowed Lee to command the American vanguard at the Battle of Monmouth on June 28,

---

[1]Joseph Hodgkins to Sarah Hodgkins, Dec. 20, 1776, in Herbert T. Wade and Robert A. Lively, eds., *This Glorious Cause: The Adventures of Two Company Officers in Washington's Army* (Princeton: Princeton University Press, 1958), 227-228. Joseph Hodgkins was a company officer in the 12th Continental Regiment (Massachusetts) in late 1776.

[2]St. Clair left Fort Ticonderoga in mid-November with three regiments from the Northern Army whose enlistments had expired. He linked up with Gates somewhere en route, perhaps with some of his soldiers who agreed to stay on. William Smith, *The Life and Public Service of Arthur St. Clair* (Cincinnati: Robert Clarke & Co., 1882), 28, 378. Stryker, *Battle of Trenton*, 354.

1778. Questions over his conduct that day led to a confrontation with Washington and a controversial court-martial, which finally resulted in Lee's dismissal from the army. It was the end of an interesting if tumultuous military career.

Lee died in Philadelphia on October 2, 1782, at the age of fifty-one. Always ascerbic and argumentative, Lee was in good form to the end. "I desire most earnestly," he wrote in his will, "that I may not be buried in any church or churchyard, or within a mile of any Presbyterian or Anabapist meeting-house; for, since I have resided in this country, I have kept so much bad company when living, that I do not choose to continue it when dead."[1]

Who knows what Lee planned if he had escaped capture at the Widow White's tavern in Basking Ridge? Lee was a volatile personality, and fate's stepping in to remove him from the scene is one of the great ironies of American history. Historian James Flexner thought that Lee's conduct on the New Jersey retreat was mutinous.[2] That is too strong a word. The general was less than enthusiastic about abandoning New Jersey, but if he was balky, he was not completely insubordinate. Perhaps he hoped to strike an isolated British outpost on his way out of the state, but no one will ever know. The intrepid Colonel Harcourt saw to that.

---

[1]Alden, *General Charles Lee*, 299.

[2]James Flexner, *George Washington in the American Revolution* (Boston: Little Brown and Company, 1967), 156.

CHAPTER NINE

The Delaware River

The reasons why general Howe did not sooner overtake the distressed fugitives, or why he cantoned his troops, without crossing the river and taking possession of the city of Philadelphia, remains yet to be investigated.
—Mercy Otis Warren (1805)[1]

To the British, the American rebellion seemed on the verge of collapse in mid-December 1776. Crown forces were in possession of New York City, Newport, Rhode Island, and much of New Jersey. Many New Jersey citizens had accepted General Howe's pardon, and hundreds of Loyalists were enlisting in Provincial Regiments. The New Jersey legislature fled before the enemy advance, moving from Princeton to Burlington to Pittstown and finally to Haddonfield. There, on the edge of New Jersey with no where else to go, legislators voted to dissolve on December 2. Members were advised to find someplace to hide. Fearing the capture of Philadelphia, the Continental Congress abandoned the city on the night of December 12. It left behind Generals Israel Putnam and Thomas Mifflin to govern the city under martial law, and granted Washington the power to direct the war on his own.[2] The

---

[1]Mercy Otis Warren, *History of the Rise, Progress and Termination of the American Revolution* (Boston: Manning and Loring, for E. Larkin, 1805), I: 335-336. Warren was the wife of the Governor of Massachusetts during the Revolution.

[2]A good summary of the situation in Philadelphia is in Benson Lossing, *The Pictorial Field-Book of the Revolution* (New York, 1855), II: 18. The Continental Congress granted Washington "full power to order and direct all things relative to the department,

delegates fled to Baltimore, and the news of their departure added to the panic in Philadelphia. Everything seemed to be falling apart.

The military situation remained bleak. General Lee was a prisoner of war and the Northern army, based at Fort Ticonderoga, was in deplorable shape. Some of the eight regiments Washington ordered to join him from Ticonderoga were marching across New Jersey under Gates; but illness and desertions had diminished them. Of the approximately twelve hundred who left Ticonderoga on December 2, only some six hundred stumbled into New Jersey on December 11. Washington privately expressed his desperation in an often-quoted letter to his brother, Lund. "Your imagination can scarce extend to a situation more distressing than mine," he wrote on December 17. "Our only dependence now is upon the speedy enlistment of a new army. If this fails, I think the game will be pretty well up, as, from disaffection and want of spirit and fortitude, the inhabitants, instead of resistance, are offering submission and taking protection from Gen. Howe in Jersey."[1]

Yet there were some encouraging signs. The army still existed. Although the Grand Army lay exhausted and freezing along 70 miles of the Delaware River, it remained in the field and defended Philadelphia. On paper, Washington had a force of 11,500, but more likely he had an effective force of 7,500. This included 1,500 inexperienced Pennsylvania militiamen under Colonel John Cadwalader and 400 soldiers from the newly established German brigade commanded by Colonel Nicholas Haussegger. Thus, if they were considerably the worse for the recent campaign, and if many of their reinforcements were untried, the rebels soldiers were still a force to reckon with; Howe had misjudged their staying power.

There was also an American buildup in northern New Jersey. The village of Morristown, an important agricultural region behind a range of protective hills, had become a gathering place for patriot resistance. It was near the newly established enemy cantonments at New Brunswick, Newark,

---

and to the operations of war." *Journal of the Continental Congress*, VI: 1024-1027; Washington to the President of Congress, Dec. 20, 1776; Fitzpatrick, ed., *Writings of Washington*, VI: 402. Washington was ill at ease with the grant of dictatorial powers, however temporary. Charles Lee, however, may have had fewer doubts. He wrote Congressman Benjamin Rush recommending the need for a military dictator and volunteering for the position, claiming that much could still be done. "Had I the powers I could do you much good," he assured Rush, "might I but dictate one week--but I am sure you will never give any man the necessary power." Lee to Rush, Nov. 20, 1776. *Lee Papers*, II: 288-289.

[1]Fitzpatrick, ed., *Writings of Washington*, VI: 347.

and Elizabeth, all of which were potential targets. By the middle of December, several American forces had passed through the Morristown area. None, however, had stopped long enough to assist or encourage the militia gathering there. On December 11, Lee's corps found a considerable militia force as they arrived in the town. Lee may have directed a few small raids at British parties to the south, but he soon continued his march, leaving the militia on their own.[1] So did General Gates, when he passed nearby with his four skeleton regiments on the way to reinforcing Washington. Worried about a British strike in their direction, yet willing to fight, the lack of Continental leadership was a matter of real concern among local militia officers.

The situation soon improved. On December 14, General Alexander McDougall, one of Lee's brigade commanders, arrived in town. Left at Haverstraw, New York, with severe rheumatism, he recovered sufficiently after eight days and tried to catch up with Lee. Reaching Morristown, he learned of Lee's capture and decided not to continue his journey unescorted. Hearing that three patriot regiments were nearing Morristown en route to Washington, he decided to travel under their protection.[2] The arriving Continental regiments hailed from Massachusetts: Greaton's (designated the 24th Continentals), Bond's (25th Continentals), and Elisha Porter's militia regiment, totaling 520 men. They were commanded by Lt. Colonel Joseph Vose.[3] They marched into Morristown during the evening of December 17.

Meanwhile, a few miles to the east, there had been fierce fighting between rebel militia and British regulars. It started when Howe learned of militia activity at Chatham. He dispatched General Alexander Leslie with eight hundred men from Elizabethtown to rout the Americans; on December 17,

---

[1]Lee informed Washington of finding a strong militia force in Morristown in a letter sent *via* Colonel Humpton, whom Washington had dispatched from Pennsylvania to establish the whereabouts of Lee. Lee reported about a thousand militia around the village. *Lee Papers*, II: 336-337; Billias, ed., *George Washington's Generals*, 38.

[2]McDougall to Washington, Dec. 19, 1776, Force, ed., *American Archives*, Fifth Series, III: 1296-1297; Roger Champagne, *Alexander McDougall and the American Revolution in New York* (Schenectady: Union College Press, 1975), 119-120.

[3]Troop returns for these regiments are in Lesser, ed., *The Sinews of Independence*, 38; and McDougall to General William Heath, Dec. 17, 1776, Force, ed., *American Archives*, Fifth Series, III: 1260. Vose's three regiments departed Fort Ticonderoga on Nov. 18; *ibid.*, 878. For Vose, see Francis Heitman, *Historical Register of Officers of the Continental Army* (Washington D.C.: Rare Book Shop Publishing Company, Inc., 1914), 561.

Leslie's troops clashed with the Eastern Battalion of Morris County Militia, commanded by Colonel Jacob Ford, Jr. The fighting took place near Bryant's Tavern, about three miles east of Chatham. The action broke off at dusk, but renewed battle was expected the following day.[1] During the night of December 17, the militia officers and "principal gentlemen" pleaded with McDougall to order Vose to stay with the militia. Without clear authority, McDougall nevertheless boldly did so. "I have ventured to advise Colonel Vose to remain in this State," he explained to Washington, "and shall post his troops, with the Militia, in the best manner to cover the country not in the hands of the enemy."[2] Vose's troops started marching toward Chatham and the expected fighting early on December 18, but General Leslie broke off and retired towards Spank-Town (between Rahway and Westfield).[3]

Encouraged by the situation, and recognizing McDougall's continued poor health, on December 21 Washington sent Brigadier General William Maxwell to Morristown. Commanding Vose's regiments, plus the militia under Colonel Ford, Maxwell was to open active operations. Washington wanted him to protect the region as best he could while "harassing" the enemy "in their Quarters" and hitting "their Convoys."[4] By the end of December, this series of events had established Morristown as a secure military base for the rebels. It was a development that would soon pay handsome dividends.

Washington also acted on another front. By December 7, he was convinced that Howe would not send part of his army to harass New England. He also knew the British fleet had sailed for Rhode Island. He therefore

---

[1]White, *A Village at War*, 78-79.

[2]McDougall to Washington, Dec. 19, 1776, in Force, ed., *American Archives*, Fifth Series, III: 1296-1297. Washington wrote to approve McDougall's action on Dec. 21. Fitzpatrick, ed., *Writings of Washington*, VI: 419.

[3]McDougall to Washington, Chatham, December 19, 1776, in Force, ed., *American Archives*, Fifth Series, III: 1296-1297.

[4]Fitzpatrick, ed., *Writings of Washington*, VI: 415. Maxwell (1733-1796) was born in Ireland and emigrated to western New Jersey with his parents when he was a teenager. Maxwell was a veteran of the French and Indian War and commanded the 2nd New Jersey Regiment in the Northern Army until that regiment was disbanded in late November 1776.

ordered Heath's Continental troops to leave Peekskill, New York, and march across northern New Jersey to reinforce the Grand Army in Pennsylvania.[1]

Heath crossed the Hudson on December 10 and learned that New Bridge, near Hackensack, was the northernmost Crown garrison. However, much of Bergen County was controlled by the British-armed Loyalist 4th Battalion of New Jersey Volunteers. The Tory troops were plundering local Whigs, and Heath decided to halt his march long enough to restore order. On December 13, Heath sent a reconnaissance party towards Hackensack and raided the town on the 14th. There were only five British soldiers guarding Hackensack, but considerable stores had been collected there for the use of the Loyalists. Heath seized them and carted off the booty to his camp at Paramus. On December 19, Heath was joined by a number of New York militia under General George Clinton. A mixed force of five hundred Continentals and New Yorkers then attacked a Loyalist camp in the vicinity of Bergen Woods (the area between modern Hoboken and Fort Lee) and captured a picket guard of sixteen men from the 4th Battalion of New Jersey Volunteers.

Worried about Heath's activities, the British began maneuvering and reinforcing their eastern New Jersey cantonments. Washington approved of Heath's activities, and he stayed in northern New Jersey until December 23. At that point, under pressure from the New York legislature to defend Westchester County, Heath recrossed the Hudson and returned to Peekskill.[2] The withdrawal forced Clinton to return to New York state with his militia.

Meanwhile, Washington had not been idle on the Delaware. From his headquarters in Newtown, Pennsylvania, he sent raiding parties back into New Jersey and encouraged the local militia. By mid-December, 1776, Washington and other officers were engaging the enemy in New Jersey on a number of fronts. The initial shock of the invasion had worn off, and the rebels were actively probing for weak points along Howe's lines and making life dangerous for small enemy detachments. Yet the significance of this activity seemingly escaped the British commander-in-chief.

Many of Howe's junior officers, however, were concerned at how dangerous the situation had become. "It is now very unsafe for us to travel in Jersey," a Hessian officer noted. "The rascal peasants meet our men alone or

---

[1]Washington to Heath, Dec. 7, 1776, Fitzpatrick, ed., *Writings of Washington*, VI: 335.

[2]There is a detailed account of Heath's activities in New Jersey in *Heath's Memoirs*, 99-103; see also Lundin, *Cockpit of the Revolution*, 182-183.

in small unarmed groups. They have their rifles hidden in the bushes, or ditches, and the like. When they believe they are sure of success and they see one or several men belonging to our army, they shoot them in the head, then quickly hide their rifles and pretend they know nothing."[1]   Colonel Rall, commanding at Trenton, the most exposed and dangerous Crown position in New Jersey, wrote that he needed major forces just to get letters safely from Trenton to Princeton. "Yesterday I sent two dragoons to Princeton with letters," he complained. "They were not gone over an hour when one of them came back and reported that the other soldier had been killed and his own horse had been shot by a concealed enemy." He then "sent immediately one Captain with one hundred men and one piece of artillery to Princeton and asked again of General Leslie to place some troops at Maidenhead."[2] For a supposedly beaten force, the rebels had become troublesome indeed.

Howe had failed to land a knock-out blow, and as December drew to a close, a number of factors worked to restore patriot fortunes. The British failure to advance across the Delaware allowed Washington time not only to gather reinforcements, but to assess intelligence on the enemy. Howe's scattered and isolated posts were obvious attractions. As early as December 14, Washington was looking for an opening for a counter-attack involving Lee, Gates, and Heath. He wanted "to attempt a Stroke upon the Forces of the Enemy, who lay a good deal scattered and to all appearance in a state of Security. A lucky Blow in this Quarter," he wrote to Governor Jonathan Trumbull of Connecticut, "would be fatal to them, and would most certainly raise the Spirits of the People, which are quite sunk by our late misfortunes."[3]

Washington struck the "lucky Blow" on December 25, 1776. The Battle of Trenton resounded through the rest of the war and into legend. He and his troops made their famous Delaware crossing in the cold darkness of Christmas night and then, at dawn on December 26, surprised and routed

---

[1]Kippling and Smith, eds., *At Howe's Side*, 7.

[2]William S. Stryker, *The Battles of Trenton and Princeton* (New York: Houghton, Mifflin & Co., 1898), 331. Rall wrote this letter on December 21.

[3]Fitzpatrick, ed., *Writings of Washington*, VI: 366. Dec. 14, 1776 is the earliest date that General Washington wrote about a counter-attack on the enemy in New Jersey. He also wrote Major General Horatio Gates on Dec. 14 with the idea of attacking the enemy in New Jersey: "If we can draw our forces together, I trust, under the smiles of providence, we may yet effect an important stroke, or at least prevent Genl. Howe from executing his plans." *Ibid.*, 372.

Colonel Rall and his three Hessian regiments.

News of the affair created a sensation among the British. Captain von Muenchhausen was at headquarters in New York City, and had just finished writing a letter home on December 26 when the first sketchy news of the American attack arrived. He mournfully added a postscript: "I have reopened this letter to report an unhappy affair. Colonel Rall, who was at Trenton with the Knyphausen, Lossberg, and Rall regiments and 50 jaegers, was compelled to surrender at dawn on the 26th, after a fight of one hour, owing partly to the suddenness of the enemy surprise....We know no further details at the moment."[1] Subsequent details were stunning. It appeared that Rall, who had looked with such contempt on the rebels, had failed to take adequate precautions to protect against surprise.[2] He paid the price: Rall, who had shown great bravery in the assault on Fort Washington, was among about 30 Hessians killed in action.[3] An estimated 919 enemy troops were captured, along with six brass cannon and 1,000 muskets. Washington quickly gathered his captives and booty and went back across the Delaware to safety.

But Washington's Christmas-night raid proved only the start of a rebel counter-offensive. Encouraged by the uprising of militia following the raid, Washington returned to Trenton on December 30 as a big enemy force advanced against him under the command of Cornwallis.[4] After several forced marches, Cornwallis arrived at Trenton on the night of January 2, 1777 to find Washington's army in a good defensive position. With his troops exhausted and night approaching, Cornwallis decided to postpone his attack until the next day, proclaiming that he would "bag the fox" in the morning.

During the night, Washington indeed showed the cunning of a fox: he ordered campfires to be kept burning and left a few men behind to march

---

[1]Kipping and Smith, eds., *At General Howe's Side*, 8.

[2]Stephen Kemble, adjutant to General Howe, summed up the problems at Trenton in an entry in his private journal at the end of 1776: "Why Post so small Detachments as to be in danger of Insult, as happened in Rall's Affair, upon the Frontiers of your Line of Communication, or why put Hessians at the advanced Posts, particularly the Man at Trentown, who was Noisy, but not sullen, unacquainted with the Language, and a Drunkard?" *The Kemble Papers*, 105.

[3]Fitzpatrick, ed., *Writings of Washington*, VI: 447.

[4]Cornwallis had planned to winter in England; he was scheduled to sail on HMS *Bristol* from New York on Dec. 27. Upon Rall's defeat at Trenton, Howe ordered Cornwallis to resume command immediately in New Jersey.

constantly in front of the blazes, making plenty of noise. He then had the wheels of his cannons wrapped in rags to muffle noise and silently marched his army on a remote farm road towards Princeton, passing within three miles of twelve hundred British sleeping at Maidenhead. The patriots emerged at Princeton the following morning (January 3, 1777) to surprise three regiments left there by Cornwallis. The Battle of Princeton ended with the surrender of hundreds of British who had barricaded themselves in Nassau Hall.[1]

At Trenton, Cornwallis was readying his assault on the seemingly-bustling rebel camp when he heard the sound of artillery from the direction of Princeton. Realizing he had been tricked, the British general raced back down the high road. But by the time he arrived at Princeton, Washington had retreated into the Millstone Valley towards his stronghold at Morristown.

Sometimes victory and success burst forth with stunning suddenness. Washington's Trenton-Princeton campaign was, simply, one of the most daring in the history of American arms. In ten days (December 25, 1776 to January 3, 1777), Washington reversed the course of the American Revolution and regained his prestige and stature. "This is an important period to America, big with great events," Nathanael Greene wrote to his wife following the Battle of Trenton. "God only knows what will be the issue of this Campaign, but everything wears a much better prospect than they have for some weeks past."[2] Greene wrote from experience. He had seen the worst of the "long retreat," and now he had seen the spirit of the Revolution restored at a stroke.

---

[1]Boatner, *Encyclopedia of the American Revolution*, 617. Washington's celebrated deception did not impress Sir Henry Clinton. Clinton was convinced that the Americans had escaped solely through the negligence of Cornwallis, who had been duped by an elementary ruse. Clinton claimed that he personally tried to cover up Cornwallis' enormous blunder because he did not want to expose "the most consummate ignorance I ever heard of [in] any officer above a corporal." Wilcox, ed., *Sir Henry Clinton's Narrative*, 60n.

The enemy troops surprised at Princeton were the bulk of the British 4th brigade (under Lt. Colonel Charles Mawhood), consisting of three regiments: 17th, 40th and 55th, plus some mounted and dismounted dragoons of the 16th regiment. David Ramsey gave this account of the incident at Nassau Hall: "A party of the British fled into the college and were there attacked with field pieces which were fired into it. The seat of the muses became for some time the scene of action. The party which had taken refuge in the college, after receiving a few discharges from the American field pieces came out and surrendered themselves prisoners of war." Ramsey, *History of the American Revolution*, I: 412.

[2]Greene to Catharine Greene, Dec. 30, 1776, Showman, ed., *The Papers of General Nathanael Greene*, I: 377.

CHAPTER TEN

Assessment and Epilogue

*It is great credit to us, that, with an handful of men, we sustained
an orderly retreat for near an hundred miles, brought off our
ammunition, all our field-pieces, the greatest part of our stores,
and had four rivers to pass.*
—Thomas Paine, *The American Crisis*[1]

Following the Battle of Princeton, General Howe abandoned his
advance posts and withdrew to the eastern half of central New Jersey. The
British also gave up Elizabethtown and Woodbridge. New Brunswick and
Perth Amboy were their principal cantonments for the balance of the winter of
1776-1777. British and Hessian soldiers often pillaged with a free hand, and
damage to the occupied towns and to the surrounding countryside and villages
was often severe. Then, in early summer of 1777, the fortunes of war changed
and Howe pulled out almost completely; the only posts the British held in the
state for any length of time were small forts at Paulus Hook (modern Jersey
City) and Sandy Hook. New Jersey was redeemed.

Long before Howe's withdrawal, however, and even before
Washington's raid on Trenton, whispers of criticism swirled about the British
commander's generalship in the New Jersey campaign. Captain Johann Ewald,
the Hessian Jaeger officer, had plenty of time to think about it while he

---

[1]Thomas Paine, *The American Crisis--Number One*, in Eric Foner, ed., *Paine,
Collected Writings* (New York: The Library of America, 1995), 98. The four rivers were
the Hackensack, Passaic, Raritan,, and Delaware.

languished at New Brunswick in early December 1776. "Why did we let the corps of five to six thousand men withdraw so quietly from Fort Lee," he asked? "Secondly, why did we tarry so many days until the enemy had peacefully crossed the Second River [Passaic River]? Thirdly, why did we march so slowly that the enemy could cross the Raritan safely?" Finally, he wanted to know "why did we not pursue the enemy at once, instead of lingering here [New Brunswick] for five days?"[1] Ewald was a good soldier, and he was frankly bewildered at Washington's escape.

The explanation was not simple. Part of it involved Howe's intentions when he invaded New Jersey. His objectives, which he had not shared with Ewald or other junior officers, were strictly limited. His first goal was to eliminate Fort Lee to give the Royal Navy unhampered navigation of the lower Hudson River. His second goal was to secure winter quarters for part of his army. Howe never thought of defeating Washington's main army, nor did he ever think seriously about seizing Philadelphia. Howe's best biographer, Troyer Anderson, has emphasized this point. "When everything has been considered," Anderson noted, "it appears that the New Jersey campaign has been somewhat misunderstood." It was not Howe's original intention to bring Washington to a showdown battle or to destroy the rebel army. The effort to catch the patriot army began in earnest only after the initial successes at Fort Lee showed how vulnerable the Continental and militia units actually were.[2]

Even then, Howe pursued within the predictable and deliberate context of eighteen-century warfare. The advance was no *blitzkrieg*. At the time of the American Revolution, logistical problems prevented armies from fighting for extended periods. Howe had been in the field since August, and in action a good deal of the time. Operations had been costly in supplies, food, forage, and equipment; with a supply line that extended 3,000 miles from England, the general required 37 tons of food and 38 tons of fodder each day to feed 35,000 men and 4,000 horses.[3] Howe needed to resupply and reorganize, and the military norms of the day argued for an end to the campaign, not an all-out effort to crush an opponent late in the season. Even Howe's seemingly poor decision to winter the army in dispersed garrisons was

---

[1]Ewald, *Diary of the American War*, 25.

[2]Anderson, *The Command of the Howe Brothers*, 208-209.

[3]Douglas W. Marshall and Howard Peckham, *Campaigns of the American Revolution* (Ann Arbor: University of Michigan Press, 1976), 34.

based largely on the need for the troops to supply themselves from local resources until spring.

Casualties were also a concern. Eighteenth-century battles could be murderous and trained soldiers were valuable. Howe was fighting far from home and soldiers lost to combat, disease, or desertion were not easily replaced. Fearful of serious losses, the general was reluctant to attack strong American positions, such as Harlem Heights or North Castle, especially after the brutal experience at Bunker Hill. Even at Fort Washington, where Howe ordered a frontal assault, he believed the rebels would abandon the fort before he had to attack.[1] An impetuous dash against Washington in New Jersey, or a bold effort to force the Delaware in the face of opposition--and American batteries on the Pennsylvania side had done some nasty work as lead British units had approached the river at Trenton--seemed only to invite needless casualties.

Another problem for Howe was his unusual dual role as warrior and peacemaker. William and Richard Howe may have had instructions, tacit if not written, to bring the Americans to terms by means short of destroying them in the field.[2] While there is no evidence that any such understanding induced General Howe to relinquish any tactical advantage, he understood that the war in America did not enjoy popular support in England. The Howe brothers probably did want to end the war through negotiations; had they done so, they would have sailed home as heroes.

Howe's strategy in 1776 was to soften the rebels by creating the impression of British invincibility and then bringing them to the treaty table. He did not want to harden rebel determination through brutality. He offered peace talks following the Battle of Long Island, and issued the proclamation of pardon after overrunning part of New Jersey. But Howe's velvet-glove failed. Much of the fault lay with his inability to control the behavior of the army. Pillage, wanton destruction, looting, and rape started soon after the British arrived in the state (and in America, for that matter) and bred hostility among the New Jersey population.[3] Atrocities and harassment turned many

---

[1]Henry P. Johnston, *The Campaign of 1776 Around New York and Brooklyn* (Brooklyn: The Long Island Historical Society, 1878), 282n.

[2]Fuller, *Battles of the Revolution*, 21.

[3]Based on their experience in Westchester County, New York prior to their assault on New Jersey, the British knew that there would be problems trying to restrain the enlisted men from looting and rape. Writing in his journal from Westchester on Nov.

neutrals into rebels. By mid-December 1776, the wave of anti-Crown fervor was so strong that some New Jersey partisans may have carried Howe's pardon, crushed in their pockets, as they fought back.

General Howe also failed to comprehend the ability of the Americans to rebuild their army. He beat the rebels in battle, but never destroyed their organization. He captured equipment, but never enough to deprive Washington of sufficient transport or artillery to move his forces and to support them with battery fire. The British drove off thousands of militia and captured General Lee; but they were unable to prevent reinforcements from reaching Washington (albeit in the nick of time), a resurgence of militia activity in December, or the continued march of Lee's troops under Sullivan. Had he remotely suspected the extent of patriot resilience, Howe indeed might have tried to destroy Washington's army when he had the opportunity in New Jersey. As it was, he had enough military skill to create the illusion of success and to hide the opportunities he let slip by in the name of peace or faith that the battered rebel armed forces would fall apart over the winter.

Some patriots were pleased enough with Howe. "It has been said, that we could not have chosen a better adversary than General Howe;" wrote Alexander Graydon, an American officer captured at Fort Washington, "and it is not improbable that one more enterprising and less methodical, might have pushed us harder." Howe was not untalented, Graydon thought, and he often fought skillfully; but he "often treated us with unnecessary respect." A more imaginative officer "might have meant to play us, as an angler plays a fish upon his hook."[1] Howe was a competent officer in a situation that required an outstanding soldier and statesman.

Under the circumstances, it seems that Washington did a better job than Howe of defining and solving problems. Some historians, however, have disagreed with this assessment, arguing that the patriot Commander-in-Chief grew increasingly unsure of himself over the course of the New Jersey retreat. One of Washington's greatest biographers, Douglas Southall Freemen, thought that the general's judgement became "clouded" and hesitant. John Shy

---

7, 1776, Major Stephen Kemble, a native of New Brunswick, New Jersey, summed up the problem: "8 or 10 of our People taken Marauding; Scandalous behavior for British Troops; and the Hessians Outrageously Licentious, and Cruel to such a degree as to threaten with death all such as dare obstruct them in their depredations. Violence to Officers frequently used, and every Degree of Insolence offered. Shudder for Jersey, the Army being thought to move there Shortly; think it very probable." *Kemble Journal*, 98.

[1]Littell, ed., *Alexander Graydon, Memoirs of His Own Time*, 214-215.

has suggested that Washington was probably plagued with self-doubt during the retreat.[1] Was Washington so exhausted by November 1776 that he was indecisive to the point of incompetence? Certainly he dithered over Fort Washington, and with disastrous consequences, and he was disturbingly lax in his failure to issue Lee a direct order to reinforce the Grand Army after the British invaded New Jersey. Yet these events, however important, were incidents, not the complete picture.

In the final analysis, Washington was a cunning and dangerous adversary. The British army never came close to catching up with him in New Jersey. Washington paced his retreat to match his opponents' advance. Even though Washington was crippled by the loss of the Fort Washington garrison and Lee's recalcitrance, it was extraordinary that when he reached Trenton on December 3, he quickly ferried his baggage to safety in Pennsylvania and started back toward Princeton with three thousand men; he was looking for a fight with an enemy estimated at ten thousand. This daring was combined with prudent planning. As the military situation unfolded in late 1776, Washington diverted Continental regiments to Morristown to encourage the militia and build a strong base of operations. His own units, if thin, were operational. The troops, if hungry, still had food; his cannon had ammunition and his horses had fodder. Washington was able to manage resources in adversity, and that fact alone made him a respectable foe. Desperation made him dangerous. There is some irony in British worries over Lee in late 1776; it was Washington who bore watching.

The New Jersey retreat was one of Washington's most notable military exploits. As Thomas Paine wrote in *The American Crisis*, the events of late 1776 became a trial of Washington's soul. The retreat took Washington not only down the muddy roads of towns such as Newark, New Brunswick, and Princeton, but also through the private thickets of his own fears and self-doubts. It was a trial that led to redemption for Washington and for the fragile hopes of an infant nation. The light of the Revolution's glory shines from many sources, but the road to eventual victory can be traced directly back to the path of Washington's long retreat through New Jersey.

---

[1]Freeman, *George Washington*, IV: 240; John Shy, "Charles Lee: The Soldier as Radical," in George Billias, ed., *George Washington's Generals* (New York: William Morrow and Company, 1964), 38-39.

BIBLIOGRAPHY

Primary Sources: Manuscripts

Avery, David. *Diary of Chaplain David Avery*. Microfilm edition of manuscript. Library, Princeton Theological Seminary, Princeton, New Jersey.

Glyn, Thomas. *Ensign Glyn's Journal on the American Service with the Detachment of 1,000 Men of the Guards Commanded by Brigadier General Mathew in 1776*. Bound original. Manuscript Division, Firestone Library, Special Collections, Princeton University, Princeton, New Jersey.

Hunter, Andrew. *Diary, 1776-1779*. Bound original. Manuscript Division, Firestone Library, Special Collections, Princeton University, Princeton, New Jersey.

William Van Vleek Lidgerwood Collection of Hessian Documents of the American Revolution. Fiche edition of transcripts. Morristown National Historical Park, Morristown, New Jersey.

Peale, Charles Willson. *Autobiography*. Undated manuscript, American Philosophical Society, Philadelphia.

Primary Sources: Books

Anderson, Captain Enoch. *Personal Recollections*. Edited by Henry Hobart Bellas. Wilmington: The Historical Society of Delaware, 1896.

Baurmeister, Carl L. *Revolution in America: Confidential Letters and Journals 1776-1784, of Adjutant General Major Baurmeister of the Hessian Forces*. Translated and edited by Bernhard A. Uhlendorf. New Brunswick, New Jersey: Rutgers University Press, 1957.

Burnaby, Andrew. *Travels Through the Middle Settlements in North America*. London, 1798.

Chastellux, Marquis de. *Travels in North America*. 2 vols. London, 1787.

Clinton, Sir Henry. *The American Rebellion*. Edited by William B. Wilcox. New Haven: Yale University Press, 1954.

Collins, Varnum Lansing, ed., *A Brief Narrative of the Ravages of the British and Hessians at Princeton in 1776-77*. Princeton: The University Library, 1906

Commager, Henry Steele, and Morris, Richard B., eds. *The Spirit of Seventy-Six*. New York: Bobbs- Merrill, 1958.

Cresswell, Nicholas. *The Journal of Nicholas Cresswell, 1774-1777*. New York: Dial Press, 1924.

Ewald, Johann. *Diary of the American War: A Hessian Journal*. Translated from the German, edited, and annotated by Joseph P. Tustin. New Haven: Yale University Press, 1979.

Force, Peter, ed. *American Archives: Fifth Series, Containing a Documentary History of the United States of America from the Declaration of Independence, July 4, 1776, to the Definitive Treaty of Peace with Great Britain, September 3, 1783*. 3 vols. Washington, D.C., 1848-1853.

Graydon, Alexander. *Memoirs of His Own Time*. Edited by John Stockton Littell. Philadelphia: Lindsay & Blakiston, 1846.

Greene, Nathanael. *The Papers of Nathanael Greene*. Edited by Richard K. Showman et al., eds, 8 vols. to date. Chapel Hill, North Carolina.: The University of North Carolina Press, 1976---.

Greenwood, John. *A Young Patriot in the American Revolution, 1775-1783*. Edited by Isaac J. Greenwood. Westvaco, 1981. Originally published as: *The Revolutionary Services of John Greenwood of Boston and New York, 1775-1783*. New York: De Vinne Press, 1922.

Hamilton, Alexander. *The Papers of Alexander Hamilton*. Edited by Harold C. Syrett and Jacob E. Cook, 26 vols. New York: Columbia University Press, 1961-1979.

Hamilton, Alexander. *The Itinerarium of Dr. Alexander Hamilton*, in Colonial *American Travel Narratives*. Edited by Wendy Martin. New York: Penguin Books, 1994.

Jones, Thomas. *History of New York during the Revolutionary War*. 2 vols. New York: New York Historical Society, 1879.

Journals of the Continental Congress 1774-1789. 34 vols. Edited by Worthington Chauncey Ford et al. Washington, D.C.: General Post Office, 1904-1937. Index published in 1976.

Kalm, Peter. *Travels In North America*. (1770; Reprint of the English edition). Edited by Adolph B. Benson. New York: Dover Publications, Inc., 1987.

Kemble, Stephen. *Journals of Lieutenant Colonel Stephen Kemble*. 2 vols. New York: New York Historical Society, 1883.

Lee, Charles. *The Lee Papers*. 4 vols. New York: The New York Historical Society, 1871-1874.

Lesser, Charles H. *The Sinews of Independence*. Chicago: The University of Chicago Press, 1976.

Livingston, William. *The Papers of William Livingston*. Edited by Carl E. Prince, vol. 1. Trenton: The New Jersey Historical Commission, 1979.

M'Robert, Patrick. *A Tour Through Part of the North Provinces of America*. Edinburgh, 1776.

Mackenzie, Frederick. *The Diary of Frederick Mackenzie*. 2 vols. Cambridge, Massachusetts: Harvard University Press, 1930.

Monroe, James. *Autobiography*. Edited by Stuart Gerry Brown with the assistance of Donald G. Baker. Syracuse: Syracuse University Press, 1959.

Muenchhausen, Captain Fredrich von. *At General Howe's Side 1776-1778*. Translated by Ernst Kipping and annotated by Samuel Steele Smith. Monmouth Beach, New Jersey: Philip Freneau Press, 1974.

Paine, Thomas. *Paine, Collected Writings*. Edited by Eric Foner. New York: The Library of America, 1995

Reed, Joseph. *The Life and Correspondence of Joseph Reed*, Edited by William B. Reed. 2 vols. Philadelphia: Lindsay and Blakiston, 1847.

Robertson, Archibald. *Diaries and Sketches in America.* Edited by Harry M. Lydenberg. New York: The New York Public Library, 1930.

Rush, Benjamin. *Autobiography.* Edited by George W. Corner. Princeton: Published for the American Philosophical Society by the Princeton University Press, 1948.

Serle, Ambrose. *The American Journal of Ambrose Serle, Secretary of Lord Howe, 1776-1778.* Edited by Edward H. Tatum, Jr. San Marino, California: Huntington Library, 1940.

Smith, Cap't George. *An Universal Military Dictionary.* London: Printed for J. Millan, 1779

Smith, Paul H. editor. *Letters of Delegates to Congress, 1774-1789.* 21 vols to date. Washington D.C: Library of Congress 1976-.

Stiles, Ezra. *The Literary Diary of Ezra Stiles.* Edited by Franklin Dexter. New York: Charles Scribner's Sons, 1901.

Stedman, Charles. *The History of the Origin, Progress, and Termination of the American War.* 2 vols. London, 1794.

Wade, Nathaniel and Hodgkins, Joseph. *This Glorious Cause..The Adventures of Two Company Officers in Washington's Army* [Diaries]. Edited by Herbert T. Wade and Robert A. Lively. Princeton: Princeton University Press, 1958.

Washington, George. *The Papers of George Washington.* Revolutionary War Series. 7 vols. to date. Edited by W.W. Abbot *et al.* Charlottesville: University Press of Virginia, 1985-.

Washington, George. *The Writings of George Washington from the Original Manuscript Sources 1745- 1799.* 39 vols. Edited by John C. Fitzpatrick. Washington, D.C.: Government Printing Office, 1931-1944.

Webb, Samuel Blachley. *Correspondence and Journals of.. 1772-1806.* Collected and Edited by Worthington Chauncey Ford. 3 vols. New York, 1893-94.

Wilkinson, James. *Memoirs of My Own Times.* 4 vols. Philadelphia: Abraham Small, 1816.

Primary Sources: Periodicals and Monographs

Bradford, William. "The Revolutionary Diary of a British Officer." *Maryland Historical Magazine,* XXVIII (March 1933).

"British and Hessian Accounts of the Invasion of Bergen County 1776." Edited by Major Donald M. Londahl-Smidt USAFR. *Bergen County History,* 1976 Annual.

Judd, Jacob. *Fort Lee on the Palisades: The Battle for the Hudson. A Historical Evaluation of Fort Lee.* Prepared for the Palisades Interstate Park Commission. 1963.

McCarty, Thomas. "The Revolutionary War Journal of Sergeant Thomas McCarty." Edited by Jared C. Lobdell. *Proceedings of the New Jersey Historical Society,* 82 (1964).

McMichael, James. "Diary of Lieutenant James McMichael, of the Pennsylvania Line, 1776-1778. " *Pennsylvania Magazine of History and Biography*, XVI, No. 2 (1892).

Smith, John. "Sergeant John Smith's Diary of 1776." Edited by Louise Rau. *Mississippi Valley Historical Review*, 20 (June 1933 to March 1934).

Strike, Henry. "A British Officer's Revolutionary War Journal, 1776-1778." Edited by S. Sydney Bradford. *Maryland Historical Magazine*, 56 (June 1961).

White, Joseph. "An Narrative of Events, As They Occurred from Time to Time in the Revolutionary War; with an Account of the Battles of Trenton, Trenton-Bridge, and Princeton." Charlestown, Mass., 1833. In *American Heritage*, 4 (June 1956). Original in Library of Congress.

Secondary Sources: Books and Dissertations

Alden, John. *General Charles Lee, Traitor or Patriot?* Baton Rouge: Louisiana State University Press, 1951.

Anderson, Troyer Steele. *The Command of the Howe Brothers During the American Revolution*. New York-London: Oxford University Press, 1936.

Bedini, Silvio A. *Thomas Jefferson, Statesman of Science*. New York: Macmillian Publishing Company, 1990.

Benedict, William H., *New Brunswick in History*. New Brunswick: Published by the Author, 1925.

Bernstein, David. *New Jersey in the American Revolution*. Doctor of Philosophy diss., Rutgers University, 1969.

Bill, Alfred Hoyt. *A House Called Morven, Its Role in American History*. Princeton: Princeton University Press, 1954.

Bill, Alfred Hoyt. *New Jersey and the Revolutionary War*. Princeton: D. Van Nostrand Company, Inc., 1964.

Billias, George Athan, editor. *George WashingtonÕs Generals*. New York: William Morrow and Company, 1964

Blanco, Richard L. *The American Revolution-An Encyclopedia*. 2 vols. New York & London: Garland Publishing, Inc., 1993.

Boatner, Mark Mayo, III. *Encyclopedia of the American Revolution*. New York: David McKay Company, Inc., 1966.

Boatner, Mark Mayo, III. *Landmarks of the American Revolution*. Harrisburg, Pa.: Stackpole Books, 1973.

Carrington, Henry. *Battles of the American Revolution*. New York: A.S. Barnes & Company, 1877.

Champagne, Roger. *Alexander McDougall and the American Revolution in New York*. Schenectady: Union College Press, 1975

Fleming, Thomas. *1776 Year of Illusions*. New York: W.W. Norton & Company, Inc., 1975.

Ferling, John E. *The Loyalist Mind, Joseph Galloway and the American Revolution.* University Park, PA: The Pennsylvania State University Press, 1977.

Flexner, James Thomas. *The Young Hamilton.* Boston- Toronto: Little, Brown and Company, 1978.

Flexner, James Thomas. *George Washington in the American Revolution.* Boston-Toronto: Little, Brown and Company, 1967

Freeman, Douglas Southall. *George Washington : A Biography.* 7 vols. New York: Charles Scribner's Sons, 1948-1957.

Godfrey, Carlos E. *The Commander-In-Chief's Guard.* Washington, D.C.: Stevenson-Smith Company, 1904.

Gordon, William. *The History of the Rise, Progress & Establishment of the Independence of the United States of America: Including an Account of the Late War....* 3 vols. New York: Hodge, Allen and Campbell, 1789.

Hageman, John Frelinghuysen. *History of Princeton and its Institutions.* 2 vols. Philadelphia: J.B. Lippincott & Co., 1879

Heitman, Francis B. *Historical Register of the Continental Army.* Rev. ed. Washington, D.C.: The Rate Book Shop Publishing Co., 1914.

Heusser, Albert H. *In the Footsteps of Washington.* Paterson, New Jersey: privately printed, 1921.

Hine, C.G. *The Old Mine Road.* New Brunswick: Rutgers University Press, 1963.

Hull, Joan C. *New Jersey: A description Of Its Military and Supply Assistance to Washington and the Continental Army During the American Revolution.* Thesis, Master of Arts, Montclair State College, 1962.

Irving, Washington. *The Life of George Washington.* 5 vols. New York: G.P. Putnam, 1855-1859.

Jackson, John W. *The Pennsylvania Navy.* New Brunswick: Rutgers University Press, 1974.

Katcher, Philip. *Armies of the American Wars 1775-1815.* New York: Hastings House, 1975.

Ketchum, Richard M. *The Winter Soldiers.* Garden City, New York: Doubleday & Company, Inc., 1973.

Lane, Wheaton. *From Indian Trail to Iron Horse.* Princeton, New Jersey: Princeton University Press, 1939.

Lefferts, Charles. *Uniforms of the American, British, French and German Armies in the War of the American Revolution, 1775-1783.* New York: The New York Historical Society, 1926

Leiby, Adrian C. *The Revolutionary War in the Hackensack Valley.* New Brunswick, New Jersey: Rutgers University Press, 1962.

Lossing, Benson J. *Pictorial Field Book of the Revolution.* 2 vols. New York: Harper & Brothers, 1851-1855.

Lundin, Leonard. *Cockpit of the Revolution, The War for Independence in New Jersey.* Princeton, New Jersey: Princeton University Press, 1940.

Maclean, John. *History of the College of New Jersey.* Philadelphia: J.B. Lippincott & Co., 1877.

Marshall, Douglas W. and Peckham, Howard H. *Campaigns of the American Revolution.* Ann Arbor: University of Michigan Press, 1976.

Marshall, John. *The Life of George Washington.* 5 vols. London: Printed for Richard Philips by T. Gillet, 1804-1807.

Mallo, John & McGregor, Malcolm. *Uniforms of the American Revolution.* New York: Blandford Press Ltd., 1975.

Mintz, Max M. *The Generals of Saratoga.* New Haven: Yale University Press, 1990

Nelson, Paul David. *General Horatio Gates.* Baton Rouge: Louisiana State University Press, 1976.

Neumann, George C. *The History of Weapons of the American Revolution.* New York: Harper & Row, 1967.

Palmer, Dave Richard. *The Way of the Fox, American Strategy in the War for America, 1775-1783.* Westport, Connecticut:. Greenwood Press, 1975.

Ramsay, David. *The History of the American Revolution.* Philadelphia, 1793.

Richardson, Edward W. *Standards and Colors of the American Revolution.* The University of Pennsylvania Press, 1982.

Schachner, Nathan. *Alexander Hamilton.* New York: Appleton-Century Company, 1946.

Sellers, Charles Coleman. *Charles Willson Peale, Early Life.* Philadelphia: The American Philosophical Society, 1947

Sellers, John. *The Virginia Continental Line, 1775-1780*, Ph.D. diss., Tulane University, New Orleans, 1968.

Silverman, Kenneth. *A Cultural History of the American Revolution.* New York: Thomas Y. Crowell Company, 1976.

Smith, William. *The Life and Public Service of Arthur St. Clair.* Cincinnati: Robert Clarke & Co., 1882.

Stryker, William S. *The Battles of Trenton and Princeton.* Boston: The Riverside Press, 1898.

Studlet, Miriam V. *Historic New Jersey Through Visitors' Eyes.* Princeton, New Jersey: D. Van Nostrand Company, Inc., 1964.

UrQuhart, Frank J. *History of the City of Newark.* Newark, New Jersey: Lewis Historical Publishing Company, 1913.

Ward, Christopher L. *The Delaware Continentals 1776-1783.* Wilmington, Delaware, The Historical Society of Delaware, 1941.

Ward, Christopher L. *The War of the Revolution.* Edited by John Richard Alden. 2 vols. New York: The Macmillan Company, 1952.

Warren, Mercy Otis. *History of the Rise, Progress and Termination of the American Revolution.* 3 vols. Boston: Manning and Loring, for E. Larkin, 1805.

Wertenbaker, Thomas Jefferson. *Princeton 1746-1896.* Princeton: Princeton University Press, 1946.

White, Donald Wallace. *A Village at War, Chatham, New Jersey, and the American Revolution*. Rutherford, New Jersey: Fairleigh Dickinson University Press, 1979.

Woodward, Carl Raymond. *Ploughs and Politicks, Charles Read of New Jersey And His Notes on Agriculture, 1715-1774*. New Brunswick: Rutgers University Press, 1941.

Wright, Robert K., Jr. *The Continental Army*. Washington, D.C.: Center of Military History, 1989

Secondary Sources: Periodicals and Brochures

"Major Aldington." *Bergen County History*, 1970 Annual

Durnin, Richard. *George Washington in Middlesex County, New Jersey*. North Brunswick:. Middlesex County Cultural and Heritage Commission, 1989.

Glover, T.N. *The Retreat of 1776 Across Bergen County*. Bergen County Historical Society (1905).

Holst, Donald. *Regimental Colors of the Continental Army*. Military Collector & Historian, Fall, 1968.

Maxwell, Henry Dusenbery. *General William Maxwell*. New Jersey Society of the Cincinnati, 1900

Mosley, Virginia. "The Mystery of Polly Wyckoff." *The North Jersey Suburbanite* [newspaper], November 12, 1975.

Robinson, Walter F. *Old Bergen Township (Now Hudson County) in the American Revolution*. Bayonne, NJ: Bayonne Bicentennial Committee, 1978.

Sellers, Horace Wells. "Charles Willson Peale, Artist-Soldier." *Pennsylvania Magazine of History and Biography*, XXXVIII, No. 3 (1914).

Spring, John. "The 1776 British Landing at Closter." *Bergen County History*, 1975 Annual.

Vermeule, Cornelius. *Proceedings of the New Jersey Historical Society*, New Series, VI, No. 2 (1921); XIII (1928); LIV, No. 2 (1936).

INDEX